Revolutionary Ideology and Political Destiny in Mexico, 1928–1934

Revolutionary Ideology and Political Destiny in Mexico, 1928–1934

LÁZARO CÁRDENAS AND ADALBERTO TEJEDA

EITAN GINZBERG

2016

Hand cover 2015

sussex
ACADEMIC
PRESS
Brighton • Chicago • Toronto

2 4 6 8 10 9 7 5 3 1

First published in hardcover 2015, reprinted in paperback 2016, in Great Britain by
SUSSEX ACADEMIC PRESS
PO Box 139, Eastbourne BN24 9BP

Distributed in North America by
SUSSEX ACADEMIC PRESS
Independent Publishers Group
814 N Franklin St, Chicago, IL 60610, USA

British Library Cataloguing in Publication Data
A CIP catalogue record for this book is available from the British Library.

Library of Congress Cataloging-in-Publication Data
Ginzberg, Eitan, author.
Revolutionary ideology and political destiny in Mexico, 1928–1934 : Lazaro
 Cardenas and Adalberto Tejeda / Eitan Ginzberg.
 pages   cm
Includes bibliographical references and index.
ISBN 978-1-84519-694-3 (hbk. : alk. paper)
ISBN 978-1-84519-777-3 (pbk. : alk. paper)
 1. Mexico—Politics and government—1910–1946. 2. Cardenas, Lazaro,
1895–1970—Political activity—Mexico—Michoacan de Ocampo. 3. Tejeda,
Adalberto, 1883–1960—Political activity—Mexico—Veracruz-Llave (State)
I. Title.
F1234.G488 2015
972.08′2—dc23

                                                                    2014046335

Typeset & designed by Sussex Academic Press, Brighton & Eastbourne.
Printed by Independent Publishers Group, Chicago.
Printed on acid-free paper.

Contents

Acknowledgements

This book could never have been written without the assistance of a great many people who supported, and guided me. I owe special thanks to the late Dr. Leopoldo Zea of the Centro Coordinador y Difusor de Estudios Latinoamericanos at the Universidad Nacional Autónoma de Mexico (UNAM), who took me under his wing professionally and academically while I was staying in Mexico between the years 1991–1992, and again in 2001. I would also like to express warm thanks to the helpful staff of the Hemeroteca Nacional, particularly the director, Aurora Cano Andaluz who allowed me to photocopy all the press material relevant to my research.

In addition, I would like to acknowledge my debt to the respective staffs of the statistical departments in the agrarian reform offices of Morelia and Jalapa (Secciones de Estadística de la Secretaría de la Reforma Agraria), who spent months systematically compiling a broad range of statistical data from 4,000 ejidal communities for me. In Morelia this was Estanislao Benomea López and the director of the department, Josefina López Vargas, while in Jalapa I was aided by the director, Yolanda Ramírez, and María Teresa Cabrera Vera. Particular mention should be made for the invaluable assistance of the federal delegate (Delegado Federal) and director of the Jalapa agrarian reform office, Lic. Luis Ordinola Heredia, who not only gave me the benefit of his extensive knowledge but also offered me all the services of his office.

Warm thanks go to the staff of the Veracruz central archive in Jalapa, headed at the time by Lic. María Elena García Díaz; to the staff of the congressional archive in Morelia, directed by a man who became a personal friend and advisor since I researched my Master's thesis in 1989 and until the present, Dr. Javier Tavera Alfaro; to the former director of the municipal archive of Zamora, Michoacán, and today the President of the College of Michoacán (El Colegio de Michoacán) Dr. Martín Sánchez Rodríguez, a friend and a scholar who brought me closer to the complicated questions of water and irrigation in the Mexican village; to the staff of the Centro de Estudios de la Revolución Mexicana "Lázaro Cárdenas", in Jiquilpan and to the wonderful team of historians at the Centro de Estudios Históricos at the Universidad Veracruzana in particular Mtra. Olivia Domínguez Pérez (today the general director of the Archivo General del Etado de Veracruz); to Mtra. Soledad García Morales and Dr. David Skerritt Gardner, who have helped me immeasurably with advice, explanations and important bibliographical references. Among my Michoacán connections, I would like to mention in particular the late Dr. Luis González y González, who welcomed me whenever I needed his advice and orientation to his home in Mexico, where he was always ready to discuss any subject, and referred me to other experts for specific aspects of Michoacán regional history.

I would like to express deep appreciation to the staff of the Colegio de Mexico (COLMEX), particularly Dr. Flora Bottón, former head of the Centro de Estudios de Asia y África (CEAA) at the Colegio; Shirley Ann Ainsworth and Mtra. Micaela Chávez the library director. All four treated me as a guest of honor and assisted me in many ways, both during my stay in Mexico and afterwards, when I needed copies of important documents that Ms. Ainsworth and Mtra. Chávez were kind enough to locate and send to me in Israel.

The enormous volume of material in the Veracruz central archive and its not indexed state, together with time constraints, forced me to enlist assistance. Without that assistance, offered intelligently and unstintingly by Nelly Ortíz Sánchez, I would never have gotten through half the sources I did. My heart-felt thanks and appreciation go to this clever woman, who continued to help me obtain important documents when ever I needed them.

I also have a great debt to Dr. Gerardo Sánchez Díaz until recently the director of the Intitute of Historical Research of the University of Michoacán who invited me several times to be his host during my post-doctorate studies and ever since, and an excellent scholar who explained to me the extremely complicated life of every Mexican farmer, once his own experience; and to my personal colleages, hosts and friends there: Dr. Eduardo Nomelí Mijangos Díaz, Dra. María Guadalupe Chávez Carbajal and Dr. José Napoleón Guzmán Ávila.

Many thanks to my friends in Mexico City, Julieta and Yoav Tzur, who welcome me with open hearts whenever I come to Mexico, who made me feel at home everytime I visited them.

Profound appreciation for Prof. Raanan Rein, from Tel Aviv University for his constant assistance and advice and helpful structuring ideas and his encouragement to publish this book, and to Mr. Tony Graham, director of Sussex Academic Press, for the consent to publish the book and for the hands-on instructions given me throughout the editing process and preparation of the book for publication.

Warm thanks to my fellow colleagues, Verónica Oikión Solano who helped me extensively in collecting the photographs for the book and always guided me with empathy and good advice in my work in Michoacán; to Chantal Cramaussel and Salvador Alvarez, for years my hosts in Zemora bringing me the secrets of Mexican history since the days of the colony to the obscurities in the research and historiography of contemporary Mexico.

Finally, I must express my warmest thanks to my teacher and guide, Prof. Tzvi Medin of the University of Tel Aviv, who was the advisor for the doctoral thesis on which this book is based; who presented me with important contacts in the Mexican academic world; and who obtained a generous research grant for me. Professor Medin is unmatched in the optimism that he imparts to his students, the extensive knowledge he offers them, and his exhortations to them to work and create. I, too, enjoyed these benefits when I had to find the strength and persistence for a long journey into Mexican history.

List of Maps and Tables

Maps

1   Veracruz and Michoacán at the National Sphere.
2   Michoacán: Names and Places.
3   Veracruz: Names and Places.

Tables

1.1   Land Tenure in Veracruz and Michoacán in 1930 (Private Properties of Over One Hectare).
2.1   New *Municipios* (Municipalities) in Michoacán, 1917–1962 (two-year periods, from 16 September of each year).
2.2   Geographic Distribution of *Municipios* Established by Cárdenas in the Period 1928–1932.
2.3   Creation of New *Tenencias* (Sub-municipal units) in Michoacán, 1917–1940.
2.4   Establishment of New *Tenencias* in Michoacán, 1928–1932.
2.5   Dismissal of Local Government Administrators in Veracruz, 1929–1932.
2.6   Municipal Upgrading in Veracruz, 1925–1933.
3.1   Elementary Schools and Teaching Staff in Michoacán, 1928–1932.
3.2   Michoacán Education Budget as a Percentage of Total State Budget, 1928–1932.
3.3   Percentage of Children Aged 6–14 Enrolled in School in Michoacán, 1928–1932.
4.1   Ejidal Petitions in Michoacán during Cárdenas's Governorship, 1928–1932.
4.2   Ejidal Petitions in Veracruz during Tejeda's Governorship, 1929–1932.
4.3   Sources of Ejidal Petitions in Veracruz by Region and Year during the Tejeda Administration, 1929–1932.
4.4   Number of Ejidal Petitions per Month during Cárdenas's Second Year as Governor (15 Sept. 1929–15 Sept. 1930).
4.5   Cárdenas's Ejidal Reform in Michoacán, 1928–1932, by Area (Settlements Actually Established).
4.6   Tejeda's Ejidal Reform in Veracruz, 1929–1932, by Area (Settlements Actually Established).
4.7   Achievements of the Agrarian Reform in Michoacán and Veracruz, 1928–1932 (in % by region).

List of Illustrations

Introduction

Background

When Luis Manuel Rojas announced the convening of the Constitutional Convention in Querétaro on 31 January 1917, the atmosphere was euphoric. The 209 delegates filled the hall with cries of "Long live the Constitutional Convention!" That jubilant moment, the pinnacle of 62 days of dogged labor inspired by the most progressive social ideals in the areas of education, labor and land, very soon gave way to the gray reality of day-to-day political praxis and the frustrating ideological compromises that went with it. The agrarian sphere, one of the main objectives of the constitutionalist discourse, suffered in the crisis that all successful revolutions seem to undergo. Very little change happened in the 10 years following the formulation of the sweeping principles of Article 27 of the 1917 constitution, which had promised a comprehensive agrarian reform that would break up the *latifundia* and distribute its land among the masses of landless peasants. The 3.2 million hectares expropriated from large estates up to 1928 were a literally a "drop in the bucket" of the 131 million hectares of agricultural land then at the nation's disposal. Moreover, a portion of the expropriated land was taken from the marginal holdings, which permitted the *latifundia* to continued operating as production units and centers of power capable of determining the future of the local peasantry. The good fortune of the 300,000 lucky peasants who received extremely small plots, only underlined the distress of the overwhelming majority of three million peasants who still had nothing. The veterans of the Revolution apparently felt that the constitutional guarantees and enabling legislation, together with the limited land distribution, would be enough to pacify the unfortunate peasants and induce them to support the new administration.

After the government had crushed an officers' revolt (March 1929) led by General Gonzalo Escobar and managed to put down the Catholic rebellion known as *La Cristiada* (1926–1929), it decided to terminate even that partial reform. As long as the government feared for its political legitimacy and internal stability, it saw land distribution as a useful way of winning support from the masses. But, once it no longer felt threatened, the Revolutionary "veterans," led by Plutarco Elías Calles, seemed to think they could jettison the "social" agrarian reform—based on *ejidos* (community-held farms)—that had been instituted in 1915. The issue became how to establish a "natural" agrarianism structured solely on the basis of market forces and free of government intervention. The reform's proponents assumed that more rational agricultural production could be based on small-sized family plots.[1] The 4,000 communities that had received land by 1929 were, in the veterans' eyes, more than enough. Millions of peasants were about to be doomed to eternal marginality within what Andrés Molina Enríquez has called *criollo* Mexican society—an extremely stratified, fragmented and poverty-stricken society that was the natural outgrowth of a republican *criollo* oligarchism—instead of a flourishing egalitarian, nationalistic and *mestizo* society he predicted. The call to end popular agrarianism was in fact motivated by the fear that continuing the *ejidal* reform would lead to accelerated politicization and radicalization of the villages. Hence, there was the possibility that these same processes might award political benefits to a string of second-rung politicians who might challenge the Veterans' hegemony but especially the *"maximato"* system developed by Calles for the purpose of perpetuating his influence on the post-revolutionary state and nation building process. The veterans, mostly middle-class northerners, could not accept the process of change with its potential for proletarianization of the political order and the attendant loss of centralized control over society. Moreover, they were suspicious and fearful that the communal agrarian reform—which was considered a temporary and partial reform aimed at the poor—would become permanent, permanently dooming possibilities to create a wealthy middle-class Mexican Homestead.[2]

The veterans' conservative attitude was anathema to the agrarianist leaders, who demanded not only the continuation of the reform but its completion in as short a time as possible. The agrarianists believed that the *ejidal* system was the correct way to transform socioeconomic structures and to integrate the peasants into the political life of the state—if done broadly, honestly, quickly and decisively. The agrarianists were thus at odds with the veterans not only with respect to the agrarian issue itself, but also—and mainly—with respect to the future image of Mexican society.

The agrarianists were represented in different branches of the administration: among the state governors, in the institutions of the Partido Nacional Revolucionario (National Revolutionary Party—PNR), in the federal Congress, and in the state legislatures. When they first began operating in 1929, they still lacked an integrated ideology and efficient power structures (and control mechanisms), although the picture began to change in 1930. Two figures prominent in this turn-around were Lázaro Cárdenas, the governor of Michoacán, and Adalberto Tejeda, the governor of Veracruz, who waged in tandem a bold campaign during the years 1930–1934 to save the reform from extinction. It became increasingly clear that the messages presented by these two men and their comrades in the struggle against "decadence" were more than simple amendments to a mistaken policy; they offered a sweeping alternative to the incumbent administration's conservative approach, which espoused a minimalist interpretation of Article 27 of the 1917 constitution.

By the end of 1932, the agrarianists' growing power, now too conspicuous to ignore, compelled the political center to take action. It compromised by coopting the moderate sector of the agrarianist movement, led by Cárdenas (this was accomplished by first nominating him in January 1933, as Secretary of War and Marine during the administration of Abelardo Rodríguez and tacitly confirming him, some months later, as the PNR's presidential candidate), and eliminating the radicals, who were grouped around Tejeda. The fact that Cárdenas had already managed to establish independent power bases on the national level—partly at the expense of radical agrarianism— yet without challenging the authority of Calles as the national strongman, may have ultimately enable Cárdenas to gain Calles's support, especially because the Tejedist option would have presented a much more united and active opposition. Calles obviously had good reasons to assume that despite Cárdenas' relative autonomy, he could be controlled.

This choice, however, rather quickly proved to be less successful than the Revolutionary veterans had hoped. The man whom Josephus Daniels, the American ambassador to Mexico had characterized in April 1934, just before the presidential elections, as "an outstanding soldier but an untalented politician" turned out to be just the opposite. Cárdenas was hardly an outstanding soldier, but he was undoubtedly a skilled politician with well-integrated views. The veterans, having been no more perspicacious than the ambassador, were quite surprised to see the "untalented politician" adroitly and energetically begin putting his ideas— aimed at the working classes' complete integration into the political life of the state—into practice from the moment that he was seated in the presidential chair. Nevertheless, the statist orientation and corporatist, bureaucratic character of Cardenistic agrarianism would ultimately prevent it from becoming the basis of a generalized social revolution leading to full democratization of the Mexican state.

The Main Characters

Lázaro Cárdenas del Río (1895–1970), a native of Jiquilpán, Michoacán, began his political career in his home state. At the beginning of 1928, the 33-year-old military governor of the Huasteca region in northern Veracruz decided to leave the army, in which he had served since 1913, and enter political life. On 15 September 1928 he was inaugurated as governor, completing his term in September 1932. During this period, he threw himself into a series of land, educational, and economic reforms that turned sleepy Michoacán into a dynamo. In June 1933 he declared his candidacy for the upcoming presidential elections and was elected as the PNR's official candidate in December. After a well-organized electoral campaign, he was swept into office as President of Mexico in December 1934 to become Mexico's most popular and praised president in the 20th century.

At almost exactly the same time, Adalberto Tejeda Olivares (1883–1960) became governor of his own native state, Veracruz. Born in Chicontepec, Tejeda was 45 years old when he took office for the second time. In the

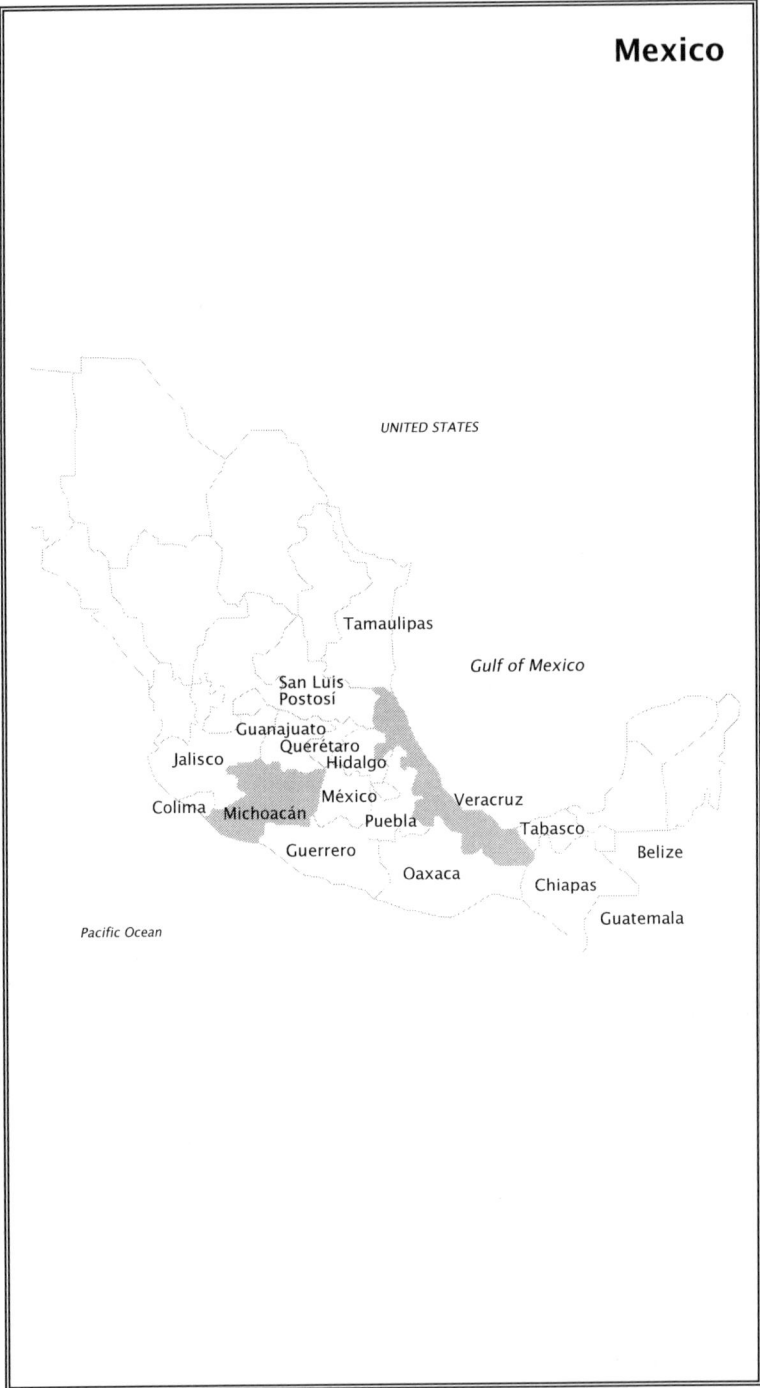

Mexico

UNITED STATES

Tamaulipas

Gulf of Mexico

San Luis
Postosí

Guanajuato
Querétaro
Jalisco
Hidalgo

México
Colima
Michoacán
Puebla
Veracruz

Tabasco

Belize

Guerrero

Oaxaca
Chiapas

Guatemala

Pacific Ocean

preceding years, he had already served as a colonel in the cavalry, military governor of the Huasteca region (1915–1916), chief-of-staff of the Eastern Division (1917–1918), senator (1918–1920), governor of his state (1920–1924), and Minister of Transportation, and later, of the Interior (1924–1928) in President Calles's government.[3] Like Cárdenas, Tejeda seized the opportunity afforded by his office to implement a series of social and structural reforms intended to make his state a pioneering model of reform worthy of emulation by the other Mexican states. Veracruz, which had been dynamically progressive even before Tejeda's administration, received an enormous boost during his governorship, taking its place at the vanguard of socioeconomic change.[4] In 1933 Tejeda established the PSI, was nominated its candidate for the next presidential elections, and conducted a miserable campaign, which destroyed his political career even though he was later appointed ambassador to France, Germany and later Spain during the Cárdenas administration.

Both Cárdenas and Tejeda were born to rural middle-class families—Cárdenas to the lower middle-class, Tejeda to the upper middle-class. Both spent years in the Revolutionary army, developing a strong sense of identification with the Revolution's social ideals that owed much to their direct contact during this period with poor, oppressed rural populations. Both of them resolved to do all they could to bring the Revolution to the villages, to relieve once and for all the peasants' material and psychological distress and onerous dependence—both physical and emotional—on the large landowners and the priests. Because Cárdenas and Tejeda both viewed the social principles and aims of the Revolution as a pledge that the regime was obliged to resolutely fulfill, they resisted the federal campaign begun in early 1930 to end the agrarian reform in Mexico.

Superficial similarities notwithstanding, the two governors differed radically in ideology and tactics. Though they both sought to establish a unified labor movement, Cárdenas saw the movement as simply another social agent, important but not necessarily hegemonic, whereas Tejeda believed in the movement's hegemony. Cárdenas put his faith in an institutional, paternalistic, supervised, and controlled agrarianism; Tejeda opted for a democratic agrarianism—spontaneous, multidimensional (combining communal and particularist land distribution, and widening social utility expropriation to urban property as well), less controlled and to be instituted rapidly. The two men also had different visions of modern Mexico. Whereas Cárdenas wanted a centralized government that would delegate power to the periphery, Tejeda advocated a federative model in which the individual states would delegate power to the center. These different perspectives led each one to follow different career paths: Cárdenas spent his years in politics preparing for his bid for the presidency, after which he planned to implement his ideas in a centrifugal fashion; Tejeda, on the other hand, was bent on making Veracruz a model of federalism that would serve as a base for centripetal construction of the national state.[5]

The Conceptual Framework

This book covers the years 1928–1934, a highly significant period for any understanding of the agrarian aspect in the debate over Mexico's future national identity. The book's major argument is that Cárdenas and Tejeda, the two prominent leaders of the agrarian movement in Mexico, were in fact driven by two opposite trends with no possibility of compromise between them. On the one hand, there was a radical trend that advocated varied, multifaceted agrarian (or in some cases, urban) redistribution of wealth, based on a rapid overall socialization of all extensive private property, followed by a total proletarization of society and federalization of the political system. On the other hand, there was a more moderate trend (yet considered radical at the time) that sought to achieve a quick, orderly, and bureaucratic redistribution of limited extensive agrarian property only, under a state-supervised socioeconomic integration, and political centralization.

These two trends—the popular and the institutional—were in effect inherently opposing approaches for advancing the Mexican working class. As we will see, they represented conflicting (or divergent) tactics to attain that aim. These approaches are in fact two opposing interpretations of radicalism: the first leading a process of democratization and federalization of Mexican society, while the second steering Mexico into a type of authoritarian regime with tight controls over society and politics.

Four critical aspects of these crucial ideological and political approach will be analyzed: unification of political bases for support of the radical national formation and state-building models suggested by Cárdenas and Tejeda; shaping a popular consciousness regarding the feasibility of those models together with the urgent need for social progress; establishment of new land distribution patterns stemming from reconstructed power bases potentials of the incipient "New State" within its own provincial realm; and the "export" of those models to wider political arenas during the 1933–1934 presidential campaign.

This study will show that during the years 1928–1932, both Michoacán and Veracruz had governors motivated primarily by a radical revolutionary ideology displaying strong moral commitment to the weakest sectors of society. By battling local oligarchies and a conservative political center, these governors managed to attain political control and develop extremely different models for a post-Revolutionary Mexican nation-state: the centralist, moderately reformist state proposed by Cárdenas, and the federalist-popular (if not proletarian) radically reformist state proposed by Tejeda. Cárdenas, leaning on Mexico's traditional centralist paradigm, maintained a delicate balance between his ideals and the political limitations imposed on the office of a provincial governor, relied on the center to implement his program; alternatively, Tejeda preferred to ignore those same constraints. He gave precedence to ideology as a guide to political praxis, irrespective of the structural restrictions placed on him as governor. This decision did not betray a lack of judgment but a conscious decision to operate within the federalist paradigm. Had he been able to generalize or 'nationalize' this model, the weaknesses of Veracruz—considered within a highly centralized national framework—could have been transformed into strengths. Consequently, while Cárdenas managed to win the trust of the Federal administration despite his ideological divergence, a tactic that paved his way to ultimately replacing that regime, Tejeda was viewed as a threat. This attitude led to attempts made by the political administration to destroy him politically and undermine the legitimacy of his government. The administration's acts effectively crippled Tejeda's political career and long-term opportunities to promote his ideals.

Four major premises guide my analysis of these historical events. First, I assume that Cárdenas entered politics with the clear ambition to promote his political career, which may have included the possibility of reaching the president's office. This led him to pursue controlled, moderate agrarian and social policies that, although intended to implement his ideals, also accommodated trends evolving in the political center. Cárdenas's designs to achieve the presidency were also the primary factor in his assumption of various national roles during his governorship, which earned him wider public recognition and better opportunities to build an individual power base in the national arena, which he would need to win a presidential campaign. Tejeda, in contrast, entered politics without any overt intentions of either running for president or extending his ideas in other directions. He did not develop this ambition until late in his governorship—too late for it to be practical.[6] Unhampered by presidential aspirations, he was able to pursue a maximalist policy with open disregard for the views of the federal center; he thereby hoped to create an impressive local model of change that would eventually be adopted by the other states, that is, imposed from outside on the "decadent" center. From this premise we reach the conclusion that Cárdenas acted within the context of long-term political time whereas Tejeda acted in short-term political time.

My second premise is that by his nature and outlook, Cárdenas was averse to social transformation through class war; instead, he sought to achieve the same result by means of general consent. Such consent, in his view, would require the social and political integration of all sectors, whether they opposed or supported the Revolution's message regarding the construction of a liberal, just and socially integrated Mexico. Accordingly, his struggles against conservative elements were circumscribed by his persistent if paradoxical efforts to rally them to his cause—a characteristic approach that ultimately helped muster wide public support for his race for president of Mexico in the 1934 elections. In contrast, Tejeda—who never defined himself as a communist and was constantly attacked by the Communist Party—believed that class war was the proven method for effecting cultural and economic transformation, and that the needs of working classes should be given unequivocal priority over those of the middle classes until full socioeconomic equality had been achieved. Although this attitude made him very popular in the agrarian sphere, especially at the provincial level and amongst radical agrarian leagues throughout Mexico, it made him very unpopular with the political establishment. However, the political elite still had sufficient political and military power to hinder Tejeda's attempts to marshal any significant support during the presidential campaign.

My third premise is that although the two governors were highly committed to the social promise of the Constitution, Cárdenas favored remaining within the existing Constitution's limits, stretched only as politically possible, whereas Tejeda discovered that despite the extensive reformist potential inherent in the Mexican Constitution, the current modus operandi effectively thwarted attempts to realize that potential outside the political control of the center. The key questions regarding the introduction of agrarian reform and its timely implementation therefore pertained to the separation of church and state, establishment of secular education, introduction of aggressive labor laws and enforcement of those articles affecting the operation of foreign firms (especially oil companies) within the different states that might further the entire country's economic independence. Application of the law within these areas suffered from a visible lack of decisiveness and urgency; their enforcement was sluggish. This realization, which gradually developed in Tejeda's mind after 1930, brought him to a decisive turning joint in his republicanism. He now demanded energetic reaffirmation of federalism and, eventually, constitutional reform.

My fourth premise is that Cárdenas's views were colored by his receptiveness to what can be termed "the Mexican experience"—a complex of historical, behavioral, cultural, and class variables that together made up multifaceted Mexican society. This complex could not be approached solely from a strictly rational perspective but was shaped largely by emotions, social sensitivity and intuition. This perspective inspired him, I assume, to seek greater consent in his campaign for social justice, a tendency that reduced somehow his ability to achieve it. Tejeda, in contrast, espoused the "imported" elements of the Mexican consciousness: rationalism, social activism if not outright socialism. Consequently, he tended to view Mexican society and its problems in a dogmatic, sometimes Manichean fashion and to look for radical, unequivocal, and extreme, rational solutions—although such solutions were sometimes impractical and possibly ineffective in the social and political circumstances of his time. Yet it was Tejeda, with his positivist origins and strong Europeanist orientation, who proved best able to identify the root of Mexico's indolent modus operandi. Thus, rather than plunge into the latent undercurrents that shaped Cárdenist intuition, Tejeda sought to break the Mexican order down into its conceptual components in order to expose their hidden contradictions and make it possible to cope with them efficiently. He viewed any other course as an abdication to the traditional oligarchic (*criollo*) interests of Mexican society, a hindrance to revolutionary momentum and its potential for change, and a mechanism for perpetuation of the inequitable status quo for generations to come.

The book's point of departure is the thesis that "revolutionary" reformism unfolded in the shadow of an historical nexus characterized by external and internal pressures in addition to political exigencies. Thus, although *agrarista* reformism burgeoned due to its attentiveness to the vital interests of various types of *campesinos* who had been empowered in the revolution's wake, the revolutionary state remained attuned first and foremost to those core political interests that were thought to guarantee its seniority. At the same time, the state acted vigorously to oppress or severely limit all autonomous political initiatives.[7] This approach transformed local or regional labor associations, which were highly conscious of their interests but had never been invited to clarify them in open public debate,[8] into marginal actors with respect to the specific components of state reformism and its practices.[9]

The same fate awaited Tejeda and similar politicians who attempted to overstep the boundaries designed by the political center, and to offer a more popular framework for discussion and practice. Such politicians were immediately "banished" from the existing political framework.[10] A similar fate was in store for all the organizations that attempted to advance their own reformist interpretation outside the framework of the state or contrary to official positions.[11] Nevertheless, despite the relative moderation of the debate, the outcomes were rather surprising: What had begun in 1930 as a disagreement regarding the future of national agrarian distribution ended in 1935 as an encompassing ideological discourse regarding the revolution's true initiators, its mission, objectives, character and, incidentally, its status as an impetus for regime change. However, this grand move succeeded because first and foremost it came from the center.

Many students of Mexican folk culture point out that from its earliest stages, the revolution provided a platform from which various social groups could express themselves as well as influence the revolutionary ideology and the associated national agenda.[12] However, few can doubt that the emergence of the agrarianists, originally as a limited power on the provincial level (1929–1932) and later as the dominant force on the national-level (1933–1940), provoked a significant about-face in the transmission and revolutionary content of their political messages to Mexico's civil society. Despite the serious internal differences regarding center-periphery relations, the desirable depth of reform, the source of authority for socioeconomic legislation and even the validity of the constitution itself, the entire agrarianist camp agreed on the need to maintain an attentive and emphatic dialogue with the peasantry, especially with groups that openly rejected the revolution. The purposes of the dialogue were many: to achieve broad, organized representation for their interests, to promote advanced strategies to further the revolutionary consciousness by means of education (a process begun by Obergón in 1921), to energize agrarian praxis and provide moral and political support to peasants and workers in the power struggles on the syndicalist and governance planes on all levels of governance, beginning with the municipal levels. This strategy was anchored in an expansive social(ist) interpretation of the constitution and in the development of a democratic-revolutionary ethos that viewed the state as an agent of the common citizenry. Social reform was thus conceived as the sole measure of the state's moral right to rule.

Cárdenas, like Tejeda, transformed members of his province's local agrarian leagues into quasi-governmental agencies for the purpose of overseeing and defending reform in addition to furthering the political and organizational crystallization of farmers and workers. They accompanied these processes with lofty revolutionary yet patriotic rhetoric imbued with a narrative that described the *campesinos* as the revolution's primary agents. According to this version of the events, the peasants had unhesitatingly committed themselves to the Revolution, observed particularly during their most critical military trials. The *agraristas* continued to expound that by doing so, the *campesinos* had won their right to socioeconomic reforms and to an honorable place in Mexican society and culture. Ezequiel Padilla, a delegate to the PNR's second convention, described this relationship and its implications in an interview held with a number of peasant women: "I asked them if they have land. They answered: 'No, sir, we are poor and they still have not distributed any land to us.' And schools for their children? 'We also don't have any of these' they responded. 'And your husbands?' " Killed in the revolution.'"[13]

The *agraristas* did not, however, remain satisfied by these steps. In order to ensure penetration of their revolutionary messages and practices into the villages, they created an impressive structure of political mediation. This structure was based on numerous agents of change. Traditional village leaders (*caciques*) who had joined the Revolution (or who had understood that circumstances had changed and that new patrons were about to achieve hegemony), teachers, students, agricultural league and syndicalist leaders, cultural missionaries, farmers and Indians who had studied in rural teacher training seminars as well as politicians of different ranks who had crisscrossed the villages within the framework of the "visits" that were slowly becoming routine. These agents of change applied a range of practices: mediation in its fundamental sense; direct aid to government representatives when establishing contacts with the local population; teaching in secular and bilingual schools; transmission of summer seminars and short "cultural" courses to adults and children (subjects ranged from occupational training to hygiene, sports to environmental protection, among others); syndicate organization, consolidation of agrarian leagues and work confederations; formation of *ejidalist* nucleus groups for the purpose of requesting land from the government as well as self-defense in the interim; organization of secular rites and celebrations (e.g., memorial days, commemoration days, sports events, farewell parties for retiring teachers, tree-planting during arbor days); intensive search for pre-Columbian archeological sites, and so forth. At the same time, histories of the Revolution were written and edited, as were textbooks, information and propaganda material, newspapers and statistical studies. The objective of these activities was formation of a collective memory regarding the nation's history and the Revolution for the purpose of reinforcing the moral and political status of the state as well as the reformist project.[14]

Approaching the villagers was not a conflict-free activity, as this book will show. The sources of conflict were the enduring gap between the two main guises of state behavior: the "giving" state with the material, emotional and political advantages it awarded on the one hand, and the "taking" state with its demands that the villages wage a cultural war against the Revolution's opponents—many of whom were *campesinos*, members of the villagers' own families—and to sometimes operate against their own interests. The anti-clerical struggle that Tejeda and Cárdenas announced against declared Catholics, often to the resentment of the *agraristas*, illustrates the first aspect of the state behavior. The requirement to adopt the *ejidal* model, which was unattractive to many farmers, and to agree to replace the religious names of settlements with "revolutionary" names or to form syndicates only within state-established frameworks illustrates the difficulties incumbent on the second aspect.[15] The prevailing context of domination in whose framework agrarian reform was implemented initiated several worrisome phenomena: Reformism was limited to the narrow proportions of revolutionary liberalism rather than evolving as a true popular yet self-managed alternative—what Adolfo Gilly labels a "popular regime of property".[16] The bureaucratic aspects of agrarian reform caused unbearable delays and exhausted many farmers. Decisions to act exclusively on the basis of the *ajido* and to reject any alternative format such as the homestead or the broader restitution of the village's common property transformed the reform mechanism into a highly limited institution with respect to its ability to offer an agricultural alternative to *latifundism*. It likewise impeded its capacity to act as the source for the development of a strong rural bourgeoisie and prosperous village community.

Nor did *agrarista* reformism prevent the emergence of an entire gallery of "weapons of the weak" or the development of local sophisticated "arts of resistance," characteristic of situations of such power relations, as meticulously documented by James Scott.[17] Resistance by the indigenous village population took multiple forms in the Mexican context: disregard of the agrarian laws that prohibited any type of sale, mortgaging or transfer of the *ajido*; severe cases of apathy, wasted resources, corruption and violence in property management; and covert practice of religious rites, to name just a few. Peasants effectively operated according to a 'public' (overt) transcript that supported the government at the same time that they acted according to a 'hidden' (covert), that frequently rejected the *ajido*, obligatory syndicalism, anti-clerical ideology and associated practices, required substitution of place names and other state dictates. The fact that moderate *agraristas* made no attempt to progress beyond the liberal-centralist paradigm, left campesinos throughout Mexico, but especially in Veracruz and Michoacán, as destitute and overburdened as they were prior to the victory of agrarian reformism and its institutionalization.[18] As late as November 1991, President Carlos Salinas de Gortari would portray this situation in the harshest of words:

> This is the reality of the Mexican countryside and it leaves no doubt: there
> is much injustice and poverty in the countryside.[19]

There is little doubt that the conceptual link between Revolution and reform could be established only because the Revolution made no claims to upset the presiding social order beyond the introduction of selected corrections. Despite the fact that these corrections were radical for Latin American standards (with the exception of Cuba and Bolivia, these reforms were never implemented on a similar scale in any other Latin American country), the Revolution's democratic-liberal ethos abstained from proletarization of Mexican society. Hence, the failure of democratization or, perhaps more correctly, popularization of agrarian reform—the flagship of Mexican reformism in general—was inevitable.

Nevertheless, even within the boundaries of agrarian reform, there was space for other mass actions, moves that were perhaps mandatory for the reform's ultimate success. These actions were initially rejected by factions ready to accommodate the regime, followed by the moderate *agraristas* who were led by Cárdenas. As the study will show, had these steps been realized, they would have changed the Revolution's democratic-liberal fabric if not the principle of private property. This category includes several initiatives proposed by Tejeda, which this study describes in great detail. In its concluding chapter, the book delves into the source of the revolutionary regime's fear of taking full advantage of the potential for those agrarian reforms inherent in the constitution and its regulatory legislation. These could have created a more prosperous rural society with more positive features than those described by Salinas de Gortari to his audience. In fact, the tension between what Tejeda considered imperative within the agrarian and syndicalist spheres and what Cárdenas considered feasible within those same arenas, will accompany this research throughout. This tension and the context of intergenerational ideological divisions that nourished it provide the readers with an appropriate discourse to consolidate their views regarding two other issues. The first concerns the question of why Cárdenist pragmatism rather than Tejedist idealism eventually triumphed over their radical sources; the second refers to whether a relationship exists between the outcome of this competition and the rural reality outlined by Salina de Gortari sixty years after the Revolution.

Methodology and Sources

This study explores the attitudes of Cárdenas, Tejeda, and their contemporaries through an examination of primary sources such as letters, speeches, personal memoirs, and press releases. It delves into the two men's political praxis as implemented in state programs, contemporary reports, statistical data, laws and legislative drafts, parliamentary debates, government circulars, and so on. To corroborate the representativeness of the selected data, I visited several of the communities involved in the reform and interviewed some of the people living there during the governorships of Cárdenas and Tejeda.

I have chosen comparative analysis as the most appropriate to my purpose for writing this book. A straightforward study of a given geopolitical area, the approach adopted by most scholars researching the history of the Mexican Revolution, would likely cloud the significance of many of the study's findings. In contrast, the comparative framework permits a multidimensional view capable of opening new vistas regarding one of the most dramatic periods in the history of modern Mexico.

Researchers of Veracruzan agrarianism have a rich literature at their disposal. The first works on the Tejeda period appeared as early as the 1940s and 1950s, when Tejeda was still alive. Leafar Agetro apparently inaugurated study on the subject in 1942 with his description of the initial agrarianist experience in Veracruz, followed by publication of Mario Velasco Gil's book in 1953. These modest beginnings provided the foundations for two prolific researchers: Heather Fowler Salamini, whose articles began to appear in *Historia Mexicana* at the beginning of the 1970s and who published her important study, *Agrarian Radicalism in Veracruz, 1920–1938*, in 1971; and Romana Falcón, who published her own major work in 1977, *El agrarismo en Veracruz: La etapa radical, 1928–1935*. Fowler examined the subject from the perspective of Tejeda's relationship with the *Liga Agraria* (Agrarian League), whereas Falcón focused on Tejeda himself.

In the 1980s other historians published Tejedist research: David A. Skerritt (1986); María Eugenia Terrones López (1989); Soledad García Morales who, with Romana Falcón, co-authored a detailed biography of Tejeda (1986); Olivia Domínguez Pérez, who studied the roots of Tejedist radicalism during his first term as governor (1986); Serafín Maldonado, who wrote an interesting Master's thesis on Tejeda's relationship with the federal government (1992), and Andrew Wood's chapter on Tejeda's political work during his two terms (2009). Relevant also to our study is the doctoral thesis of Helga Baitenmann (1997) on the agrarian history of central Veracruz 1915–1992 Large parts are dedicated to Tejeda's work during his first and second governship. In addition, the doctoral thesis of Erasmo Hernández García (2010) on the social movements' history in Veracruz 1920–1970, where a full chaper is dedicated to Tejeda's work was found significant.

Historians are very sympathetic to Tejeda, who is generally perceived as a heroic if occasionally pathetic figure, a man ahead of his time who embarked on a relentless struggle against anyone he designated as an enemy of the peasants and the workers. Fowler undoubtedly made a breakthrough when she pointed out that Tejeda, the non-working-class "outsider," galvanized the League's radicalism, and not the other way around, as might have been anticipated given the League's ideological stance in the 1920s, a period when it was still closely associated with the Mexican Communist Party (Partido Comunista Mexicana—PCM). The present research reaffirms this thesis but tries to take it further, examining the factors that contributed to

Tejeda's radicalism, the point at which that radicalism became sufficiently extreme to threaten the liberal order, in addition to its implications for Tejeda's leadership and political fate. Hence, my focus rests on Tejeda, not on the League. My re-examination was facilitated, I should note, by the opening of the main State archive (Archivo General del Estado de Veracruz) in 1991 that were unavailable to Fowler.

In a sharp departure from the sympathetic historiography to Tejeda is the work of Baitenmann. According to her, Tejeda's main motives in his Agrarian League Organization and the rural guards that was composed of league members was to gain political power that would have enabled him to be better prepared for the battle for the Presidency. The result was the creation of a violent, oppressive rural Bossism which mainly served the wealthier farmers and sometimes the wealthy who were not farmers at all. Tejeda, points up Baitenmann, abandoned the poor farmers who could no longer pay for the lands that they had supposedly received for free, but not so. The farmers had difficulty going against landowner whom they identified with and had a close relationship, or they just refused Tejeda's offer of land because it demanded them to be at once commited league members, and conduct campaigns against farmers who refused to join the ranks of the agrarianists. This situation where the league administered the rural area including the municipal authorities, created two levels of citizens: a high level of agrarianists and a lower for no agrarianists. Baitenmann's work attempts to espouse an alternative historiography. Sometimes it goes well but sometimes it imposes itself on the facts, taken from limited informative corpus. This book affirms more than once the findings of Baitenmann but presents a more balanced picture that many times affirms the findings of Fowler.[20]

Very little material exists on Michoacán during Cárdenas's administration; to date only a short monograph by Alejo Maldonado Gallardo (1985), an article by Enrique Guerra Manzo (1999), and a broader study by Ginzberg (1999) have been written directly on the subject. In 2004 a very good chapter on Cárdenas's period was added by Verónica Oikión Solano in her huge study on the political history of Michoacán between 1924–1962. However, many authors have researched Michoacán in the framework of wider studies of Cárdenas as governor and president. Two conflicting historiographic schools have since developed in this area. One lauds Cárdenas; it includes, notably, Jesús Padilla Gallo (1935), William Townsend (1952), Nathaniel and Silvia Weyl (1955), Nathan Whetten (1969), David Raby (1973), Jesús Múgica Martínez (1982), Diego Hernández (1982), María del Carmen Nava (1984), Alejo Maldonado Gallardo (1985, 1993, 1995, 1997), Jorge Zepeda Patterson (1986, 1988, 1992), Gerardo Sánchez Díaz (1990), María Teresa Cortés-Zavala (1995) and Christopher Boyer (2003). The other, put forth by Victoriano Anguiano (1951, 1989), Arnulfo Embriz Osorio (1982, 1984), Marjorie Becker (1995) and, to some extent, Luis González y González (1968), criticizes Cárdenas as an insensitive and anti-clerical manipulator who forcibly imposed a formula for socioeconomic change that was inappropriate and unnatural for the Michoacán village, thereby abolishing any possibility of more natural, voluntaristic change.

The reason for the great difference in the number of studies and approaches to the two governors apparently lies in their respective political fates. The fact that Tejeda never rose above the rank of governor has led historians to concentrate on Veracruz, where his political career was born and died. Cárdenas's governorship, in contrast, was relatively short, an episode less important than his term as president. Historians have consequently chosen to focus on the seemingly more significant period of his presidency, and neglected the period that preceded it. In this respect, the present work will fill a conspicuous gap in the historiography of the Revolution in Michoacán, and provide an additional link in the historiography of the Revolution in Veracruz.

This text itself is divided into seven chapters. The first discusses the conditions prevailing in Veracruz and Michoacán when Tejeda and Cárdenas entered office, specifically, the readiness of two governors to adopt radical socioeconomic ideas. Chapter 2 describes how political power bases were established in the two states to facilitate implementation of the reforms planned by their respective governors. The chapter describes how the reforms operated, were supervised and controlled. Chapter 3 explains how Cárdenas and Tejeda used the public education system and anticlericalism to create a rationalist, secular, popular consciousness receptive to the reformist messages of the Revolution. These programs accelerated the social change that the two men sought to institute in their respective states. Chapters 4 and 5 focus on the struggle to promote agrarian reform, a Revolutionary platform that gave rise to the great agrarian epic in Veracruz, and to a momentous turning point in the social and economic evolution of Michoacán. Chapter 6 deals with the campaign to erase Cárdenas and Tejeda from the political map which succeeded in Veracruz but failed in Michoacán. Cárdenas survived because he had managed to establish power bases in the political center without challenging the hegemony of the federal government over Mexican political life. Tejeda, in contrast, had not taken such precautions; as a result, he was dependent on relatively weak and vulnerable local power groups that, on top of everything else, espoused a federalist ideology that was anathema at the time. The book's Conclusion discusses the two governors' fates, their contributions to Mexican agrarianism, and the implications for the ultimate shape of the Mexican republic; it closes with Cárdenas's success and Tejeda's failure in the presidential elections of 1934–1940.

1

Veracruz and Michoacán on the Threshold of a New Era

Background

A combination of land, precipitation patterns, and climate has given Veracruz the most bountiful agricultural heritage in Mexico. In 1930, it had more arable land and richer pasturage than any other state in the country, as well as particularly extensive plantations.[1] Beginning in the last quarter of the nineteenth century, Veracruz had enjoyed an unprecedented economic and demographic boom. During those years of prosperity, a liberal policy on foreign investment provided the stimulus for the exploitation of oil fields in the north of the state, as well as the establishment of large textile industries in the center and enormous new agricultural concerns (*latifundia*) producing coffee, sugar, tobacco, tropical fruits, and rare woods.[2] This accelerated economic growth attracted a massive influx of workers, making Veracruz the most populous state in Mexico in 1930, with 1,377,293 inhabitants living on an area of 72,815 square kilometers,. It also had the highest rate of demographic growth, and, by some measures, of economic growth (after the federal district).

Nature had been less kind to Michoacán (a Nahuatl name meaning "land of fishermen"), which in 1930 had a population of 1,048,381 inhabitants living on an area of 60,093 square kilometers. It had only half the annual precipitation rate of Veracruz, and its rainfall was limited to a single season; climactic conditions were harsh, and the topography made agriculture difficult, since some 52% of the state was mountainous (compared with only 20% of Veracruz). In addition, both its subterranean resources and its geopolitical location were very much inferior to those of Veracruz.[3] Owing to these circumstances, at the end of the 1920s Michoacán was primarily an agricultural state in which eight basic crops—corn, wheat, sesame, barley, sugar cane, beans, rice, and tomatoes—constituted about 94% of total agricultural production (1950 data). Corn alone accounted for 51.3% of that figure.[4]

The economic and demographic boom in Veracruz had no parallel in Michoacán, where the population grew by only 12% during the years 1900–1930, as opposed to Veracruz's 40%. In Michoacán income per unit of cultivated land was about a third lower than in Veracruz, and dependence on subsistence farming was double the rate in Veracruz.[5]

When Cárdenas and Tejeda took office, 71% of the population in Veracruz and 74% of the population in Michoacán lived in villages or small communities inhabited by fewer than 1,000 people. At the time, Michoacán had 6,123 population centers, including 11 cities—only one of which had more than 20,000 inhabitants. There were 7,991 population centers in Veracruz, 24 of them cities, of which three had 20,000 or more inhabitants.[6] Compared with Michoacán, Veracruz was an "urban" state, with about 14.5% of the population living in seven cities with populations exceeding 10,000 inhabitants; Michoacán, in contrast, had only four cities with populations greater than 10,000, and a mere 8% of the total population lived in them. *á*

Villages in both states suffered the same characteristic pattern of poverty—a low standard of living, a high illiteracy rate, and deep religiosity—but in Michoacán conditions were worse in all respects: nutrition, housing, wages, purchasing power, and land access. In 1930, rural wages in Veracruz were some 40% higher than in Michoacán, and purchasing power was almost double. The proportion of peasants able to obtain land in Veracruz was about 20.5%, as compared with 12% in Michoacán.[7] Although the two states were similar in many respects, their differences—particularly in measures of urbanization, access to land and income—were all in Veracruz's favor.

Indices of Industrialization and Political Sophistication

The two states differed widely in their levels of industrialization (excluding the mining and oil industries). Slightly more than 35,000 workers were employed in industry in Veracruz in 1930, producing 101.3 million pesos' worth of goods yearly, while Michoacán had fewer than 12,000 industrial workers, producing goods worth 19.6 million pesos yearly.[8] The average daily industrial wage in Veracruz was 1.77 pesos, compared with less than 0.70 pesos in Michoacán.[9] Mexico's first industrial survey (1935) confirmed Veracruz's marked industrial advantage over Michoacán across the board, recording ratios of 2:1 in industrial installations, 9:1 in invested capital, 2:1 in labor employed in industry, at least 10:1 in monetary yield, 5:1 in economic value of the industrial product, 2:1 or more in the average wage, and 8:1 in energy use. Similar disparities characterized the mineral industries of the two states—particularly gold, silver, copper, and lead in Michoacán, and oil in Veracruz.[10] These differences reflected not only Veracruz's much higher degree of industrialization and standard of living, but also its workers' greater bargaining power, which derived from their

Michoacán

La Piedad

Puruándiro

Sahuayo

Zamora

Jiquilpan

Cuitzeo

Jacona

Maravatío

Zacapu

Ciudad Hidalgo

Cherán

Angangueo

Los Reyes

Morelia

Jungapeo

Pátzcuaro

Uruapan

Zitácuaro

Tacambaro

Apatzingan

Ario de Rosales

La Huacana

Coalcomán

Aguillia

Huetamo

Arteaga

Verarcuz

- Tampico
- Pánuco
- Tempoal
- Tantoyuca
- Tuxpan
- Tihuatlán
- Poza Rica
- Papantla
- Martínez de la Torre
- Tlapacoyan
- Altotonga
- Jalapa
- Perote
- Xico
- Veracruz
- Córdoba
- Alvarado
- Orizaba
- Tlacotalpan
- Tierra Blanca
- Catemaco
- Coatzacoalcos
- Acayucan
- Minatitlán
- Jesús Carranza

high level of organization and their developed political and class consciousness.[11]

The great disparities in agricultural, industrial, and mineral production reflected Veracruz's much greater sociopolitical dynamism, as expressed in the development of a local labor movement shaped by various competing organizational and social ideologies. By the same token, Veracruz became the headquarters of a number of labor organizations: the Confederación Regional Obrera Mexicana (CROM—Regional Confederation of Mexican Labor), the largest labor organization in the Republic; the Confederación General de los Trabajadores (CGT—General Confederation of Labor), the labor union of the anarchist movement; and the communist labor organizations sponsored by the Partido Comunista Mexicana (PCM—Mexican Communist Party). This political sophistication facilitated the establishment in Veracruz of one of the first and strongest agrarian organizations in Mexico, the Liga de Comunidades Agrarias y Sindicatos Campesinos del Estado de Veracruz (Veracruz League of Agrarian Communities and Peasant Unions), which in 1926 spawned the Liga Nacional Campesina (LNC—National Peasant League), a national federation of regional peasant leagues that boasted 310,000 members in the year of its establishment.[12]

Agrarian Structure as an Index of Revolutionary Dynamism

A comparison of the agrarian *status quo* in the two states in 1930 indicates that conditions were much more difficult in Michoacán, as reflected in Table 1.1

Table 1.1 Land Tenure in Veracruz and Michoacán in 1930 (Private Properties of Over One Hectare)

State	Haciendas (more than 1,000 hectares)	Ranchos (100–1,000 hectares)	Small land-holdings (1–100 hectares)	Total land-holdings	Total Ranchos and Haciendas
Veracruz	822.00	5,267.00	59,339.00	65,424.00	6,089.00
% of Total Area	59.34	27.57	13.09	100.00	86.91
Michoacán	609.00	1,812.00	26,599.00	30,232.00	2,421.00
% of Total Area	68.96	19.31	11.73	100.00	88.27

Source: *Primer Censo Agrícola-Ganadero*, Tables 1–3, pp. 35–51.

The most important fact reflected by this table is that agrarian division in Veracruz was double that of Michoacán in all parameters, even though Veracruz's total area was only 20% larger than that of Michoacán (72,000 square kilometers as compared to 60,100 square kilometers). The table also shows different land-tenure patterns in the two states: In Michoacán landholdings tended to range from large to very large, while in Veracruz large and medium-sized properties were most common. In Veracruz 158 haciendas larger than 5,000 hectares accounted for some 32% of total land area, whereas 97 haciendas of that size took up about 42% of the land in Michoacán; the 40 haciendas measuring over 10,000 hectares in Michoacán accounted for 31% of total landholdings, while the 59 haciendas of that size in Veracruz constituted "only" 22% of total holdings in the state. Thirty-one percent of agrarian property in Michoacán consisted in medium-sized and small holdings, as opposed to about 41% in Veracruz.[13]

These different patterns of land distribution were also reflected in the status of the peasantry and their access to land: More than 60% of the peasants of Michoacán were peons residing on hacienda grounds (*peones acasillados*),[14] as opposed to only 9.4% in Veracruz, according to 1921 data (these figures had dropped considerably by 1930).[15] Moreover, in Veracruz, where there were more independent peasants working for a daily wage (*peones alquilados*), it was customary to rent out even large private plots, thereby giving more peasants access to land. In Michoacán, with its more restricted peasantry, landowners preferred to entrust the management of their property to administrators, or to set up sharecropping arrangements.

The preference for land leasing in one state and sharecropping arrangements in the other reflected two different labor cultures and different levels of social and economic consciousness. These differences would later influence both the nature and the quality of the agrarian reform instituted in each state. Where sharecropping was the custom, the reform tended to follow the ejidal pattern. Where land leasing was preferred, the reform tended to take two other forms: the creation of private smallholdings and the compulsory leasing (*arrendamiento forzoso*) of uncultivated lands that were expropriated for a limited time. This type of reform was best suited to the relatively free use of land embodied in the rental system.

The patterns of land distribution in Michoacán and the traditional system of agricultural production there were not conducive to the development of a labor or class consciousness nor to the arousal of any special enthusiasm for agrarian reform. Not only was there little pressure for land, but the political weakness of its governors blocked all possibility of any agrarianist boom until 1928.[16] In Veracruz, however, the situation was completely different. Just before Tejeda took office as governor, demand for land was high and agrarianism was strong, a trend that had been encouraged by every governor of Veracruz since Cándido Aguilar, the first constitutional governor.

Agrarian reform statistics for the years 1915–1927 reflect these differences. During those years 134 ejidos were established in Michoacán (on a provisional basis) on 172,666 hectares, while during the same period 299 ejidos were set up in Veracruz, on an area of 294,171 hectares. In Veracruz, with a population 31% larger than that of Michoacán, the extent of the reform was 45% greater than that implemented in Michoacán.[17] This imbalance was also reflected in the volume of petitions for land (*solicitudes*), which expressed substantially different levels of receptiveness to change: Whereas during the period in question 707 petitions were filed in Veracruz—the highest number in the Republic—only 266 were filed in Michoacán.[18]

Grassroots Organization and Its Influence on the Development of Agrarianism

In Veracruz agrarian reform had begun in the early 1920s. During the Porfirio Díaz years (1876–1911) the local economy enjoyed rapid growth, which created many employment opportunities and facilitated access to land. The resulting population increase, the famine engendered by the warfare of the Revolution, and the Revolution's pioneering agrarian law (in January 1915) gave rise to the first significant demands for land. The first petitioners were Italian day laborers in the sugar refineries in central Veracruz, who had been initiated into syndicalism in their land of origin.[19] This underlined a fact that was to become increasingly clear: Regardless of circumstances, agrarianist policies could not be implemented in the absence of a class and worker consciousness.

The return to Veracruz of the agrarianist leaders who had served in the Revolutionary army—for example, José Cardel, a *ranchero*, and Marcos C. Licona, a tenant farmer—helped spread the agrarianist message among the small tenant farmers in central Veracruz, who were hard-pressed to pay the high rents demanded of them. The peasants acquired the ideological foundation they had hitherto lacked from Communist propagandists who had gained experience in 1922 in a violent tenant campaign, headed by Manuel Almanza, Ursulo Galván and "a handful of other founding members of the Veracruz Syndicate" (Revolutionary Syndicates of Tenants—Sindicato Revolucionario de Inquilinos), for fair rental and living conditions in the city of Veracruz.[20] The landowners' organized resistance in the framework of the Junta de las Uniones de Propiedades y Agricultores del Estado de Veracruz and the ensuing series of bloody clashes between the two groups—which reached a climax in the Puente Nacional episode on 9 March 1923[21]—radicalized the principle of struggle in the peasant consciousness, a consciousness that was bolstered by the myths and symbols engendered by the conflict.

The establishment of the Liga de Comunidades Agrarias y Sindicatos Campesinos del Estado de Veracruz (hereafter Veracruz Agrarian League) on 23 March, 15 days after the Puente Nacional affair, was a direct expression of months of organizational activity, peasant struggle, and ideological maturation. Its foundation created a basis for expanding the circle of land petitioners to include independent peasants, who were generally unlikely to develop the consciousness necessary for political struggle and organization. The agrarianist camp now began to take on the shape of a mass movement.[22] The League's success in mobilizing agrarianists against the Adolfo de la Huerta revolt that lasted from October 1923, to May 1924, earned it the prize of an alliance with the state government of Veracruz that continued throughout Tejeda's second governorship.

The creation of the Veracruz Agrarian League, its role in the rebellion's suppression, and the agricultural crisis of 1924–1925 all expedited the appearance of rural unions organized under the aegis of the CROM and the CGT. Conditions were ripe for a joint struggle by workers and peasants in which each group reinforced the other: The workers could threaten to call up the agrarianists if they did not receive better working conditions, and the peasants could threaten worker strikes if they were prevented from organizing to qualify for land grants. The overall result was a marked increase in the rate of reform. In the first phase of agrarian reform—up to 1920—64 communities were founded; in the second (1920–1924) 154; and in the third (1925–1928), 184.[23]

In Michoacán, however, the agrarian reform stagnated. Its structural weakness and the ideological and political limitations of Michoacán's successive governors, further compounded by the Cristero Rebellion and an efficient opposition mounted by the rural oligarchy and urban business sectors reduced it to almost nothing. The meager 53 petitions for land filed in the years 1925–1927 (compared with Veracruz's 207 for the same period) clearly indicated the dismal state of agrarianism in Michoacán.[24]

In contrast to the dynamic agrarianist organization in Veracruz, the Liga de Comunidades y Sindicatos Agraristas del Estado de Michoacán (the Michoacán Agrarian League)—founded in December 1922, by Primo Tapia of Naranja—could not provide any real support for the weak local agrarianist base. It was not strong enough to contend with the powerful Noriega family, who owned land in the Zacapú area, where the League was based; it could not suppress the fierce infighting among its own leadership and develop a clear operational strategy; and it was unable to compete with the Church's militant social Catholicism and win the support of the state, which would not forgive Tapia for sitting on the fence during the De la Huerta revolt.[25] The peasants' fear of both the Church and the Noriega family was so great that on one occasion, when Primo Tapia was trying to organize an agrarian committee to sign petitions for land, he was forced to pretend that the purpose of the meeting was to draft a letter to the Church administration in Morelia asking it to send a priest to tend to the community's religious needs. Once he had obtained 109 signatures by this ruse, he changed the letter into an agrarian petition which was then duly sent off to the Comisión Local Agraria (CLA—Local Agrarian Commission, the state branch of the Comisión Nacional Agraria).[26] In short, the Michoacán League lacked the Veracruz League's two outstanding advantages: a unified leadership and political and unionist support. Tapia's murder in April 1926, apparently on Calles's orders,[27] put paid to the modest beginnings of an agrarianist movement in the state, and, of course, to any organizational continuity such as the Veracruz League enjoyed.[28] When in April 1928, Cárdenas returned to Michoacán to wage his election campaign after three years as the divisional military commander in Huasteca in northern Veracruz, he found only remnants of the old Michoacán Agrarian League—still kicking, if feebly, but completely insignificant politically.

Given the different conditions of agrarian reform in the two states, the new governors faced different problems. In Michoacán the main question was how to resuscitate the reform, whereas in Veracruz the challenge was to accelerate it. Although both governors talked of fully implementing the reform during their terms of office, only for Tejeda was this goal actually possible; for Cárdenas it was a pipe dream.

Tejeda's Road to Power

Tejeda took office in 1928 thanks to a successful combination of political circumstance, manipulation, and clever planning. The circumstance that allowed him to serve a second term as governor was the amendment of Articles 82 and 83 of the federal Constitution canceling the prohibition on reelection (thereby allowing Obregón to run for a second presidential term), which prompted a similar amendment of Article 85 of the political consti-tution of Veracruz in October 1926.[29] From the moment he realized the relevance of the "Obregón amendment" to his own situation, Tejeda began to take energetic measures to weaken opposition to his reelection in Veracruz. The spearhead of that opposition was the state's military commander, General Arnulfo Gómez, and one of the two Veracruz senators, Arturo Campillo Seyde. Gómez's opposition was not particularly difficult to overcome: All Tejeda had to do to have Gómez put aside was to show Calles that he constituted a threat to the integrity of the Republic. Gómez's aggres-sive tirades against the supporters of reelection and his threats to rebel if his road to the presidency were blocked left no doubt as to his intentions. His eventual revolt in October 1927, and resultant elimination removed the first obstacle from Tejeda's path.[30]

Taking action against Seyde was more complicated. Obregón was partial to him and disliked Tejeda, who besides being too radical for his taste was a supporter of Obregón's rival, Calles.[31] Given this delicate situation Tejeda wisely decided to set up a joint electoral apparatus for himself and Obregón. This clever move neutralized Seyde, who, forced into a corner, collected around himself all the Veracruz anti-reelectionist forces that had been lead-erless since the execution of General Arnulfo Gómez and Francisco R. Serrano in the fall of 1927. His anti-reelection campaign, although directed at Tejeda and his efforts to win a second term as state governor, naturally made an enemy of Obregón as well, since the latter was also seeking reelec-tion. At the same time Tejeda courted Calles's support by reinforcing the *Callista* power bases in Veracruz. The idea that Calles would replace Obregón in 1934 was not unreasonable given the new constitutional amend-ment, and Calles had an interest in guaranteeing Tejeda's support for his future candidacy by backing Tejeda now.

To judge by statewide manifestations of support for Tejeda's candidacy, the campaign for governor began unofficially on 31 March 1927, almost 16 months before the elections. Tejeda's idea was to start early in order to get a head start over his rivals.[32] On 30 August 1927 a group of Obregonist-Tejedist students in Jalapa, spurred by their fear that Arnulfo Gómez would revolt against the government, formed a committee to promote Tejeda's candidacy and to combat what they called Arnulfo Gómez's "reactionary" views. The danger that threatened the Republic, they explained, obliged them to "stand by the government in the sole interest of safeguarding the institutions created by the Revolution," in order to ensure the continuation of "the well-being won by blood [spilled in the Revolution]."[33] On 9 November 1927 this committee was expanded into a joint Obregonist-Tejedist front, inaugurated at a meeting in the Limón Theater in Jalapa attended by 500 representatives of worker and peasant organizations. On November 25—and, to judge by the time lapse, probably not without considerable hesitation—Obregón gave the new association his blessing.[34]

On 4 January 1928, a further step was taken: The front became a political party called the Gran Partido Socialista Veracruzano de Obreros y Campesinos (Great Veracruz Socialist Party of Workers and Peasants), which was in fact an umbrella organization for dozens, if not hundreds, of committees and subcommittees, as well as 11 parties constituted mainly by workers in the large cities. The latter included the Partido Ferrocarrilero Unitario (Unitary Railway Party) of Veracruz and Jalapa, run by Hernán Laborde, one of the founding fathers of the Mexican Communist Party (PCM). On 1 January 1928, Laborde told Tejeda "the workers of Veracruz enthusiastically support your candidacy for governor of the state."[35]

The pro-Tejedist front was united and very stable. It managed without difficulty to put Gómez, who had mustered all the anti-reelectionist forces, out of the running for president. It also defeated Seyde's efforts to undermine Tejeda's legitimacy through court action brought on the grounds that the "Obregón amendment" did not apply to state governors, since Article 115 of the Constitution, concerning governors, had not been amended to accord with Articles 82 and 83.[36] In the meantime, the electoral campaign officially began on 4 May 1928. Gómez's assassination at the beginning of November 1927, and Seyde's failure to win sufficient public support for his challenge to the legality of Tejeda's candidacy left Tejeda as the sole contender when the time came to submit the candidate lists, on 18 July 1928. The assassination of Obregón on the same day shattered Seyde's last hopes—if he still had any.[37]

The sophisticated support system that Tejeda developed for himself reflected great political talent and a deep understanding of the people operating in the federal arena. Interestingly, most of his support within Veracruz came not from the peasants, who were divided by the battle against Seyde, but from the workers, who were united behind him—according to a letter from Marte Gómez, then-president of the Comisión Nacional Agraria (CNA—National Agrarian Commission, the body responsible for administering the land reform law), who wrote to his friend Portes Gil, the governor of Tamaulipas, that in Veracruz Campillo Seyde would "fight with the support of the agrarianists and Tejeda with the support, perhaps, of the workers and with the personal friendship of Calles."[38] Yet the power Tejeda derived from the workers, though significant, was a transient phenomenon with no roots in the past.[39] This curious fact reflected a problematic truth about him: his rather sectoral appeal, which handicapped his ability to form a lasting political coalition.

Although his victory was virtually assured, Tejeda embarked on a formal campaign tour. In an interview accorded to the Veracruz daily *El Dictamen* on the eve of the tour, he revealed his plans to seek contact with different sectors of society and to study the ways he could help them as governor. His top priority, he asserted, would be economic and social issues. He would address the issues of industrial functioning and the textile slump, land-use problems, education, and moral and intellectual life in the village. Tejeda also promised to consider the thorny question of Veracruz's decaying land-based communication system. "Although this tour is like political propaganda," he told his interviewer, "its main purpose is to study the various problems in each of the regions of Veracruz, to get to know them well, and to develop appropriate solutions."[40]

On 28 November 1928, two days before taking office, Tejeda told a reporter from *El Dictamen* about his political program, which was based in part on what he had learned during his campaign tour. The wording of the program was very down-to-earth and devoid of the philosophical rhetoric that characterized his later speeches, but indicated a deep social commitment. Tejeda promised to solve the urbanization problems of the city of Veracruz by making use of the pasture land between the city and the shore to build spacious, hygienic housing for workers, expand the harbor, build public structures, and pave the road from Jalapa to Veracruz and other places. Turning to agrarian matters, he spoke of the need to create an atmosphere propitious to voluntary distribution of land by the owners. With modern agricultural methods, he said, it was no longer necessary to work thousands of hectares to turn a profit; on the contrary, the greater the territory, the less disposable income the owners had for investment. Even Calles's own ranch near Mexico City, he noted, measured a mere 200 hectares, on which he raised beef, vegetables, and alfalfa—producing more than most of the great *latifundia* in Veracruz did on their 10,000 hectares or more, because on the *latifundia* "the owner expect[ed] everything to come from the work and initiative of the tenant or sharecropper without any effort on his part." The present situation was intolerable, Tejeda stressed, since it denied many households access to the land they needed for their livelihood. He concluded by warning the *hacendados* that the state would not release them from the debt they owed it. His underlying message was clear: The landowners would be better off breaking up their estates voluntarily than waiting for them to be expropriated.[41]

In the same interview, Tejeda promised to promote the ejido system by establishing a bank for ejidal credit that would help ejidatarios exploit the full agricultural potential of the land they received. Similarly, he promised to found a central agricultural school similar to those established in some states during Calles's presidency, as well as large numbers of rural schools, each one of which would receive land for agricultural training so that it could give its students a more practical education. He also pledged to begin irrigation projects, and to encourage the establishment of small agricultural and industrial cooperatives of workers and peasants that would promote a solid, orderly economic regime in Veracruz, "since Veracruz has such good lands for getting products that can be industrialized."[42] In the industrial sphere, Tejeda promised, first of all, to rehabilitate the entire sugar industry, which was inefficient, lacked an adequate technological basis, and was suffering a commercial decline, and to promote the rest of the state's "big industries" (presumably he meant primarily the textile industry) "in the spirit of labor legislation."

Thus, the Tejeda program was mainly economic in nature, focusing for the most part on the land issue. It could not have anticipated what would take place in Veracruz in the years to come, although Tejeda did seem to be preparing public opinion for the necessity of breaking up large properties and reorganizing them according to modern economic criteria. He may have refrained from proposing a specific program to break up the *latifundia* in order to appear moderate, at least until his rule was firmly established; or perhaps at that point such a radical policy had not yet occurred to him. Both possibilities are equally plausible; but even if he was thinking of an energetic agrarian campaign of the sort pursued, by his account, in Italy, France, and other European countries, he was neither ideologically nor practically ready for it, and lacked the necessary political clout to implement it.

Cárdenas's Road to Power

Cárdenas's road to power was easier than Tejeda's, legally, politically, and publicly. He was able to give his campaign tour the aura of a manifestly revolutionary mission firmly based on a well-integrated social program, that encouraged the radicals but apparently did not frighten the conservatives. He, too, began his campaign contacts a relatively long time before the election, early in 1927, when he was still commander of the Huasteca region. At that time, Michoacán citizens began to urge him to declare his candidacy for governor. The Michoacán Congress itself took the initiative, in February 1927, of declaring that it considered Cárdenas as its candidate for the office. The flow of appeals increased towards the end of the year, when delegations of workers, peasants, and friends began visiting his headquarters to try to persuade him to run.[43]

Three major bodies, representing a very wide political spectrum, stood behind these appeals: a collection of ad hoc pro-Cárdenas local parties[44]; the Unión de Partidos Socialistas de Michoacán (Union of Socialist Parties of Michoacán), led by Silvestre Guerrero, a supporter of the radical Francisco José Múgica (erstwhile governor of Michoacán); and a confederation of conservative, bourgeois parties, the Confederación de Partidos

Revolucionarios de Michoacán (Confederation of Revolutionary Parties of Michoacán), headed by Melchor Ortega, an active member (*diputado*) of the local and the national parliaments and a rich *hacendado* from the Tierra Caliente area who had been one of Governor Múgica's most fierce opponents.[45]

This blend of organizations indicates that both the Left and the conservatives saw Cárdenas as a viable candidate; and as a Calles man he aroused no more anxieties among landowners than had his predecessor, Enrique Ramírez. Thanks to his army career, which had included military and political posts in Michoacán itself, he was well-known and widely respected by the public, who saw him as a solid, honest, law-abiding, authoritative man able to cope with organizational questions on a broad scale. When the time came to choose a candidate for governor, Múgica's followers remembered him, and so did residents and public figures of all the communities where, as a military officer back in the early 1920s, he had striven to eliminate banditry and impose public order. The bourgeoisie, for its part, was looking for an authoritative figure to stamp out the Cristero Rebellion, which was threatening public safety in the state, and to resolve the economic crisis that had handicapped business in Michoacán since 1925.[46]

Cárdenas, with his keen political sense, kept his supporters in suspense. He was waiting for Calles and Obregón to endorse his candidacy. The lessons he had learned from Obregón's forcible removal of Múgica in 1922, and from his own observations of post-Revolutionary Mexican politics (amply documented in his correspondence with Múgica) made him particularly careful not to appear too eager to be governor.[47] In the meantime, time was not working in his favor. Letters he received from Múgica on 27 December 1927 and on 24 and 30 April 1928 informed him that another man had begun to conduct "a vigorous propaganda campaign" in Michoacán and that in some areas it was difficult to promote Cardenist candidates for the local Congress.[48] To Cárdenas's gratification, however, he finally received Calles's blessing towards the end of 1927, thereby becoming the sole candidate for governor.[49]

In bestowing that blessing, Calles gave due consideration—as he had in Tejeda's case—both to Cárdenas's loyalty and abilities and to his own political needs, given the possibility of rotating the presidency between himself and Obregón.[50] At a certain stage Obregón, too, extended his support to Cárdenas. Obregón was pleased with this young officer, who had supported him against Carranza in 1920 and De la Huerta in 1923–1924, and had even helped him block Múgica's return to local government in 1923.[51]

This was clearly the moment to announce a general political platform and to begin the election campaign. On 10 January 1928, Cárdenas published a proclamation to the Michoacán people, and on 20 January he declared his candidacy for the governorship. Unlike Tejeda's cautious, ambiguous program, Cárdenas's platform was trenchant and unequivocal. He declared himself as an agrarianist, a sworn democrat, a legalist faithful to the 1917 constitution, and an uncompromising champion of the Revolutionary prin-

ciples laid down in that constitution—particularly those concerning the rehabilitation and protection of the working classes. Cárdenas clearly indicated
that he intended to make radical changes in all spheres of life, but would
concentrate on three main issues: agrarian reform, educational reform, and
economic rehabilitation. He saw these aims not only as a political mission,
but also—and primarily—as a moral mission, since they derived from the
revolutionary postulates he had undertaken to implement. This commitment
was completely personal, a matter of subordinating his own interests to the
collective good, and would constitute the yardstick by which he measured
his own political success.[52]

This well-developed program and its assertive spirit reflected Cárdenas's
considerable self-assurance and his carefully thought-out ideology, qualities
that Tejeda lacked at the time. Undoubtedly the wide support for his candidacy for governor, the fact that he did not have to break the sacred
Revolutionary principle of "*no reelección*," and his efforts to conceptualize
Mexican reality all contributed to his image as a man of vision rather than
just another slick politician—a man who had greater confidence in the future
than Tejeda did.

Like Tejeda, Cárdenas decided to embark on a tour of the state in order
to become acquainted with the population and its problems. On this tour,
which began in April 1928, he had the opportunity not only to see for himself
Michoacán's wretched situation, but also to clarify his views and adjust his
plans for reform. While visiting Zacapú, he met with the remnants of Primo
Tapia's agrarian league, about which he wrote afterwards to his friend
Múgica:

> I consider that there we have the basis of a peasant organization that,
> forming a single front in the State, will respond effectively in the social
> struggle carried on by the peasants of our state—a struggle from which
> they have had less benefit than in other states because of bad political
> elements who remember them only when elections are approaching.[53]

This letter underlines an issue that influenced Cárdenas throughout his
political career: the fact that the agrarian reform in Michoacán failed to
achieve much because the peasants were not effectively organized. As a
result, they were cynically exploited by various politicians for political
purposes without receiving much in return. In Cárdenas's view, the way to
remedy this was to organize the peasants in one united front that would
promote the reform and work to apply the agrarian laws to the fullest.

The campaign tour was encouraging. Almost everywhere Cárdenas went,
"the revolutionary behavior and suppression of fanaticism we mentioned
were received with applause," as he wrote to Múgica. Nevertheless, in some
regions—Zacapú, for example, which was "rich in priests and monks"—
"reaction was still alive." Not all the valley communities responded
favorably to Cárdenas's impassioned speeches about the importance of
agrarianism and the need to eliminate religious fanaticism.[54] His conclusion

was that, along with zealous educational and agrarian reforms to cut the Gordian knot between religion and the abject poverty of the countryside, the number of priests in the state had to be reduced. These were the two facets of his government's future program, which was to be formulated along the lines of what he called, in a letter to Múgica, the "moral and constructive basis of the Revolution."

Cárdenas was also concerned about the Cristero Rebellion and the way it was undermining the power of the local government. To protect his administration, he decided that after election day (10 June) he would put himself at the service of the war and navy ministry, since he wanted—as he wrote to Múgica—to take active measures to eliminate the "fanatic rebels." "I have a particular interest," he wrote, "in ensuring that President Calles sees the country at peace before he leaves the Government, and I need peace in this state so that my own Government will not be a failure."[55] Accordingly, immediately after his victory at the polls he reenlisted in the army, receiving a commission as military commander of Michoacán until he took up his duties as governor on 16 September.[56]

Cárdenas was well-prepared for his role as governor. His conscientious election tour, his observations of Michoacán reality "in the field," and his meeting with Múgica in Huasteca all taught him vital lessons about the ramifications of Mexican politics, while his ideological and political maturity, which his friend Múgica defined as "seriousness in radicalism," equipped him to cope with the whole range of urgent problems in Michoacán: the Cristero Rebellion, a limping agrarian reform, a government with no clear ideological orientation, an unorganized populace, a rigid and conservative municipal administration, strong attachment to the Church among the people, and an education system in crisis.

Towards a New Era?

Veracruz, by virtue of its physical, demographic, social, and economic characteristics, was ready for Tejeda's programs. Michoacán's basic profile, in contrast, was much less propitious. Nonetheless, since the issues of grassroots organization, class consciousness, and land ownership were on the agenda in both states and the politicians at the helm were unusually dynamic and determined, it was only to be expected that in both states agrarianists would clash with the rural oligarchies, the middle class and the Church institutions—in a struggle that would escalate into an ideological confrontation. The past history of these institutions, especially the rural oligarchy, should have suggested as much. Since the Revolution the rural oligarchy in Michoacán had made every effort to eliminate the beginnings of agrarianism, and had produced the murderers of the first agrarianist leaders, including Miguel de la Trinidad Regalado, Izaac Araiga, and Primo Tapia, as well as of later leaders—notably Rafael Picazo.[57]

The Veracruz oligarchy, largely composed of foreigners, was very powerful, militant, and highly experienced in anti-agrarianist battles. One such battle culminated in the murder of José Cardel, and another in the murder of the agrarianists at Puente Nacional. At the end of the 1920s this oligarchy found a leader in the person of Manuel Parra, the owner of the Almolonga hacienda. Parra set up a terrorist organization called Mano Negra that sowed fear in central Veracruz for more than 20 years, killing many hundreds of agrarianist activists and leaders.[58]

Both Cárdenas and Tejeda apparently realized they would have to strive to implement their views systematically, rather than in patchwork fashion as circumstance dictated. In the past, such ad hoc attempts to advance social issues had failed or at most achieved only partial success. This indicated that a strong political power structure would be needed in order to impose the elbow room needed to implement the goals of the Revolution. In this respect, Veracruz's basic geopolitical profile gave it a clear advantage over Michoacán.

2

Towards Reform:
The Development of
Leadership Patterns and
a Political Infrastructure

Priorities and Modes of Operation

The lessons of the past in Michoacán and Veracruz had clearly shown Cárdenas and Tejeda that a sophisticated power base was indispensable for political freedom of action. Equally important was the adoption of methods of control and supervision to ensure that the power base performed its function and did not rise up against its creator. Both governors directed their efforts—though with varying degrees of emphasis and energy—into four main channels: organizing the masses; taking over the sphere of local government; arming the peasants; and promoting their own status in the local and federal contexts. In Michoacán, the central issue was organizing the grassroots. In Veracruz, which already had an organized popular infrastructure, the main challenge was gaining control of the municipios (basic political-administrative units roughly equivalent to counties). However, although the two states differed in focus, they were alike in the extraordinary level of determination, perseverance, and daring their governors demonstrated in pursuing the focal issues.

Organizing the Masses

The Veracruz Agrarian League: Organizational and Ideological Bases

From the day of its inception until it joined the Confederación Nacional Campesina (CNC—National Peasant Confederation) in 1937, the Veracruz Agrarian League was an agrarianist and rural syndical league. All attempts to extend its control to urban workers failed. Even in its limited sphere of operation, however, the League managed to achieve extraordinary power, becoming a large and effective organization with a finger in every pie. It shaped agrarian ideology, organized extensively on the local and national levels, and undertook agrarian, legal, financial, educational, military, and administrative field work of unprecedented scope. By 1932, the League seemed to have become the democratic popular alternative to the paternalist, interventionist party structure that Calles had designed for Mexico. Before it lost its autonomy in 1933, it undoubtedly represented the last hope of building a decentralized "rural democracy," as Arturo Warman calls it; the great pains the central government took to break it up after Tejeda left office confirm this.

The League was founded as a class-based organization with a Marxist orientation, and its ambitions went much further than the ambit of Veracruz alone. Its goal was to develop a socialist, revolutionary consciousness in the peasants that would prepare them, when the time came, to replace the capitalist liberalism that had engulfed Mexico despite the Revolution with a proletarian socialism. The League's ideologue, Manuel Almanza, did not see the League's agrarian achievements as the be-all and end-all of its existence. In his view, agrarianism was something to which the bourgeoisie paid lip-service, a way of keeping the peasants quiet while maintaining their inferior position in society. The League's real achievement, Almanza felt, must be measured by its success in instating the peasants in their true position in society, as part of a ruling proletariat class. The "social question," he stressed, could be resolved only "by the proletariat's final triumph over the capitalist class."[1]

The Veracruz Agrarian League's basic platform was ratified at its second convention, which took place in Jalapa from 28 November to 4 December 1924. On that occasion, the League asserted that it would adopt the principles of Articles 27 and 123 of the federal constitution as the basis of a minimum short-term plan to safeguard the rights of both ejidatarios and wage-earning peasants. It also endorsed the cooperative ejido as one of the social and economic bases of national development. For the long term, however, the League outlined a more ambitious program for socializing all land and other means of production. It also presented the peasant problem as an international rather than merely Mexican issue, and as such important in its own right. It had to be solved in cooperation with the urban workers "without [whom] it would be impossible to fulfill all [the proletariat's] supreme aspirations." The members of the convention decided that the League would do everything it could to improve the *campesinos*' material, economic, moral, and intellectual situation, and that it would also seek to liberate them from the Church's influence, which clouded their recognition "of the economic tyranny that [kept them] mired in poverty, and of the ignorance that [retarded their] integral development." The League's flag was to be red and its slogan would be "*tierra y libertad*" ("land and liberty").[2]

The League also passed a series of resolutions designed to settle political accounts with all the members of the oligarchy who had taken part in the

Escobar–Aguirre revolt, forcing them to pay compensation to peasants who had suffered losses from the revolt, whether in lives or in property. In addition, the League called for an accelerated expropriation of the collaborators' lands so that they could be distributed to the petitioners still waiting for grants. It further advocated arming the peasants and organizing some of them into military colonies, as well as providing permits to bear arms for all those currently mobilized in the 86th agrarianist battalion that had fought against the rebels within the framework of the federal army. The League saw itself as the proper body to take charge of the arming process, and called on all the agrarianist committees in the state to send it lists of peasants eligible to carry arms. At the same time, it began lobbying Calles, then just beginning his term as president of the Republic, and the local and federal Congresses for the necessary permits.[3] Issues affecting the *campesinos'* daily life, such as the establishment of an agricultural credit bank and various cooperative enterprises, agricultural inputs, efficient and experimental farming methods, and pest control, which had been on the official convention agenda, were postponed to future conventions. The preoccupation with lofty ideals left no time for these more prosaic subjects.[4]

The League was dominated by ideological tension until March 1929, when it broke with the Communist party over the latter's support for the Aguirre revolt. At that point, undoubtedly a decisive historical moment, the League began to move towards closer ties with Tejeda. The League needed a patron and Tejeda needed a popular power base. This symbiotic relationship allowed the League to become the largest, strongest, and most influential organization in Veracruz.[5]

The Veracruz League as a Power Base

In addition to its ideology and operational orientations, the League brought to its relationship with Tejeda a substantial organizational dowry consisting of a unified leadership, a team of local activists and representatives in many of the rural unions and agrarian committees, and an advanced system of policy- and decision-making. The League's rich experience in dealing with all kinds of land issues allowed the state administration to use the organization as an all-purpose agrarian agency—it merely had to be strengthened and given more influence in the formal power centers.[6] The task, then, was to begin introducing the League into the municipal, parliamentary, military, and administrative spheres—in short, into public life in general.

Two years of intensive activity in this direction proved fruitful: The League gained control of at least 100 municipios and held 12 of the 21 seats in the state legislature in 1930 (and 7 out of 14 in 1932); it set up an impressive militia of 22,000–30,000 people, the largest in Mexico;[7] it infiltrated many branches of the state administration; and it became a central arbiter of both agrarian policy and a great deal of public policy. "Owing to its numerical strength and political influence," an *El Dictamen* reporter wrote in October 1931, "this [agrarianist] majority bloc carried the other, minority deputies along with it in its decisions so that the agrarianist bloc, the real representative and parliamentary mouthpiece of the state League of Agrarian Communities, came to achieve great political ascendancy."[8]

Arming the organized peasants was a natural step in Veracruz, which had been an important base for most of the rebellions of the 1920s. The Escobar–Aguirre revolt had prompted the Veracruz Congress, on 14 March 1929, to give Tejeda emergency powers for a period of six months so that he could amend regulations in the fields of defense and the economy.[9] Four days after receiving these powers Tejeda published an edict establishing a local volunteer militia (the *guerrilla*) and calling on all the citizens of the state, particularly the peasants and the workers, to come to the defense of the institutions "conquered by the Revolution." He based his authority to issue this edict on various articles of the state constitution, on the special powers he had been granted a few days earlier, and on the increased authority that the president had vested in the state governors as a way of bolstering internal security during a period of crisis.[10]

The enabling law for the edict establishing Tejeda's militia (24 June 1929) went one step further and stipulated that the *guerrilla* would be made up exclusively of agrarianists. It also provided, doubtless with ulterior motives, that the militia units would be organized in groups of 10–30 men based in rural centers and anywhere else that the government saw fit.[11] In addition, the authority to enlist "volunteers" was vested not in the local police commanders, but in the League. As a result, many ejido heads and presidents of ejidal executive committees (*comités ejecutivos*) became militia commanders, while League leaders trained and coordinated the militia units.[12]

When the state Congress's summer session opened in 1931, Tejeda was able to boast that the peasants were now organized in two frameworks, the League and the agrarian militia. He exulted, "Despite the efforts to discredit the organized peasant, it can be asserted that the immediate result of this organization is peace and quiet in the countryside."[13] Given the tensions in the villages of Veracruz, the establishment of the militia had a crucial impact on the nature, scope, and ultimate fate of local agrarianism, as well as on government control of the countryside.[14]

Besides protecting agrarianists, the militia units had dozens of other tasks. They kept an eye on the *hacendados* and Church supporters—including teachers, administrative officials, and municipio functionaries, as well as simple peasants who clung to religious observance despite its prohibition since July 1931. They also monitored small groups of Cristeros operating in the state, and battled crime and "unrest," the latter attributed by Tejeda to "immoral politicians who do not hesitate to incite fanatical elements against the government." Another task of the *guerrilla* was to combat "moral" transgressions, and it pursued gamblers, prostitutes, and producers of bootleg alcohol. In short, it took an active interest in every circumstance that deviated from the legal, moral, and political norms of the Tejedist administration.[15]

At times the militia abused its great power. Various administrative offices, particularly the interior and justice departments and the office of Tejeda himself, received many complaints from agrarianists that some *guerrilla* units were collaborating with landowners against the peasants. In a typical complaint, a group of ejidatarios from the Jamapa municipio, who claimed to represent many members of different agrarian committees throughout the municipio, told Tejeda at the beginning of November 1931, that the peasants were being persecuted relentlessly by the militia, which laid murderous nighttime ambushes for them, burned their homes, attacked their daughters, protected sacred icons that had been ordered destroyed, and so on. They noted that although the local militia had been relieved of its weapons once already, the *hacendados* had rearmed them. Accordingly, they asked that the force be disarmed once again, and disbanded.[16] Thus, while some peasants were submitting requests for permission to establish militia units, others were petitioning for their dissolution.

Since the League was a semi-official government agent, the administration felt obliged to finance it, but had to exercise caution in publishing figures; the government budget could not include an institution that was not part of the formal administrative structure of the state. Tejeda did not conceal the fact that his government provided the League with office space and equipment, publicity, and training, since it was customary for the state administration to assist any organization that requested support for its social activities. But the financial assistance received by the League was cloaked in secrecy, suggested only by a budgetary category cryptically entitled "special expenses" (*gastos extraordinarios*).[17]

At the beginning of 1932 the League's power and influence were at their height. Partly because of this, that year witnessed the most radical developments in agrarian reform. On 13 May, the president of the Veracruz Agrarian League, José García, wrote to League representatives around the state that the organized peasants' historic mission to "socialize" the land could be achieved only by seizing power. "This goal will never be achieved," he wrote, "through democratic use of ballots, but through the organized power of the revolutionary workers."[18] With 140,000 members, organized and integrated institutions, a majority in the local Congress, a large armed force, control over many local authorities, close to 2,000 agrarian committees, and many unions, the League was ready for the next, truly revolutionary stage of agrarianism, essential for any real agrarian reform.

Why Veracruz Had No United Proletarian Front

Tejeda put most of his energy into building up the League rather than trying to create a united proletarian front. Few historians have addressed the complex question as to whether this was a conscious decision based on his view of the countryside as the primary focus for socioeconomic change, or whether the power and independence of the major urban workers' organizations of Veracruz left him no choice. David Skerritt claims that Tejeda decided not to create a single proletarian front because the undisciplined and unfaithful CGT could not be trusted, and the CROM was too closely linked to the federal center, which might have limited Tejeda's freedom to maneuver. Tejeda also feared that a single front would constitute an overly strong power center that would be dangerous to himself. In addition, Skerritt writes, Tejeda's main problem was not in the cities but in the country. That was where the state's largest population sector lived—a sector that was also the weakest and the easiest to control; and it was the source of the primary opposition to his government. Accordingly, Tejeda spent more time organizing the peasants and less on the urban workers, who were less important to him. Nevertheless, he took pains to encourage dissension among the different urban organizations so that, playing the part of the impartial arbitrator, he could maintain some degree of influence over them.[19] Skerritt—together with Romana Falcón and Soledad García Morales[20]—argues that Tejeda's failure to establish a united front could be attributed to a mixture of pragmatism and independent political decision. In this case there is no need to talk about failure, but rather Tejada's informed decision based on political expediency.

Another factor that should be taken into account, however, is Tejeda's general approach to organization. Creating a "pan-Veracruz" labor confederation was certainly a very daunting project, but it was not an impossible one. Although a large percentage of workers were already members of autonomous national or local organizations, there was still a large untapped reservoir of unaffiliated workers in Veracruz, and considerable popular support for Tejeda himself as a result of his great attentiveness to workers' interests and needs.[21] Enlistment efforts could have taken advantage of such political circumstances as the outlawing of the Communist party in 1929, Calles's withdrawal of patronage from the CROM and its workers' party (Partido Laborista Mexicano—PLM) from 1929 on, and the CROM's internal leadership crisis and loss of national influence (though the crisis had less impact in Veracruz). Tejeda's firm grip on the city of Veracruz from 1931 on and his energetic efforts to build worker housing as part of a campaign against profiteering landlords also gave him a certain leverage in his relations with the CGT and the independent unions in town. Yet although he capitalized on that to strengthen his own position, he never tried to control them or to unite them in a single framework.[22]

Apparently the main factor inhibiting Tejeda from taking over at least part of the labor movement was his own belief that freedom of syndical organization was essential for the development of a proletarian consciousness and an authentic leadership. In his view, the democratic Mexican state had to arise out of an autonomous labor movement organized from the bottom up—like the Agrarian League—since an organization imposed from above would doom the workers to a position of permanent weakness, dependence, and irrelevance in their struggle against powerful foreign interests and the capitalist tendencies of the political center, forcing them into galling compromises. That is why Tejeda emphatically opposed the bureaucratic and paternalist model of the PNR and supported the Communist unions even after their party had been outlawed; and that is why he was on close terms with the anarchists, helping them set up new unions in the Veracruz port in order to rescue the port workers from the coercive organizing tactics of the veteran unions there.[23] In his opinion, freedom to organize and organizational spontaneity were intrinsic to proletarian democracy. Consequently, any efforts to unify the proletariat in Veracruz were never more than sporadic attempts by one local PNR committee or another; and Tejeda himself never initiated such attempts, or thought of joining them.[24]

Similarly, Tejeda never sought to take over the leadership of the Agrarian League (as Cárdenas did, for example), or pressured it to unite with the PNR. From the day the Veracruz League was established most of its leadership came from the *campesino* grassroots, and this remained the case throughout Tejeda's administration.[25] Although he used the League to reinforce his own power and worked with it very closely, he never tried to impose any particular organizational structure or agenda of his own on it. By the same token, he also refrained from intervening in the organization's internal power struggles.[26]

Despite Tejeda's class and monist views, which would presumably have dictated a proletarian unity of action and organization, he was reluctant to try to impose such unity from above and before the time was ripe. In his opinion, the unification of the proletariat had to come as the result of a mature revolutionary consciousness that sprang from an autonomous proletarian democracy in action—meaning decentralized. In this view, the state's role was only to coordinate and encourage, pave the way and reinforce—never to direct or unify. The League and the other labor organizations were supposed to act as independent partners of the state, while at the same time lobbying it to intervene in the interests of the peasants and workers. These organizations would in fact replace the state once a mature class consciousness and proletarian unity had been achieved and the proletariat had taken over the means of production. The labor organizations, rather than the state, had to be the historic subject of the revolutionary process, while the state was to be the object—the opposite of the trend that had prevailed since the Revolution.

According to this reasoning, promoting the League as a separate but privileged organization was merely a temporary expedient until a balance could be achieved between capital and labor in the country and between rural labor and urban labor, since the latter enjoyed syndical advantages that rural workers had never known. At that point of equilibrium, the separation between the two components of the labor movement would supposedly lose its rationale, and the workers would unite spontaneously and democratically as a natural result of their improved material conditions and heightened consciousness. Unlike Almanza and Cárdenas, who saw proletarian organization as a necessary condition for solving the agrarian problem, Tejeda saw it only as an essential result of that solution. In his view, until the agrarian problem could be solved, a union between urban and rural workers was a functionally unjustified and unethical imposition.

Tejeda did preach proletarian unification, however. In a speech on 8 April 1931 at a mass rally of the Federación Sindicalista de Trabajadores de la Ciudad de Veracruz (Workers' Syndical Federation of the City of Veracruz), he said: "It gives me great satisfaction to see female workers gathered here. Women have a role to play in the social struggle that is vitally important for the unification of workers and peasants." [27] Later he said, "The state government has been a friend to the workers in the social struggle and has always striven for the total unification of the working class [not only] of the state of Veracruz or of Mexico, but of the whole world . . . and to achieve it the workers must eradicate their fatal predilection for politics." [28] This untypical rhetoric sounded more like good advice than an actual political goal, however. Tejeda's remark about casting out the "fatal predilection for politics" showed clearly the basis of his fears concerning the imposition of unity on the workers.

The Basis of the Michoacán Labor Confederation

"The Revolutionary classes of Michoacán undoubtedly brought me to power to guarantee and nurture their rightful aspirations to betterment," wrote Cárdenas in his announcement of the founding convention of the Confederación Revolucionaria Michoacana del Trabajo (CRMDT— Michoacán Revolutionary Labor Confederation), which was distributed throughout the state at the beginning of January 1929. He went on to say, "to achieve my aim of guiding the workers within an exclusively social organization, it is essential to unify the labor collectives of the State completely, since labor unions are not a definitive and efficient force unless they are united in action." [29]

A few days after taking office, Cárdenas called together a group of friends, including former Múgica supporters and members of the original Michoacán Agrarian League and with their help drafted the charter and program of the new organization, which was born in Pátzcuaro at a gala founding convention on 7 January 1929. The CRMDT was guided by three basic principles: agrarian reform, the socialization of property, and the inculcation of a civic consciousness in the working classes. [30] Land, the emancipation of labor, and education consequently became the organization's three main interests. The Confederación was to be based on a united proletarian front of urban and rural workers and peasants "in the framework of a class war," and would work for the socialization of land, production, and the means of production. It would establish an educational infrastructure at all production sites— particularly haciendas and rancherías in remote areas—and would develop a system of cooperative labor and credit to replace exploitation and speculation. Finally, it would instill a new consciousness in its members, teaching them the rights that were theirs by virtue of "the principles of the Revolution and universal solidarity." At the same time, however, the CRMDT was to be an apolitical organization focusing on the social welfare of its members, under the slogan "*unión, tierra y trabajo*" (union, land, and work). [31]

This syndicalist program strongly reflected the CRMDT's resolve to fight for the enforcement of the labor law in Michoacán and even to add a few improvements—notably an eight-hour workday, a minimum daily wage of 1.50 pesos (instead of the one peso stipulated in the existing law), and full implementation of the decisions of the boards of conciliation and arbitration (*juntas de conciliación y arbitraje*).[32] The organization promised to assist any group comprising at least five workers, and to open schools in every rural community, large or small, and in every rancho and hacienda. It announced a wide-ranging and intensive organizing campaign targeting all unaffiliated workers. In addition, the syndical program called for concluding solidarity and cooperation agreements with proletarian organizations outside Michoacán, as well as, with all labor bodies that did not want to affiliate themselves with the CRMDT. To this end, Cárdenas signed a solidarity pact with the CROM, which maintained a strong presence in the mining areas of Tlalpujahua and Angangueo and in the textile region of Ciudad Hidalgo in eastern Michoacán. Cárdenas, of course, would have liked to include the CROM workers in the CRMDT, but he did not want to provoke a confrontation with Calles, the CROM's patron at the time, or to show too much political fervor in general, since that might endanger his position vis-à-vis the central government. Like Tejeda in his dealings with the CROM in Veracruz, Cárdenas was designated as arbitrator in disputes between the CRMDT and the CROM.[33]

The CRMDT's agrarian program called for the distribution of ejidal land to all rural communities and the restitution of any lands taken from them in the past, and underlined the need to shorten the waiting periods entailed by these processes. It also promised congressional action to abolish the exemption of *peones acasillados* (peasants residing on haciendas) from the benefits of the agrarian law, and a campaign to organize production cooperatives in the countryside. It stressed the importance of distributing arms to the peasants, developing autonomy in the villages, and unionizing all the peons on the haciendas and ranchos to help them push for the implementation of the laws affecting their welfare. An interesting and particularly delicate issue raised by the program was the problem of creating greater equality within the ejido by breaking up the *compadrazgos*—protectionist cliques comprising ejidal officials and their pals among the ejidatarios. The fact that the program addressed this subject at all was strong evidence of the existence of an ejidal *caciquismo* (that is, informal leadership by village "bosses") that threatened the egalitarian aspirations of agrarianism.[34]

Functionally, the CRMDT was intended to serve as a government party in all respects. At its third congress, in July 1931, a large majority approved a resolution proposed by Luis Mora Tovar, a party founder, that the Confederación should be entitled to play a role in politics under the direction of its political action committee and in coordination with the PNR.[35] This resolution revealed the political nature of the CRMDT, which in structure, program, and concept was, in fact, based on the PNR. Just as the PNR was designed to serve as an efficient power base for Calles and to provide an

infrastructure for institutionalizing the Revolution, so the
supposed to act as an efficient power base for the institut
Cárdenas's rule in Michoacán. Nonetheless, the CRMDT's d
it was putting itself under the authority of the PNR was a cl
that Cárdenas did not envisage the CRMDT as an independent
but as part of the official political establishment.

The CRMDT expanded rapidly. Within two years it gained 75,000–
100,000 new members, who made up between a quarter and a third of the
labor force in Michoacán.[36] To encourage still more workers to join, in
December 1928, the state government amended the local labor law to eliminate the requirement for notarization of new unions' regulations (to certify
that the syndicates were labor unions rather than employer, or "white,"
syndicates), and gave unionized workers preference in both hiring new
workers and concluding labor agreements.[37] In addition, from now on only
unionized workers were eligible for election to the boards of conciliation and
arbitration. These joint worker-boss committees received a significant boost
as well; the law shortened the deadline for execution of their judgments
(usually fines) to 24 hours (instead of 72 hours or more), and made the
boards themselves the agents of enforcement. This special amendment established the authority of these boards at the expense of the courts, thereby
strengthening the status of organized labor in the state.[38]

To encourage rural and Indian communities to join the CRMDT,
Cárdenas established the Federación Agraria y Forestal de Michoacán
(Michoacán Agrarian and Forest Federation) at the beginning of 1930. His
original intention was to set up two separate agrarian federations, one of
peasant unions and rural communities, and the other of indigenous forest-
dwelling communities, designed to accommodate Michoacán's large Indian
population. This plan, however, foundered on the Indians' aversion to the
idea. Instead, the CRMDT itself included a separate department for the
Indian forest communities. The leader of the veteran Agrarian League, José
Solórzano (Primo Tapia's successor), was elected as secretary-general of the
new Federation, which replaced Tapia's old League for good.[39]

In addition to these two cardinal measures, Cárdenas placed all the officers of the CRMDT in key positions in the local administration,[40] and
achieved some success in opening the organization to young people, women,
students, teachers, civil servants, and intellectuals. He even tried to reach the
landowners themselves, inviting them (in vain) to the founding convention
of the new Federación Agraria. The CRMDT developed a strong presence,
reinforced by Cárdenas's election as its permanent president and the election
of his friends to all the seats in the Comité Central Confederal (CCC—
Confederal Central Committee) of the League, to the executive of the
Federación Agraria, and to all the key positions in the local PNR.

Arming the peasants was another focus of the CRMDT and of grassroots
organization in general. This, too, was done discreetly, and presented as a
practical rather than political act. *El Universal* was the first to report, on 30
March 1929, that peasants were being armed and rural guards were being

established; the federal defense ministry had sent army officers to Michoacán to begin training such guards.[41] Cárdenas apparently did not want to publicize this step too much, being well aware of the great complications of maintaining paramilitary militias alongside the regular army. Yet he could not do without them, since he needed them to strengthen the agrarianists loyal to the state and protect them from the distrustful if not actually hostile rural population that surrounded them.[42]

These militias grew steadily stronger throughout Cárdenas's rule. The discreet silence enfolding their operation makes the calculation of yearly totals difficult, but towards the end of 1932 the US ambassador to Mexico estimated their number at some 17,000 men. It was the second-largest popular army in Mexico, following that of Veracruz and preceding that of San Luis Potosí, which numbered only 10,000. Thus, Cárdenas had managed to create a very large paramilitary force without arousing all the adverse publicity that hounded the Veracruz *guerrilla*. Clearly it was not the numbers involved, but the manner of the force's establishment and, particularly, its use that accounted for the vastly different public reactions to the creation of the respective militias of Veracruz and Michoacán.[43] Cárdenas did not allow the militias to deviate from the very strict instructions they received. If they overstepped their authority or showed undesirable initiative, they were immediately disarmed.[44]

These rural guards ultimately played a highly significant role in Michoacán. It was thus no wonder that the Morelia chamber of commerce, the political mouthpiece of the landowners and industrialists of Michoacán, did everything it could to discredit them and to convince the central government and the national press that they should be disbanded. It loudly blamed every murder in the state on the rural guards. The Michoacán representatives in the federal Congress were faced with the never-ending task of refuting such accusations and allaying all suspicion that violent anarchy was prevailing in Michoacán. Senator Dámaso Cárdenas, Lázaro Cárdenas's brother, said at a meeting of senators and deputies he had convened in the federal Congress in February 1933: "The national army, the army of the Revolution, must consider [the rural guards] as its main partner in preserving public order in the rural areas and implementing the principles of the Revolution—guards that have always been, and always will be, the first to give their blood for the definitive consolidation of the institutions of the Republic." He was clearly admonishing the landowners and industrialists to treat the agrarian militias with some respect, since their loyalty to the Revolution—unlike the loyalty of the propertied class—was unimpeachable.[45]

In contrast to Tejeda, Cárdenas took care to maintain respect for the army and did not portray the rural guards as an alternative to it—even if in practice they were. He developed close personal relationships with the most important generals in Mexico, particularly the highly influential minister of war and the navy, Joaquín Amaro, and with all the military officers stationed in Michoacán. He bolstered these relations by rendering important services to the army—for example, establishing a school in Michoacán for the offspring of the military[46]—by involving the army in various social projects for material improvements, by vehemently defending the army every time the agrarianists attacked it as the champion of the latifundists, by limiting the rural guards' freedom of action so they could not antagonize and compete with the army in preserving public safety, and, finally, by developing an ethos that focused on the army as a shield of the Revolution. It was this orientation that put General Manuel Avila Camacho, commander of the Zamora area, in the city's Junta de Mejoras Materiales (Council of Material Improvements),[47] and that mobilized the army to work on public works projects—for which it won wide praise, both in the yearly speeches made by Cárdenas and his temporary stand-ins, and in remarks by leaders of the state Congress.[48] Moreover, when Avila Camacho was censured at the CRMDT's third convention, in July 1931, for "constantly harassing the peasants of the region" and hindering the advancement of agrarianism, the Congress took his side, even though the CRMDT's complaint was obviously justified.[49]

Organization as a Reflection of the Concepts of the State and of the Nature of Social Change

Cárdenas's and Tejeda's respective approaches to organization revealed identical political attitudes. Both felt the state should play a decisive role in grassroots organization. Both assigned it the task of creating the conditions for socioeconomic change in accordance with the principles of the Revolution and the constitution. Both believed the state should watch over the interests of the collective. "In an age when humanity is awakening," said Cárdenas in a speech summing up his rule in Michoacán,

> and when evolution oscillates fatally between individualistic egoism and a wider, more noble conception of collective solidarity, the State, as an organization of public services, cannot remain inert and cool, static in the face of the social phenomenon developing before it. It must assume a dynamic, conscious attitude, providing whatever is necessary for the proper guidance of the proletarian masses, pointing out paths for the firm and progressive development of class war.[50]

Tejeda expressed very similar ideas in a speech summing up his term of government, when he spoke of socialism's being preferable to other social philosophies because it was the only one that defended collective interests from personal, egoistic liberties. Human existence, he said, was characterized by two forces basic to human nature and always in conflict: the instinct for self-preservation, and the instinct for preservation of the species. The first instinct saw the individual as the basic unit of the social order, whereas the second instinct was interested in the collective above all. Evolution and the history of humankind, he asserted dialectically, would synthesize these contrary forces and achieve a proper balance between them that would, in the main, be biased towards the strong side of this evolutionary parallelogram of forces—that is, towards the overriding interest of the collective.[51] The state's centrality in the process of social change was also a concept familiar to Tejeda from the positivist philosophy he had embraced since his years in the national high school (Preparatoria Nacional). After all, positivism, too, despite its individualistic foundations, recognized the state's centrality in the process of socioeconomic change, a change it defined as evolutionary.

However, while Cardenist statism was centralist—that is, all state action started in the center and worked its way out to the periphery—Tejedist statism was decentralist, giving priority to the federated states. When Cárdenas talked about the state, he meant the central government. The subordination of the CRMDT to the PNR was a prime example of Cárdenas's promotion of the center at the expense of the periphery. Tejeda, in contrast, stressed the role of the federated state, an approach reflected in the Veracruz League's independence from the PNR. This ideological difference predicated different patterns of behavior as well: Cárdenas had to tailor the CRMDT's activities to suit the interests of the central government, whereas Tejeda ignored those interests as long as he was certain that the center would not eliminate him politically.

The two men differed substantially, too, in their conception of social change. Despite Cárdenas's activist rhetoric, he saw social change as a gradual process—hence his integrative approach to organization, which required an atmosphere of social peace. The CRMDT was first and foremost an organization designed to protect the collective interests of the popular sector—workers and peasants—but it was also joined by teachers, students, civil servants, and other bourgeois idealists. Tejeda, in contrast, held that successful social change must involve conflict and struggle in order to sharpen class differences. Eschewing Cárdenas's cooptive approach, Tejeda, the philosophical disciple of strife, took up the cudgels against everyone who did not belong to the Veracruz proletariat, including the business community, landowners, students, part of the bureaucracy—in general, the latifundist oligarchy and the bourgeoisie. The differences between the two governors were also directly reflected in the way each used his grassroots power base: Cárdenas kept the CRMDT moderate and measured, while Tejeda encouraged the Veracruz League to be activist and radical.

Taking Over the Sphere of Local Government

Rationale and Techniques

Article 115 of the Mexican constitution provided: "The States shall adopt for their internal government the popular, representative, republican form of government; they shall have as the basis of their territorial division and political and administrative organization the free municipality. . . . "[52] The political constitutions of Veracruz and Michoacán echoed this principle, making the free municipio the basic territorial, administrative, and political unit and giving it a solid legal status and a wide field of responsibility.[53] Since the local authorities were empowered and, in fact, obligated to take steps "without delay" to break up large properties into small rural holdings, they were clearly a key element in the process of agrarian reform and social change.[54]

The advantages of the municipios' hegemony were clear to both Tejeda and Cárdenas. Their problem was how to keep that hegemony in their own hands when the most influential people in each region were usually large landowners. Each governor found a different solution: Cárdenas promoted his own authority by instituting new—and loyal—municipios and promoting existing villages to municipio status, while Tejeda simply waged war against all the municipios that did not implement his social goals, dissolving them without hesitation. Nor did he hesitate to make changes in the internal workings of the municipios, although unlike Cárdenas he emphasized those changes that appeared to strike directly at the *latifundistas* and downplayed those they might consider reasonable. There is no real evidence for the claims of Victoriano Anguiano, Cárdenas's close friend and later his fierce critic, that Cárdenas waged a direct battle against the municipios, though he may have had a hand in various and sundry political appointments.[55]

Integration of Power in the Michoacán Municipios

Table 2.1 (overleaf) shows that between the years 1917–1962, Cárdenas was the governor who initiated the most municipios. Between the years 1940–1962 (and after 1962 as well), no other governor of Michoacán established more than three new municipios in the course of a four- or six-year term. The conservatives among them, such as Ortiz Rubio, Sidroño Sánchez Piñeda, and Benigno Serrato, established only two in the entire seven and a half years of their rule. Thus, the establishment of new municipios was obviously a policy adopted by the more radical governors of Michoacán, and essentially linked to the preparation of a suitable infrastructure for social reforms.

Cárdenas hurried to set up new municipios in his first two years in office, most of them in the more populous and economically important northern areas of the state— areas that represented a potentially significant source of power. This geographic distribution is shown in Table 2.2 (overleaf).

The municipio's political preeminence under Cárdenas is exemplified by the case of Tocumbo. On 27 November 1929, the inhabitants of Tocumbo, then part of the Tinguindín municipio, sent a letter to the president of the state Congress and Cárdenas explaining that their town's population of 3,000 earned a scant but respectable living as muleteers and small-scale farmers. The town provided a reasonable level of municipal services, including a basic economic infrastructure, some 20 businesses, and two

Table 2.1 New *Municipios* (Municipalities) in Michoacán, 1917–1962 (two-year periods, from 16 September of each year)

Years	New Municipios	Governor/s during the period
1917–1920	1	Pascual Ortiz Rubio
1920–1922	5	Francisco José Múgica
1922–1924	1	Sidronio Sánchez Piñeda
1924–1926	1	Enrique Ramírez
1926–1928	2	Enrique Ramírez
1928–1930	7	**Lázaro Cárdenas**
1930–1932	1	**Lázaro Cárdenas**
1932–1934	–	Benigno Serrato
1934–1936	2	Rafael Sánchez Tapia, Rafael Ordorica Villamar
1936–1938	1	Gildardo Magaña
1938–1940	2	Gildardo Magaña
1917–1940	23	
1940–1950	7	
1950–1962	4	
1917–1962	34	

Source: These data are taken from a file recording municipio changes between the years 1920–1968 (no title or bibliographical identification), in AHCMO.

Table 2.2 Geographic Distribution of *Municipios* Established in Michoacán by Cárdenas in the Period 1928–1932

Name of Municipio	Date established	Region
Ocampo	17 January 1930	Center-North
Churumuco	24 January 1930	South
Charo	24 January 1930	North
Tocumbo	11 February 1930	Center-North
Tarímbaro	18 February 1930	North
A. Obregón	18 February 1930	North
Tzintzuntzan	1 September 1930	Center-North
Turicato	9 March 1932	Center-South

Sources: See note 56.

schools that did not function properly owing to a lack of teachers and principals. Nonetheless, they wrote, they were concerned that their children should "receive the best possible instruction to prepare them for the possibility that political-economic-social reforms aimed at the well-being of humanity will be implemented in the Republic." Tinguindín's treatment of Tocumbo, they said, bordered on "tyranny," and derived from a contemptible selfishness deeply rooted in history and particularly out of place in "these times of profit and progress." They concluded their letter by declaring their complete solidarity with the principles of the Revolution and requesting permission to establish an independent municipio. This act, they said—using the rhetoric common at the time to denote legitimacy—would be "a work of true progress" that would open to the inhabitants of Tocumbo and the rancherías that would be annexed to it "the possibility of enjoying the advantages of the Revolution, the beneficent shadow of which has, unfortunately, not yet touched us."[57] Tocumbo's petition elicited mixed reactions: Most of the villages it wanted to annex were amenable to the idea, but a few were strongly opposed.[58] Concerning the La Esperanza hacienda, which was to be transferred from the Tinguindín municipio to Tocumbo, Francisco Quijano de la Parra asserted:

> It is undesirable for us to become part of a largely illiterate village that is scheming and rebellious, as can testify all Governments to date, which have suffered its constant criticism . . . this application to become a municipio is nothing more than the desire of half a dozen ambitious schemers who are trying to live off others, while their honorable, hardworking neighbors realize that these people are motivated solely by ambition and are too ignorant to know what they are asking.[59]

The summary report of the congressional commission appointed to deal with the subject ignored the arguments against granting Tocumbo's request. Instead, it presented—at length—the legal and "revolutionary" grounds for granting Tocumbo's application, and recommended that the Congress approve it. The Congress accepted this recommendation unanimously.[60]

Some believed that Tocumbo was a wretched town doomed, "sadly," to remain far from the "generous protection of the Revolution's advantages"; others, that it was a town rife with rebellion that had managed to pull the wool over the eyes of a Congress mobilized for the revolutionary cause. There was evidence for both views—as well as for the view that the administration had seized on the opportunity to exploit an ancient feud between the two communities, not necessarily connected to the Revolution, and, by driving a wedge between them, engage the support of one of them. In this way a new geopolitical nucleus of support was established in the far west of the state, in the middle of a conservative area where the Cristeros were still active. No one could prove that the state had initiated the application for a change in status, or that it had deviated from the law. Everything appeared to be legal; but the main motive for establishing a Tocumbo municipio was undoubtedly the one tacked on to the end of the list of justifications submitted with the application: ideological and political interests.[61]

A similar policy was adopted with respect to *tenencias* (the smallest municipal unit authorized to elect its own administration), as shown in Table 2.3.

Table 2.3 Creation of New *Tenencias* (Sub-municipal units) in Michoacán, 1917–1940

Period	New tenencias	Governor
1917–1920	–	Ortiz Rubio
1920–1922	4	Francisco J. Múgica
1922–1924	–	Sidronio Sánchez Piñeda
1924–1926	2	Enrique Ramírez
1926–1928	7	Enrique Ramírez
1928–1930	6	Lázaro Cárdenas
1930–1932	10	Lázaro Cárdenas
1932–1934	4	Benigno Serrato
1934–1936	–	Sánchez Tapia, Ordorica Villamar
1936–1938	–	Gildardo Magaña
1938–1940	–	Gildardo Magaña
Total	34	

Sources: These data are taken from a file recording municipio changes between the years 1920–1968 (no title or bibliographical identification), in AHCMO and Periódico Oficial, 1928–1932.

Additional aspects of this activity during his governorship are reflected by Table 2.4. Of the 16 tenencias Cárdenas established, 10 had previously been haciendas. Geographically, 12 of the tenencias were situated in the two northernmost regions of the state. Eight were established on the premises of former haciendas in the last month of Cárdenas's term as governor, seven of those on his last day! This last act alone changed the status of some of the largest haciendas in Michoacán—Guaracha, Nueva Italia, Lombardía, Copándaro, Cantabria, and Tepenahua. Clearly, besides simply achieving new bases of power, Cárdenas wanted to weaken the influence of the large haciendas in the state. The tenencia, as the smallest municipal unit authorized to elect its own administration, represented the beginning of the road to full political independence for the *campesinos* and, consequently, to a stronger syndicalist, agrarianist, and anticlerical potential. This is why one of the main reasons invoked in the state Congress for creating tenencias was to allow communities to take advantage of "the benefits of agrarian legislation, particularly in the labor sphere."

The Surumbeneo rancho, for example, did not meet any of the minimal demographic, economic, or infrastructural criteria to qualify as a tenencia (at least, not according to the president of Charo, the municipio to which it belonged). This, however, did not prevent the Congress from granting its request so that its inhabitants could "enjoy the benefits of the agrarian laws."[63] Similarly, the motive for changing Zurumuato's municipal status was to accommodate the wishes of the grassroots, the inhabitants of the

Table 2.4 Establishment of New *Tenencias* in Michoacán, 1928–1932

Tenencia	Date of establishment	Previous status	Previous name
1. Emiliano Zapata	25 October 1929	Hacienda	Guaracha
2. Ibarra	25 October 1929	Colony of railway workers	Encargatura del Orden de la Estación de Pátzcuaro
3. Surumbeneo	24 January 1930	Rancho	Surumbeneo
4. Cuto	18 February 1930	Rancho	Cuto
5. Téjaro	18 February 1930	Rancho	Téjaro
6. Pastor Ortiz	24 January 30	Hacienda	Zurumuato
7. Mariano Escobedo	7 September 1931	Rancho	S. Lorenzo Acumbreo
8. Salto de Tepuxtepec	18 August 1932	Hacienda	El Salto
9. Copándaro	5 September 1932	Community annexed to Copándaro hacienda	Copándaro
10. Nueva Italia	15 September 1932	Hacienda	Nueva Italia
11. Lombardía	15 September 1932	Hacienda	Lombardía
12. Tepenahua	15 September 1932	Hacienda	Tepenahua
13. Pedernales	15 September 1932	Hacienda	Pedernales
14. Briseñas	15 September 1932	Hacienda	Briseñas
15. Chaparro	15 September 1932	Hacienda	Chaparro
16. Cantabria	15 September 1932	Hacienda	Cantabria

Sources: See note 62.

region whom governmental inattention had forced to take action on their own behalf.[64]

In the case of Guaracha the atrocities committed by the landowners and their overseers against the peons living there, were one of the main justifications for changing the hacienda's status. The state congressional commission that dealt with the Guaracha application discovered that the peasants of Guaracha were paid 37–50 centavos for a 12-hour workday; that the "white guards" took people from their houses every day by force to work on the hacienda—people who were subjected to "cruel and inhumane treatment when they were too sick to work"; and that the hacienda, in violation of the law, still ran the notorious *tienda del raya*, a store where workers were forced to spend their wages and which "everyone knows is a gold mine for the owner of the hacienda." In this case, the commission's recommendation was unequivocal: Guaracha must be converted into a tenencia for "the unfortunates who were born there and who work for the master," and who "have not been permitted to experience the Revolution's overwhelming and progressive effects."[65] The name chosen for the new tenencia—Emiliano Zapata—was another indication of the ideological orientation of the change.

Cárdenas turned to the establishment of tenencias primarily towards the end of his term because he wanted to avoid potentially explosive conflict in two municipal spheres at once. Simultaneous campaigns to establish both municipios and tenencias would have torpedoed his effort to give the municipio "improvement" process a practical facade that would cover up the obvious political motives behind it. He also wanted to avoid drawing the criticism of the national press and the political center, which—as the Veracruz case shows—were very sensitive to such power plays.[66] Moreover, while he was still trying to talk the landowners into joining the Federación Agraria, it was not in his interest to take steps that they would perceive as directly hostile to them. Later, however, when it became clear that the landowners would not be full partners in the agrarian reform, Cárdenas added the tenencia issue to his political agenda, in the name, of course, of the "new spirit pulsing through the state" and the new possibilities that "the laws, especially the agrarian and labor laws, [had] opened to the peasants"— key phrases in the municipal improvement process.

Integration of Power in the Veracruz Municipios

In Veracruz, the name of the game was confrontation. It began as soon as Tejeda took office, and it continued unabated to the end of his term, as shown by Table 2.5. In his first year alone, Tejeda dismissed 41 municipio councils and presidents in 13 out of the 190 municipios then in existence. In 1930 the pace slowed, only to pick up again in 1931, with 54 dismissals. In his last year as governor, the number of dismissals returned to the general level of 1930. These ups and downs were linked to the dates of local government elections: In September 1929, and September 1931, the municipio elections for the years 1930–1931 and 1932–1933, respectively, took place. Before each election campaign, Tejeda took care to purge not only the municipios that did not properly accommodate his social-agrarian vision, but also those that might jeopardize the results he sought from the elections.[67]

One hundred and ten dismissals—considered provisional for three months until a parliamentary inquiry could be completed and a court decision handed down—eventually became final. Tejeda's zealous action affected 78 municipios (41% of the total). In a substantial number of particularly "obstinate" municipios, Tejeda carried out two or three such purges in the course of his governorship. Actopan, Atoyac, Ixhuatlán, Jalacingo, Temapache, Tempoal, and Villa Cuauhtémoc were some of his targets.

This maneuver was already a tradition in Veracruz. In 1925 Heriberto Jara had dismissed five municipio councils and two municipio presidents, and in 1926 he dissolved eight councils. Vázquez Vela, who succeeded

Table 2.5 Dismissal of Local Government Administrators in Veracruz, 1929–1932

Action	Total	1929	1930	1931	1932
All dismissals and transfers in local government	168	42	35	54	37
Municipios involved	78	31	14	30	18
Dismissal of municipio presidents	16	5	3	4	4
Dismissal of governing councils	94	31	16	30	17
Dismissal of municipio agents	55	5	14	20	16
Reinstatement of municipio presidents and councils	3	1	2	0	0

Source: *Gaceta Oficial*, 1929–1932.

Tejeda, sent 24 presidents and councils home in 1933 alone—most of them, of course, Tejedists (*sic transit gloria mundi*). Tejeda, however, exceeded even the norm for Veracruz, turning his authority to dissolve governing councils into a prime means of political expression—to the point, in fact, that even his own agrarianist Congress viewed his actions with visible unease, fearing for the survival of lawful, stable government in the state. Supporters of the system, of course, had no misgivings, as witness a speech by Deputy Rafael García during a debate over the dissolution of the San Antonio Tenejapan administration at the beginning of July 1930:

> Until now we had not complied with the Law of Free Municipios; but now, with this ruling . . . we have, and are respecting the needs of the villages that, having tired of their authorities, ask the Executive and this Chamber to suspend them, as in the present case. . . . [We] must put a stop to the evil that we have ourselves implemented. We must give complete support to the administrative work that the Executive is carrying out and which is not in all cases supported by the governing councils . . . If only the Chamber would see it as a penalty not only for members of the governing councils and civil servants, but also for individuals; on that day . . . the State [will] lead the entire Republic.[68]

Even more significant than the unprecedented number of dismissals was the role Tejeda gave to the organized agrarianists. The agrarianists' complaints against the municipios over all sorts of violations of the agrarian process and infringements of the agrarianists' status and security were holy writ to Tejeda, and an immediate justification for dissolving the municipio in question.[69] The composition of the bodies appointed to replace municipio councils, the *juntas de administración civil* (civil administration councils), was the Veracruz Agrarian League's responsibility. If an appointed council did not do its job to the League's satisfaction, the League did not hesitate to demand the council's immediate replacement.[70] A typical case occurred in

Tomatlán, where the League allowed Tejeda no time to think before sending him, immediately after the dissolution of the municipio council, a proposal for forming a civil administration council that would include "elements close to our ideas of the struggle, who will be, above all, guarantors for the peasants and the entire population."[71]

It was an incessant round of provocation that constantly increased tension in the state, involving fierce wrangling, the publication of caustic manifestos in the local and national press, and proceedings in the federal Congress to depose Tejeda. Eventually the battle for hegemony in the municipios ended successfully—for Tejeda—at the end of 1931, as exemplified by the case of the city of Veracruz, one of the main battlegrounds and the acid test for the whole Tejedist campaign to gain control of the municipios.

The Takeover of the City of Veracruz

The city of Veracruz constituted the largest municipio in the state, with some 72,000 inhabitants in 1930, and it was a stronghold of the opposition, including the Obregonists, the anti-reelectionists (who opposed the principle of reelection that Obregón had consecrated with his 1927 amendment to the constitution so that he could run for president again), the anarcho-syndicalists, the communists, foreign industrial and commercial capital, and others.[72] It was typical of Tejeda, fresh from an election campaign that was still reverberating among the city's anti-Tejedista opposition, to start off by dismissing, on 28 December 1928, the city's governing council, headed by Nicolás Hernández, on the charge of "unethical administration." Instead of Hernández, an administrative council was set up under the stewardship of the engineer Benigno Mata.

The desperate protests of the Federal deputy Pedro Palazuelos, a native of the city who had made the trip from the capital especially for the occasion, were futile, as were claims that the outgoing governing council was the best elected council the city had ever had. Nor was anything gained by protests against the appointment of Benigno Mata, who allegedly did not live in the city and was an untalented, "notorious anti-reelectionist" of bad repute who was unlikely to meet the expectations of the city's residents. Tejeda stood by his decision. The members of the outgoing council, he fulminated from the state congressional podium, had exploited every good plot of urban land, lining their pockets with some 100,000 pesos. Mata and his team, said Tejeda, were "remote from politics." Nor would he agree at first to Palazuelos's proposal to replace Mata with Tomás Pérez Morteo, a friend of Tejeda's who had assisted him greatly in his election campaign. Tejeda wanted an outsider for the job, someone who would not come under pressure—and definitely not one of the local Obregonists. Tejeda did not reorganize the municipio council until after the Aguirre revolt in March 1929, when he in fact did appoint his friend Pérez Morteo, a local deputy at the time, to replace Mata—perhaps in an effort to calm tempers in the city.[73] Tejeda's diatribe against the outgoing council provoked a tempest. All the hurt, deposed mayor could say was "My conscience is clear. I have not done evil to anyone. Everything will become clear with time."[74]

The Obregonists were helpless, bursting with accusations against the local deputy of their party, Benjamin García, whom they accused of betraying them and contributing to the fall of the municipio. Tejeda's success in unifying most of the Congress members around himself silenced the few Obregonists in the Congress, and on 20 March 1929, the Congress finally dissolved the city council, which had been provisionally deposed at the end of the previous December. In its decision it said that the judicial inquiry undertaken against the council had revealed not only the magnitude of its corruption, but also that the council had played a role in the Aguirre revolt. The Congress did not have hard evidence of this, but relied on what it considered to be well-founded accusations. The decision not to investigate those accusations fully was prompted by the Congress's desire to wind up the affair quickly, and in any case it already had, it said, "a bulging file concerning the accusations against the aforementioned body."[75]

In April 1929, shortly after the suppression of the Aguirre revolt, Tejeda began to prepare for the municipio elections scheduled for September. At the forefront of the struggle for control of Veracruz he placed no less a personage than Ursulo Galván, then president of the Liga Nacional Campesina (LNC). Tejeda's successful campaign against De la Huerta, in which he speedily mobilized some 3,000 agrarianists and brought them to the city under his own command even before the army arrived, earned Tejeda effusive praise from the national press[76] and gave him the confidence not only to set his sights on gaining control of Veracruz, but also to dissolve, in the month of March alone, 17 municipios on the charge of direct or indirect collaboration with the rebels. Compared to other cities, Veracruz did not have enough of an agricultural hinterland to allow the development of a rural peasant movement that might serve as a counterweight to the city's bourgeois establishment. Tejeda therefore faced a difficult battle.[77]

On 16 April 1929 an article appeared in *El Universal* summarizing a review by *El Dictamen* of the candidates who would stand for the presidency of the Veracruz governing council in the September elections. *El Universal*'s view (developed on the basis of letters received from members of the public) was that none of the three viable candidates—Ursulo Galván, Alfonso Mendívil, and Ricardo Ángulo—was suitable. "The public does not want one more council composed of illiterates or scholars who, instead of administering the city, spend all their time in political activity."[78] In July *Excelsior* wrote that nearly all the political groups in the city wanted Juan de Dios Lara for president.[79] Dios Lara was a young, moderate agrarianist connected with the PNR and on amicable terms with Tejeda. In those years he was a member of the Córdoba city council, and later, in 1932, he became head of the PNR in Veracruz and a federal deputy who aspired to the senate. A cautious and thoughtful politician, he could have been a good president—but not during a period of such keen political conflict, in which Tejeda was playing for very high stakes. Only the uninhibited Galván, loyal to Tejeda above all, was the right man for the times.

The anti-Tejedists, led by Campillo Seyde, a federal senator, were determined to prevent Tejeda from taking over the city. Seyde, who as a general had also fought against Aguirre and shared in the glory of victory, assured his followers in the Veracruz Socialist party that Tejeda's days were numbered. He promised that when Pascual Ortiz Rubio, the new president-elect, took office in December (in the end he did not do so until February 1930), Tejeda would be "sent packing" and he, Seyde, would be governor.[80] His party kept feeding Ortiz Rubio with "incriminating" material against Galván (and by extension, of course, against Tejeda), accusing him of being a "Communist" who was collaborating with Ortiz Rubio's enemies in the city in order to improve the chances of Rodríguez Triana, Ortiz Rubio's Communist rival for the presidency of the Republic. This, of course, was disinformation pure and simple, since Rodríguez Triana was not nominated as the Communist candidate until after Galván had left the party to protest its support for Aguirre.[81]

Tejeda, of course, retaliated. He took care to keep Ortiz Rubio up to date on events as seen from his point of view, and even promised he would "take good care of Seyde," who was in charge of propaganda for Ortiz Rubio's campaign for the presidency as the PNR candidate.[82] Tejeda did his best to present himself as neutral, even winning an admiring headline in *El Universal* on 29 June: "Impartiality in Veracruz Elections . . . Vindicates Governor Tejeda's Policy "[83]

The election campaign began on 23 June 1929. Galván proposed a "class-based administration without communism, based on honest, lawful intentions," and explained that he had been expelled from the Communist party because of disagreements with the party leadership concerning the attempt to instill in Mexico "principles that are not the ones needed here." For his part, he promised to employ "highly advanced systems and tactics. . . . "[84] Tejeda himself backed the struggle at the federal level. In the months from May to August, he defeated attempts by Campillo Seyde and Manlio Fabio Altamirano, another of Veracruz's representatives in the federal Congress, to exploit the political enmity that had built up against Tejeda in the capital in order to have him deposed. They circulated the information that Tejeda had dissolved 142 municipios since taking office, thereby highlighting the issue of local power as a central factor in the public debate concerning Tejeda's behavior and ability to continue governing his state. This debate was conducted both in the federal Congress and through the medium of the national and Veracruz press.

The threat to Tejeda was not an empty one. On 29 May Alfonso Medina, the governor of Zacatecas, was deposed by the court of the federal Congress, in part on charges of violating the *Ley de Municipio Libre* (Law of Free Municipios) passed by the city council of Zacatecas. Tejeda's enemies in Congress wanted to use the Zacatecas precedent to depose him; and in fact, while the debate on Alfonso Medina was still going on, a number of deputies led by Seyde and Altamirano launched a public attack on Tejeda, making the same accusations against him that were being made against Medina and whipping up public opinion preparatory to similar proceedings against him. Meanwhile, they submitted a formal request to the federal Congress for Tejeda's removal.[85]

The process gained momentum, reaching its peak in August. When, on the tenth of that month, the Veracruz Congress met to express its opposition to the attack on Tejeda, Deputy Benjamín García declared that the instigators of the proceedings against Tejeda had solemnly promised all their comrades in the capital that "next Wednesday" Tejeda would be deposed. Those "satraps of the Revolution," as García called Altamirano and Seyde, only wanted, he said, "to cause trouble, with the sole object of satisfying their own mean interests."

The Veracruz Supreme Court held a special session to examine the accusations against Tejeda, and concluded its deliberations by deciding to send representatives to Mexico City to meet with President Portes Gil and explain to him that there was no basis for the charges against Tejeda. The head of the Ortiz Rubio faction in the state Congress intervened as well, sending a letter of protest to the PNR to condemn the "maneuver" against Tejeda and to ask the party to try to stop the proceedings. Tejeda himself delivered an impressive and assertive speech in Congress, in which he refuted unequivocally the claims that he and the president were at odds, or that there was some "social or political motive that had created a breach between Veracruz and the Federation." He rejected the charges that affairs in Veracruz were not conducted through the proper channels, and called on all Veracruz and Revolutionary patriots to condemn the proceedings against him and to confirm the fact that the government of Veracruz was "the most trustworthy social product of the national institutions," and that he and his government were dedicated to the defense of those institutions.[86]

The tension in the Tejeda camp eased slightly once it became clear that Portes Gil would not lend his hand to overthrowing Tejeda, and that Seyde and Altamirano's initiative lacked the support it needed in the federal Congress. Altamirano now did an about-face and swore by all he held dear that he had had nothing to do with the intrigue. In an extraordinary emotional speech in the federal Chamber of Deputies, he asked the house to certify that he had never been involved, neither "individually with any deputy" nor through the majority faction, in mobilizing support for the campaign to topple Tejeda. This plea aroused such a storm that no debate took place that day—only a clamorous row that ended with the overwhelming defeat of Altamirano's bizarre proposal.[87]

The danger had passed for the moment, but it did not disappear completely. The warring sides abandoned the confrontation in the national arena only to square off again in the local elections scheduled for 22 September 1929. Five lists were entered, including Seyde's, that of the Veracruz Socialist party, and that of Ursulo Galván's new party, called rather ironically "Partido Unificador Veracruzano" (Veracruz Unifying Party). The election campaign took place in an atmosphere of great tension, heightened by strong accusations made by Galván and his colleague Enrique Hernández, head of the local Tejedist party, against the outgoing civil administration council, remarking on the fact that after the council had expressed support for Alfonso Mendívil, head of the Seyde list, he had indeed won the election. These accusations were only part of a general attack on the council's conduct of the elections. The congressional committee that investigated the elections concluded that the election procedure had involved "serious aberrations and irregularities," and it advised the local Congress to invalidate the election and appoint an administrative council until new provisional elections could be held. On 24 October a resolution along these lines was passed.[88] The system that obliged the Congress to confirm or invalidate the results of municipio elections was widely exploited to veto the results of elections not only in Veracruz but also in 20 other municipios in the state (11% of the total), in which some 17% of the population lived.[89]

By law Tejeda was required to hold interim elections within a year after the voiding of the previous ones. He did so in all the municipios on 21 September 1930—except in Veracruz, apparently because of Galván's death in June of that year. Contrary to both the usual procedure in such cases and the municipio election law, Tejeda decided to wait until the regularly scheduled elections of September 1931. He left Orizaba, the largest industrial city in Veracruz, in similar circumstances, since there too, he had had trouble getting his agrarianist supporters into the CROM-controlled governing council. Accordingly, he preferred to have the city governed by a temporary *junta* rather than by the elected representatives of his rivals. Similarly, in Córdoba, the third largest industrial city in Veracruz, several Congress members had mounted an abortive attempt to dissolve the city council, which, like that of Orizaba, was controlled by CROM men.[90] Yet despite all this great political manipulation to create a pro-Tejedist front on the municipio level, by the end of 1931 Tejeda had not yet managed to achieve total control over the municipios, particularly the large cities. Moreover, his undemocratic methods continued to draw harsh criticism from all quarters.

On 1 June 1931, Tejeda convened an assembly of the presidents of all the municipio councils in Jalapa. Only 48 people came, a number reflecting the relatively meager support he enjoyed in the municipal periphery, and perhaps also a tacit protest by many of the municipio heads in his state. Although the quorum required for such meetings was 91 people, the assembly went ahead, nonetheless, to perform its designated task of preparing for the coming September's municipio elections. The events of Minatitlán repeated themselves as the gathering turned into a platform for fulminations against Tejeda's agrarian policy and his practice of dissolving municipios. The agrarian reform, said many of the municipio presidents, was slow and offered no real benefit to the peasants, who continued to suffer from wages and living conditions inferior to those of industrial workers.[91]

The stinging criticism left Tejeda unmoved, merely strengthening his resolve to use the upcoming elections to complete the process of taking over the municipios and open them to agrarianism once and for all.[92] Accordingly, whereas up until the beginning of June Tejeda had dissolved "only" seven municipios, in the months remaining before election day, he dismissed an additional 20, and another seven by the end of the year. He was equally unfazed by the displeasure of local agrarianists, who opposed the efforts of Agrarian League leaders to dissolve certain municipios. Tejeda also ignored the great violence that accompanied these proceedings, violence that led to the murder, on 1 April 1931, of Juan Jacobo Torres, a devoted agrarianist and leading member of the local Agrarian League, as well as a deputy in the state Congress. Torres's move to dissolve the elected council of San Andrés Tuxtla in the south and to replace it with an administrative council (a move that was eventually accomplished on 9 June) had cost him his life.[93]

As doggedly as ever, Tejeda continued to prepare for the last and most significant municipio election of his term of office, and this time he was determined not to suffer another defeat. Since Galván was dead, he put his friend Epigmenio Guzmán, a local deputy and one of the League's most active leaders, in charge of Veracruz. He appointed Carolino Anaya, a close confidant and another League leader, in Jalapa, and other League members in the rest of the municipios.[94]

An attempt on Tejeda's life on 25 July 1931, which he barely escaped, only added to his resolve. About two hours after this attempt, Guzmán himself was involved in the murder of two young priests in the Asunción church in the city of Veracruz, in front of a group of children who were receiving religious instruction from the priests at the time.[95] According to a report by the American consul in Veracruz, Guzmán had been sent to the city to organize the agrarian party there in preparation for the elections.

As expected, Guzmán won the election on 20 September.[96] At the same time other League members carried the day in the vast majority of municipios in the state. In districts important to Tejeda where his candidates lost, such as Orizaba, Córdoba, and Huatusco, the state Congress—in which the agrarianists were now much more heavily represented than in September 1929—voided the elections and allowed Tejeda to appoint administrative councils. "Contrary to the usual disorders, killings, etc. which have heretofore accompanied these elections," wrote the American consul to his superiors in Washington, "there was no disorder or violence in any part of the State except at Orizaba, the industrial center of the State, where the labor party outnumbers the members of the National Revolutionary Party. . . . Elsewhere in the State, the agrarian and anticlerical element dominated the situation so completely that there was no opposition and consequently no violence." In Veracruz, he wrote, Deputy Epigmenio Guzmán had been elected, "the most violent partisan of the agrarians and anticlericals."[97]

Reaping the Fruits of Success

For the first time in the history of the Veracruz Agrarian League and in Tejeda's own political experience, most of the municipio heads were League activists. Finally the agrarian policies of the League and the Tejeda administration had a chance of being implemented fully, since that implementation depended on the initiative of the municipio administrations. Incomplete control over local government prevented the League from supervising its representatives in the municipios and ensuring that they acted in accordance with its policy. As a result, in more than a few instances municipio presidents elected on the League ticket severed all contact with the organization—even written correspondence—once they had taken office, and began to cooperate with the *latifundistas*, who were eager to buy their services.[98] Thus, September's victory allowed the agrarianists to tighten their supervision.

The Agrarian League's newly improved control was reflected in two gatherings that took place at the end of that year. The first was the League's seventh congress in November. The second, defined as the second special session of the November congress, took place on 21–23 December. In addition to the League's 40 regional representatives, the meeting was attended by the 100 new municipio heads who had been elected under League sponsorship in the September elections. The aim of the gathering, according to a report in *El Dictamen* on 23 December, was "to show that its members can govern as well as anyone else."[99]

Now criticism was no longer being directed at Tejeda and his activist municipal policies, but at the heads of the municipios and their lukewarm agrarian policies. At the November congress, harsh censure was heard against "the great agrarianist leaders of yesterday who have become the *hacendados* and *latifundistas* of today"—the turncoats who had betrayed their mission and exploited their class in the service of the landowners. "These senior agrarian leaders, the fruit of our loins," the *El Nacional* reporter wrote sarcastically in his account of the event, "have amassed very handsome private fortunes, and . . . the national treasury would be insufficient to satisfy the greed of our redeemers. . . .This time," continued the reporter—probably a member of the central League—"we will not allow them to mortgage the ejidal funds, which represent the effort, the sweat, and the life of impoverished peasants." In case any doubt remained as to whom he meant, he went on,

> It is all very well that the magnates of today, who glory in their revolutionary fervor who just yesterday were poor, anonymous, and miserable, should build themselves fancy houses, enjoy a profusion of valuable jewelry, maintain elegant mistresses, and cut a dash in expensive cars. But we will not allow the deputies and municipio heads from our own ranks to imitate such disgusting behavior. [Agrarianism] should be a sacred mission, but unfortunately it is not. At least we will take care not to get infected with the rot of the bourgeois ethic.[100]

During the December session of the League congress, at which the League executive declared the need to provide guidance for the new municipio presidents, the speakers again denounced the treachery of the agrarianist officers of the previous term. This time the League went further, however, demanding from its 100 representatives an explicit undertaking to work towards the League goals. To ensure that they kept their word, it made them sign blank letters of resignation. These letters were stored in the League's main offices so that the organization could use them any time it felt the signatories were deviating from the correct agrarianist-proletarian orientation or had been "infected" by the "bourgeois ethic." The signatures also allowed the League to circumvent the lawful procedure for dissolving a municipio council and to transfer control of the council from the state to the League.

Tejeda did more than wave an admonitory finger at the new municipio presidents, however. He encouraged them with promises that they would enjoy the assistance of the state government, and expressed his certainty that they would do revolutionary work that accorded with the ambitions of the people, if only because they themselves were of peasant origin. He also promised that his administration would not intervene in their internal affairs as it had in the past, because "you are members of the League, of peasant origin, and you will act for the good of the working classes." He assured them that the League would also provide broad assistance, since it was working "zealously and efficiently to form the consciousness of the Veracruz peasant, and [their] own consciousness as well, since [they, too, were] peasants." In passing, he reminded his audience that the League held its elected members in an iron grip, and exhorted them: "I am sure that all of you are going to prove that in the State of Veracruz there are honorable, sincere hearts, that in the State of Veracruz there are men able to do their duty; you are going to prove that the State of Veracruz, as always, will know how to provide a noble example of public spirit and, today more than ever, of revolutionary spirit."[101]

It was not until the end of 1931 that Tejeda could regard the results of his campaign to take over local government with any satisfaction. His successful partnership with the Veracruz Agrarian League had finally borne the political fruit he desired, though there was still room for improvement; the representatives of more than a few municipios—approximately 90—had not attended the Jalapa congress. Tejeda continued his strategy of dissolving governing councils in 1932, dismissing 20 presidents and governing councils in that year alone, and the fact that complaints about the anti-agrarianist behavior of many municipios continued to stream into Tejeda's office indicated that not all municipios followed the administration's radical line.

Undoubtedly Tejeda's success in overpowering the intransigent city of Veracruz represented the ultimate consummation of his campaign in the municipios, and reflected the great change in his status in the state. It proved the efficiency and vital importance of the political relationship that he had developed with the Agrarian League; and it reflected a certain increase in worker support, particularly in the city of Veracruz, where he had won some workers over with his advocacy for the tenant movement and his efforts to solve housing and unemployment problems. He had taken an important step in his relations with the tenant movement at the beginning of 1929 by allowing Hernán Proal, the movement's militant leader, to return to the city, from which he had been banished by the city authorities in January 1926.[102] Another step was to ensure that the head of the city council's department of tenancy affairs was always a member of the tenants' movement.[103] At the same time, Tejeda promoted legislation in the spheres of tenancy, construction, and even agriculture, providing urban workers with family garden plots and raising the official status of workers' neighborhoods (*comunas*) to that of *congregaciones*, as well as trying to move them from "bad" (meaning non-agrarianist) municipios into the precincts of "good" (agrarianist) ones.

By September 1931, then, Tejeda could feel he had accomplished something, and begin to think about the political and social benefits to be derived from that accomplishment. He had the full backing of the state administration, the League had been reinforced in virtually all spheres, and most of the municipios were in his hands. Satisfied with these initial results, Tejeda was now in a position to present his social-moral vision to the participants in the second session of the League's seventh congress, in the hope that by implementing that vision Veracruz would set an example for all Mexico. "Now, with the creation of this trilogy of State Government, local authorities, and League, I am certain that we will do effective work, work that will make history in the State of Veracruz. Although I myself will not be in your company for more than half the period, we will have opportunities to demonstrate that we know how to do our duty," he said.[104]

Interesting questions are raised by Tejeda's great zeal for reorganizing the municipios, a zeal that never diminished as long as he was in office. Why did he ignore the heavy criticism of his reorganization policy inside and outside the state, and why was he willing to risk both his life and his position as governor to pursue this campaign?[105] The answers seem to lie in the feeling of urgency that goaded Tejeda throughout his second term as governor. Tejeda feared that if he did not achieve his objectives at once, he would never do so. He probably suspected that after his governorship of Veracruz he would not be able to climb any higher on the political ladder. His positions on all the key issues—issues involving labor, the national debt, relations with the United States, the agrarian question in general, the governor's role, the structure and modus operandi of the PNR, and the status and role of workers and peasants in Mexican society, among others—differed from the views of the political center, and after 1930 they afforded him no room for compromise. Although all these issues reached maturity during the elections for the presidential term of 1934–1940, they were already ripening during Tejeda's term as governor. His plan was to push the process of change in his state past the point of no return, so that it could continue even without him and develop into a select model—ideological, political, legal, and practical—that the rest of Mexico would adopt. The crucial link between control of local government and agrarianist progress, clearly reflected in the political and legal relations between the municipios and the state administration, was also manifested in the speeches by municipio heads at the Jalapa congress in June 1931. Tejeda's recognition of this link, together with his consciousness of the limited time at his disposal, was the source of the fervor and determination he showed in his interventions at the municipio level.

Politico-Administrative Reclassification of Villages

Tejeda, like Cárdenas, understood the importance of municipios that were loyal to the government. Unlike Cárdenas, however, he did not attribute any special significance to the technique of establishing new municipios; after all, his own system of direct action, though unsubtle, produced the same results. Thus, while Cárdenas established eight new municipios (9% of the total number of municipios in the state), Tejeda established only five during his entire term of office (2.6% of the total), although there were exactly the same reasons for creating new municipios in Veracruz as in Michoacán. Two of the new municipios in Veracruz, Angel R. Cabada and Tenochtitlán, were established at the initiative of local agrarianist organizations and "residents in general." The petitioners based their request on the remoteness of the seat of the municipio (*cabecera municipal*) to which they belonged and the fact that they could not promote a development policy based on the ideals of the constitution as they wanted to. They also claimed that under the present circumstances they were unable to benefit from the "Revolutionary principles of justice and liberty," nor to receive "recompense for the sacrifice of our brothers and near ones" to the Revolutionary cause. In their decision, Tejeda and the congressional committee that examined the petitions were influenced not only by objective administrative criteria, but by the idea that in creating the new districts the state government would be able to show its willingness "do justice to our peasant comrades," since such gestures were "the only way of obtaining guarantees for our political and civil interests."[106]

A variation on this ploy, unique to Tejeda, was the transfer of settlements or villages from one municipio to another, or, alternatively, the transfer of the *cabecera municipal*—that is, the location of the offices and administrative apparatus of the municipio—from one city to another in the same district. As in the creation of new municipios, the many changes involved in transferring *cabeceras* gave rise to unprecedentedly fierce political battles, in which the victorious side was always the one that managed to give the best proof of its progressive views and uncompromising loyalty to the Revolution "in the most difficult moments."[107]

Another strategy unique to Tejeda in this sphere was the politico-administrative reclassification of individual villages or settlements, a proceeding for which he showed extraordinary enthusiasm. The aim was to make as many communities autonomous as possible by classifying them as *congregaciones* (the equivalent of the Michoacán tenencias) or better within the existing municipios, *congregación* being the minimum status entitling a community to receive public land (*fundo legal*) and to elect its own leader (*agente municipal*). This status also entitled it to conduct an independent local development policy and to participate in the agrarian reform, which the law limited to communities of a recognized political category (thereby excluding colonies of *peones acasillados*).

From a modest and relatively slow beginning in the first year of Tejeda's term, the reclassification of rural communities reached an intensive rate in the second year and remained there throughout his governorship. *Poblados* were elevated to the status of *rancherías*; *rancherías* became *congregaciones* or *pueblos*; *pueblos* were promoted to *villas*, and *villas* to *ciudades*. A smaller number of *congregaciones* were upgraded to the status of municipio *libre*. As Table 2.6 shows, Tejeda was responsible for the greatest volume of munic- ipal upgrading in the history of Veracruz, both before and after his term. Twenty-nine of those upgrades (27.6%) were made in the first two years of his governorship, and 76 (72.4%) were made in the last two years, for a total of 105. These unprecedented statistics reflect the frenzy that seized Tejeda as he approached the end of his term of office—the last gasp of his general effort to create an irreversible new social reality in Veracruz.[108]

Table 2.6 Municipal Upgrading in Veracruz, 1925–1933

Year	Rancherías upgraded to Congregaciones	Other municipal frameworks created, including new municipios	Total
1925	0	2	2
1926	1	4	5
1925–1926	1	6	7
1929	10	1	11
1930	12	6	18
1931	33	7	40
1932	34	2	36
1929–1932	89	16 (2 *rancherías*, 4 *pueblos*, 3 *villas*, 2 *ciudades*, 5 *municipios*)	105
1933	13	1	14

Source: Gaceta Oficial, 1925–1933.

Cárdenas would undoubtedly have been happy to achieve what Tejeda did. Unlike Tejeda, however, who sought to change the structure of local government as quickly as possible, even at the cost of confrontation with powerful interests and, in some cases, the Veracruz grassroots as well, Cárdenas took a more cautious approach, foreseeing the danger inherent in an all-out war in the municipal sphere. Accordingly, he was chary about municipal upgrades and he refrained from employing Tejeda's tactic of systematically voiding any local election results not to his liking. The local Congress, too, had strong reservations about its role in confirming or canceling election results. Most of the members felt that this should be the responsibility not of the Congress, but of the municipios themselves. The Congress even took the step of approaching the PNR institutions that had initiated a public debate on the issue with a request that they prepare a federal draft law reflecting its position.[109] Undoubtedly this initiative was motivated by the fear that excessive intervention in the municipal field would give rise to a backlash when the administration changed.

Establishing Personal Authority in the Local and National Spheres

Cárdenas and Tejeda took substantially different approaches in their relations with the political center. Cárdenas was inseparably associated with it. He had not abandoned his relations with the army when he went into politics; as mentioned earlier, he asked to participate in the military campaigns against Escobar and the Cristeros. In October 1930, he took on the job of president of the PNR, and at the end of August 1931, he moved on to the position of interior minister in Ortiz Rubio's government.[110]

Throughout his years in the army and in politics, Cárdenas was careful to maintain close ties with Calles, providing him with important services and never challenging him. He stalwartly supported Calles after the death of Obregón, did the dirty work when he felt that Calles had had enough of Ortiz Rubio, and orchestrated the collective resignation (on 14 October 1931) of all the minister-generals in Ortiz Rubio's government. Cárdenas never tried to operate outside the framework of the party and the federal government.[111]

Tejeda took exactly the opposite course of action as governor. He never sought positions in the central government, not even for limited periods, although he received a certain number of offers. As mentioned earlier, he disapproved of the PNR and consequently never joined it. He did not cultivate his relations with Calles, even though he supported him for many years. Tejeda did not approve of the position Calles had appropriated for himself as the strong man of the Revolution, and deplored the difficulties he caused to independent forces in both the central government and the periphery, Tejeda included.

Tejeda was well aware of the fact that Calles's manipulations had paved the way to his own second term as governor of Veracruz in 1928.[112] Although he did some manipulating of his own, he had trouble accepting the fact that the Revolution was gradually becoming institutionalized and infringing on local autonomy—an autonomy that Tejeda saw as the bastion of his own power and the basis for the establishment of a democratic, modern Mexico. Consequently, Tejeda not only refused to join in the ritual pilgrimages to Calles's house in Mexico City and his various vacation homes around Mexico, but he publicly opposed him on social and governmental issues, established an independent electoral base of his own in the presidential elections, and developed a revolutionary sociopolitical program that went far beyond Calles's own institutional conservative vision.[113]

Cárdenas attributed great importance to maintaining a personal presence in the Michoacán village. He visited even the most remote villages often, meeting with the villagers and listening calmly to their complaints, requests, expectations, and hopes. His visits left a deep impression on many peasants in Michoacán, and undoubtedly contributed to the creation of the Cárdenas legend in Michoacán.[114] These unmediated visits were considered a means of calming unrest in the villages, which were riven by ethnic, religious, economic, and political tensions, and they gradually became an institution, providing Cárdenas with an accurate picture of reality and a strong base for policy making and evaluation. His committed personal relationship with the *campesinos*, who had hitherto experienced nothing but disappointment in their contacts with the government, gave them a certain measure of confidence that this time the promises would be kept. These visits were more than just a political weathervane, however; they were a pedagogic means of teaching the masses the importance of change and of stimulating motivation to participate in the reform proposed by the state.

In addition to these visits, Cárdenas took care to participate in all political or public functions, large or small, that took place in Michoacán. Both as interior minister in the Ortiz Rubio government and as secretary of the PNR, he did not let a single event go by without making an appearance. The warm, spontaneous welcome he received at every federative or confederative congress of the CRMDT, for example, at municipal and party gatherings, and even at private affairs attested to his great popularity. This popularity had an important political value; so what had begun as a habit eventually became an institution, and ultimately a unique political culture.[115]

Cárdenas made strenuous efforts to bring peace to Michoacán—increasing the peasants' security by organizing and arming them, paying his frequent visits to the villages, and constantly meeting with agrarianists, Cristeros, official rural leaders, teachers, cultural delegates sent to the village, CRMDT agents, and others—and achieved considerable success. Michoacán became a relatively quiet place that hardly appeared in the statistics on violence that the US embassy in Mexico sent to the State Department in Washington every three months.[116] Within two years Cárdenas had managed to create for himself a good working environment for the implementation of the ideals in which he believed.

Tejeda put less energy into attaining the stature of a popular leader. He did not tour the countryside the way Cárdenas did, and as a result he did not always know at first hand what was happening in the vast expanses of his state. This problem was compounded by Veracruz's defective communication system. Because of the rough traveling conditions, his own shaky position, and his fear of ambushes, Tejeda made few trips to the north or south of Veracruz, or, indeed, out of the state. His visits were so rare that even the elders of the Actopan municipio, which borders the Jalapa municipio, could not remember ever seeing Tejeda in their villages. Their first opportunity to see him came only at the end of November 1932, when they were invited to a ceremony in the Jalapa university stadium at which he transferred the reins of government to Vázquez Vela.[117] In Michoacán, in contrast, many peasants—even those who lived furthest away from Morelia, the capital—remembered Cárdenas (although they were not always certain whether he had visited them as governor or as president).

Tejeda's leadership style forced him to supplement his knowledge of what was going on in the state with the help of a secret intelligence service employing 100 agents. Officially, this service was established after an attempt on Tejeda's life in July 1931, but in fact it had been set up as soon as he took office.[118] Its purpose, according to Tejeda, was "to counter the activities of the clergy and the ideological enemies of this Government."[119] Actually, however, its primary purpose was to protect Tejeda's life, to keep tabs on his political rivals, and to identify centers of opposition. Accordingly, agents were stationed in the city of Veracruz and in the industrial cities of Orizaba and Córdoba, where they were instructed to observe the activities of the CROM. Other agents were posted in the Jalapa train station so they could report whenever a local or federal politician, military officer, *hacendado* or civil servant left or entered the state. Agents were also sent to other states in Mexico and to Mexico City to monitor the Congress and the national press. Their mission was to spy on the Veracruz representatives in the federal Congress and to watch out for subversive activity against Tejeda among the Cristeros. Still other agents were planted in concentrations of Veracruzian immigrants in the United States, particularly in Texas.[120] Tejeda himself did not even go out to the movies unless he was surrounded by agents. The fear for his safety was so great that ten full rows in the movie theater had to be reserved for his bodyguards.[121]

Tejeda learned from his agents' reports, for example, that the central government was making great efforts to find out the actual size of the Veracruz local militias. It was also from them that he discovered that Ortiz Rubio had sent his nephew, Rubén Ortiz, to the city of Veracruz on 8 February 1932, accompanied by General Vicente López, to try to find out the quantity of arms with which Tejeda's government was "irrigating the country."[122] Still another piece of information Tejeda gleaned in this way was that Church activists in the Islas Marías, Puebla, Michoacán, and other places were arranging for attempts on his life.[123]

This intelligence service supplemented the local militia. While the latter maintained the peace in Veracruz and served as the long operational arm of the administration, the intelligence service concentrated on preventive action. The militia was limited to Veracruz itself, but the intelligence service was deployed in every "danger" spot in Mexico and even abroad—for the notion of "ideological enemies" had no frontiers. Since Tejeda thought in such terms, he saw every political rival as an ideological enemy who must be watched. Among his most prominent "enemies" was the federal government itself, whose institutions and officers were under permanent surveillance by Tejeda's agents in Mexico City.

Cárdenas apparently did not need secret agents of this kind; his accounting books showed no expenses that would indicate the existence of such a service. However, a similar function was performed by many of the CRMDT members working in the Michoacán state administration, who furnished Cárdenas with a steady stream of reliable reports. He solved the problem of control by means of his frequent visits to the various districts and cities of the state, by holding posts in federal institutions, and by frequent pilgrimages to Calles's dominions. Cárdenas had the sense to realize that it was smarter to maintain a personal presence around the state and in the political center, thereby seeing which way the wind lay at first hand, than to find out what was going on by proxy and from a distance.

Political Power and the Test of Recognition

Both Tejeda's Veracruz and Cárdenas's Michoacán witnessed the institution of original and highly impressive political power systems that gave the governors presiding over them a remarkable freedom of action. Both governors enjoyed infinitely better conditions than those of their predecessors in office, and, in Tejeda's case, than those he had had to contend with in his previous term as governor. As we have seen, however, each system was born of a different approach to the organization, implementation, and objectives of power.

Cárdenas preferred an integrative, controlled, and centralized approach, a power structure that combined formal and informal aspects, in which organizations played a part without impinging on his own role as a popular leader, and in which groups and people from all walks of society would cooperate. He preferred a system that was subordinate to the political center and that received maximal recognition from both the center itself and the local and national public.

At the same time, he took care not to alienate the opposition, and maintained good relations with other elements of power, in particular the traditional agricultural oligarchy, the military, and the Church (which will be discussed more fully in a later chapter). He purposely did not limit his political sphere of action to Michoacán, but expanded his power base and influence to the national level; besides his many functions in federal government and his extravagant efforts to curry favor with Calles, he began—supposedly as an envoy of the PNR and undoubtedly with Calles's blessing—to take over the radical and influential Liga Nacional Campesina Ursulo Galván (LNCUG, or the Ursulo Galván National Peasant League, as the LNC had been renamed in July 1930, after Ursulo Galván's death) in Veracruz, beginning at its convention in February 1931.[124] He managed to complete the process by completely vanquishing this League at its eleventh convention in Mexico City on 1 June 1933,[125] and establishing the Confederación Campesina Mexicana (CCM—Mexican Peasant Confederation) on its ruins—an organization that would be a major asset to Cárdenas in his progress towards the presidency.[126]

The Cardenist power structure mirrored his integrative approach to the different groups making up Michoacán society. His relations with these groups were characterized by three different types of integration: ideological, statist-cooptivist, and personal-charismatic. He sought ideological integration for all the groups that joined the CRMDT, including the village and urban agrarianists and unionists and some of the students, the student teachers, the teachers, and the government officials. He extended statist integration to all the groups that were not members of the CRMDT, including the rural Indians and some of the Cristero peasants, the *rancheros*, the *latifundistas*, and members of the chamber of commerce, the Church, the federal army, and parts of the academic establishment of Michoacán. The relationship between all these groups and the state was mainly functional, based on give-and-take relations conditioned by the specific interests of each group.

The common denominator that linked and complemented these two types of integration was Cárdenas's taciturn intimate leadership, which achieved another kind of integration on a personal, caudillist basis—one that included all the social groups of Michoacán. It was a unifying factor born of Cárdenas's gift for dialogue and his ability to establish direct links with all elements of society and make them into friends of the regime. More than just the offshoot of a special personality, this ability was the combined product of three basic principles: first, a functional concept of modern, progressive society as a complex entity based on a wide range of complementary interests and power groups; second, the premise that a sturdy, functional relationship required a certain degree of socioeconomic equality between the different groups of society; and third, a concept of the Revolution as not only a historical opportunity but also a kind of mission to bring about a dramatic turning point in the development of Mexican society—a society founded on positivist, Darwinist, and protectionist liberalism, the creed designed to supply the "creole oligarchy" (to use Molina Enríquez's term) with the tools it needed to preserve its privileged status in society.[127]

The central aim of all three types of integration was ultimately to concentrate most of the groups under a single ideological roof. Cárdenas assumed that the right integrative policy would break down the barriers between the different groups and attract individuals and groups away from the non-revolutionary camp—the largest and most diversified in Michoacán society—and into the revolutionary camp. This sophisticated thinking was very Mexican in nature, being based on a deep perception of social reality that somehow combined ideological, historical, and pragmatic tools. It also recognized that in Mexico no progress could be made in a situation of strife or deep conflict. "In an underdeveloped state like ours, where a majority of people live in poverty," Cárdenas wrote in his diary on 30 November 1950, "one must govern tolerantly, in accordance with the principles of the constitution."[128]

Tejeda built his power base on completely different assumptions. Power was supposed to be autonomous, sectarian, unlimited by definition, and exploited to its full potential; its structure would link similar organizations in different states to each other and to one common organization that owed nothing to the existing political system, its views, or its legal bases, but answered only to the interests of the peasants themselves. The organizational and operative links holding the Tejedist power base together were primarily ideological, and seldom incorporated other forms of integration such as appeared in Michoacán. The leadership had to come from the ranks of the organization rather than from the political system per se, a requirement that from the outset limited Tejeda's impact as a charismatic leader within that organization, and almost totally effaced him outside it.

Tejeda's power evidently took this form for a number of reasons. First, he and his followers saw strife and conflict as possible and perhaps even desirable conditions in the process of social change. Second, their social-democratic creed viewed society as a class-based society in which the proletariat, as the majority, constituted the foundation that shaped it and defined its culture. Third, in their federalist conception the emergence of the state was a process that had to move from the periphery towards the center rather than vice versa. And, finally, they took a practical and very sober approach in analyzing the ills of concrete reality, but sought radical solutions that appeared dogmatic even when they were very logical.

Time was another strong, if not crucial, factor in Tejeda's political work. He was overly ambitious in his goal, expressed more than once, of creating an irreversible *fait accompli* that would make Veracruz an example to other states and a national pioneer both in agrarian reform and in the development of Mexico's image and government. He radicalized ideology, the relations between the state and bourgeois society (and in some cases the more moderate sectors of proletarian society), and the relations between the state and the political center. Under these circumstances, establishing a broad cooperation between different classes of society, or even between different sectors of the working class, was unthinkable—let alone finding allies in the political center. Thus, while Cárdenas was able to make Ortiz Rubio and Calles his friends despite their different views, Tejeda made them his enemies.

Tejeda therefore failed the test of recognition. Although the power structures he set up were strong and efficient, they never won sufficiently broad federal and public recognition. From the beginning of his term in government, Tejeda's activities in the spheres of the municipios, paramilitary defense, and grassroots organization came under heavy attack. The media, initially very favorable to him, later turned against him, mockingly or hostilely describing everything he did as political, "office-seeking," "communistic," destructive, or borrowed from foreign sources. Even Veracruz deputies and senators tested their strength with various maneuvers designed to topple him, while elements in the opposition merely waited for the opportunity to rid them of him. Under such circumstances, Tejeda had no alternative but to exploit the trappings of his power as fully as possible, coming to rely increasingly on his formal authority and making great use of the civil guards, the secret service, and the police—which combined to give Veracruz the aspect of a state within a state.

Cárdenas lacked Tejeda's oppositionist, impatient—even hasty—nature. Unlike Tejeda, he managed to achieve the public and federal recognition (from the successive federal presidents, the Congress, the PNR, and the national press) he needed both to operate his power bases safely and effectively and to become a leader of national stature, known for his merit and integrity. The national press was at his feet. Calles and the Calles-sponsored presidents (Ortiz Rubio and Rodríguez) all invited him to serve in their respective governments, and various political sectors, particularly the moderate agrarianists, saw him as their leader and a worthy candidate for the next presidency. With great insight, the American ambassador in Mexico to Washington, writing in October 1930, described Cárdenas as an outstanding personality who would implement the Revolution quietly, promoting harmony and unity in the Revolutionary family.[129]

3

The Shaping of a New Civil Consciousness

Motives for Developing a New Consciousness and a Revolutionary Ethos

"Although we are considered radicals within the revolutionary ideology," Tejeda asserted in his valedictory speech to the Veracruz Congress in November 1932, "we are neither destructive nor suicidal. Quite the contrary: We are actually advocating a plan for rapidly and effectively constructing a new life for the people based on their culture and economy, the factors that determine their well-being."[1]

Cárdenas, in turn, said the following in a speech before the PNR's plenary convention in Querétaro on 6 December 1933: "It is . . . only right to declare categorically . . . that I see myself as united, in act and in responsibility, with all the old fighters who through their efforts contributed and continue to contribute to the creation of a new social state and a regime with a redemptive orientation."[2]

For the two governors respectively, the terms "new life for the people" and "new social state" expressed the essence of the Revolution and of their mission as its implementers. Their point of departure was a total negation of the pre-Revolutionary positivist, authoritative and oligarchic 'reformist' past (but nonetheless, as shown by the new historiographic current, modernizing, involving national and foreign investments where owners, chiefs and peasant communities participated in a dynamic context of national economic development opportunities).[3]

Traditional village life, which Cárdenas and Tejeda knew at first hand, was in no way picturesque or romantic, contrary to the school of thought that blames the Revolution for the cultural annihilation of the villages.[4] It was harsh, rough, and real, and its history was characterized by misery, degradation, and exploitation, well-documented in many sources.[5] The Revolution had to address that reality—not the myths of a marvelous "authentic culture," or the illusion of "rural freedom" that obscured the true situation prevailing in the countryside.

In their efforts to examine and conceptualize the social reality of their time, both Tejeda and Cárdenas adopted some Marxist concepts. Cárdenas became exposed to them undoubtedly by a number of eminent Marxist mentors, in particular Luis Mora Tovar, a poet and labor leader; Alberto Bremauntz, one of the shapers of socialist education during Cárdenas's presidency; Rafael García de León, a local supreme court judge and a graduate of the Michoacán University of San Nicolás—a "well-dressed socialist," according to Luis González y González; and a group of teachers at the local university, including the rector, Jesús Díaz Barriga, the university secretary, José Campistro de Cáceres, and the head of the law faculty, Gabino Vázquez, a supreme court judge who deputized for Cárdenas as governor on a number of occasions.[6]

Tejeda had his own mentors, including prominent Communists such as Manuel Almanza and Ursulo Galván, two of the founders of the Partido Comunista Mexicano, although he seems to have made the transition to Marxism on his own. The development of his thought can be traced easily in the explanatory preambles to a succession of draft laws that he proposed in the Veracruz Congress and in his ideological justifications for the expropriation of land in the public interest (*utilidad pública*). None of the 29 direct expropriation decrees by which thousands of urban plots were obtained to build worker housing (a form of expropriation virtually unique to Veracruz until 1931) had included any prefatory ideological discussion; the usual formula was a laconic legalistic enumeration of the reasons for the expropriation and the basis of the government's authority to implement it. However, this began to change in 1931, a year in which 70 expropriation orders of different kinds were issued. Of those, 25 emphasized ideological reasons for the measure proposed, and from August on no other kind of justification appeared at all. Most of these "ideological" decrees harshly denounced capitalism, describing it as an oppressive, profiteering, and socially perverse regime that constituted a major obstacle to the progress and prosperity of nations.[7]

Tejeda's ideological development reached maturity in the course of 1932. His opening remarks in the speech summarizing his governorship constituted an impressive digest of social philosophy that linked (as Terrones López has justly noted) the Kantian concept of individual freedom with Marxist collectivism, portraying the collective as an appropriate sphere in which to achieve individual freedom.[8] In a statement to the press in July 1933, Tejeda summed up his ideological development by saying that Marxism was the natural sequel to the education he had received as a boy, since communism was the logical continuation of positivism.[9]

The problem was that not all the *campesinos* were amenable to the doctrine of change. In fact, the general tendency in rural areas was to continue the traditional way of life—a tendency particularly strong in Michoacán and noted with some frustration by Cárdenas, who saw the peasant resistance to agrarianism as the result of several factors: the "clerical dictatorship," the "fanaticism of the confessional," the pressure exerted by the rural oligarchy, and the "reactionary spirit that continues to breathe in the people." That reactionary spirit posed a great challenge for the agrarianists, who had decided to return to the sources of the Revolution and interpret it anew. They sought to portray the Revolution as a turning-point in the course of Mexican history, a dramatic historical event that had spawned a new social and national ethic. That turning-point was the moment when the bourgeois revolution became a popular, peasant-led revolution; the moment when the political revolution became a social revolution demanding equality and social justice; the moment when the Revolution began to divert Mexican history from the strictly liberal path it had followed since the *Reforma* (Reform) to a popular path that put the interests of the collective before those of the individual.[10]

The agrarianist interpretation was based on a critical view of both the Revolution and society. It pointed out the Revolution's failure to change in any fundamental way the structural inequality of the Mexican social system, even though the Revolutionary constitution had acknowledged the deep-rooted social distortions and undertaken to implement radical reforms. The new revolutionary ethos developed by the agrarianists was a complete alternative in every way—values, concepts, and emotions—not only to the Revolution as implemented at the time, but to the liberal philosophy in general. At the same time, this new ethos was intended to pull down the great barriers to moral and economic renewal created within that culture by years of subjugation. The agrarianists wanted to give the rural population a sense of self-value and belonging—a feeling that it had a role to play in the new democratic state formation of Mexico.

Under these circumstances, it was natural to turn to education. This strategy was not completely new; the idea, at least, of developing a secular, humanistic, rational, activist, and democratic education had originated back in Porfirio Díaz's presidency, and had been promoted considerably under Obregón.[11] The innovations offered by Cárdenas and Tejeda were their radical social message, the priority they gave education in their government policies, and their determined persistence in pursuing their educational objectives.

The Education System before the Advent of Cárdenas and Tejeda

The education systems of Michoacán and Veracruz were not suited to the role the Revolution assigned them. They did not have the right educational philosophy; they did not have clearly defined goals; and they did not have suitable curricula. They suffered from severe shortages of schools, teachers with pedagogical and ideological training, teacher-training colleges, supervisory systems, and money for development and equipment. The compulsory-education laws were not enforced, and most children did not go to school at all.[12] The drop-out rate was very high, and a deep gulf existed between the schools and the community. Other disturbing problems in both Michoacán and Veracruz were the starvation wages paid to teachers—when they were paid at all—and the absence of any link between the academic system and the day-to-day practice of teaching.

In a report submitted to the Michoacán Congress on 15 September 1928, the then-governor, Luis Méndez, said:

> The sad state of the Public Treasury . . . prevented my Administration, as it did that of my predecessor [Ramírez, 1924–1927], from accomplishing what we would have liked to do in the educational field. Budgetary restrictions did not permit us to realize the desired transformation in the economic conditions of the teaching profession . . . In fact, the Government has concentrated on collecting as much statistical data as possible concerning teacher qualifications, curricula, textbooks, and buildings so that in the next four-year term General Lázaro Cárdenas, a progressive and enterprising man, will, with more time and better preparation, be able to solve this problem which is of such great concern in the normal life of the State. Accordingly, I expect this Legislature to offer its wholehearted support to General Cárdenas in implementing what will undoubtedly be the keystone of his Administration, an Administration that I confidently expect to be of great benefit to the State of Michoacán.[13]

In response, the president of the Congress confirmed that education had been neglected "owing to the anomalous conditions prevailing [the Cristero rebellion]," and expressed the legislature's "fervent hopes that the new Administration beginning its term today [would] confront [the problem] decisively." To that end, he said, it would require "broad cooperation and staunch unity from all the social classes . . . so that [the government] may itself punctiliously fulfill its obligations to the people, on the basis of the postulates of the Revolution."[14]

Cárdenas was well aware of the deficiencies of the education system in his state. In a report to the Michoacán Congress at the end of his first year as governor, he declared that Mexico had done nothing but "copy unthinkingly the educational systems of other countries without adapting them intelligently to our environment."[15] A year later he remarked that about 400 villages still lacked schools, and at the end of his term he claimed that although two additional teachers' colleges had been founded, they were not adequate to meet the need.[16] His successor, Benigno Serrato, confirmed this, and noted that of the 965 teachers employed by the state-funded education system in 1932 (as opposed to teachers whose salaries were paid by the federal government, private bodies, and the municipios), 400 were untrained.[17] The Church, for its part, did its best to persuade parents not to send their children to the state schools. The Cristero Rebellion was an additional complication, effectively preventing education in the villages.[18]

The situation in Veracruz was even worse. In January 1929, the director-general of the federal education ministry, Luis Hidalgo Monroy, attacked the state of Veracruz for no longer compelling graduates of the Rebsamen teachers' college in Jalapa to work in the state for a few years, as he himself had done after graduating from that college. Graduates preferred to seek their fortunes in Mexico City rather than tolerate the wretched salary and working conditions in Veracruz.[19] Paying a surprise visit to Veracruz in mid-April 1929 (in part for political motives), Hidalgo Monroy uncovered serious deficiencies. He disclosed his findings to a reporter from *El Universal*, who gave the resulting article the following headlines: "Elementary Education a Failure in the Veracruz Schools"; "The Director-General of Public Education Makes Pointed Statements about the Incompetence of Teachers and Teaching Methods."[20] In the newspaper interview, Hidalgo Monroy explained that during his visit in Jalapa he had discovered that the children who attended school were sadly wasting their time; they knew almost nothing. The teachers were still using antiquated teaching methods, and were causing profound damage to the children in their charge. The supervisor had found fifth-graders unable to solve simple arithmetic problems. A similar situation prevailed in the teaching of the sciences, which suffered, he said, from "the lack of a clear orientation."[21]

These revelations by the federal director-general of education were not very different from what Veracruz teachers themselves described again and again in letters to Tejeda: severe shortages in teaching staff and classrooms, resulting in an average of 100 pupils to every teacher; starvation wages that were frequently withheld; a pupil absentee rate of some 30%; and the impossibility of meeting the stringent requirements of the local education department, which forced teachers to hold evening classes for adults on their own time and without additional pay. In both Michoacán and Veracruz, teachers could only dream of the two pesos daily that the federal government had established as a minimum wage for teachers.[22]

This situation is also confirmed by a letter Tejeda received from a teacher friend of his, Jacinto Lara, about a week before taking office. In the letter, Lara, who had once been secretary of the department of Indian education in the federal education ministry, complained about the lack of any concept linking education with the needs of the community, particularly the rural community; the focus on teaching only reading, writing, and arithmetic "which are forgotten in any case, since they are not used"; and the inferior textbooks, which were fit only for the rubbish bin. He also spoke of the severely felt absence of agricultural and vocational schools, a lack that resulted in huge losses in vegetable, citrus, and fish yields, since the peasants knew nothing of agriculture and believed simply that "things grow because they grow." More than once, he said, peasants went hungry because they had sold their produce at a loss without any commercial justification. Lara also complained that the academic sector shrugged off all responsibility for rural education, preferring to foster the liberal professions.[23]

Cardenist Education as a Revolutionary Mission

Cárdenas's solution to the education problem was two-pronged. One line of approach was the one normal to any education system: improving the physical and organizational infrastructure, enforcing the existing laws, tightening educational supervision, improving teachers' pay and working conditions, and so on. The other consisted in defining new goals for the education system and fostering the sense of a revolutionary educational mission in the teaching staff and the students while trying to organize them as an active body within both the CRMDT and the state.

The first challenge, of course, was to extend the education system throughout the state. The relevant statistics are shown in Table 3.1 despite missing data, it is apparent that during the years 1928–1930 the number of schools increased by about 500, certainly a substantial increase. Particularly interesting is the role of the ranchos and haciendas, which, under government pressure, increased the number of schools they financed from 75 in 1928 to 379 in 1931. This undoubtedly represented a major victory for the administration in its battle for the minds of the *campesinos*' children, who were the targets of Decree #74, the new education law (December 1930).[24]

Table 3.1 Elementary Schools and Teaching Staff in Michoacán, 1928–1932

Year	1928	1929	1930	1931	1932
Type of school					
Rural federal	175	201	199	274	294
Rural state and municipal	152	152	200	230	No data
Rural private	75	255	300	379	248
Total rural schools	402	608	699	883	542*
Urban federal	13	12	11	11	11
Urban state and municipal	323	323	598	206	421
Urban private	18	30	47	47	34
Total urban schools	354	365	656	264	466
Total schools	820	979	1372	1164	1023*
Teachers	1275	1649	No data	No data	2232

*Partial data.
Sources: *Informes del Gobierno*, 1928–1933 Foglio Miramontes, *Geografía económicó*, II, pp. 194–208; Gallardo, *La lucha por la tierra*, pp. 60–62; Raby, "Los principios de la educación rural," p. 578; "Funcionan en el país 6,480 escuelas rurales," *Excelsior*, 30 July 1933.

This surge of educational development petered out in Cárdenas's last two years as governor, however, the main reason apparently being the drop in investment (see Table 3.2) occasioned by the world economic crisis and accompanying fears of decreased revenue (which in fact proved unfounded, since the state still had a surplus of 534,795 pesos at the end of the year).

Table 3.2 Michoacán Education Budget as a Percentage of Total State Budget, 1928–1932

Year	Education expenditure	State budget	Education expenditure as % of the budget
1928	614,478	2,234,604	27.50
1929	956,227	2,303,763	41.50
1930	1,005,097	2,436,331	41.25
1931	1,081,513	3,056,019	35.40
1932	927,172	2,455,256	37.80

Sources: Gallardo, *La lucha por la tierra*, p. 63; Foglio, *Geografía económicó* III, p. 381.

The closure or merging of schools due to changes in state revenue reflected the education system's great vulnerability and the difficulty of predicting growth trends. Another problem was the relatively stable percentage of children who never attended school at all, despite all the efforts to establish as many schools as possible (see Table 3.3).

Table 3.3 Percentage of Children Aged 6-14 Enrolled in School in Michoacán, 1928–1932

Year	Estimated number of children in Michoacán	% of Michoacán children enrolled in school
1928	218,773	30.40
1929	221,617	37.52
1930	224,475	43.21
1931	230,655	40.35
1932	236,396	41.75

Source: Foglio Miramontes, *Geografía económicó* II, p. 205.

While in 1928 some 70% of school-aged children in Michoacán were not enrolled in school, in 1932 the figure had dropped to 60%. If the drop-out rate, which remained high, is taken into account, as well as the unreliability of the figures themselves,[25] the picture is fairly dismal. At the same time, however, the table shows steady enrollment even after 1930, reinforcing the hypothesis that the decreased investment in education was offset by a certain rationalization of resources that prevented serious impairment of the educational enterprise. Cárdenas had greater success in improving the image and self-concept of teachers as social missionaries. A teacher, Cárdenas wrote, must teach "the new revolutionary ideology"; he or she must be exalted to the level of "social guide" (*guiador social*) a person who would bravely enter the revolutionary struggle, who would step firmly into "the fields of the organized peasant and the workshop of the worker strengthened by unionization" to defend "the interests and aspirations of both and to guarantee the economic conditions of both."[26]

The natural place for the development of an idealistic teacher was the CRMDT. Cárdenas encouraged teachers to organize in the framework of the Confederación and, through it, mobilized them for work in the rural districts, teaching adults in night schools and fostering village culture during weekends, holidays, and summers. The unionized teacher was supposed to introduce the values of proletarian organization and agrarian reform to the village, and to serve as the local "modernizer."[27]

Cárdenas did not rely solely on the CRMDT, to which no more than a few teachers belonged, but also took governmental measures. From 26 December 1928 to 18 January 1929, the Michoacán education department offered short courses designed to give the 487 teachers who attended it a sense of educational mission that would, "according to more just and equitable norms . . . introduce them to spiritual peace, provide them with an orientation in doctrines and tendencies, guarantee the concept of *socializing the schools* [original emphasis]." The courses also encouraged them to organize as a cooperative, unionized sector so that they could develop solidarity with the workers and express that solidarity in their educational work.[28] Thus, teachers were to be trained to provide a new sort of education, one that would turn schools from dull, passive, insipid places into "essentially dynamic, active, *social* [original emphasis] institutions that created better habits and customs; [that were] free of prejudice and religious, political, and social fanaticism, [that] forged deep feelings of solidarity, cooperation, and fraternity." The graduates of the new schools would be, according to the Cardenist ideal, "real human beings, as strong spiritually as physically . . . men of *action and enterprise* [original emphasis], better suited to work in the sectors of agriculture, business, industry, and the manual arts . . . "[29]

The subject content emphasized by the new education included social solidarity, knowledge about Mexico and nature, physical and esthetic education, and, in general, studies that would train pupils for an enlightened, healthy, well-planned, and productive life—productive for themselves and for the community and the state.[30]

In his governmental report, Cárdenas stated that the foundation was already being laid for the new educational approach. The construction of state and private (rural) schools had been stepped up, the new pedagogical principles were being put into practice "in accordance with our ideology," and a number of new institutions had been established to link the schools with the community—namely, "*sociedades de padres de familia*" ("associations of household heads"), "*sociedades protectoras de la educación*" ("education protection associations"), and "*juntas de vigilancia escolar*" ("school vigilance groups"). These liaison organizations were intended to help ensure that children were sent to school, and to limit the drop-out rate and provide support for the teachers. Another of their tasks was to help set up evening courses for workers on day-school premises that would provide instruction in the principles of citizenship, hygiene, and syndical and cooperative organization.

Cárdenas also reported that efforts had begun to create a unique Mexican educational discipline—desperately needed, according to him—that would address the Mexican need for a "democratic school that faithfully reflects our institutions, minus their defects." Michoacán, he said, needed to "systematize the school experience" in the framework of "teachers' technical committees" that would work together with household heads in an effort to expand the number of people able to read and write and to try to put into practice the technical and disciplinary reforms "that must be instituted in our schools." To date, 61 such committees had been established, noted Cárdenas, and their contribution could already be felt.[31]

The new approach, reinforced by a strong national emphasis, was incorporated in the regulatory educational law of January 1931. Not only did this law reaffirm the substance of Law #74, but it also stipulated that education in Michoacán would be "national and democratic," an education "for equal opportunity, liberty, and participatory government" that would "emphasize the individual's role in social improvement, and instill in pupils an awareness of the principles established by our Social Revolution and recorded in the Mexican Constitution."[32] The law paid specific attention to rural schools, viewing them as "socializing agents" needed to "create a communal consciousness concerning local problems." To meet this noble aim, the school was supposed to take on the functions of a social-service agent completely adapted to the Michoacán village's communal way of life. In this framework various organized services would be developed: an anti-alcoholism campaign, a child protection agency, a campaign for cleanliness and community health, a tree conservation crusade, the household-heads' association, a communal library, a peasant reading group, and so on.[33]

Another aspect of the facelift undergone by Michoacán education was the improved working conditions of the teachers and the enhancement of their status as professionals with a revolutionary public mission. This was one focus of Law #76, which established an impressive teacher's bill of rights. From now on, any teacher who had worked for 15 years was entitled to a silver medal and a special certificate attesting to his or her contribution to education. A teacher who had taught for 20 years was entitled to a gold medal and an appropriate certificate. These medals were supposed to be awarded with due pomp and ceremony every year within the framework of the celebrations for "Teacher's Day." Teachers who sought early retirement after 20 years of employment were entitled to a monthly pension amounting to 75% of their last salary; and a teacher who had to leave the profession after 15 years owing to poor health received, by law, a pension equaling two-thirds of his or her last salary. A teacher who retired after 30 years received a full pension (100% of his or her last salary). If a teacher died after at least 15 years on the job, his or her family was entitled to claim funeral expenses and half of the teacher's salary until the last of his or her children reached the age of 18.[34]

The changed attitude towards teachers was apparent even before Law #76 went into effect. One example was the impressive ceremony held on 2

October 1930 to honor the teacher Evangelina Rodríguez of Tanhuato. The celebrations lasted the entire day (the teacher's birthday), as public officials, teachers, city residents, and peasants from all the surrounding rancherías came to pay the teacher homage with speeches, songs, music, and dance. All this, wrote an *El Nacional* reporter, was an expression of gratitude for "her good organization in all the education centers, which as a natural result will change [the peasants] from pariahs to free men."[35]

During Cárdenas's time, an effort was also made to pay teachers on time. As early as September 1929, in his annual speech, Cárdenas announced that his administration had given instructions that the payment of teachers' salaries would take priority "so they may return immediately to their places of residence to begin the school activities of the current year. . . ."[36]

Another step towards establishing a new kind of education in which teachers propagated revolutionary ideology was the local Congress's ratification, on 9 October 1930, of a draft law proposed by Deputy Enrique Ramos that transferred responsibility for the teachers' colleges from the university department to the state education department. The principal justification cited by the parliamentary committee handling the draft law was that transferring control of the primary-school teachers' colleges to the public education authority would give them greater material resources and—perhaps the real object of the move—inspire them with a "revolutionary orientation." The result of all this was the *Ley Orgánica de las Escuelas Normales* [Organic Law of Teachers' Training Colleges].[37] Another interesting step taken immediately after the removal of the teachers' colleges from the university authority was to combine, in the spirit of equality, the men's college with the women's college to form the *Normal Mixta* of Morelia. More than a token gesture, this move reflected the administration's social-integrationist orientation and the modernizing, secular tendency of the "new education."

Yet another important endeavor was the effort to win over the students of the Michoacán University of San Nicolás to the Cardenist ideology and its educational goals, a project that began to take shape in July 1931. On 14 July Cárdenas received a letter from Múgica stressing that since the students were the avant-garde of cultural-educational transformation, students' committees should be set up to disseminate the "right" professional ethic in both the country and the city.[38] Accordingly, at the beginning of August 1931, Cárdenas invited 60 lecturers and students from the University of Michoacán to his home, including the rector, Jesús Díaz Barriga. The university itself had already established the custom of holding bimonthly faculty-student meetings, intended as informal gatherings for the enjoyable exchange of ideas on various current subjects. Now Cárdenas was the host. His intention was to turn this "*círculo de café*" ["coffee klatch"]—which apparently included the radical student and university leaders—into a nucleus for disseminating his ideas. That same day, Cárdenas wrote in his diary of the need for student participation in propagating education and culture among the working masses. This participation could take the form of student committees that would be responsible for "ideological dissemination and means of economic advancement." In the open debate he had conducted with the students and faculty members, Cárdenas wrote in his diary, a number of decisions had been reached. One of them was particularly important: "to propose a draft law socializing the professions, under which the candidates accepted by San Nicolás [would] be obliged to lend their services for a certain time in the areas indicated by the State (this provision [would] be extended to the teachers' colleges)."[39]

On 4 August, only three days after the meeting at Cárdenas's house, a group of "revolutionary" university students was invited to a congressional meeting. The impetus for this visit had come from the students themselves, who—undoubtedly with Cárdenas's encouragement—had sent a letter to Congress urging the enactment of legislation to close down the "free schools" (that is, the Catholic schools) of Michoacán on the grounds that they "injured the country's modern educational interests, particularly those of the University [of San Nicolás] itself, and they were not in harmony with the basic principles of the Revolution." Ernesto Ruiz Solís, the house speaker, noted that the Congress had invited representatives of the students to explain their petition and what they wanted from the Congress, and he expressed his confidence that all the deputies would support that petition. And indeed, after a debate filled with impassioned revolutionary socialist rhetoric, during which a number of students spoke in favor of "socializing the professions" and closing the free schools, Deputy Antonio Meyes Navarro, the CRMDT's secretary of education, took the floor and declared his support for the students' initiative, which, he said, meshed with the views of the CRMDT. Their appeal, he stressed, was justified not only with respect to the free schools, but also as a measure "against all the reactionary professionals who cleverly exploited the working class." At the end of the debate, the president of the Congress declared that the legislature would support the students not only in this matter, but on all other issues as well.[40] Thus, the Congress in fact promised to enact a law that restricted or closed down the private preparatory schools and the free law school.

Faithful to the promise he had made to the members of the "coffee klatch," on 16 February 1932 Cárdenas placed before the Congress a law designed to adapt professional training and education to the needs of society. This goal was targeted in two ways. First, the law allowed the government to regulate the number of people working in specific professions by giving it the authority to close temporarily or permanently—or even prevent the establishment of—academic departments and private schools that trained people for jobs that were already in short supply, including religious posts. Second, it also allowed the government to compel the University of Michoacán itself and all the institutions associated with it to "impose the new artistic, industrial, scientific, and philosophical orientations that the advancement and progress of nations demand from the intellects of the young if they are to become an entity or element of positive production and effective yield for well-being and social exaltation." Thus, in addition to its regulating function, the law was supposed to help modernize the teaching and vocational-education systems in Michoacán.[41]

A month and a half after the "coffee party," Gabino Vázquez, who was temporarily standing in for Cárdenas, noted that the students and faculty of San Nicolás were already developing a habit of regular contact with the masses and making active and fruitful efforts to spread knowledge, whether through popular events or conferences they organized, or through cultural and social "missions" that operated all over the state during school vacations. The university, Gabino Vázquez asserted, was itself instilling a new outlook in its students. They were learning to think of themselves not only as individuals but as members of a community, as members of a certain race and of humankind. They were taught a system of values and ethics that would influence their behavior, including recognition of the value of education and the idea of an *"escuela única"* ("single school"), concepts that they would be expected to disseminate throughout the community. The students of both the university and the teachers' training colleges, said Vázquez, were working together with the CRMDT to do away with the Church-administered "free schools."[42]

The Michoacán administration's intensive activity produced quick and visible results. The close relationship forged between the state, the local authorities, the university, the teachers' colleges, the labor confederation, and the parent-teacher committees turned the school into a significant factor in the promotion of the Revolution's social principles. Cárdenas revealed some of his great political ability in developing a complex, efficient, integrative system powered by the force of a progressive world view. By means of this system, Cárdenas was able to spread the gospel of nationally directed social education throughout the state. Linking all the education sectors together was certainly a highly successful move, without which any change in consciousness would have been virtually unthinkable.

Nonetheless, the day-to-day routine of education was beset with difficulties. Not all teachers identified with the Cardenist educational concept, and many village parents' committees were unhappy with the revolutionary messages being conveyed through the secular curriculum.[43] More than once the traveling cultural missions were attacked on their way to perform educational functions, and teachers could not long stand up against the outbursts of violence against them—violence that sometimes ended in murder.[44] The state did not manage to establish schools everywhere, nor was it always able to contend successfully with the powerful influence of the Church and the private schools that operated under the Church's aegis.[45]

The necessity of placating the Cristeros in the districts they controlled handicapped efforts to institute "the new education" in those areas. The task was particularly difficult since some of the rebel commanders, who were almost completely uneducated, had been appointed as educational supervisors, in which capacity they strove to eradicate from the curriculum anything that suggested "socialism" or "communism." One supervisor, for example, said:

[. . .] the Municipal President of the district of Coalcomán, Michoacán, appointed me as Inspector of Rural Schools in my district in order to prevent the bad teaching provided by the socialist, atheist government teachers and loathed by the parents, who were quarreling with the teachers to the point of banishing them from the schools or killing them, as they did in various parts of the district.

I could do no less than to interview the teachers of the various schools already operating in my district [and using] all possible communist means to eradicate Christianity from the young and make them nothing more than materialists. I went from school to school telling the teachers to confine themselves to teaching reading, writing, and counting . . . [because] there the parents' wishes held sway, not the will of the filthy liberal socialism that wants to appropriate what does not in good conscience belong to it.[46]

Although more and more rural schools were founded, they did not meet the real need for educational facilities, as can be seen in Table 3.3. These problems and limitations overshadowed Cárdenas's educational achievements to some extent, and his speech at the close of his term reflected his frustration over the dragging pace of the mental metamorphosis he was seeking to effect and the "fatal state of anarchy" that still lurked in the collective consciousness.

Nonetheless, there is no doubt that ideologically a completely new educational foundation had been laid in Michoacán. The new education was not for children alone, but had an all-inclusive communal, cultural, and national orientation. Such an education skillfully combined with the syndicalist and agrarianist praxis of the time, indeed began to bring about the change Cárdenas sought in the popular consciousness, but it was a very slow process.[47]

The Rehabilitation of the Veracruz Education System

Tejeda's term of government was not distinguished by any significant increase in the number of schools: 1,310 schools were operating at the end of 1928, and four years later this total had risen to 1,428 (789 of them rural schools), including 15 kindergartens and one teachers' college in Jalapa. The system employed 2,322 teachers to educate 81,455 children.[48] However, the agrarianists in the state were eager to build increasing numbers of rural schools. Their enthusiasm was reflected in the debate over the 1932 budget; at a time when the state was preparing for a 36% cut in its budget,[49] the agrarianist lobby was firing off innumerable memos to the Congress demanding significant increases for rural education. Deputy Jesús Ramírez Ordoñez, for example, suggested eliminating the state school supervisory staff and using its share of the budget—some 70,000 pesos—to build rural schools. He offered an interesting rationale:

If we eliminate the [. . . school supervisors] from the budget, we free the teachers of a burden, allowing them to devote more time to their duties, [since currently] teachers are burdened by fear of the boss whose favor they must retain at all costs, and thus they end up being the object of intrigues and prejudices.[50]

This proposal, which gave rise to a very stormy debate in Congress, was, of course, defeated. Its opponents explained passionately that the supervisors were the very persons who would "interpret most correctly and properly the revolutionary ideology that should govern the education of the people . . . "[51]

Moisés de la Torre, the head of the Unión Revolucionaria Anticlerical (URA—Anti-clerical Revolutionary Union), had an even more revolutionary proposal. In a letter to Tejeda he suggested nothing less than closing down all the upper-level state-funded high schools (*escuelas preparatorias*), temporarily closing all the middle schools (*escuelas secundarias*), and using the money saved thereby to establish additional rural primary schools. One high-school student, he claimed, cost the state as much as 20 poor village children. The state would be able to save half the money gained by closing the high schools—an advantage in itself during a period of economic difficulty—and to invest the remaining 68,460 pesos in the establishment of 20 rural industrial schools, or, alternatively, 70 ordinary rural schools. This would not harm the high-school students, De la Torre insisted, since they were perfectly capable of financing their studies with their own money, and in any case they constituted a small, insignificant group that did not justify the large sums being invested in them. After all, they were a conservative group remote from the Revolution, comprising "young people of the aristocracy, very few from the mesocracy, and scarcely any from the proletariat."[52]

The high schools continued to operate, of course. All these imaginative proposals, however, indicated both the very heavy "proletarian" bias of the educational climate and the great difficulty of obtaining the resources needed both to build rural schools throughout the state and, in general, to make educational reality conform to the government's vision.

As part of his effort to reinforce rural education, Tejeda established three experimental teachers' colleges for rural teachers in 1929. Two of them (Chicontepec in the north and Acayucan in the south) became permanent regional teachers' colleges in 1931.[53] Tejeda tried to recruit potential teachers from the rural communities themselves, asking each agrarian committee to find at least one worthy candidate. He explained to the committee members that the graduates of the training colleges would work for the liberation of the Indians, for agrarian organization along revolutionary lines, and for the creation of a "collective spirit."[54] At the same time, in August 1930, Tejeda instituted a "cultural mission" (*misión cultural*) comprising four teachers and a small technical staff. This delegation was supposed to travel from village to village and hold extension courses lasting a few weeks for untrained rural teachers. While Tejeda was in office, the cultural mission managed to cross the state from north to south and to establish dozens of training centers.[55]

Like Cárdenas, Tejeda sought to resolve the thorny problem of meager teachers' salaries and delays in payment. In a congressional debate over the budget at the beginning of 1929, Deputy Torres pointed out the injustice of a situation where a textile worker earned a comfortable wage of 4.5 pesos a day (a sum Torres claimed covered a family's daily expenses) and a clerk who could barely read and write received about 150 pesos a month, but a teacher, "a cultural pioneer who had to prepare the next generation," made only 50 pesos a month. Deputy Montiel suggested taking 100 pesos off each deputy's monthly salary in order to augment the education budget.[56] In the end, nothing actually changed, however. The majority—some 500—of rural teachers continued to earn 60 pesos a month, while the remaining 200 received an "improved" salary of 75–100 pesos per month.[57]

Another chronic problem was the constant delays in paying these salaries, particularly the salaries of teachers appointed directly by the local authorities. Under these circumstances, teachers naturally tended to spend less time teaching than moonlighting in other jobs, as Tejeda discovered soon after taking office.[58] Tejeda's appeals to the municipios to expedite payment did not achieve much. Some of them told him that they lacked the money to do anything.[59] This response, and the continued failure to pay the salaries that were due, led Tejeda to attempt a more systematic approach. In June 1930, he sent a circular to all the municipios explaining that the delay in paying teachers' salaries was very harmful to the pupils, since the teachers were compelled to leave their "exalted mission" and invest their energies in other spheres. His government, convinced of the need to correct this anomaly, begged the municipios to amend their budgets and order the regular payment of the teachers' current salaries and, as soon as possible, those owing from previous years.[60]

Subsequently, on 26 December, Tejeda proposed a draft amendment to the general education law of Veracruz that was supposed to solve the problem. This amendment provided that if a municipio did not pay the salaries of its teachers within two months, responsibility for its schools would be transferred to the state administration. Tax funds would then be deducted from the municipio treasury, at the state government's discretion, and transferred partially or entirely to the state "for the purpose of duly and appropriately maintaining the aforementioned schools." This amendment was approved on the spot.[61] From then on, Tejeda responded to each failure to pay teachers' salaries on time with great severity, confiscating rent-yielding municipal assets and dissolving offending municipios.[62]

The issue of salaries arose again in Law #222 (24 November 1932). This law in essence reaffirmed Article 68/XLIV (f) of the state constitution, holding the officials and employees of the educational administrative system legally liable for the payment of teachers' salaries.[63] The provision of judicial remedies was a recognition of the failure of efforts to solve the problem by ordinary bureaucratic means. Law #222 in fact lumped together in one legal and ethical category those officials who were negligent in implementing the agrarian reform and those who were negligent in the payment of teachers' salaries. At the same time, however, since the threat of legal action was apparently of rather limited efficacy, Tejeda tried to ease the teachers' situation by setting up teachers' colonies on government land. In this way, he thought, teachers would be saved having to pay rent, and would be able to eke out their meager earnings by growing fruits and vegetables. A number of such colonies were established.[64]

Tejeda, like Cárdenas, also took energetic measures to improve the image and social status of teachers. In Veracruz this process had begun even before Tejeda took office, with the enactment of a decree on 10 September 1928 that gave teachers life insurance. Covering teachers who had worked for at least three years, the decree entitled the families of deceased teachers to a payment of 1,000 pesos, a large sum by the standards of the time. On 18 May 1931, Gabriel Lucio, the director of the Veracruz education department, sent out a circular to all the teachers of the state explaining a plan to extend the benefits of the 1928 decree to education workers who were not teachers. Insurance payments would be increased from 1,000 pesos to 1,100 pesos, and they would be paid to the family within eight days from the insured individual's death. These provisions were enacted on 30 June, amending the 1928 insurance law. The new Law #212 extended insurance coverage to new teachers from their first day in the education system, and to all other employees of the education system as well upon payment of a three-peso membership fee and an additional payment of one peso upon the death of the policyholder. On the same day another law, Law #213, was passed, which instituted pensions for teachers for the first time in the history of Veracruz.[65] Tejeda's administration invested about 40% of the state budget in education, making Tejeda, together with Cárdenas, the Mexican governors who invested most heavily in the educational field.[66] In Veracruz as in Michoacán, however, the results were very modest in terms of both the number of children who attended school and the number who actually completed their education.[67]

The Ideological Orientation: Socialist Education in Veracruz

Up until mid-1931, the Veracruz education system lacked any clear pedagogical orientation. On 17 January 1930 a new director, Professor Gabriel Lucio, was appointed to the local education department, but before he could address any serious ideological or pedagogical issues, he had to contend with much more prosaic problems stemming from the deficiencies of the state education infrastructure.

These problems were not the only reason for the delay in defining Veracruz's educational goals, however. The main difficulty lay in Tejeda's own ideological nebulousness. It was not until his personal views began to crystallize at the end of 1931 that a clear orientation began to appear in the education system as well, to the point that in May 1932, it was defined as "socialist." Combating ignorance, fanaticism, and "intellectual backward-ness" among the working classes was now seen as the general aim of education. The goals of teacher-training were defined as creating "a mentally healthy and physically strong society in whose spirit pulse noble, disinter-ested ideals, inspired by a true morality," and making teachers into "mentors conscious of their lofty mission and indisputable agents in prosperity and the rapprochement of the masses [to the Revolution]." The keystones now were scientific instruction deriving from a "pedagogical plan of action based on broad rational and psychological criteria," and active training for practical work that "favor[ed] the solidarity and fortitude of our race as an indispen-sable basis for reinforcing our nationality."[68]

The struggle against religious fanaticism (which began in June 1931) provided a means of changing the spirit of education in Veracruz. Tejeda believed that the schools' participation in his campaign against the Church would instill Revolutionary principles in the young and prepare them to take control of their futures. His notion of these principles was quite specific: He meant "the Mexican socialist Revolution." Although this concept first appeared in his own rhetoric, he felt very optimistic about the possibility of implanting it in the popular consciousness. From his point of view, the anti-clerical campaign had already begun to bear fruit. The peasants, he believed, were undergoing a "mental transformation," and were beginning to see the schools as "the guarantee of the Revolution's future and the well-being of humankind," as well as a place where the coming generations could receive "the best possible preparation . . . to achieve a better social condition."[69]

This was also the moment to change the antiquated definitions of educa-tion laid down in the 1917 political constitution of Mexico, a document that had been the work of a small group of middle-class politicians, military men, and intellectuals.[70] Tejeda decided to organize an educational congress (Congreso de Educación) to renovate Mexico's educational philosophy at the end of 1931, to be attended by representatives of the people—teachers, peas-ants, workers—as well as representatives of the state and federal governments. The purpose of the congress would be to produce "a potent new educational orientation that completely fulfill[ed] the hopes and needs of the Veracruz proletariat, thus pursuing one of the noble ideals of vindi-cation that stir[red] in the spirits of the proletarian classes." In this respect, the congress would provide a strong boost for education.[71]

After several postponements, the socialist Education Congress opened in June 1932. By now Tejeda was running out of time; he wanted the congress to deal with practical matters rather than theory and ideology. Accordingly, the gathering took the form of a "technical" conference (Comisión Técnico-Pedagógica) for teachers, peasants, and workers rather than the "educational" conference originally planned, and Tejeda gave it a mandate to draft amendments to the constitutional articles. Its goals were to guarantee "economic and technical autonomy for teachers" and to permit "full development of the educational process" according to "the new social imperatives" so that the schools would cease to be "a bourgeois institution [and] become a frankly proletarian institution...." The new education would have to conduct an energetic campaign against alcohol, "that social plague" and "barrier to [the worker's] economic and spiritual liberation," and shape a consciousness that would orient children radically towards "the overriding necessity of transforming the present social system in such a way as to satisfy the longings for proletarian justice."[72]

Three months after the conference had begun its labors, Tejeda called on it to mold a school system that would prepare communities to take "active part in the socialized exploitation of wealth, in order to benefit the working classes and to polish the proletariat culturally and institutionally."[73] In other words, the conference was supposed to develop socialist education.

Socialist schools were to be cooperative community institutions, characterized by solidarity with the surrounding culture. They would involve fathers in the educational process and encourage the establishment of pupil cooperatives. Such cooperatives would help children appreciate the value and importance of proletarian solidarity and teach them the mechanisms that gave rise to it. This type of school would foster the image of the "social teacher" as an agent of change in the village who educated adults, encouraged peasants to organize in cooperatives, and promoted cooperation among the various agrarian committees.[74] Teachers would be trained as "social guides" (*guiadores sociales*) by the teacher training colleges, which would foster "a materialistic viewpoint . . . as a basis for a firm concept of the new human morality" and impel "future teachers to firm, resolute action to vindicate the exploited."[75] They would teach their pupils to identify with the peasants, encourage them to take part in the anti-clerical struggle, and spur them to join in the class struggle to achieve political and syndicalist organization and the implementation of the labor laws and the agrarian reform.

In imposing all these responsibilities on the schools, Tejeda was virtually declaring them as an instrument for preparing the proletariat to take over political power. This was not said openly, of course, but by giving the schools the responsibility for providing doctrinal and practical training for socialized life while reducing the influence of the productive and commercial bourgeoisie, he clearly indicated what he thought should be the ultimate goal of not only education, but political endeavor in general.[76]

In order to expedite the work of the upcoming education congress and to point it in the right ideological direction, Tejeda had decided to institute socialist education in five primary schools in Jalapa beginning with the 1931–1932 school year. These schools, which were henceforth called "proletarian schools," were given a new curriculum that combined theoretical Marxist teachings with practical experience. Thus, the children studied issues such as the various "sources of labor," labor legislation, systems of trade organization, forms of class struggle, and ways of cultivating solidarity among workers. They gained practical experience in agricultural work, manufacturing workshops, and school administration, and were drilled in the "Marxist language," which was supposed to prepare them to serve as agents of change when they grew up. They also learned about the existing proletarian organizations in the state, and their goals and modes of operation. Finally, in addition to general cultural studies, they were taught "the history of social-economic exploitation and the class struggle," with particular reference to Mexican history.[77]

The experience of these five schools was discussed by the technical conference, which formally resolved to recommend the institution of socialist schools throughout Veracruz. This resolution noted that the schools would constitute both work centers, where pupils learned to produce goods for social and utilitarian purposes, and laboratories in which would be synthesized a fundamentally socialist ideology and a culture able to provide a rational explanation of the principles of labor, production, and the class struggle.[78]

The conference's recommendation became law (Law #222) on 24 November 1932. Tejeda had succeeded—at least on the formal, legislative level, in melding his own world view with both the goals of education and the turbulent social reality of his state. Law #222 laid the foundation for an education system that cultivated the popular consciousness necessary in order to institute a socialist government and way of life in Veracruz.[79] The socialist education developed in Veracruz was adopted by the PNR convention of December 1933, as a component of the party's Six-Year Plan and after Cárdenas became president it was extended to the entire nation. Cárdenas, however, unlike Tejeda, made no attempt to link education with the establishment of a genuine proletarian state in Mexico.[80]

As its new ideological approach crystallized, Tejeda's government began to attack any educational institution it suspected of being "bourgeois" (and therefore "reactionary," "neo-clerical," "conservative" and so on). Its targets were many, and included private schools, the university-linked high schools (*escuelas preparatorias*), and even the middle schools (*escuelas secundarias*), in addition, of course, to the fledgling Veracruz university, which even then was already Tejeda's bête noire.[81] He wanted to lead a public campaign to close down these institutions and destroy the organizational base for "the reserves of the conservative bourgeoisie." "The Government is not in a position to cover the costs of [the law school's] maintenance," declared Tejeda in his annual speech in September 1932. "[To do so it would] have to sacrifice resources needed for rural and primary education, the fundamental source of the Nation's future." The government had no intention, he said, of investing in the training of professional classes who "unfortunately" did not identify with the needs of the working classes but sought personal advantage among the capitalists, even if it hurt collective and national interests."[82] This campaign was more verbal than anything else. Taken up by the local and national media, it elicited a shower of scathing criticism that led Tejeda to back down from his plan to close down the "bourgeois" institutions completely. In practice, only the decree closing the private schools (28 September 1931) remained in force, and even it was not enforced systematically.[83]

One of the "anti-bourgeois" campaign's main failures was its treatment of the university. Unlike Cárdenas, who made strenuous and largely successful efforts to enlist the support of both the students and the university as an institution, Tejeda unwisely threw away his own opportunity to do so. The first stroke against him was the substantial delay in the foundation of the Veracruz University, a delay apparently rooted in his own ambivalence to the project. Moreover, unlike Cárdenas, Tejeda did not have the wit to ingratiate himself with the law school, an institution whose graduates were employed by the judicial authority that was so important for the expedition of Tejeda's social reforms. Lacking a loyal judiciary, Tejeda was obliged to spend his entire term fighting *amparo* rulings (appeals protecting constitutional rights) that again and again canceled out his efforts to implement agrarian reform, and voided a number of important agrarian laws.

It was strange that he should not have understood something so basic to the success of his reforms, most of which, once all possible political steps had been taken, ultimately depended on the rulings of the court. In his eagerness to bring down the law school, he was carried away by the Agrarian League's radical approach to the issue, eventually having to take direct action against the state supreme court. This episode ended stormily with the resignation en masse of all the Supreme Court judges in October 1930. The Veracruz Congress devoted three consecutive sessions to the matter between 4 and 13 November 1930. In the turbulent congressional debate over both the judges' resignation and the scandalous fact that only pro-agrarianists were chosen to replace them, a deep gulf developed between members of the CROM, for whom the whole affair was a thorn in the flesh, and members of the Veracruz Agrarian League, whose aims were well served by the change. The damage was thus twofold: Not only was the government dragged into a serious constitutional debate, but the incident created a crisis in the labor movement itself. The League and Tejeda had isolated themselves in Veracruz by crossing the fine line between the rule of law and anarchy. There is no doubt that these antics were viewed with great severity by the federal government, and constituted one of the factors that hastened Tejeda's political end.[84]

Tejeda also showed little acumen in his relations with Veracruz university students, which never attained any modicum of mutual respect. One of the incidents that exacerbated the enmity between Tejeda and the students was Tejeda's closure of *El Dictamen* for 40 days, in August 1930. Most of the students sided with *El Dictamen*, adding greatly to the loud protests that reverberated through the national press and the Veracruz chamber of commerce. Although protest had been expected from the chamber of commerce and the press, it had not been anticipated from the students, and accordingly took the administration and labor circles completely by surprise.

The breach between Tejeda and the university became irrevocable a month later. On 14 September a general student congress was held in the city of Veracruz for all the students of Veracruz University. Endorsed by the Mexican Federación Nacional de Estudiantes (National Student Federation), it was supposed to discuss common student interests, and was expected, if not actually designed, to express opposition to the closure of *El Dictamen*. The proceedings were conducted by no less a personage than the university rector, Ignacio García Tellez, who "happened" to be in town.

The government's fear was that the student conference's resolutions would be tacitly supported by faculty members, ranging the entire university against Tejeda. Tejeda, who could not afford such a humiliating position, offered the conference's organizing committee a 500-peso subsidy, hoping that this donation would pour oil on troubled waters and possibly even win him a vote of sympathy, which a group of his student supporters from Jalapa had volunteered to propose at the conference. This placating gesture was doomed to failure, however. The students of the city of Veracruz refused to interrupt their philippics against Tejeda so that the Jalapa students could engineer the desired tribute as a return for the 500 pesos. The Veracruz students announced they would reject any resolution sympathetic to Tejeda on the grounds that it would constitute "complete servility."

Seeing there could be no "positive" solution to the crisis, Tejeda transferred the 500 pesos to his Jalapa supporters, who organized a *"congresito"* ("little congress") in the capital as a counterweight to the big congress taking place in the port city. As chairman of the *congresito*, Tejeda appointed the head of the university department in the Tejedist government, Genaro Ángeles, a clerk with no academic background who was directly subordinate to Tejeda.[85] A schism thus developed between the small minority of Veracruz students who supported Tejeda, and the overwhelming majority who opposed him. A delegation from the "Jalapa conference" who requested permission to be present at the general student conference in the city of Veracruz was prevented from entering the conference hall. Despite the retraction of the aid Tejeda had offered, the conference took place, financed independently and with the contribution of an additional 100 pesos from the central branch of the Student Federation.[86]

The *El Dictamen* affair was not actually the main factor in the breach between Tejeda and the students; it merely focused a long-standing enmity that became the talk of the Veracruz Congress in September of that year.[87]

Here, as in other spheres, Tejeda did not know how to unite the major agencies of power and influence. Handicapped by his Manichean view of the world, he missed his chance to give rural education—and primary and technical education in general—an immediate boost by sending cultural missions composed of students and lecturers into the villages. He also passed up opportunities to link his agrarian reform with scientific research in the fields of agriculture, marketing, soil science, hydrology, and so on, as Jacinto Lara had suggested when Tejeda took office. His conflict with the students and, apparently, with the heads of the university also precluded the possibility of establishing an institute for social research such as Cárdenas founded at the University of San Nicolás in Michoacán, an institute that could expand academic research to cover the entire social field and promote both agriculture and agrarian reform.

Instead, Tejeda's impatience and extremism led him away from a vitally important reservoir for socialist education. If Tejeda had been more attentive to the students and provided some incentive for their loyalty, like the privileged status with which Cárdenas had rewarded "his" students, he would undoubtedly have won their allegiance. But he chose not to, or was carried away by the Agrarian League's anti-bourgeois propaganda, which focused on fighting the class war rather than running a state government. He purposely—perhaps making a virtue out of necessity to some extent— enlisted the support of the rural graduates of the teacher-training colleges. This handful of people was all he had to take the educational revolution into the villages—an impossible mission, of course, by any rational criteria.[88] Thus, on one hand, Tejeda declared war on all the educational institutions that resisted him; on the other, he promoted all those he believed likely to contribute to the establishment of a socialist consciousness, from the "socialist" kindergartens upwards.[89] This approach may have produced occasional random achievements, but it was very unlikely to succeed on a system-wide basis.

Despite the obstacles described above, the measures taken by the government to promote socialist education in 1932 (the definitive year in terms of both education and ideology) were very impressive. That year saw a great increase in the establishment of rural schools and continuing-education schools. In addition, the administration gave increasing numbers of rural schools two-hectare plots of land so that they could instruct their pupils in agricultural techniques. Feverish—though ultimately unsuccessful—efforts were made to establish a proletarian university as an alternative to the "bourgeois" university. At the same time, a sociology and current affairs program was set up in the Jalapa teachers' college—yet another effort to enlist the spoiled urban student teachers on the side of the government and the proletariat.[90] Compulsory courses in sociology and social economics were instituted for all middle- and high-school students, to initiate them into "the nature of the world social movement and in particular the problems in this respect in our own country."[91] The Veracruz Agrarian League and various workers' organizations were given financial aid for the purpose of expanding their independent school systems, and scholarships were provided to allow 89 children of impoverished peasants and workers (including peasant and labor leaders) to study in Jalapa. These children were housed in a special educational community built in the city with state funds and received the best of care from a staff of trained teachers.[92]

It is very difficult to gauge the success of Tejeda's socialist education in Veracruz. Researchers of the period claim that Tejeda failed on three counts: in the battle against ignorance, in the advancement of socialist education, and in the promotion of anti-religious education. De la Peña maintains that the regional (rural) seminars were a total disappointment. He claims that the campaign against ignorance was pursued more slowly in Veracruz than anywhere else in the Republic, and that conditions of teachers' salary were never stabilized, leading competent teachers to abandon the profession. In the Córdoba district in 1942, for example, only 82 of the 287 urban primary-school teachers had teaching certificates, while only five of the 82 rural teachers employed in the district were qualified. The drop-out rate remained very high, and even by 1945 only 70% of the children enrolled attended school regularly. According to De la Peña, the provision of evening classes at the expense of the teachers themselves for adults and children unable to attend school otherwise was also a resounding failure.[93] Olivia Domínguez Pérez, for her part, has noted the inability of government efforts to make instant socialists out of the children of Veracruz, most of whom lived in a religious—even fanatically religious—environment. This debacle reconfirmed the iron-clad rule that changes in political or social consciousness are by nature slow and gradual.[94]

Ragueb Revuelta, a researcher of socialist education in Mexico, holds similar views. Socialist education in Veracruz was, according to him, no more than radical demagogy designed to channel social demands through ideology. The government wanted this education to be "an accelerating factor in the process of social transformation" and a tool for educating the masses about the class struggle, which the government saw as the way to achieve its radical social goals. Revolutionary ferment, the crisis of capitalism, popular dissatisfaction with the achievements of the Revolution, the emergence of a charismatic young leadership that established direct contacts with the masses, the implementation of radical reforms that presented a formidable local opposition to the federal administration—all these factors had contributed to the view that the social aims of the Revolution could be achieved only through class struggle. Under these circumstances, education seemed a reasonable way of preparing for that struggle. However, the socialist educational ideal that Revuelta disparagingly calls *"educacionismo"* (educationism) in fact had nothing to do with education's true capacity for effecting change, and was accordingly impossible to implement.[95]

In my view Revuelta's skepticism concerning Tejeda's motives is unfounded. Beyond the political motives underlying Tejeda's approach to education was a growing belief that in Mexico change was possible only in the context of a class struggle—in the radical social-democratic rather than the communist sense. Tejeda believed that education should instill this belief in both schoolchildren and the community by breaking it down into its cognitive, emotional, and ethical components and channeling it into practical conduits. Revuelta is correct, however, in his comments about Tejeda's quick-fix approach to introducing socialist education. His efforts were overly ambitious even for a socially dynamic state like Veracruz which was open to revolutionary ideas, and they repelled and alienated people who under less antagonizing circumstances might have participated in the endeavor to institute a new kind of education in Veracruz.

Tejeda and Cárdenas: A Parting of the Ways

Until mid-1931, Cárdenas and Tejeda defined their educational goals similarly. They were equally resolute in pursuing what might be termed "social" reforms in education. The resemblance ended, however, from the moment that Tejeda turned towards socialist education while Cárdenas carried on with "social" education. Tejeda saw education primarily as a means of promoting class struggle. The school, he said in a speech in the city of Veracruz at the beginning of 1933, "lays the groundwork for the victory of proletarian ideas while serving as the redoubt against which all the attacks by the enemies of the proletariat . . . shatter."[96]

All the factors in Tejeda's ideological extremism contributed to his espousal of socialist education: the approaching end of his governorship, with no clear political future in sight; the decision to operate outside the federal establishment and to subjugate its interests to those of the federated states, turning Veracruz into an exemplary national model; the increasing pressure by an Agrarian League anxious over the approaching end of its patron's governorship; the tendency to view reality in theoretical rather than pragmatic or "Mexican" terms; the effects of the unyielding battle against the Church and the rural oligarchy for control of the education system; the world economic crisis's harsh repercussions on the situation of Veracruz workers and peasants, and the resulting pressure on the government to seek radical solutions to alleviate their suffering; and, finally, the absence of any educational master plan covering the entire four years of Tejeda's term as governor. In its stead was only a feverish sense of working against time—a condition that could produce only extremism.

Cárdenas, in contrast, entered office already well prepared to deal with the issue of education. The manifesto of January 1928, and a 1929 report to Congress recording his orderly and systematic work during his first year as governor, offer incontrovertible proof of this.[97]

The two men's substantially different approaches generated another major difference between them: the methodical, straightforward Cárdenas managed to maintain control over the different factions active in the field of education, even using them to enlist the support of still other groups (university students, teachers, professors, urban high-school students, and parent committees, for example). Since Tejeda, initially vague and subsequently extreme, had to obey the dictates of the Agrarian League, he inevitably alienated other power groups that could have exercised a moderating influence on the League by working in or with it. Lacking any clear program or system of operation, Tejeda was in a constant tug-of-war with various educational forums organized by unruly groups of workers and peasants to pressure the government into promoting a radical public education that would meet their needs.[98] Only a political atmosphere as highly charged as that of Veracruz in 1931 could have given rise to a wild idea like closing down all the channels of "bourgeois" education in order to invest more heavily in rural education and agrarian reform.

The education issue revealed once again the deep ideological and political differences between Cárdenas and Tejeda. While Cárdenas revered social unity, sought ways to join the mainstream, and subsequently instituted a school system that played a social rather than primarily political role, Tejeda glorified class struggle, the establishment of a proletarian regime in Mexico, and consequently a politicized school system. The Veracruz experience, with its live demonstration of the dangers of such a system, was what led the federal education ministry to try to remove rural education from the authority of the states in 1932.[99]

Despite their different orientations, as revolutionaries Cárdenas and Tejeda shared certain basic views: the belief that school was the place to eradicate the values—or ingrained fears—that the Church had instilled in Mexican children; the belief that school was the place to reinforce working-class and peasant children's sense of self-worth as human beings and as citizens with equal rights and equal opportunities in national society; and the belief that school was the place to train working, activist, creative, rational young people eager for change. Both Cárdenas and Tejeda believed that to strengthen the influence of the new education, the Church's influence had to be substantially diminished—but only Tejeda set out to do the job all-heartedly.

The results of the educational reform in the two states were on the whole very similar in both quantitative and organizational terms. In both states, the education system never managed to enroll more than a third of the children in need of instruction. The drop-out rate remained very high, and the available facilities did not come close to meeting the needs of universal education. The teaching corps remained relatively small, inadequately trained, and grossly underpaid. The Church continued to exert a strong influence on the field of education, as Cárdenas admitted in a speech summing up his governorship. In that speech, as mentioned, he remarked that Michoacán remained prey to "a fatal state of anarchy." Every attempt the administration had made to exert some kind of supervisory control over the private schools had been "easily neutralized by the conservative or delaying spirit that dominates them."[100]

The Battle against the Church

While running for governor Cárdenas, who had a very strong personal bias against the Church, ceremoniously promised to fight to the death against "the vise of confessed fanaticism." Once elected, however, he underwent a complete metamorphosis. Just before the final offensive against the Cristeros in June 1929, he asked to be given the command of the Michoacán front, knowing that he would be able to end the rebellion without bloodshed and take advantage of its peaceful termination to open up a dialogue with the Cristero leaders and their *campesino* followers. The result was what *El Universal Gráfico* called, in January 1929, "*un labor de convencimiento*" ("a job of persuasion").[101] He recruited the leaders of the rebellion into the state apparatus as commanders of civil guard units, police officers, and government supervisors in various sectors, including the state elementary-school system.[102] Cárdenas was unreservedly faithful to the June agreement between the government and the Church leadership, which had concluded the struggle with a compromise. Immediately after it was signed he stopped all persecution of priests—a practice that had been virtually a national sport during the rebellion—and gave orders for the immediate release of all those who had been detained. He also ordered the prompt reopening of all the churches that had been closed by a federal decree issued in August 1926, despite protests by citizens and the CRMDT.[103] In his visits in the villages, Cárdenas sought out the believers who had fought so well against the state during the rebellion, and tried to win them over to agrarianism. This was a very difficult task, since three years of bloody struggle had left the Cristeros hostile to the government. At no point did he raise the possibility of direct action against the Church. Officially, the relationship between the state and the Church was once again governed by Law #62 (8 March 1926), which permitted one priest for every 6,000 inhabitants, although in practice this quota was more flexible. The conciliatory atmosphere prevailing in Michoacán led many inhabitants to ask Cárdenas to cancel even this law, but Cárdenas refused. The moderate Law #62 remained in force as part of the status quo, expressing the right that the revolutionary government assumed to impose supervision on the Church and on religious life in the state.[104]

Tejeda underwent the opposite process. He began his political career in 1920 with a moderate attitude towards the Church, but became more extreme as a result of the Cristero Rebellion, which had given him a great deal of trouble during his stint as interior minister in Calles's government. Tejeda had trouble accepting the "fiction," as he called the *arreglos* ("arrangements") of 1929 which concluded the rebellion. In a caustic letter to President Portes Gil, he wrote,

> [The priests] want to return to the pulpit, to the confessional, to the schools, etc., in order to recommence their monstrous task of deforming the people's conscience and spirit, impeding their liberation and their progress. The people do not need them; they have acquired, with . . . the suspension of religious worship, the higher consciousness of the truth given them by the Revolution, and they basically expect you, as a worthy leader of the Nation . . . not to permit the violation of the Reform Laws and the Constitution now in force.[105]

Once elected governor, Tejeda used both the Veracruz Agrarian League and the government machinery to hinder the activities of the Church. The League urged the citizens of Veracruz not to let priests enter their homes, not to have their children baptized, and not to send their children to the Church-sponsored private schools. Tejeda wrote to parents telling them that they should not lend themselves to the "humiliating and shameful act of . . . prostrating oneself at the feet of those satanic satyrs," exposing family secrets to ears for which they were never intended.[106] Tejeda refused to reopen all the churches as required by the 1929 agreement, and subsequently seized some of those that had been reopened. He handed over still other churches to the schismatic Church that he fostered through the medium of Bishop Joaquín Pérez, "the Bishop of Veracruz and Puebla."[107]

In the meantime, Tejeda promised to promote enabling legislation for Article 130 of the state constitution that would handicap the Catholic Church's activities in Veracruz. Such legislation would eliminate the comfortable conditions established for the Church by the Jara law of 1926. On 16 June 1931 Law #197 was duly passed, changing the relations between Church and state beyond all recognition. From the moment it went into effect on 25 July 1931, only 13 priests were allowed to serve the entire state—one priest for more than 100,000 inhabitants. When the Church refused to comply, Tejeda promptly closed all the churches in Veracruz. A grim battle ensued between, on one side, the Church and its supporters, who were concentrated mainly in the country and in the city of Veracruz, and, on the other side, the state government and its partisans among the agrarianists, the workers, and the anti-clerical intellectuals. In the course of this conflict, an attempt was made on Tejeda's life, bloody clashes took place in a number of municipios between believers and agrarianists and between believers and government and municipal officials, Church property was destroyed, and communicants continued their religious observance in secret by means of a Church "underground" that spread throughout the state.[108]

At the same time, the government began to purge the ranks of government employees, including teachers, and to expell students and pupils, even young children, who protested the anticlerical content of their lessons. Uncooperative private schools were closed. A government intelligence network was set up to uncover clandestine Church connections and to locate the believers and other opponents of the law who were ranged against Tejeda and the state. A local anti-clerical movement was formed, the Unión Revolucionaria Anticlerical. The state instituted mandatory anti-religious courses that all teachers and government officials had to attend, and widespread efforts were made to replace religious worship with secular ceremonies, giving rise, for example, to the celebration of "socialist" marriages, "baptisms," and burials. I

In August 1932, a law was enacted permitting name changes for towns with religious appellations, and subsequently more than 200 towns and villages received new names with revolutionary or secular meanings. A new, anti-clerical literary group founded by the Freemasons under the name "Estridentista" sponsored the distribution of thousands of books, leaflets, and broadsheets denouncing the Church, and vendors of religious articles, collectors for charity (who were always religious), church-bell ringers, and any other conspicuous believers were all ruthlessly hunted down. Believers who used the national colors in church ceremonies were punished for their temerity in trying to appropriate the patriotic symbols of "true" Mexicans.[109]

1 Primo Tapia: Founder and leader of the first agrarian league in Michoacán, December 1922.

2 Simón Cortés Vieyra: A Cristero commander and the first to sign a peace agreement with the local government of Michoacán, January 1929.

3 Demonstration of campesinos in Zamora, in honor of Lázaro Cárdenas, the newly-sworn President of the Republic, 1 December 1934.

4 Front view of the farmhouse (*casco*) façade and chapel of the Hacienda de Guaracha as seen today.

5 Cárdenas in his headquarters as the military commander of the Huasteca Region in Veracruz, May 1925.

6 Cárdenas with Federal Senators and Deputies after being nominated as official candidate of the PNR for the Presidency of 1934–1940 (Xochimilco, México D.F., December. 1933).

7 Evidence of a progressive agricultural activity at the beginning of the twentieth century: The rice mill of the Hacienda de Nueva Italia of the Italian family Cusi.

8 Veracruzan local government palace in Jalapa in the early 1920s.

9 Portrait of the deceased Úrsulo Galván behind the banner of the Veracruzan agrarian league, 1931.

10 Úrsulo Galván accompanied by members of the Veracruzan agrarian league delegation of Córdoba, Veracruz, circa 1930.

11 Manuel Almanza García, one of the founding fathers of the Veracruzan Agrarian League, and since 1930 its leader, salutes a group of campesinos in Salmoral, Veracruz, 1925.

12 Adalberto Tejeda with organized workers of the Fábrica Textil de Cerritos, Orizaba, Veracruz, 1931.

13 Adalberto Tejeda (in center) at a gala dinner during the sixth congress of the Agrarian League of Veracruz, October 1930.

14 Celebration of the sixth congress of the Agrarian League of Veracruz, Jalapa, Veracruz, October 1930.

15 Demonstration of delegates of the Agrarian League of Veracruz, marching in Jalapa, with Tejeda in front, 24 March 1932.

16 The famous Lions Gate of the ancient Hacienda de Almolonga's farm house (*casco*) as seen today.

17 Inner courtyard of Almolonga's farm house as seen today.

18 Almolonga's private chapel.

19 Almolonga's aqueduct.

20 Manuel Parra, his wife and a prominent churchman. A picture that still hangs today in Almolonga's farm house.

21 A large group of farm workers, employed in Almolonga, marching from their hacienda towards Jalapa with Manuel Parra in front, in support of the new elected Governor of Veracruz, Jorge Cerdán, 1 December 1940.

The Church establishment's protests against the arbitrariness of Law #197 were to no avail, and neither were President Ortiz Rubio's pleas for moderation. Tejeda steadily increased his attacks on the Church, and even demanded that the federal government terminate the Church's activities by declaring all priests as agents of a foreign power (the Vatican) and, as such, enemies of Mexico. Under Tejeda's influence, Veracruz established a numbers of bodies designed to combat the Church and religion in general: the Liga Revolucionaria Anticlerical, the Liga Femenil Liberal Revolucionaria Veracruzana, and the Liga Anticlerical de Maestros, as well as numerous organized groups for secondary- and primary-school pupils. On 6 October 1932 the Veracruz Congress took another drastic measure: It debated an initiative to amend Article 37 of the federal constitution, which governed the conditions under which Mexican citizenship could be withdrawn. The proposed amendment would have denied Mexican citizenship to priests on the grounds that they were citizens of a foreign state (the Vatican, since the 1929 Concordat with Mussolini). As foreigners subject to the terms of Article 33 of the constitution, they could be asked to leave the country en masse. The next day a copy of this draft amendment was sent to all the state Congresses, to the federal Congress, and to the PNR. If it had been adopted at the federal level, Mexico would have become a completely secular state. In Tejeda's hands, the campaign against the Church became a campaign against religion in general—there was no room for religion in Tejeda's school of revolutionary consciousness.

However, Tejeda would never have been allowed to go as far as he did if there had not already been a social climate in Mexico that permitted it. The spark that ignited the tinder of the anti-clerical campaign was the preparations for celebrating the 400th anniversary of the appearance of the Virgin of Guadalupe, which Tejeda termed "one of the greatest, and certainly the most productive, of historical lies" and was an event that aroused the anger of most of the federal politicians. It was a superb opportunity to make impassioned speeches against an enemy shared by all and easy to attack, while postponing for the moment more substantive questions concerning the revolutionary social struggle. It was also a stroke of luck for Calles, since the campaign against the Church provided a convenient means of further weakening Ortiz Rubio's already shaky position. For that purpose, he was willing to cooperate temporarily even with the intransigent Tejeda. Since he was Minister of Defense at the time, he ordered the replacement of the military commander of Veracruz, General Miguel Acosta, a man congenial to the Church, by someone more to Tejeda's taste, General Eulogio Ortiz. It was important to him that the anti-religious efforts in Veracruz should proceed successfully. Once it seemed clear that the Church was not inclined to renew the Cristero struggle, Calles told all the governors to amend their religious laws the way Tejeda had. One of the first regions to do so was the Federal District itself, which in December of the same year passed a law setting the priest quota at 34—that is, roughly one priest for every 30,000 inhabitants.[110]

Like all the other governors, Cárdenas, too, was compelled to address the issue. Unlike Tejeda and others, however, Cárdenas did so out of political necessity rather than any genuine zeal. Long-range considerations did not permit him to reject Calles's orders to recast the state's relations with the Church, which in Michoacán, as mentioned earlier, had, since March 1926, been based on a very moderate law containing only four articles. The pressure the CRMDT had been exerting for months also made the issue increasingly critical. The result was Law #100, passed on 12 May 1932. This law, 33 articles long (21 of them dealing with penalties) to all appearances greatly weakened the Church's position in the state, since it imposed a limit of three priests for every 100,000 inhabitants, as well as a series of other restrictions. Nevertheless, in the congressional debate over the draft law on 10 May, Cárdenas had managed to defeat more radical proposals, such as a limit of only one priest for every 100,000 inhabitants—"as in the states of Tabasco and Veracruz, and other revolutionary states," said Deputy Hector Varela—or at most one priest for every 50,000 inhabitants, as suggested by other deputies. To the more extreme deputies, the "high" ratio of only 33,000 inhabitants per priest threatened to make Michoacán one of the more backward states, unable to meet the challenges of the times.[111]

That the Michoacán Church did not regard Cárdenas's law as any real threat was evident from the views expressed by two of the three heads of that Church, the archbishop of Michoacán and papal nuncio, Leopoldo Ruíz y Flores, and his assistant, Bishop Luis María Martínez (whose close ties with Cárdenas made him the Pope's first choice for the position of archbishop of Mexico in 1937). Immediately after the Michoacán Congress passed Law #100, María Martínez wrote to the papal nuncio: "According to what I've been told, they don't make any intolerable conditions—rather, it is more or less like the previous law [Law #62]. . . . My opinion is: Tolerate the law, subject to protest, then let the tolerance go, little by little."[112]

Cunningly, Cárdenas took care not to publish Law #100 in the *Periódico Oficial* of Michoacán, thus preventing it from taking legal effect. However, he did have it published in the state press and the federal Congress so that he would be seen to be doing his revolutionary duty. The Bishop of Tacámbaro, Leopoldo Lara y Torres, dubbed it "a thieves' law," fearing it would be enforced even though it had not been officially published. However, when, disregarding the views of the Michoacán archbishop, he sought to organize mass protests against the law so that he would not be suspected of neglecting his "pastoral duties," he was dismissed from his position and transferred to the post of Bishop of Halicarnassus.

Regardless of Law #100, Cárdenas in fact remained faithful to the law of March 1926, and the 1929 agreement with the Cristeros. He sought social tranquillity and the integration of the Cristeros into the state rather than segregation and conflict. The campaign of incitement espoused by Tejeda, which whipped up all Mexico into an anti-clerical frenzy, ultimately forced Cárdenas to respond with a law of his own, but he never intended it as anything more than a propitiatory gesture. His friend Múgica, realizing this, told him that the new law had no popular action mechanism to ensure its enforcement. Cárdenas's response was brief and evasive: "Religious Law— popular action will be the responsibility of committees organized for the purpose."[113] Clearly the scenes of Veracruz would not be repeated in Michoacán. As one who ruled the CRMDT with a firm hand and had managed to derail every popular action the organization had taken against the Church since June 1929, Cárdenas had no intention of permitting one now. A realist who knew that most of the Cristeros were simple, impoverished peasants, many of them Indians, he realized that he could not form a revolutionary consciousness on the basis of anti-clericalism and certainly not anti-clerical extremism. Becoming governor had forced Cárdenas to confront all the complexity of the religious question and its direct impact on the Michoacán way of life; as a result, the extreme anti-clerical views he had expressed in his election campaign underwent a complete transformation. The need to calm Michoacán in the wake of the Cristero uprising, the strong ties between the Church and its peasant congregants, the spirit of compromise and the return to the status quo that had prevailed in Mexico since the end of the rebellion, and Cárdenas's integrative social and political approach all led him to the conclusion that he must take an unequivocal stand to defend the status quo and the principle of mutual respect.

Fanning the flames over the religious issue was also unwise in terms of Cárdenas's political career. Social ferment of this sort was likely to fortify precisely the veteran revolutionaries and the *Maximato*, which, anxious over its declining public support, was delighted by the anti-clerical campaign. Peace, in contrast, strengthened the agrarianist opposition and allowed it to enlist the Church's support for Cardenism in preparation for the presidential elections in 1934.

Cárdenas's conciliatory policy towards the Church may also have reflected a certain subjective good will born of personal meetings and private conversations with priests. These meetings showed that Cárdenas did not completely reject the Church and did not disapprove of all priests as such. On the contrary, he made a distinction between priests who identified with the peasants and those who supported the *hacendados* and sought to insulate the peasants from agrarianism and the other principles of revolutionary change. It is no accident that Cárdenas is remembered in the Tarascan Indian region of Michoacán, which was a Cristero stronghold, more as a supporter of the Church and its priests than as their persecutor. He is also less remembered for banishing priests than he is for his sincere friendships and cooperation with them for the good of the working public at large. One such priest was Father Arcadio Martínez, a well-known Cristero in the Meseta Tarasca area who was arrested towards the end of the war for celebrating clandestine masses. Taken to trial in Morelia, he happened to meet Cárdenas and their meeting gave rise to an exchange still recounted today in the Tarascan region. Introducing himself, the new governor said to the unfortunate man, "Look, make your confession to God, because they're going to execute you." The priest answered, "I have always confessed to God, but I have something to ask of you: If I am to be executed, please, be the executioner yourself; do not let anyone else do it." At these courageous words, Cárdenas released him and authorized him to open the churches in Cherán, Nauatzen, and Capácuaro in the middle of the Tarasco region, with the assistance of the army unit stationed in Cherán.[114]

Similar recollections I heard from Father Daniel, the parish priest of Nahuatzen in 1992 and once the rector of the sanctuary of Totolán (near Jiquilpan). Despite his relative youth, he was a personal friend of Cárdenas. According to Father Daniel, Cárdenas, who often shared his thoughts and spiritual doubts with him, was clearly a religious man at heart, or at least not anti-religious. His abhorrence was reserved for those priests who used fear of the Devil to bend the ignorant, fearful public to their will and to withhold from it its economic and spiritual salvation. He knew how to appreciate the other sort of priest, however, even though they were his obdurate opponents on the issue of freedom of religion.[115] The complexity of Cárdenas's relations with the Church was also reflected in his friendships with other devout Catholics: the priest Federico González Cárdenas, a cousin of the historian Luis González y González; the brother of his wife, Amalia, who belonged to a very devout Catholic family from Tacámbaro, one of the bastions of the Church; and the mentioned above auxiliary Bishop of Morelia, Luis María Martínez.

While the anti-clerical campaign was not to Cárdenas's taste, it suited Tejeda very well. He was not blind to the possibility of using it to facilitate reconciliation with Calles, as warmer relations with him would ease the weight of criticism against the Tejedist administration's aggressive social policies. According to Carlos Martínez Assad, the battle against the Church was Tejeda's last-ditch effort to save his political power bases, which had been dwindling away as a result of several factors: Ursulo Gálvan's death in 1930, pressure from the federal government, the weakened status of his associates in the Veracruz and federal branches of the PNR, and the LNC's decline on the national level. In Martínez Assad's interpretation, Tejeda was seeking to regain his former freedom of action within Veracruz and his political equilibrium between Veracruz and the federal center, apparently in hopes of ensuring his participation in the presidential elections—perhaps even as the PNR's candidate.[116]

This interpretation finds some corroboration in the timing of Tejeda's attack on the Church, which began not long before the 400th anniversary of "the greatest lie in history," 12th of December. The political center's protests against the increasingly strong religious awakening were still rather muted. The first person to raise the issue could expect media exposure and a place of honor in the revolutionary gallery. Under such circumstances, removing Tejeda from office would be inconceivable, even if he was using that office to promote drastic agrarian, labor, and educational reforms. Moreover, his choice of accusations against the Church was perfect: He emphasized its foreignness, its alienation, its traitorousness, and its subversiveness, interweaving nationalist, patriotic charges with constitutional and moral ones.

This would seem to be a prime example of the use of a political technique to obtain an approval that was in fact limited in scope and pointless in public terms.

These explanations are very logical. Nonetheless, it is difficult not to see Tejeda's pioneering and extremist move as an expression of a deep-seated personal anti-clericalism that had found an extraordinary historical opportunity to reveal itself. The fierce, angry dispute Tejeda waged with the Bishop of Veracruz, Rafael Guizar y Valencia, from June to September suggests this. Tejeda accused the Church, or rather "that vast commercial transaction controlled by the Catholic Church," of many things: It was a foreign capitalist business, cold and alien, that sapped the strength of the poor believers, taking advantage of their ignorance to frighten them and manipulate them emotionally; it was an organization that did not contribute even one peso of its legendary wealth, accumulated year by year at the expense of the poor, to the rehabilitation of those hurt by seasonal floods, earthquakes, and plagues, or to the advancement of burning social issues; it was an institution that plunged the weak deep into the mire of evil, ignorance, and idolatry, pressing them to accept their destinies instead of encouraging them to establish a culture of social and cultural activism and reform; it moved against the agrarianists, attacking the cooperatives and the labor laws and silencing the organized peasants with Catholic agrarianism in order to divide and weaken their forces. The Church, said Tejeda, presented itself as the representative of the godly, transcendental, irrefutable world, and as such somehow entitled to penetrate to the depths of a person's soul and consciousness, enslaving him or her with torturous emotional, spiritual, and economic ties. It employed these measures cynically in order to enrich itself, so that it could build, undisturbed, more and more chapels and churches, and send, with triumphant fanfares, millions of pesos to the Vatican every year.[117]

If Tejeda did not have a personal bias against the Church, it is difficult to account for his total commitment to the attack, the fanaticism with which he pursued every believer—even children[118]—and his pedantic supervision of school textbook revision in order to expunge any religious overtones. Equally incomprehensible is his stubborn refusal to listen to the many agrarianists who despite their desire for reform could not accept the persecution of the Church. Years later, one of those men, Pedro Pérez Cervantez of Mozomboa in Veracruz, recalled (in an uneasy undertone, as though a Tejedist agent might be listening even after all these years) his feeling of being torn between his duty to the League and Tejeda on one hand and the Church on the other. He himself, like many others in his village and the neighboring villages, had decided to practice his religion secretly at night in the home of Ursula Mota, the widow of a local *hacendado*, Don Ramón Domínguez.[119]

It is very doubtful whether political circumstances alone would have led Tejeda to feud so fiercely with towns and villages that refused to change their religious names to secular or revolutionary ones. He denounced the inhabitants of San Juan Evangelista (St. John the Evangelist), for example, as having "limited discernment" merely because they had the temerity to complain—

with reason—that the name Villa Santana Rodríguez proposed to them by the government was not the name of a revolutionary, but rather of a "bandit and murderer, who committed so many crimes within the compass of this Municipio."[120]

If Tejeda had been opposed solely to the religious establishment, he would not have bothered to deploy an intelligence network covering every corner of the state or to encourage citizens to report any religious activity they saw, big or small. Under other circumstances Tejeda would have been more tolerant of violations of the religious law, particularly in the rural areas, and he would not have incited the rural guards against transgressing peasants, causing bloodbaths of the sort seen in Huatusco in June 1931, or Tlapacoyan in October of the same year.[121] Finally, if the campaign had been a purely political matter, he would not have shown such astonishing determination and rage. These reactions came from deep within, from the realm of values, experiences, emotions—not from a sober political mind.

Thus, under the same circumstances Tejeda and Cárdenas acted quite differently: One gave the signal for a mass offensive against the Church, while the other in fact resisted the mainstream tendency. This difference reflected the wide gap between the respective personal philosophies of these two governors and their different degrees of commitment to them. They were of one mind about the Church's reactionary role in society. They were also of one mind about the obstacles the Church raised to the formation of a consciousness of change and a popular revolutionary ethos. Their conclusions, however, were different: Whereas Tejeda embraced direct struggle, Cárdenas wanted to avoid conflict at all cost. Their attitudes were influenced by the different contours of the religious issue in the two states, the different behavior patterns acceptable to each of the two men, their personal assessments of the political and social benefits of anti-clerical measures, and, as in many other spheres, their respective political life expectancies. The result was that Tejeda undertook a very courageous and dangerous initiative, while Cárdenas opted for minor, pragmatic action; Tejeda opted for a sweeping ideological response, while Cárdenas showed cautious political judgment; Tejeda espoused a conception of rapid, militant, and focused radical change, while Cárdenas preferred gradual, integrative change through the established system.

Paradoxically, then, in Michoacán, where the Church was very active and had the power to disrupt seriously the process of implementing agrarian reform and instilling the spirit of the Revolution, only marginal action was ever taken to restrict it; while in Veracruz, where the Church was tolerant of agrarianism and revolutionary change, the struggle against it became a central tenet of Tejedist policy. This contradiction suggests that the Church's relative strength was not the factor that ultimately determined the nature of the resistance to it, but rather a combination of each governor's personal views and his tactical position. Cárdenas was able to differentiate between the two; Tejeda either was not able or did not want to do so.

4

The Salvation of Agrarianism: The Ejido Issue

Introduction

Agrarian reform in Mexico was the perfect test of a politician's views. The whole question of universal access to property was a thorny issue from the end of the 19th century and through the tormented revolutionary years of 1910–1940, and further until the end of the 20th century and the beginning of the 21th century. Actually it was a never ending dispute, a period that saw the development of the major theories of capital's socioeconomic role and legal status. It also saw the development of different ways of turning these theories into reality. The key instrument of reform for our purposes was Article 27 of the 1917 constitution, which declared that ownership of all land and water within the borders of Mexico was vested in the nation, and that the nation alone had the authority to dispose of these resources, as warranted by the public interest. This revolutionary idea created a completely new conceptual basis for rural property ownership, which had been the main source of wealth in Mexico in the first decades of the century.[1] The redistribution of rural property therefore seemed a promising means of achieving the economic and social rehabilitation of the peasants of Mexico. It was this potential that led Article 27 to be the focus of heated ideological debates, poignant and emotionally charged, to legal and political controversy, to complex legal battles and to violent political exploitation that continue to present times.[2]

The implementation of Article 27 was very difficult. While the *agraristas* tried to advance the reform, others sought to block it. The opponents of Article 27 included peasants (many of them deeply committed to the Church, which rejected land confiscation, to their *terratenientes* and generally speaking to traditional property-labor relations), the large landowners, and entrepreneurs from the ultra-conservative chambers of commerce and agriculture, and senior politicians from among the Revolutionary old guard.

These were the forces against which Tejeda and Cárdenas had to contend. Their experiences were in fact the prototype of the struggle between, on one hand, those who wanted either no reform at all (Cristeros, peones, comuneros and smallholders[3]) or a limited one dictated by short-term political needs (the veteran revolutionaries); and, on the other hand, those who saw reform as the whole purpose of the Revolution.

Missed Opportunities for Agrarian Reform

The 1917 constitution offered the possibility of a magnificent agrarian reform. It presented the historic and moral rationale for such a reform and, after clearly defining both the basis and the social role of land ownership, established the state's authority to link the two. It instituted possible routes to reform (private and collective), established the rules for land expropriation and compensation, and laid down guidelines for enabling legislation.[4] Indeed, in December 1920, the notation of land as communal-collective (ejidal) property, given to organized farmers' groups, was regulated by the central government, following the guidlines of Article 27 of the Constitutional. Meanwhile, between the years 1915 to 1923, at least 18 federative States' legislatures, Michoacán and Veracruz among them, accomplished executing *latifundia* division laws, that enabled them to deliver fragmented small to medium sized family units (called also homesteads), to interested farmers, who had to pay for them in a long term payments, while forming colonies (colonias) of privateers. This process followed other constitutional guidelines that granted Federal States exclusivity in the creation of small family properties.[5]

However, very little progress was made in agrarian reform until the beginning of the 1930s. Every administration since Carranza had preferred to steer clear of the *latifundia*, which were the main source of agrarian land. When, 12 years after their enactment, Cárdenas revived Laws #45 (1919) and #110 (1920), which had been instituted in order to break up the *latifundia* and distribute the land to the Michoacán peasants on an individual basis, he remarked: "despite the time that has passed since the publication of these laws, the *latifundia* in Michoacán have not been divided up, nor do the peasants have the land they need for their support and development; they constitute a great number of people and families lacking work and every means of subsistence."[6]

Tejeda made a similar comment in 1931. Farmers who managed to obtain land under the provisions of the Veracruz expropriation laws, the first of which had been passed back in 1918, found themselves "constantly anxious over their rights, which, although acquired legally, could not be enforced when required before any competent authority." He added, "although laws are in force extending a usufructuary right to land when necessary, this precarious possession does not resolve the problem definitively, since the law grants only temporary usufruct, not naked ownership."[7]

An attempt to avoid direct conflict with the landowners by creating private property out of state-owned land did not succeed either. The federal "free land" (*tierra libre*) (1923), colonization (1926), and loan and invest-ment laws designed for this purpose were scarcely implemented. The public lands were unpopular in any case, being remote from the main population centers and of poor quality, and the loans needed to develop them were diffi-cult to obtain; but their main disadvantage was the uncertainty concerning the practical implementation of the laws governing their distribution. A decree dated 10 June 1926 froze the Veracruz free land law, and consequently the related colonization law as well.[8] By the time the law came back into use in July 1930, at the height of the debate over the future of the ejido in Mexico, it was too late. The agrarianists, who in the interim had grown stronger, were now striving to obtain expropriated private land suitable for agriculture rather than the worthless public land.

Legal and political problems also prevented the exploitation of unused land (*tierras ociosas*). Neither the states responsible for legislating the issue nor the municipios responsible for actual implementation made much progress, due to the low motivation, political pressure, violence, the excru-ciatingly slow pace of overly pedantic court proceedings, and so on.[9] For that matter, even the ejidal reform, the only mode of reform in operation though on a small scale was undermined by the uncertain status of the land involved, as Luis Cabrera explained in 1931: "The Revolution has done no more in agrarian matters than to grant ejidal land to the villages. Unfortunately, even the ejidal policy leaves much to be desired, and ejidal ownership continues to be uncertain and sterile."[10]

In the early 1930s the federal government decided to terminate even this reform, proposing a grace period of a few months to wind up current cases, after which, as Calles said in July 1930, there would be "not a word more on the matter."[11]

Saving the Ejido: The Ideological Dimension

Cárdenas and the Ejidal Ethos

Cárdenas never accepted for a minute the revolutionary veterans' view that the ejido was a failure and merited immediate termination. From the begin-ning of his political career his enthusiasm for the ejido was apparent; he believed that the ejido could and should serve as a primary, integral substi-tute for the *latifundio*. In January 1928, in a manifesto addressed to the citizens of Michoacán, he asserted: "I am a supporter of the agrarian policy because it is one of the postulates of the Revolution, and because solving the problem of land is a national necessity and a stimulus for the development of agriculture."

This view was reflected in the CRMDT's agrarian program from January 1929, on. At the time, Cárdenas did not believe that the ejido would ever erase all memory of the *latifundio*; he envisioned the ejido system gradually reducing the *latifundio* to the dimensions of a medium-sized private holding, without actually destroying it completely. Consequently, he saw nothing incongruous about inviting Michoacán landowners to the founding convention of the Federación Agraria y Forestal del Estado de Michoacán (Michoacán Federation of Agrarian and Forest Communities—hereafter Michoacán Agrarian Federation) in January 1930, or about trying to organize them in an "owners' league" to help implement the agrarian reform. Nor did he doubt his own ability to "grant land to all communities as soon as possible, so that the owners can organize credit . . . and cultivate the land they have left."[12]

While the landowners and the political center vilified the ejido, Cárdenas saw it as a source of great creative enthusiasm: "Our ejidal population has shown a keen interest in its schools, and requests for teachers stream in constantly, particularly for night schools. In many cases the ejidatarios themselves have lent effective personal and economic support to the construction of schools."[13] When he was elected president of the PNR in October 1930, he did not conceal his delight at the excellent opportunity his new position afforded him to fight for the ejido as "a soldier of the Revolution." Just before leaving for the capital, he remarked that as president of the party he would have obligations that could be met only through unceasing, energetic activity, with a full awareness of the nation's social problems. His meaning was clear.[14]

On 6 November 1930 Cárdenas was in Michoacán to inaugurate the Instituto de Investigaciones Sociales (Institute of Social Research) of the Michoacán University of San Nicolás de Hidalgo, which had been founded at his own instigation. In a speech to the university staff members invited to the event, he said "the ejido is not a failure; people talk about the failure of the ejido not because it is true, but because the enemies of the Agrarian Law—all of them—have an interest in saying so." Agricultural production had not declined as a result of the reform, he insisted, and, despite what the media reported, the ejidos were not being abandoned. On the contrary, yields had increased, and "the producing *campesino* presently consume[d] what he need[ed] for the proper nourishment of himself and his family, whereas prior to the ejidal distribution he was limited to the amount permitted by his scanty wages or the miserable share allocated to him by the owners of the land." The ejido, he declared, "will be the basis for the country's prosperity."[15]

On 30 November 1930, Cárdenas spoke out against the Calles supporters who persecuted those governors who had not heeded the call to end the reform. Defending the governor of Tamaulipas, Francisco Castellanos, he claimed that the PNR had to show complete solidarity with all the governors, and afford them the conditions they required to "devote all their effort . . . to developing their governmental programs, particularly those aspects concerning the political, social, and economic reconstruction of the states of the Union." Subsequently he added: "I am firmly convinced that the local governments . . . will study their internal problems carefully, contriving to resolve them satisfactorily in order to avoid conflicts."[16]

At the beginning of December he attacked, through the medium of the press, all the enemies of "revolutionary and renovating labor" who made a practice of systematically attacking "governments of advanced ideology." Very categorically, he announced that the party would oust not the reformist governors, but the conservative governors who obeyed the order to halt the reform.[17] Moreover, that same month he announced that from now on the party's support for candidates for various elected positions would depend on their "social action." In a period in which collective interests took precedence over individual ones, he explained, only this criterion could be a basis for political activity. Politics was no longer merely a means to achieve personal advantage and power; now it had to serve the social ideology of the Revolution.[18]

Towards the end of January 1931, Cárdenas spoke out still more strongly in defense of the ejidos, in angry response to Luis Cabrera's animadversions on the Revolution—particularly his criticism of the "three defects of the ejido," which included the conception of the ejido as a goal in itself rather than a means to an end (an homestead), and the fact that the reform appropriated the haciendas' best rather than their inferior lands. Cárdenas linked the debate on the ejido issue to an understanding of the whole Revolution. According to Cárdenas, Cabrera did not understand the significance of the Revolution's development since 1917, and particularly since 1920, the years marking the birth of a proletarian and agrarian social doctrine based on the idea that the land belonged to the peasants of Mexico by right, not charity. The agrarian policy would continue, he asserted, with the adjustments needed to "eliminate the mistakes notable at the outset," though the government would not pause in "the granting and restitution of lands that by right belong to the villages."[19]

In April Cárdenas went a step further and made ejidal reform a condition for achieving democracy in Mexico. Democracy was not a technicality, he explained at the PNR congress on the 28th of the month; it was an expression of values, a kind of mission that obliged all party members serving in the government to ask themselves if they had really worked to fulfill the aspirations of the collective—"aspirations" meaning land.[20]

With considerable adroitness, Cárdenas slowly drafted the ideological and practical blueprint for a different revolutionary approach—one that gave clear priority to the collective and its needs. This approach was designed above all to undermine the political approach to the agrarian issue that had established itself in the political center and in the PNR. Cárdenas wanted to transform agrarianism from a limited socioeconomic issue into the cornerstone of the whole process of change in Mexico, both a symbol of the Revolution and its most concrete manifestation. The abased, temporary, marginal ejido of the original revolutionaries now took center stage, becoming the basis of a national ethos and the main justification of the enormous price exacted by the Revolution in both blood and material damage.

As he developed the ideological context of the issue, Cárdenas embarked on a vigorous campaign to instill it in the consciousness of the entire Mexican population, his aim being to present the ejido as the Revolution's primary achievement, as a fundamental social ideal, and as the main criterion for assessing policies. To this end, he set off on a long series of well-publicized visits to rural villages, accompanied more than once by the president himself. He held innumerable personal meetings with the peasants, established official or quasi-official party organizations to advance the agrarian reform and rural education, and promoted regional development programs based on the ejidal system, including model projects under the aegis of the PNR. He spent a great deal of time organizing the peasants under the auspices of the party, a step that both strengthened the peasants and forced the party to accord the ejido a recognition that went beyond the program outlined in its platform.[21]

Thus, in the course of 1931 the PNR became the ejido's national sponsor. Under Cárdenas's leadership, the party showed great enthusiasm for the task of mediating between the agrarian communities and the reform institutions, encouraging the communities to use its services to forward their land petitions to the competent government bodies. It helped peasants obtain temporary land, credit, and advanced agricultural equipment, and facilitated the organization of ejidal cooperatives. The party organ took up the ejidal cause with gusto, covering its successes extensively and increasingly describing the ejido in terms of social justice and as the only social and economic alternative to large landholdings.[22]

Through all this Cárdenas managed to stand fast against the political center without arousing its enmity. Assisted by a firm ideological grounding and a superb control of political tactics, he was able to challenge the federal government without creating the impression that he was rebelling against it—mainly because he never directly attacked the center, but only "the opponents of the Revolution" and other anonymous "enemies of the ejido." Cárdenas always referred to the criticisms by Calles and his supporters in the anonymous third person—"it is said," "it is claimed," "those who . . . " and so on—never attributing them to any specific person or group. The conflict with Cabrera gave him a wonderful opportunity to present his criticism of the federal administration without identifying it as such.

Similarly, Cárdenas made no attempt to persuade the federal government to change its policies with respect to the ejido or anything else. Nor did he intervene in the events that led to the decision to halt the agrarian reform: the Montes de Oca-Lemont agreement of August 1930, regulating the national debt to the United States, which necessitated stringent economies; and the decision to slash the national expropriation budget. Instead, Cárdenas was careful to defend the institution of the presidency at all times; maintaining his amicable relations with Ortiz Rubio, he even tried to win him over to the ejidal cause, inviting him to tour Michoacán from time to time, where he was feted in the villages with as much honor and gratitude as if he had been the greatest agrarianist in the Republic.

By these means, Cárdenas slowly fostered a general recognition of the ejido as the center of the social entity, as the legitimate source of the Revolution, as the basis for Mexico's economic recovery and development, and as the source of the energy and social power that would lead to national integration. Its success would be the success of the Revolution, the achievement of the opportunity the Revolution had provided to build a truly democratic society in Mexico.

Tejeda and the Ejidal State

Tejeda was completely unmoved by the national debate on the ejido issue. In his view the ejido had always been the central component of revolutionary agrarianism. "Veracruz," he thundered in the valedictory speech of his governorship, "[is] an essentially ejidal state. The land and water grants made to the *pueblos* under the licit mandate of 6 January 1915 agrarian law unquestionably constitutes one of the most transcendent factors in the economic and social transformation of the country, and the firmest postulate of the ideology of the Revolution."[23] In May 1932, he remarked: "The resolution of the agrarian problem in its ejidal phase is one of the issues that has most intensely interested this Government, which is convinced that [the ejido's] complete development will offer well-being and progress not only to the peasant class, which will thereby achieve complete economic liberation, but to all the social classes, through the development of agriculture. . . ."[24]

Tejeda embraced agrarianism for a number of reasons. He believed that both natural and manufactured wealth had always been, and must remain, the wealth of the collective; that throughout history this wealth had been controlled by a handful of people who used it to oppress and impoverish the collective physically and spiritually; and that the Revolution had entrusted the task of rectifying the situation to the state. Tejeda did not negate the principle of individualism in itself. He claimed that the state fully recognized the axiom that it was "elementary social justice for every individual to be master of what he produces." However, he added, the state also thought that "collective effort [was] better than isolated effort."[25]

Thus, to Tejeda the ejido was not a sacred principle, but a practical expedient that must on no account be abandoned at that stage of Mexican social development. This pragmatic approach may have made him much more open than Cárdenas to other possibilities of agrarian distribution. And unlike Cárdenas, who was very cautious in his implementation of agrarian reform—at least while the debate over the ejido was at its height—Tejeda charged ahead regardless of obstacles. Until the end of 1931, when the anti-agrarian policy of the central government began to change, his administration managed to establish more ejidos than any other state government in Mexico. He himself bragged,

> The betterment of the peasant class through the application of the agrarian laws can be felt all over the Republic, but especially in the State of Veracruz, where the agrarian program has reached its peak development

compared with any other entity of the Union; it can safely be asserted that more than a third of the total population of the State enjoys the benefits of ejidal distribution, as a result of resolutions by my administration.[26]

Eschewing the low profile adopted by Cárdenas, Tejeda initiated a series of protests against the federal government's policy. In February 1930, he sponsored a national peasant convention (Convención Nacional Campesina) in Veracruz, which rejected the idea of setting a deadline for the termination of the reform and called on the government not to stop distributing land as long as there were peasants who needed it. The assembly also demanded that the reform be extended to *peones acasillados*, and that in the meantime peons and all other landless peasants be paid a wage—for an eight-hour workday—that would cover their needs (meaning five to eight times what they were already earning, by the standards of the time).[27] On 22 September, the Veracruz Agrarian League sought out Ortiz Rubio— presumably with Tejeda's knowledge and perhaps even with his encouragement—in order to protest pressure by the powerful Morelia chamber of commerce to end the reform. The League urged Ortiz Rubio to consider reversing his decision to end the reform so that he would not appear to be collaborating with the oligarchy against the peasants.[28] At the end of October, at the sixth convention of the Veracruz Agrarian League in Jalapa, Tejeda attacked the Montes de Oca-Lemont agreement before an audience of 1,000. He was also involved in the state Congress's decision to urge the federal government to postpone payment of Mexico's foreign debts and completely cancel the agrarian debt, on the grounds that "it was not worth having sacrificed so many *campesino* lives to carry out a land-buying revolution" (a reference to the government's efforts to reimburse landowners for the land taken from them). Similarly, the convention decided, in complete defiance of the federal government, to continue the ejidal grants [*dotaciones*], and implicitly threatened the federal government that if frustrated the peasants might seize land by force."[29]

In general, the convention became a platform for criticism against the federal government. Serious accusations were made concerning the use of the federal army against the peasants "as in Díaz's time." There were bitter recriminations about the division of the Revolutionary family into two camps: the "*claudicantes*," who had abandoned their principles and embraced capitalism and imperialism, and the revolutionaries, who continued to defend the interests of the workers and peasants. Similarly, very lightly veiled threats were heard as to the likelihood of civil war if the government did not reverse its decisions on agrarian policy.[30]

At the beginning of December, a delegation of three League leaders who were also members of the Veracruz Congress—Antonio M. Carlón, Gonzalo N. Cruz, and Juan Jacobo Torres—arrived in Mexico City to ask the president and the federal Congress to postpone the debate on Ortiz Rubio's new agrarian law, scheduled to take effect in January 1931, because the Veracruz Congress considered it "necessary to hear first the opinion of the peasants who [would be] affected by the proposed reforms." The minister of agriculture, Manuel Pérez Treviño, whose position made him the recipient of the Veracruz delegation's complaints, rejected them categorically on the grounds that the government "should not become the protector of a single class or faction, but must be the guardian of the interests of the entire Nation . . . "[31] Subsequently softening his tone somewhat, he sought to allay the delegation's concerns about the restrictive sections of Ortiz Rubio's law, particularly those designed to reduce the number of people eligible for land grants.

Tejeda continued to hound the federal government in connection with other stifling restrictions on the reform. He sought to extend the ejidal exemption from *amparo* proceedings (an achievement of the agrarianists in the federal Congress) to all kinds of agrarian reform. He also sought the cancellation of the federal law on administrative responsibility, which imposed criminal liability on officials who disobeyed federal orders to terminate the reform. In addition, he wanted to change a few provisions of the new labor law of August 1931, which in his view were detrimental to the interests of rural workers.[32] Tejeda was in no sense the high-minded gentleman that Cárdenas was. The federal center was the enemy, and as such a fair target for attack.

Cárdenas and Tejeda both succeeded in their missions, each in his own way. Towards mid-1931 the ejido regained—or even strengthened—its former ideological and logistical ascendancy in the PNR. This success facilitated the cancellation of the *amparo* remedy in December of that year,[33] and attracted back to the agrarianist movement both the sober-minded conservative Pérez Treviño, who had succeeded Cárdenas as president of the party on 29 August 1931, and the minister of industry, Luis León, one of the leaders of the campaign against the ejido. Thus it was that during a visit to the state of Mexico these two men were able to tell the peasants there that the battle for the ejido had been won. Michoacán now became a "promised land," and Tejeda's local government and agrarian work was defined as nothing less than "the example of the state of Veracruz." The minister of war, Joaquín Amaro, who had been vacillating, suddenly declared that the army stood with the agrarianist forces, and proclaimed its social-revolutionary role.[34] At the same time, the Chamber of Deputies, which was growing increasingly pro-agrarianist, rejected a proposal by the Sindicato Nacional de Agricultores (National Union of Farmers) to privatize the ejido, on the grounds that the ejido was prospering. The Chamber also completely ignored an extremely pessimistic description of the agricultural situation presented by the Cámara Nacional de Comercio, Agricultura e Industria (National Chamber of Commerce, Agriculture, and Industry).

The renewal of the struggle against the Church undoubtedly was a factor in the federal government's change of heart. As a result of Tejeda's efforts, agrarianism came to be seen as a social and spiritual alternative to the populism of the Church. The administration could present no more solid competition to religious humanism than agrarianism. Luis León actually said, in December 1931, that "if Christ returned, he would be an agrarianist." In other words, the salvation of humankind would be first and foremost an agrarianist salvation.[35]

The intensity of the agrarianist battle was a function of not only the political needs of Tejeda, Cárdenas, and other governors—such as Vargas Lugo in Hidalgo and Castellanos in Tamaulipas—but also the great pressure exerted by the agrarianists themselves. Their organization was based primarily on pragmatic needs reinforced by clear ideological principles. Under these circumstances, eliminating the reform was unthinkable. Hence, the different modes of response displayed by Cárdenas and Tejeda were attributable not only to the differences in their personalities, their different attitudes to change (integrative change as opposed to conflict-based change), and the different timeframes in which they operated, but also the different margins of operational freedom enjoyed by their respective agrarianist organizations. Tejeda's response undoubtedly reflected the greater latitude enjoyed by the Agrarian League in his state—a league able to dictate actions that Tejeda himself might have chosen to carry out more circumspectly. Examples include the local Congress's decision to send a delegation to Mexico City at the height of the agrarian debate, and the threats and diatribes against the federal center at the sixth Agrarian League convention. Cárdenas could not have conceived of such scenes; Michoacán agrarianists, organized under his direct authority, could not escape his control in order to mount noisy, impetuous protests that verged on open rebellion.

Another way of battling federal negativism was to carry on with the reform as though no one had ever suggested terminating it. Both governors adopted this ploy, though to differing degrees. Tejeda worked at full steam to achieve maximal reform through all available channels, on a catch-as-catch-can basis, and endeavored to provide temporary land during the extended waiting periods required by the agrarian distribution process; Cárdenas, in contrast, sought optimal reform, limited primarily to ejidal distribution, and offered fewer temporary solutions. Both, however, faced a particularly difficult task in educating the peasants themselves about the ejido and agrarianism in general, in strengthening them against the tough opposition put up by the big landowners, and in preparing the implementational frameworks of the reform to cope with the anticipated increase in agrarianist activity.

Saving the Ejido: Organization and Consciousness-Raising

Reinforcing the Administrative Framework

At the height of the public debate over the future of the ejido, both Cárdenas and Tejeda set about making necessary adaptations in the system to expedite agrarian reform in their states. An efficient administrative apparatus would shorten the time the petitioners had to wait between submitting their ejidal petitions and actually moving on to the land, a crucial factor in the survival of the ejidal communities, since they faced heavy pressure from the moment they filed their applications. Both governors saw clearly that at the current rate of ejido establishment, it would take generations to complete their mission: 230 years in the case of Michoacán, which had the capacity for 2,026 ejidos but, up until 1928, was establishing only eight new settlements a year; and 270 years in the case of Veracruz, which had the capacity for some 3,300 ejidos but was authorizing only 12 new settlements a year.[36] The skimpiness of the CLA technical staffs responsible for processing ejido petitions—18 people in Veracruz and three in Michoacán—made long waiting periods and sluggish implementation inevitable.

As a first step in remedying this problem, Cárdenas added three new employees to the payroll —an engineer and two surveyors—in the 1929 budget, the first budget of his governorship.[37] In September 1930, in his annual speech, he said that the 27 new settlements that had been founded that year (compared with 11 the previous year) were an inadequate achievement attributable to lack of trained manpower. By November, he said, staff would be doubled. He also urged the federal government to send engineers of its own as reinforcements for the Michoacán team, to expedite the ejidal review process as had been done in the states of San Luis Potosí and Morelos, as well as in the federal district.[38]

The president of the federal Congress, Enrique M. Ramos, responded by saying he welcomed the promise to increase the technical staff of the CLA (Comisión Local Agraria) in order to resolve the agrarian problem more quickly. However, he added that the federal government would lend its assistance "not because of a misplaced radicalism, but out of our deep conviction that ejidal distribution is one of the most just demands of the Mexican Revolution," and that it was one of the main tools for solving Michoacán's difficult economic situation.[39] Both the request for federal assistance and Ramos's response suggest that at the end of 1930, two years after Cárdenas took office, Michoacán was not yet ready, practically or politically, to implement a significant agrarian reform. The central government considered agrarianism as a narrow political issue best left alone, to avoid giving rise to "the wrong impression," as Ortiz Rubio's minister of agriculture, Francisco Elías, explained in December 1931. Elías warned the state governors against agrarianist radicalism, and called for the creation of an "organized agrarianism" (that is, slow and carefully supervised) adapted to the pace and requirements established by the federal center.[40]

As president of the PNR, Cárdenas responded to these pressures by saying, "Enemies of the Revolution have been asserting that the national agrarian agitation is thoughtless and inspired by alien communist ideas. I can tell you that only the thoughtlessness of agrarianism's detractors can explain the adjective that the enemies of the ejido apply to agrarian reform."[41]

As usual, however, he stopped short of outright defiance. The 1930 federal budget reduced the CLA's technical staff to five people; the promise to double it was not kept either that year or the next. In fact, the 1931 budget left the CLA in even worse straits, since although it left the meager 1930 workforce intact, it reduced the organization's operating budget. In July 1931, however, the situation took a turn for the better: The CLA budget was increased and the agrarian technical staff was reinforced by an additional seven people, bringing it to a total of 12.[42] Meanwhile, a branch of the CLA was set up in Zamora, in the western part of the state with a staff of seven (four of them trained personnel). A staff of 18, eight of them technically trained, remained to work in Morelia. Thus, from the administrative standpoint at least, the implementation of the agrarian reform only began to accelerate midway through 1931. At that point, the establishment of new ejidal communities jumped dramatically: 60 ejidos were founded in 1931, and 65 in 1932. The administrative push became possible from the moment that Cárdenas felt politically free to make it, and it exactly paralleled the weakening of federal efforts to eliminate the ejido and the first signs that the agrarianists had won the battle.

In Tejeda's Veracruz there was none of the Michoacán dilly-dallying, nor any gap between rhetoric and action. The fervor for ejido creation was great, generated mostly by the Veracruz Agrarian League with the blessing of the state government. Tejeda was not content with adding a few engineers to his CLA staff; he augmented the CLA's power and budget from one year to the next by increasingly larger amounts. The 1929 budget made provision for 18 technical workers, 15 of them topographers, and 13 clerical employees, for a total of 31 people. Their budget came to more than 80,000 pesos, three times the budget of the corresponding body in Michoacán. The 1930 budget increased the technical staff to 24 people, including 20 topographers, for a total staff of 38 and a budget of 105,000 pesos, five times the Michoacán CLA's budget for the same year. In the 1931 budget the technical staff had grown to 34 people (30 of them topographers), bringing the total staff to 50—a number that rose in the 1932 budget to 66, 45 of those technical personnel. The budget rose accordingly, to 167,000 pesos, more than three times that of Michoacán for the same year (47,000 pesos).[43]

Unlike the Michoacán Congress, which was infected by the Cárdenas administration's hesitation, the Veracruz Congress played a key role in the rapid growth of the CLA. In a debate on the 1929 budget, the government suggested a total of 12 technical personnel. Deputy Carolino Anaya, an Agrarian League member, proposed the addition of three first-class topographers, a proposal the Congress approved. Explaining his initiative, Deputy Anaya said that the CLA had a backlog of 240 cases, and the staff proposed by the government was too small to cope with them. Deputy Fernández de Lara gave the issue moral overtones when he said, "All the deputies are convinced that the rural sector is in the most wretched conditions. . . .The lack of engineers has meant that in various cases the *campesinos* have not obtained provisional possession, and naturally, as representatives of those workers, we have the duty to defend their rights in the Chamber. . . ." He added that he thought Tejeda himself would support the proposal, since he had always been known as a defender of rural workers.[44]

The climax of Tejeda's efforts in this field was undoubtedly the debate over the 1932 budget. During this debate all the agrarianist deputies took a united stand against the government's intention to reduce the CLA's technical staff to 25 people, apparently as a result of the economic crisis, which necessitated a 20% budget cut. The agrarianists demanded the addition of ten engineers and five assistants to the workforce proposed by the government— a demand that was accepted at the end of the debate.[45] During the same debate, Deputy Isaac Fernández proposed the establishment of a new "body of organizing agents and agrarian and cooperative propagandists," which, although part of the CLA staff, would be responsible for meeting the Agrarian League's propaganda and organization needs in the field. Such an initiative was important, he said, because "it would be unjust for a Government claiming to be proletarian to leave the campesinos to seek their economic betterment completely on their own initiative while benefiting the country with their efforts to increase ejidal production"; the limitations of the budget made it difficult to finance emissaries to carry the good news of revolutionary agrarianism to the farthest corners of the state. If the current regime was ever to be replaced by one based on true social justice and recognition of the class struggle, he added, they would have to transmit the victories of the Revolution to those far corners by recruiting workers into the ranks of the CLA. With the close assistance of the Veracruz Agrarian League, these recruits would organize production and consumers' cooperatives and obtain financing for new agricultural techniques, modern machinery, and new roads to improve access to markets.[46] Unsurprisingly, Fernández's proposal was accepted. The 10 agents he had suggested were integrated as a new body into the department of agriculture and livestock (Departamento de Agricultura y Ganadería), with exactly the budget Fernández had proposed—10,800 pesos.

The Battle over Ejidal Petitions

The next challenge was to help peasants overcome their psychological inhibitions against participating in the agrarian reform and to put a stop to the landowners' hostile reactions to that participation. The formation of the ejidal group, the drafting of the constitutive document (*acta constitutiva*) and the petition for land (*solicitud ejidal*), and the dispatch of the petition to the state governor were all critical moments. By joining together, the would-be *ejidatarios* showed they had conquered their strong fear of alienating themselves from the long-standing traditions and customs that characterized village life and its productive relations. That first meeting also proved they had managed to overcome their worry about the pressures to which they would be subjected for the next two to five years (at best) by their village non-agrarianists fellows, who wanted to maintain the status quo, and by the Church and the large landowners, who employed a variety of means to

prevent the filing of ejidal petitions. Those means included bribery, entice-
ment, social ostracism and religious excommunication, extortionate terms
for sharecropping and land-leasing, dismissals, crop-burning, property
damage, and the murder of activists and leaders.[47] The founding meeting was
in fact a moment of symbolic significance, since it changed the peasants into
agrarianists henceforth identified with the state, both in their own eyes and
those of others.

The organization of the ejidal communities and the submission of land
petitions were formally the responsibility of the municipios, the CLA, and
the Procurador de Pueblos (the CNA official in charge of the ejidal settlements). This chain of responsibility had to be well coordinated in order to
bring the peasants to the point of requesting land. The municipios were not
only the main source of the data the law required for the petition review
process, but also were called upon, through their representatives, to approve
both the *actas* (constitutive documents) and the elected leadership bodies
(*comités ejecutivos*) of the new ejidal groups; to protect the agrarianists
during the delicate initial stages of the application process; and to help them
find sources of income until they received their land. Once the ejido was actually established, the municipio's task was to integrate it into the local
economy. The campaigns that both Cárdenas and Tejeda conducted, each in
his own way, to ensure that the municipios were favorable to the state
government facilitated this integration. The inhabitants of the rancho La
Estancia de la Trinidad, for example, in the municipio of Puruándiro in
Michoacán, emphasized in their ejidal petition that they were applying for
land on the advice of the municipal president of Puruándiro.[48] In another
ejidal petition, the inhabitants of Agostitlán thanked the president of the
Hidalgo municipio, who had helped them organize for the purpose of
drafting their "humble" (*humilde*) ejidal petition.[49] Needless to say, the
municipios, like everyone else involved in the reform, had to contend with
pressure intended to prevent them from cooperating with the state government in agrarian reform. In more than a few cases municipio officers lost
their lives as a result, a famous example being the murder of the municipio
president of Vista Hermosa in northwestern Michoacán at the end of July
1931, who was killed by local landowners.[50]

The key to efficient collection and review of ejido petitions was to ensure
that CLA staff and CNA emissaries were both sympathetic to the reform and
impervious to bribes and threats.[51] In this respect, in April 1929, Tejeda
asked federal deputy Pedro Palazuelos to take steps at the ministry of agriculture to prevent a certain CNA employee, Rubén Morales, from processing
the Veracruz files, because he discriminated against the peasants.[52] At the
beginning of 1930, Tejeda managed to engineer the appointment of the
agronomist Salvador de Gortari, a sworn agrarianist and head of the CLA,
as head of the CNA delegation in Veracruz.[53]

In a letter to Pérez Treviño, the agriculture minister, on 22 March 1931,
Cárdenas asked, on behalf of the Revolutionary government and the peasant
classes, that all the Michoacán ejidal files be processed by a certain engineer

by the name of Figueroa instead of the engineer who had dealt with them to date, because the latter did not employ "revolutionary" criteria. Cárdenas also asked that a number of people in the CNA delegation in Michoacán be replaced, because, he claimed, they had promised the owners of expropriated lands to reduce the number of eligible beneficiaries before the final confirmation of the ejido, thereby reducing the amount of land that could be expropriated.[54] As a result of his request, the entire CNA delegation in Michoacán was replaced. The new delegation was headed by Carlos Peralta, a fervent agrarianist and competent engineer, who worked dauntlessly and energetically to advance agrarian reform in the state.[55]

On top of these efforts, in July 1932, Tejeda introduced a law of administrative responsibility regulating the obligations of the government employees of Veracruz. Although the law did not mention agrarian reform specifically, it was undoubtedly designed to facilitate that reform, since it was enacted at almost the same time as Ortiz Rubio's law of administrative liability governing federal officials, which was intended to block the agrarian reform. Tejeda's law, then, was meant to counteract the federal law, which was a last-minute measure passed just before Ortiz Rubio was removed from office.[56]

Cárdenas did not sponsor any law of administrative responsibility, but he did occasionally remind administrative officials and municipio presidents of their duties with respect to agrarian reform. In May 1932, for example, he sent a circular around to these officials, threatening them with dismissal and other penalties if they did not scrupulously comply with the law on unused land in the state.[57]

The CNA-appointed Procurador de Pueblos was the third level in the chain of responsibility. His task was to encourage the villages to file ejidal petitions, help them draft the petitions in the standard form required by the regulations, defend the villagers from attacks by local landowners, build their confidence, and both speak for them and respond to their complaints.[58] The Procurador's importance was very concretely reflected in the agrarian petitions themselves, most of which paid glowing tribute to his central role in their preparation.

Yet even all these assists were not enough to integrate all communities into the agrarianist movement. Despite everything, implementing the reform was a very slow process, as the Michoacán Procurador de Pueblos acknowledged in a letter to the president of the Zamora city council on 20 Feb. 1931:

> Since to date there are many population centers in this State that out of ignorance have not asked for ejidal land . . . I ask that you be so good as to find out and let me know as soon as possible the names of those communities that . . . have not claimed the benefits of the law in force . . . so that their respective petitions for land can be made and they can be morally and economically emancipated from the tutelage of the *hacendados*, who in most cases exploit them wickedly.[59]

Tejeda also referred to this problem in his valedictory speech: "Considering that not even half of the cases filed with the Local Agrarian Commission have been resolved . . . and that many population centers entitled to ejido lands have not yet filed petitions, it is clear that the organization of agricultural production in Veracruz will have to undergo a radical transformation once these petitions have been settled . . . "[60]

Thus, joining the agrarianist movement was clearly not axiomatic; despite all the pro-agrarianism activity both within and outside the establishment and the educational work, spreading the agrarianist creed was slow work. This was the reason for the energetic efforts in both Veracruz and Michoacán to create their Agrarian Leagues as additional, unofficial and ideologically oriented mechanisms of reform. Only bodies displaying such strong faith in the cause as these did were capable of mobilizing the forces needed to reach the most isolated communities and to persuade them of the justice and benefits of agrarianism, as well as to help them organize so they could receive those benefits. Only bodies such as these had the power to organize agricultural workers, *peones acasillados*, tenant farmers, and sharecroppers into unions, to instill in them a sense of confidence and personal liberty, and to spur them, ultimately, to apply for land. Attempts to organize the peasants on an administrative rather than an ideological basis, such as were made by the Procuradores de Pueblo, were apparently inadequate at that historical juncture.

Soon after its foundation, the CRMDT, too, became a notable influence in the promotion of agrarianism. Many ejidal petitions, the peasants' main medium of expression in this respect, stated specifically that the peasants subscribing to them had been led into the agrarianist fold by the CRMDT itself or one of its associated organizations. In an ejidal petition addressed to Cárdenas, the inhabitants of the Zicuirán hacienda in the La Huacana municipio proudly identified themselves as being affiliated with the CRMDT.[61] Similarly, the residents of the El Calvario neighborhood of Queréndaro wrote in their ejidal petition on 6 July 1931, "we recognize the Michoacán Agrarian and Forest Federation [affiliated with the CRMDT] as the parent of our Organization . . . and we designate its offices as our official mailing address."[62] On another occasion, the inhabitants of the El Zinciro hacienda explained to Cárdenas in their ejidal petition (15 October 1930) that they recognized only two people as their representatives: the Procurador de Pueblos and José Solórzano, the current secretary-general of the CRMDT.[63] Certain formulas used by dozens of communities in drafting their ejidal petitions also stressed their connection with the CRMDT. Although the standard closing motto for such letters was "*sufragio efectivo, no reelección*" ("effective suffrage, no reelection"), many petitioners substituted the CRMDT's slogan: "*Unión, tierra y trabajo*" ("Union, land, and work").[64]

Even the number of ejidal petitions and their distribution over time are indicative of the CRMDT's role in this field (see Table 4.1). The jump in petitions from 1930 on reflects the efforts of the CRMDT and the agrarian

Table 4.1 Ejidal Petitions in Michoacán during Cárdenas's Governorship, 1928–1932

Year (Sept. to Sept.)	Number of petitions
1928–1929	36
1929–1930	136
1930–1931	109
1931–1932	144
Total	425

Source: Agrarian files (*expedientes agrarios*) of the State of Michoacán for the years 1929–1932, ASRA, Delegación Michoacana, Morelia, Michoacán.

league (the Federación Agraria y Forestal) it founded in January 1930. Similarly, examination of the hundreds of files in the Zamora archives classified under *Fomento* ("development") shows that of the 50 files directly concerned with agrarian issues for the period 1929–1932, only three were from 1929, as opposed to 19 from 1930—and in all those 19 the involvement of the CRMDT and its Federación Agraria y Forestal was clear. This fact is better evidence than anything of the robust beginning these organizations made in early 1930.

Cárdenas did not leave the job of consciousness-raising among the peasants completely up to the CRMDT. He himself visited dozens of villages where he encouraged the villagers to exercise their agrarian rights. These visits were an important means of discovering the enormous pressures brought to bear on the peasants to keep them from applying for land, including propaganda designed to make them believe that agrarianism was bad for farmers. It was these visits that gave rise to Cárdenas's image as a man who spoke directly to the peasants, a man who hunkered down and broke bread with them while listening to their problems, and then persuaded them that the agrarian reform was their best hope.[65]

During these visits, justice had to be demonstrated, not merely invoked. On one occasion Cárdenas was visiting the area of his birth in western Michoacán, in his capacity as president of the PNR and accompanied by President Ortiz Rubio. During his visit (26 February 1931), several members of the ejidal committee of the Las Zarquillas rancho, which was under the jurisdiction of the formidable Guaracha hacienda, complained to him of an attack the day before by two hacienda administrators and 15 armed members of the *guardias blancas*, in retaliation for the ejidal petition the community had filed on the 23rd of that month. The men from Guaracha gave the Las Zarquillas community six hours to vacate the place, after which they destroyed the agrarianists' houses, loaded the possessions of those who had refused to leave on carts, and dumped them beyond the borders of the hacienda.

Upon hearing this story, Cárdenas immediately appointed himself as mediator in the conflict, with the consent of Gabino Vázquez, the provisional governor, who had also accompanied him on the visit. Cárdenas carried out a day-long investigation which revealed the truth of the complaints and the terroristic tactics of the hacienda. On 27 February he set down a number of decisions in writing. First, he called on the state to expedite its review of the community's request for ejidal land, because the petitioners had already lost their jobs on the hacienda. Second, he recommended that the two administrators be dismissed immediately, that the *guardias blancas* be disarmed, and that a federal army unit be stationed in the area to protect the residents. He also demanded that the public prosecutor conduct a comprehensive investigation and bring charges against those responsible for the events. Similarly, he suggested that proceedings be undertaken for the indemnification of the residents and that severe warnings be sent to the management of the hacienda and the non-unionized peasants who worked there to leave the organized workers alone. Finally, seizing the opportunity to publicize his rigorous enforcement of justice in the village, he decided to show all his findings and his decisions to the president of the Republic and the minister of war. Cárdenas's involvement was very beneficial to this particular ejido, which, rather unusually, received its land relatively quickly, on 21 September of that year, exactly seven months after filing the ejidal petition.[66]

On this occasion, Cárdenas purposely exploited an occurrence indirectly connected with a hacienda against which he already had a grudge. In October 1929, he had begun direct action to undermine the status of this hacienda by raising it to the category of *tenencia*, his first act as governor in the field of local administration. By upgrading the hacienda he sought to liberate the peasants who lived in the hacienda *casco* (compound) from their status as *peones acasillados* and to incorporate them into the agrarianist movement. In the course of 1930 these peasants did in fact organize, finally submitting a petition for land on 1 July 1931. Even the murder of the head of the first *comité ejecutivo*, Pablo Canela, did not stop the ejidal application process, which culminated in the issue of a presidential decree authorizing the ejido's establishment on 29 October 1935.[67]

In any case, Cárdenas's showy action in Las Zarquillas was widely publicized, earning him warm congratulations from Tejeda, Manuel Almanza (then president of the Veracruz Agrarian League), Isauro Acosta (a League member and federal deputy for Veracruz), and various rural communities. They all expressed their satisfaction over the support agrarianism was receiving from the local government, the PNR, and the federal Congress.[68]

Undoubtedly Cárdenas managed to allay to some extent public suspicion concerning the agrarian reform in his state, and to instill in most of the municipios (88 out of 99)[69] a certain measure of faith in the reform and in him. This was reflected in many of the ejidal petitions sent to him. The residents of the Indian community of San Miguel in the Tacámbaro district, for example, stated in the preamble of their petition: "the aims and principles that served as the standard of the revolution that demanded human rights have been completely realized in your Government's program."[70] Similarly, the residents of Manzana de Guadalupe wrote in their petition:

> All the undersigned, citizen Governor, have viewed with real satisfaction your lofty democratic sentiments, your lofty aspirations for the revival of our village, which suffers under the yoke of misery and illiteracy. You know those sufferings well, since you have lived partly with us. That is why we do not doubt for a moment that you will lend your valuable support to our just petition, and we and our children will inscribe with affection and respect the name of our worthy Governor Lázaro Cárdenas.[71]

Even more significant than the flattering, even obsequious, content of these petitions, however, and a strong indication of the new spirit Cárdenas had infused into the Michoacán village, were the slogans that concluded many of the ejidal petitions: "*Tierra, trabajo y patria!*" ("Land, work, and country!"), "*Tierra, justicia y educación!*" ("Land, justice, and education!"), "*Tierra, justicia y libertad!*" ("Land, justice and liberty!"), and "*Tierra, trabajo y justicia!*" ("Land, work, and justice!").

Veracruz was in even greater upheaval, though this was not reflected in ejidal petitions as in Michoacán, since the editors of the *Gaceta Oficial* put all the petitions into a succinct, official formula. Nor did Tejeda travel much in Veracruz or report his impressions; he left the task of mobilizing the peasants to the emissaries of the Veracruz Agrarian League, who were dispersed all over the state and operated under the protection of the *guerrilla*. Their informative reports about their own activities and the parliamentary initiatives introduced by the League in order to obtain financing for additional emissaries indicate the great momentum of agrarianist mobilization in the state. The constant calls by Tejeda's secret service agents for more League emissaries in the villages to organize the peasants and counter the Church's propaganda war against the state administration reflected their faith in the benefits of the agrarian reform process, as well as a recognition of the importance of changing the social and spiritual mores of the village.[72] This agrarianist boom has been confirmed in interviews with ejido elders in Veracruz, who, although unsure when and whether they had ever seen Tejeda, remembered well the League agents and the *guerrilla* recruits who had encouraged them to apply for land and had protected them after they had done so.[73]

In May 1931, Tejeda reported that throughout the state no fewer than 1,443 petitioners' committees (*comités particulares ejecutivos*) and administrative committees of existing ejidos (*comités particulares administrativos*) were in operation. All together they represented some 100,000 peasants, most of whom belonged to the Agrarian League. Thus, 1,443 ejidal requests had been filed in the state of Veracruz since the beginning of the reform.[74]

In Veracruz just as in Michoacán, the volume of ejidal petitions grew in tandem with the burgeoning strength of the League. Table 4.2 shows that in Veracruz the boom in agrarian reform began as soon as Tejeda took office.

Table 4.2 Ejidal Petitions in Veracruz during Tejeda's Governorship, 1929–1932

Year (Jan. to Dec.)	Number of petitions
1929	224
1930	246
1931	365
1932	326
Total	1,133

Source: Agrarian files (*expedientes agrarios*) of the State of Veracruz for the years 1929–1932, ASRA, Delegación Veracruzana, Jalapa, Veracruz.

The number of ejidal petitions filed in his first year was more than three-fourths of the total (281) petitions filed during the entire four-year term (1925–1928) of his predecessor, Heriberto Jara. The big jump in petitions in 1931 paralleled both the maturation of Tejeda's philosophy and the establishment of the Agrarian League as a major center of power in the state. The drastic decline in the number of ejidal petitions in 1933—the year the federal government broke the League completely—corroborates this conclusion.[75]

The Veracruz League's key importance in the state agrarian reform is also clear from the geographical distribution of communities submitting ejidal petitions, some 94% of which are represented in Table 4.3. This table shows that the League managed to elicit about half of the petitions from the periphery (where 51% of the total state population lived). Of these petitions, 18.6% came from the far north and the far south, a clear indication of the League agents' efficient geographical coverage. The Tejedist administration, with the help of the League, managed to obtain petitions from 94.3% of the municipios (compared to roughly 90% in Michoacán). Moreover, although petitions from the central region increased by only 6% between the first half of Tejeda's administration and the second, the increase over the same period for the entire periphery was 118.5%! These circumstances help explain Isaac Fernández's call for a budget increase to finance the League's activities on the periphery—and the government's willingness to comply, despite its difficult financial situation. They also bear out Tejeda's assessment that the League could be credited with having roused the peasants from a "centuries-long lethargy."[76]

Analysis of the average monthly totals of ejidal petitions shows a surprising disparity between Veracruz and Michoacán. While the number of petitions in Veracruz rose more or less steadily from one month to the next, in Michoacán totals tended to rise and fall. In the 16-month period from March 1930, to June 1931, when the CRMDT was already fairly well-established and the Federación Agraria y Forestal was very active, Cárdenas's government received an average of seven petitions a month. In the preceding

Table 4.3 Sources of Ejidal Petitions in Veracruz by Region and Year during the Tejeda Administration, 1929–1932

Region	Municipios submitting petitions	1929	1930	1931	1932	% of the total
Far north	19	5	30	41	37	10.7
Southern north	24	43	23	65	47	16.7
Northern center	44	57	81	62	90	27.2
Southern center	54	57	73	81	51	24.4
Northern south	17	21	27	40	52	13.1
Far south	24	9	3	32	40	7.9
Total	182	192	237	322	317	100.0

Source: Agrarian files of the State of Veracruz for the years 1929–1932, ASRA, Delegación Veracruzana, Jalapa, Veracruz.

year and a half, from the end of the Escobar and Cristero rebellions in September 1929, up to February 1930, the average was 16–17 petitions a month, while in the months from July 1931, until the end of Cárdenas's governorship, the average was 13 per month. The difference between the first half of his term and the second was very pronounced, with a sharp decline in the number of ejidal petitions beginning with the month of March 1930 (see Table 4.4, overleaf). This slow-down continued through the third year of his term, the number of petitions remaining small in comparison with the totals for his second and fourth years. Only in September-October 1931 did the pace of applications increase to the averages for October 1930—January 1931; though it never regained the levels recorded at the end of 1929 and the beginning of 1930. This slowdown did not occur by chance; Cárdenas encouraged it in order to accommodate the wishes of Ortiz Rubio, who became president of Mexico in February 1930. This was also the period during which Cárdenas served as president of the PNR and interior minister in Ortiz Rubio's government—political roles that compelled him to maintain a relatively low profile as an agrarianist. Consequently, although he continued to preach the agrarianist creed, he preferred to keep his activism on a back burner.

This hypothesis is corroborated by the fact that the decline in ejidal petitions in Michoacán coincided with, variously, the height of the public debate on the agrarian reform, the apex of Ortiz Rubio's power, and Cárdenas's political offices in the center of the country. A similar correspondence can be seen between the renewed acceleration in the submission of ejidal petitions from September 1931 (when 28 petitions were filed) and Cárdenas's return to Michoacán, Ortiz Rubio's declining power (from mid-1931), and the end of the agrarian debate.[77]

However, the heady excitement of the end of 1929 and the beginning of 1930, when Portes Gil was president, was never repeated. Even after Ortiz

Table 4.4 Number of Ejidal Petitions per Month during Cárdenas's Second Year as Governor (15 Sept. 1929–15 Sept. 1930)

Month	Number of ejidal petitions
16–30 September, 1929	9
October, 1929	22
November, 1929	23
December, 1929	17
January, 1930	17
February, 1930	10
March, 1930	8
April, 1930	9
May, 1930	6
June, 1930	4
July, 1930	2
August, 1930	5
1–15 September, 1930	4
Total	136

Source: Statistical summary of monthly data on ejidal petitions in the state of Michoacán, 1928–1932, SESRA—Delegación Michoacana.

Rubio's influence had faded, Cárdenas did his best not to appear as a radical, although the power and status of the CRMDT were such that he could have obtained many more ejidal petitions than he did. He was held back by his reluctance to arouse Calles's suspicions at a time when Cárdenas wanted his support in the upcoming contest for the presidency. Thus, during the same period that Tejeda was receiving a fairly steady average of 25–26 ejidal applications per month—his peak—Cárdenas's average was a mere seven petitions per month. This disparity reflects both the two men's different attitudes towards their power bases—Tejeda allowed free rein, Cárdenas maintained constant control—and the differing degrees to which they practiced what they preached: Tejeda's praxis matched his ideology, while Cárdenas's actions generally fell short of his principles (and his rhetoric).

Protecting the Nascent Ejido

The long waiting period before ejidal land could be received was very difficult for the petitioners. In Michoacán, for example, only some 7% of petitioners received a definitive response within the year, while 32% had to wait two years and 57% had to wait three years. Many communities, in fact, waited several years for their cases to be decided. This red tape was a boon to the enemies of the reform, providing them with many opportunities to

break up the ejidal community before it could complete the entire application process. The long waiting period also gave landowners time to sell land
destined for ejidal expropriation or to distribute it among family members,
to dismiss the petitioners from their employment or worsen their tenancy or
sharecropping conditions, to take over the ejidal committees through the use
of "*caballos negros*" ("black horses"—peasants in the pay of the landowners
who infiltrated the ejidal committees in order to sabotage them), to break up
communities of ejidal petitioners by force and kill their leaders, and to
prevent the CLA engineers from doing their work.[78]

Implementing the Reform in the Field

The first step in coping with these hostile actions was to create conditions in
which the CLA engineers could carry out their work unhindered. A letter
from Segundo Maldonado, an engineer employed by the CNA, to the federal
delegate of the Agrarian Reform Office in Veracruz in October 1942,
provides interesting insights into the threatening atmosphere that weighed
upon everyone involved in expropriations:

> Having been commissioned by yourself to establish the boundaries of the
> ejido definitively granted to the village of Actopan, seat of the municipio of
> the same name . . . , I take the liberty of informing you of the following:
>   During 1928 1929, and 1930, I worked intensively on agrarian matters
> in the municipios of Actopan, Alto-Lucero, Cardel, Puente Nacional, and
> Jalapa. . . . At the time the owners of country estates obstinately resisted the
> application of the agrarian laws in force, and I was obliged to obtain and
> use the necessary means for my own personal safety and that of the peti-
> tioners for ejidal land, to the point that I was able to obtain the
> disarmament of a militia, headed by Eligio Palmeros and Crispin Aguilar,
> that protected the interests of the owners of country estates.
>   [. . .] Naturally these gentlemen, remembering my past actions, want to
> retaliate against me now that I am within their domains and completely
> defenseless. I therefore ask you to relieve me of all topographical work in
> the . . . area, or else to take the necessary steps to guarantee my safety while
> I carry out the task that you have conferred on me in the aforementioned
> village of Actopan.[79]

Recognizing this problem, Cárdenas and Tejeda warned landowners
severely against any attempt to interfere with the work of the CLA.[80] In
cases where the CLA workers were tried too far and the situation seemed
likely to fly out of control, Cárdenas organized brigades of engineers who
spread throughout the problematic area and carried out together all the
work necessary to implement the various stages of the land redistribution
as quickly as possible. One such operation was carried out in the Huetamo
municipio in January 1932. After two bloody clashes at the end of
December 1931, in which four leading local agrarianists lost their lives at

the hands of thugs hired by the large landowners in the area, a group of five engineers and auxiliary staff was sent to Huetamo to perform en masse the work required for the establishment of 20 ejidos. The group was divided into five teams, and within a short time completed the formalities for eight ejidal petitions, which were submitted in May-August 1932, for Cárdenas's approval, eventually resulting in the establishment of seven ejidos in January 1933.[81]

Under Tejeda's administration, disturbances of this kind were sufficient cause to dissolve any municipio council that was involved in or had failed to prevent them. Nor did Tejeda hesitate to use his agrarianist militias in areas affected by violence. Where he was unable to offer such remedies, he armed the local peasants so they could form militias themselves.[82] In other cases, such as that of Segundo Maldonado, Tejeda disarmed the guards employed by the landowners, including those of Manuel Parra of Almolonga, who learned to be wary of Tejeda; he became genial, hospitable, and scrupulously law-abiding even while wrangling with the ejidos that sprang up on the property that had once been his.[83]

Generally speaking, the process of land expropriation and redistribution progressed fairly quietly in Veracruz under Tejeda. The *guerrilla* units, the direct arming of the peasants, the forceful measures taken against recalcitrant municipios, the disarming of "white guards," the omnipresence of the Agrarian League, and Tejeda's statewide network of intelligence agents, militia commanders, and League representatives all permitted the Veracruz governor to pinpoint centers of tension and violence and neutralize them immediately.[84] Similar success was achieved in Michoacán. A contributing factor here was Cárdenas's restriction of actual implementation of the reform (as opposed to the encouragement of ejidal petitions) to the northern part of the state. In this respect, the action he took in the Huetamo municipality, in the southeast, was something of an aberration, designed to prove that he, rather than the owners of the El Palmar hacienda and other local strongmen, was master in the district.

In addition to the measures taken to protect the implementers of the reform and the nascent ejidal communities, ways had to be found to guarantee the livelihood of the petitioners while they waited for the results of their applications. One expedient—which relied on local labor laws and, after August 1931, the federal labor law—was to supervise the petitioners' working conditions as wage earners, sharecroppers, or tenant farmers very carefully to ensure that they were not fired or subjected to any abuse as a result of their agrarianism. Another means was to give them land on a temporary basis, under the provisions of the 1920 federal law on unused land (*Ley de Tierras Ociosas*). The ejidal reform stimulated efforts in both states to make this law more easily enforced by reducing the obstructive effects of the *amparo* remedy. Of the two governors, however, it was Tejeda who raised the expedient of provisional expropriations to an art. Cárdenas made relatively moderate use of this tool, but relied more heavily on peasant and worker unions.

Arrangements to Help Potential Ejidatarios Survive the Waiting Period: Veracruz

The use of provisional expropriations began in Veracruz a few days after Tejeda entered the governor's office. On 11 December 1928, the local Congress renewed Law #297 on temporary expropriations (introduced by Heriberto Jara in July 1926).[85] This land-leasing law declared it to be in the public interest to hand over to landless peasants for their own use all lands in the state exceeding 50 hectares that were not being used for "industrial" crops, for oil extraction, or for federally regulated agricultural settlement. The law entitled every such peasant to take possession, within three days, of a parcel of uncultivated land measuring 10–25 hectares for an unlimited period of time. The municipios were given the task of enforcing this provision, as well as collecting an infinitesimal rent of up to 4% of the fiscal value of the land established by law (which was usually low to begin with) and transferring it to the lawful owners.[86] Wanting to afford the peasants complete freedom of action and to protect them from the strong-arm tactics of the large landowners, Tejeda ignored the restrictions that the federal *Ley de Tierras Ociosas* imposed on the leasing period; the Veracruz law did not limit the lease to a period of one to three years, as the federal law did.[87] The state department of agriculture and livestock was made responsible for processing the many applications for temporary land, assisted by the CLA and the Agrarian League.[88]

The renewed Law #297 went into effect immediately, and became a lifesaver for many peasants otherwise doomed to misery. A typical, though difficult, case was that of 50 erstwhile tenants from the La Pastoría community. The high rent they had been forced to pay for years decided them to seek relief by applying for ejidal land. Once they had done so, however, their lives were threatened by hired killers sent by the owner of the lands that they had hitherto rented but were now requesting for their ejido. One encounter with these killers, already well known as the murderers of four other peasants in the area, was enough to make the petitioners abandon the area, now bereft of any means of making a living. In desperation they turned to the regional president of the Veracruz Agrarian League, who was also responsible for agrarian issues in their community, and asked him to secure land for them under the provisions of Law #297 so they could maintain themselves until they received their ejido. He in turn forwarded their request to Salvador de Gortari, president of the Veracruz CLA, who passed it on again to the department of agriculture, asking for a rental arrangement to "tide them over" until the finalization of their ejido grant, which was, he said, still under review.[89]

The absence of a time limit on such leasing arrangements and the 24-hour deadline set for appeals against the expropriation made Law #297 a constant target of *amparo* proceedings (*juicios de garantía*). In December 1930, the federal Supreme Court canceled Law #297 on the grounds that it was unconstitutional.[90] Accordingly, Tejeda decided to introduce a new law that would correct the litigation-generating aspects of Law #297 and adapt it better to the role he wanted it to play. On 16 December 1930, a few days after the Supreme Court ruling had been published; he sent a new draft bill to the state Congress. The amended law shortened the expropriation process, lengthened the period during which an appeal could be filed, and provided for payment of compensation to temporary lessees for any improvements they made to the land (such as buildings and the cultivation of perennial crops). In Tejeda's view, these amendments made the old law an ideal law for the ejidal transition period: This bill, he said, "avoids these evils, and, in general, seeks to fill a need in the transition period that begins with the submission of the ejidal petition and ends with the grant of provisional possession—a period when *campesinos* frequently suffer from the hostility of the owners, who try to make the centers of rural population stipulated in the law disappear, thereby avoiding [expropriation]."[91]

The two congressional committees that debated Tejeda's draft law saw it as a valuable measure against the proliferation of *amparo* proceedings and the resulting dearth of possibilities for the army of poor, starving, unemployed peasants unable to pay the "capricious" rents demanded by "a handful of landowners who profited from fat rents." The new Law #208 was accordingly passed. From the day of its publication on 10 July 1931, it governed all issues arising during the wait for ejidal land. The Veracruz Agrarian League deployed large forces to publicize the law and promote its implementation. In some cases the League advised Tejeda to give peasants provisionally, under the terms of Law #208, the same lands that would eventually constitute their ejidos, to prevent the *hacendados* from destroying the land in their attempts to ward off the anticipated ejidal expropriation.[92]

Laws #297 and #208 were in a way local interpretation of the federal *Ley de Tierras Ociosas*, although not enabling legislation for it; their independence gave the Veracruz government certain flexibility in dealing with the issue of uncultivated land in general. This greatly annoyed the federal government, which wanted Tejeda to adhere closely to the explicit provisions of the 1920 federal law. Tejeda capitulated, and on 3 August 1931 he laid before the Congress regulatory legislation for the federal law—a bill that would constitute an additional means of expropriating land on a temporary basis. In the preamble, he explained that he had decided the law was necessary because every time land was expropriated under the terms of the federal law on unused land (rather than Law #208 or its precursor, Law #297), the owners of the land inevitably won it back by bringing an action in *amparo*. Such actions were easy to win, because the municipios, which were responsible for enforcing the law, had no clear legal criteria for determining what constituted uncultivated land (*tierras baldías*); since the definition necessarily depended on the crop, the season, and the area, a specific schedule was required by which the municipio could determine at what point land within its jurisdiction could be defined as uncultivated.[93]

The new law did not take effect until April 1932, although Tejeda had already had all the agricultural data he needed to draft it in 1931. He

undoubtedly preferred to rely on Law #208, which offered a more convenient way of protecting the agrarianist communities. An investigation carried
out by two Veracruz Congress members, Isaac Trigos and Jesús Ramírez
Ordóñez, in May 1931, in the Tlapacoyan archives corroborated this. They
discovered that the agrarian communities (*comunidades agrarias*) tended to
use the federal law on unused land, while the agrarian committees (*comités
agrarias*) preferred Laws #297 and #208.[94] In addition, the data concerning
the actions carried out under the terms of Law #297 indicated that Tejeda
had been unduly pessimistic: the majority of petitions for forced expropriation were in fact ultimately approved and the *amparo* appeals filed against
them were rejected.[95] This fact raises the possibility that Tejeda was
purposely disseminating disinformation to win public approval for the enactment of Law #208 and to lend greater legitimacy to Veracruz's demand for
the complete elimination of the *amparo* remedy in the agrarian sphere.

However that may be, Tejeda's use of both Law #208 and the federal *Ley
de Tierras Ociosas* was very successful. According to the data in his final
report to Congress, on the basis of these two laws (it is not clear whether he
was including Law #297, which he did not specifically mention at all), he
gave the peasants 97,749 hectares of tillage and pasture land. This astonishing figure, achieved during a period generally hostile to agrarianism,
testifies to the colossal effort made in Veracruz to implement the ejidal
reform.[96]

Arrangements to Help Potential Ejidatarios Survive the Waiting Period: Michoacán

Cárdenas did not draft a law of his own governing uncultivated land, preferring to enact enabling legislation for the federal *Ley de Tierras Ociosas*,
which had languished in oblivion until his administration. Nor did he begin
work on an enabling law immediately. For unknown reasons, political or
technical, he waited 20 months to present, in May 1930, a draft enabling
law eventually passed as Law #110. During that period there was no organized system for protecting the ejidal petitioners. Cárdenas did not in fact
define his law as having any connection with the wait for ejidal land. Based
very generally on the provisions of Article 27 of the federal constitution, the
law gave everyone in the rural sector equal rights, and did not favor the ejidal
enterprise in any way. Law #110, a regulatory land law, established two basic
principles in its preamble: the social right to work the land and enjoy its
fruits; and the duty to exploit the land's full potential, as an imperative of
the public interest.[97]

Law #110's cautious terms, which closely followed the anemic provisions
of the federal law, were not really calculated to make life much easier for the
ejidal petitioners. Cárdenas apparently did not want to invite a confrontation with the political center on knotty constitutional issues, as Jara and
Tejeda had done, preferring instead to remain on firm ground legally and
politically, even if it threatened the stability of the agrarianist communities.

I have no concrete data concerning the enforcement of the law, but it appears to have been seldom used. The relevant files in the Zamora archive show, for example, that in the years 1929–1932, only one peasant community, from the rancho El Sauz de Magaña, filed a petition for land under this law.[98]

In his annual speech, in September 1931, Gabino Vázquez, then the provisional governor, did not say a single word about the issue of unused land. Similarly, Cárdenas, in his valedictory speech, did not provide any details about the implementation of the law, but merely mentioned a circular (*circular reglamentaria*) from 6 May 1932 regulating Law #110. Moreover, to forestall any suspicion that the law was used to support ejidos, he reemphasized that it was intended to benefit individuals. Even so, Law #110 presented many problems of enforcement, which cast doubt on its suitability as a solution even for individual peasants. Gabino Vásquez said expressly: "in future we will avoid the difficulties that have resulted in practice from mistaken interpretations of the legal precepts involved."[99]

A study carried out by Foglio Miramontes in 1935 showed that at the time there were still large tracts in the state that were considered to be unproductive land and that could have been transferred under the terms of the law on unused land. According to Foglio Miramontes, 95% or more of the *campesinos* of Michoacán were unfamiliar with agrarian law or were unable to interpret it correctly.[100]

The first person to mention the law's implementation was Benigno Serrato, who, in September 1934, not only spoke of the law's role as a life raft for ejidal communities while they awaited the outcome of their petitions, but also presented data on 109 organized petitions filed for land in the framework of the law during the 1933–1934 fiscal year (although he did not give statistics on the number of hectares involved). Of all these petitions, 75 were approved, for unknown amounts of land.[101] Serrato also mentioned something that underlined the importance of Law #110: According to him, the unused lands were lands that had previously been cultivated by the peasants who became *ejidatarios*. When these peasants joined the agrarianist movement, they were thrown off the *latifundia*, and the lands they had once worked as farm laborers, tenant farmers, or sharecroppers became unused land. In other words, part of the problem of unused land had been created by the landowners' battle against ejidal groups, a fact that merely underlined the need to return the land to those communities somehow.[102]

On 16 July 1932, Cárdenas introduced the *Ley de Aparcería Rural* (Law of Rural Sharecropping), the main purpose of which was to regulate the relations between sharecroppers and their landlords. Certain articles of this law, however, were intended to support the village's agrarianist potential. First, permanent residents in the area were given preference as sharecroppers. Second, every sharecropping arrangement had to be formalized by means of a written contract with a term of at least one year, and, in cases where the sharecropper made improvements on the land, up to three years. Third, the law compelled the landowner to allow the sharecropper to live on the sharecropping land and to use the pasture and forest land of the hacienda rent-free, without the sharecropper thereby becoming a *peon acasillado*. Finally, the law gave preference to unionized peasants, and obliged the owner of the property to negotiate with them collectively, if that was their wish.[103] Since sharecropping was widespread in Michoacán, these protections did offer some relief to the peasants. The fact that the law favored organized peasants also strengthened the CRMDT, and accordingly wage-earning rural workers in general, who were unionized within the framework of the Confederation.[104]

The Implementation of the Ejidal Reform: Quantity and Quality

The differences in agrarian policy between the two governors—clearly expressed in such parameters as ejidal petitions, establishment of agrarian administrative systems, the distribution of the Agrarian Leagues in the states and the uses made of them and the enactment of legislation to ease the ejidal waiting period—were also, of course, reflected in the actual results of the reform. Cárdenas, moderate and deliberate as always, concentrated most of his agrarian reform efforts in the northern region of Michoacán (see Table 4.5).

Table 4.5 Cárdenas's Ejidal Reform in Michoacán, 1928–1932, by Area (Settlements Actually Established)

Area	North	Center	South	Southern Mountains	Total
Municipios Affected	37	15	9	0	61
Settlements Established	142	31	8	0	181

Source: Agrarian files of the state of Michoacán for the years 1929–1932, ASRA, Delegación Michoacana, Morelia, Michoacán.

Tejeda's freer approach promoted agrarianism all over the state, as indicated in Table 4.6 (overleaf). If we compare these results in percentages, we obtain the results shown in Table 4.7 (overleaf).

These tables indicate that more municipios were involved in the reform in Michoacán than in Veracruz (about 62%, as opposed to 50%), but that in Michoacán most of the ejidos were concentrated in one region (78.5%, versus about 64% in Veracruz). In other words, in Veracruz communities in the periphery accounted for about 36% of the reform (14.3% of them very remote from the center), while in Michoacán the figure was 21.5%, corresponding to ejidos in the central and southern regions. Not a single ejido was established in the southern mountains during this period. Unsurprisingly, Veracruz under Tejeda established more than twice the number of ejidos that Michoacán did under Cárdenas. Of the total number of ejidos established in both states together, Veracruz accounted for 67.7% and Michoacán 32.3%.

Table 4.6 Tejeda's Ejidal Reform in Veracruz, 1929–1932, by Area (Settlements Actually Established)

Area	Number of Municipios in which reform was implemented	Number of ejidos established	Ejidos as % of total
Far North	7	38	10.1
Southern North	10	35	9.3
Northern Center	32	133	35.3
Southern Center	33	108	28.6
Northern South	8	47	12.5
Far South	9	16	4.2
Total	97	377	100.0

Source: Agrarian files of the State of Veracruz for the years 1929–1932, ASRA, Delegación Veracruzana, Jalapa, Veracruz.

Table 4.7 Achievements of the Agrarian Reform in Michoacán and Veracruz, 1928–1932 (in % by region)

State	Municipios affected	Ejidos established		
		North	Center	South
Michoacán	62.0	78.5	17.1	4.4
Veracruz	50.7	19.4	63.9	16.7

Table 4.8 Indicators of the Quality of the Agrarian Reform: Michoacán and Veracruz Compared, 1928–1932 (Land in Hectares by Soil Quality and Suitability for Cultivation)

State	Number of Farmers (Ejidatarios) surveyed	Average area per Farmer	Average area suitable for agriculture per Farmer	Average area of irrigated or wet land per Farmer
Michoacán	19,316	6.10	3.04	1.1
Veracruz	2,464	6.12	4.34	0.7

Source: Agrarian files of the States of Michoacán and Veracruz , 1928–1932, ASRA, Delegaciones Agrarias de Michoacán y Veracruz.

Comparison between the reforms in the two states also reveals differences in quality. Although both states had similar quantities of irrigated or wet lands (Michoacán had more irrigated land, but the Veracruz land was of much better quality), the extent of land suitable for agricultural cultivation in Veracruz was 43% greater than the equivalent in Michoacán (where 3.04

hectares=100). Taking into account the better rainfall and great natural fertility of the land in Veracruz, the Veracruz peasant had many agricultural advantages over his Michoacán counterpart (see Table 4.8).

Defending the New Ejido

Even after an ejido was finally established, its future was by no means secure. The first years were very difficult, both because the *ejidatarios* had to learn to manage a farm on their own and because the ejido's fate still depended on the president's final authorization. The large landowners found this time favorable for continuing the attacks and abuses described previously, in order to discourage the peasants and persuade them to abandon their ejidos, to neglect their fields, or to rent them out (which was against the law). The question was whether the new ejido would manage to become a viable alternative to the traditional way of life, or whether it would remain a shaky proposition, barely holding on. Both Michoacán and Veracruz addressed this delicate issue, but only Veracruz dealt with it systematically and efficiently.

The Cooperative Basis: Veracruz Did More

The economic basis of the ejido was cooperative. This had a significant impact on the mobilization of capital, the exploitation of natural resources, the organization of labor, marketing, and, to some degree, the cost of consumption. The statutory bases and powers of cooperative organizations were established in January 1927, by the federal law on cooperative societies (*Ley General de Sociedades Cooperativas*), which permitted the establishment of cooperatives without special local legislation.[105]

Cooperativism was a central tenet of Tejeda's philosophy, being considered "one of the most effective means of achieving economic independence." The government therefore took a strong interest in it.[106] A resolution passed at the Agrarian League's fifth congress, on 29 October 1930,[107] constituted a first step in the direction to which Tejeda had committed himself in an interview with *El Dictamen* in November 1928. At that time he had spoken of the need to organize production on a cooperative basis in order to avoid the influence of speculation, to create "social wealth," and to deal with the problem of foreign ownership of industries and services in the state. In December 1930, Tejeda began to work on a large, ambitious plan to establish a cooperative hydroelectric company in Minatitlán. This project was supposed to be the beginning of a larger program to build a cooperative national economy, thereby restoring to local hands the exploitation of the state's natural resources and promoting efficiency and social justice. The hydroelectric plant, which was formally inaugurated on 16 April 1931, was defined as a joint-stock company whose shares would be purchased by "all the inhabitants of the Tehuantepec Isthmus." This project, Tejeda wrote, would show that "an enterprise of great magnitude could be carried out with Mexican capital, Mexican labor, and Mexican brains."[108]

In January 1931, Tejeda took another step forward when he founded, at the League's instigation, a state cooperative credit fund (the *Refaccionaria*) designed to provide a financial basis for the work of all the cooperative firms in the various economic sectors of Veracruz. In a prime example of Marxist rhetoric, Tejeda explained the reasons for the institution. Normally, he said, the worker—whether peasant, craftsman, civil servant, or industrial worker—lost his power to bargain over what he created if he did not have some margin of financial security. Under such circumstances, workers stayed poor, living on a pittance inadequate for their survival. The people raking in the profits from their work were, of course, speculators and merchants—that is, the various middlemen, the few people able to obtain credit. That situation, according to Tejeda, had to be changed through the creation of a popular credit system that would eschew the principles of classic capitalist credit. Hence the plan to establish a workers' credit fund that would also serve as a savings institution rescuing the workers from the evils of the current system. "This will be a continuation of Ursulo Gálvan's ideas on the subject," Tejeda said in conclusion.[109]

Tejeda linked the goal of organizing village life on a cooperative basis with the Agrarian League, and both of them with the ejido, by means of the "Biennial Agricultural-Economic Program" for the development and modernization of the agricultural sector, a program that the League approved at its seventh congress, in March 1932, partly on the recommendation of the state government. In the last speech of his governorship, Tejeda explained why the connection with the Agrarian League was necessary:

> Taking advantage of the existence in the State of such an advanced and complete peasant organization as the League of Agrarian Communities, which controls almost all the Agrarian Committees in the State—close to 100,000 peasants organized within the advanced and truly progressive program of that institution—it has been suggested that the League should develop a basic Economic and Agricultural Plan that will govern its activities for the period of two years. The Department [of Agriculture and Livestock] is already working on the initial blueprints for this program. . . .[110]

The cooperative program, which was under the supervision of the Cooperativa Central Agrícola de la Liga de Comunidades Agrarias (Agricultural Central Cooperative of the League of Agrarian Communities), was immediately made compulsory for all members of the League. It was decided that agricultural inputs, the use of mechanical equipment (which would be provided in the framework of the program), all phases of work, storage, and marketing would all be managed cooperatively, under the supervision of the Central Cooperative. This central office would be assisted by both the *Refaccionaria* and a number of additional agencies, such as a central marketing body and equipment centers. The program also called for efforts to incorporate even private consumption into the cooperative framework by means of consumers' cooperatives that would be established in all ejidos.[111]

Immediately after the League congress, the program was put into operation in a number of ejidos. Begun on an experimental basis, it gained momentum and was working well by the second half of the 1931–1932 fiscal year.[112] Towards 1932, the League was sending Tejeda increasing numbers of requests from villages wanting government advisors to help them organize cooperatively. The ejidos' interest in the subject had in fact begun during the seventh League congress itself, and testified to the effectiveness of the League's public relations and promotion campaign in this sphere, as well as to the mutual interests of and good relations between the League and the government.[113]

From the moment they were founded, the cooperatives began to apply to the credit fund (often through the intermediary of Tejeda or the League) for seeds, plows, cultivators, fertilizers, seed drills, and so on. Some requested direct financing for various agricultural projects, or guaranties for joint purchases from commercial establishments. Still others sought support in disputes they were having with the ejido administration; typical examples were disputes over the rates of internal tax imposed on pottery-manufacturing cooperatives that dug the clay they needed in the ejido's common land. Every request was quickly attended to, to judge by the short span of time between the application and the provision of the assistance requested.[114]

Despite all this activity, however, the cooperative approach never became widespread. Fowler claims that it was a failure.[115] Tejeda himself, in May 1932, mentioned 27 cooperative companies operating in Veracruz at the time, one of them belonging to the League itself, which had decided to combat commercial speculation in the city. In July of the same year, Tejeda noted that a number of urban producers' and consumers' cooperatives had mounted a "successful" (his word) cooperative effort in the state, but that the performance of the ejidos had been less satisfactory in this respect.[116] All these comments indicate that actual implementation did not always measure up to intention—especially in the villages, which remained, despite all the efforts to instill a "progressive" consciousness, suspicious towards modern organizational structures.

Cárdenas, too, was a great believer in labor cooperativism. He saw the cooperative as a fundamental component of proletarian organization. Both were supposed to make the worker a free agent enjoying economic power, master of himself and unaffected by the pressures of capitalists.[117] This aim was first established in January 1929, in Article 12 of the CRMDT's official platform, though it was not specially emphasized. It was expressed again, in an equally low key, by Cárdenas himself during a debate with Luis Cabrera and Antonio Díaz Soto y Gama in January 1931. In that debate he linked accelerated agricultural development with, among other things, "the collectivization of agricultural exploitation."[118] In July 1931, he began to work on organizing a federation of logging cooperatives in the Meseta Tarasca area to liberate the Indians living there from the profiteering lumber companies that were exploiting their forests. Moreover, in his many visits to individual villages, he missed no opportunity to encourage the peasants to set up cooperatives.[119] The issue became more significant with the enactment of the law on ejidal and small-farmer credit in January 1931, which stipulated that only cooperative societies would be eligible for credit.[120]

Nonetheless, there was never any strategic decision to promote cooperatives in Michoacán as there was in Veracruz. In this respect, despite much rhetorical enthusiasm for the subject, Cárdenas was a follower rather than a leader. This is indicated by the fact that he did not set up a state credit fund, or any cooperative institution within the CRMDT. Similarly, no attempt was made to collect information on the extent of cooperative organization in the state until after he left office, when the federal government studied the subject preparatory to drafting new legislation on cooperative societies. This study revealed that the Zamora municipio, which included five ejidos all built at the same time, did not contain a single cooperative.[121] Of course, this was not necessarily representative of other municipios, particularly those containing many ejidos; but it is very likely that Zamora did reflect a broader picture—especially since Cárdenas's valedictory speech as governor did not devote a single word to the subject. Thus, in Michoacán, as in Veracruz, a considerable gap existed between intentions and reality. The cooperative activity that did exist was concentrated in Veracruz rather than Michoacán, in the local credit fund's provision of agrarian aid to some of the state's peasants. The absence of such a fund in Michoacán deprived the peasants of even that pittance.

Easing the Ejidos' Tax Burden: Conflicting Trends

One way of helping the ejidos stand on their own was to exempt them from taxes. This measure was widely implemented in Veracruz, but not in Michoacán. In a series of some 25 decrees, Tejeda systematically exempted most of the ejidos in the state from all taxes. The first of these decrees (October 1929) exempted all ejidatarios from tax liability until the end of December 1928, on condition that they paid all their taxes for the year 1929. This exemption was defined as a reward for the ejidatarios' contribution to the suppression of the Escobar revolt, a cause to which they had rallied "as one man," and as a result of which "they were obliged to abandon their fields and agricultural work, [which] caused the penury and difficult economic situation in which they now find themselves."[122]

The next decree (December 1929) extended the tax exemption for 1928 to the end of January 1930, to compensate for the ejidatarios' continuing economic difficulties and a series of natural disasters that had ravaged Veracruz. Still another decree (June 1931) extended most of the ejidos' exemptions to the end of 1932.[123] Each application for an exemption was meticulously evaluated, and only then was the size and type of exemption decided—whether an exemption from state taxes, municipal taxes, or both. This assistance was a matter of principle for Tejeda, and in providing it he completely ignored the severe economic crisis in which the state was mired for most of his administration. Although in November 1931, he was forced to reduce government spending drastically—cutting government employees' salaries by 10% and canceling the subsidies enjoyed by labor organizations and special deductions for certain entities—he continued to exempt many ejidos from taxation. In general, he did everything he could for them, because he realized, from ejidatarios' letters to the Agrarian League, the Congress, and himself, that the survival of the ejidos hung by a thread. Precisely in the context of the economic crisis Tejeda showed extraordinary leadership and perseverance, motivated by his conviction that the needs of the peasants rather than the state of the treasury should dictate his economic policy.[124]

A completely different atmosphere prevailed in Michoacán, where every request for tax exemption after 1929 was systematically refused. During a congressional debate on 5 November 1929 concerning an application for exemption from the Tarecuato ejido, Deputy Ruiz Solís said that given the quantity of other applications and Cárdenas's insistence that every application be examined individually, the debate on Tarecuato should be postponed until a comprehensive, egalitarian solution to the problem could be devised.[125] Accordingly, at the end of January 1930, a decree was passed that exempted all the ejidos from 80% of their taxes for the year 1929, as long as they paid the remaining 20%.[126] This was the only decree on the subject during Cárdenas's time. Isolated applications for exemption submitted to the Congress at later dates were rejected because of Michoacán's empty treasury. When, for example, in July 1930, the Huiramba ejido applied to Congress for an exemption on grounds of economic hardship, it was turned down because of the state's own economic hardship.[127]

It can be concluded, then, that despite the Michoacán ejidos' shaky position, which was undoubtedly similar to that of their Veracruz counterparts, Michoacán's assistance policy was minimalistic. Although it is impossible to point to ejidos that broke up as a direct result, this orientation probably restricted ejidal development *ab initio*, and was one of the factors that led to the concentration of ejidos in the north of the state to the exclusion of other areas. In a letter Cárdenas sent in March 1968 to Ezio Cusi, the former owner of the large Lombardía and Nueva Italia haciendas which he had broken up in 1938, he said that while governor he had received ejidal petitions from the peasants of Lombardía and Nueva Italia and neighboring villages, but he had been prevented from granting them the two haciendas' lands owing to shortage of funds. The lack of credit and budgetary funds, he said, would not have permitted these peasants "to keep their grant lands [*dotaciones*] under cultivation, a fact that was brought to the knowledge of both the petitioners and the Señores Cusi themselves."[128]

The fact that Cárdenas did not establish a local credit fund as Tejeda did undoubtedly did not help matters. His efforts to assist the ejidos indirectly by developing the highway system (for example, the Michoacán section of the road from Mexico City to Guadalajara, and the road from Morelia to Apatzingán), building access roads to the ejidos, setting up power plants, carrying out river drainage projects in the north (Duero, Lerma), and so on may have had an impact on the ejidos in the long run; but there was little chance of an ejido's being saved by the 4% tract allocated it from the 14,400 hectares yielded by the land drainage project in the Zamora valley, for example.[129] For that matter, Tejeda, too, undertook a certain number of infrastructure projects that benefited the ejidos as well as other communities, notably emergency measures to rescue the sugar, coffee, and textile industries from the effects of the world depression; damming the state's great rivers to prevent the flooding that devastated villages every year, and laying the road from Jalapa to the city of Veracruz. Such projects, however, were no substitute for more direct financial assistance to the ejidos, particularly the credit arrangements and tax benefits enjoyed by ejidos in Veracruz but not in Michoacán. In this respect Tejeda created a much more supportive environment for the ejido than Cárdenas did.

Both governors knew well how important the development of a modern economy was for the reinforcement and consolidation of the ejido. They emphasized different aspects, however: Cárdenas gave greater weight to land communications, while Tejeda tended to invest more in the development of the production and labor systems. These different priorities reflected their different approaches to the issue of economic modernization in general: Cárdenas saw local control as crucial to this process, while Tejeda gave first importance to resolving sectoral crises, unemployment, and problems in labor relations. Both approaches were beneficial, but given their nature it was to be expected that while the ejidos in both states would enjoy long-term benefits, only those in Veracruz were likely to enjoy significant advantages in the short term.

The Salvation of the Ejido: A Pyrrhic Victory?

The economic reinforcement of the ejidos was unquestionably crucial not only for the survival of individual ejidos already in operation, but also for the survival of the whole ejidal approach as a central factor in the process of socioeconomic change. Once the ejidatarios took possession of their land, their political recruitment into the Revolution had begun; this process was reflected very clearly in contemporary sources. One example is the ejidos' enthusiastic responses to such government initiatives as the anti-clerical crusade and the enactment of educational and agrarian legislation and legislation governing labor issues and sharecropping. Further evidence was the enormous increase in the number of labor unions and organizations affiliated with the central Agrarian Leagues in each state, and the parallel rise in the number of yearly conventions and assemblies held by the Veracruz Agrarian League, the CRMDT, and their regional branches—mass shows of strength that each year became larger, more festive, and more widely publicized. Yet another indication of the ejidatarios' political mobilization was their involvement in municipio power struggles, the administrative upgrading of many communities, and the increased demand for the construction of rural schools. Without a doubt, the marked upswing in agrarianist, antireligious, and educational legislation during the last two years of Cárdenas's and Tejeda's respective terms in office could not have taken place without organized popular support, greatly reinforced by the growing ejidal base in the villages and in society in general, as well as the village unions, which were a major source of future ejidatarios.

Tejeda and Cárdenas defeated Calles and the revolutionary old guard in the battle over the future of the ejido by leaving behind them not only a strong, vital agrarianist movement, but also a public awareness and an organizational, legal, and political infrastructure capable of ensuring its continued existence and prosperity. This infrastructure was evidence of a more global political turning point that marked the advent of the organized peasantry as a significant player on the national stage. The ejidal struggle between the veteran revolutionaries and the agrarianists was therefore not primarily a battle over which agrarian system would best serve the country's needs, but rather a battle for control of the largest social and political group in Mexico. The winner, as both sides knew, would enjoy federal hegemony for many years to come. This was the reason that Calles and his followers sought to bury the ejido and strengthen the middle class instead, and it was the reason that their rivals strove to do the opposite—and proved that doing so would produce political benefits on both the state and national levels.

The old guard lost the battle because from the outset they had approached agrarianism as a political issue. Once the agrarianist movement came into its own at the end of the 1920s, it could not be suppressed. The passing years saw the flourishing of large peasant organizations and a strong agrarianist leadership whose members began, slowly but surely, to fill political posts across the nation, as state governors, as municipio presidents, as members of state Congresses, as members of the ruling party, its branches, and institutions, as members of the federal Congress and other institutions. At the same time, the power of Calles and the revolutionary veterans waned, for two main reasons. First, Calles never managed to develop a radical social ideology that would convince the peasants and their leaders of his commitment to implementing the social goals of the Revolution as laid down in the 1917 constitution. The second reason was that he failed to devise a comprehensive, long-range agrarian program that clearly showed how he intended to resolve the social problems of the *pueblo*—if not by the ejidal system, which he rejected, then by some system based on individual land distribution, which, in theory at least, he preferred—the *pueblo* as a legal, social and territorial unit.[130] Callesism failed, then, as Tzvi Medin has put it, to extend the political mechanism of the *Maximato* "beyond the barricade of short-term political intrigue."[131]

In late 1933, the end of the ejidal crisis came in sight. Harsh denunciations of the ejido could still be heard, but in that year some of the limitations imposed by the Ortiz Rubio law of January 1931, were eliminated. The agrarian code of March 1934, changed the political impact of previous legislation still further. It gave even *peones acasillados* access to land (for the first time in the history of Mexican legislation), reduced the quantity of land exempt from expropriation (so-called "industrial land"), and lifted all restrictions on ejidal expansion (*ampliación ejidal*).[132] The ejido's survival, especially from the perspective of the radical states, demanded a compromise between the new provisional president, Abelardo Rodríguez (who had replaced Ortiz Rubio in September 1932), and the agrarianist camp. That compromise entailed supporting the moderates in the camp, Cárdenas and his followers and eliminating the radicals, Tejeda and his followers. This division was possible precisely because the agrarianist camp was not monolithic, and lacked both ideological and practical consensus something that cost the peasants and workers dearly, as will be shown: They lost the chance to use the agrarian reform as a springboard to a less authoritative and intervening State in Mexico that would have drawn its inspiration, as Tejeda had hoped, from the Danish or generally Western European model.[133]

5

From Ejidal Agrarianism to Total Agrarianism

The Importance of Private Land

Ejidal agrarianism's many limitations made it unable to supply satisfactory solutions for all rural needs. *Peones acasillados,* who were not entitled to participate in the reform; peasants for whom no land could be found in a radius of seven kilometers from their homes; peasants unwilling to suffer the extended wait for ejidal land and the pressures it involved and independent farmers who because of their entrepreneurial approach desired free and direct ownership of their agrarian fields (homesteads) without hindrances from the state. All these groups remained outside the ejidal reform.

Others, specifically the Indians of the forest communities in western Michoacán, had a different problem: They were ineligible to receive land because they were considered landowners, even though since the beginning of the century contracts with foreign companies, concluded without their consent, had barred them from their own land.

It is difficult to say how many people were unable or unwilling to receive ejidal land. A survey of some of the ejidos that received land during the period in question seems to indicate that in relatively large communities of 50–100 families, such as Actopan, Mozomboa, Palmas de Abajo, and Coatepec in Veracruz, or Capula, Emiliano Zapata, and Villamar in Michoacán, only a minority of ejidal petitioners actually received land. In communities smaller than 50 families, in contrast, few of the inhabitants did *not* receive land. By my calculations, more than half of the Mexican peasantry was unable or unwilling to take advantage of the ejidal reform. Different solutions had to be sought for these people, particularly in the period when ideological awareness was high and land reform was a central tenet of revolutionary thought.

During this period of worldwide economic depression, declining income and rising unemployment, the urban workers' sufferings could not be ignored. They needed land for housing and even plots on which they could grow a few vegetables to improve lives made miserable by high rents, crowded living quarters, lack of hygiene, and poverty. Increasingly, too, land was demanded to help striking workers and badly paid members of the liberal professions—such as teachers and clerical workers—make ends meet. The ejidal reform could not help all these people, and it required great moral fortitude of those it did help. Clearly other, supplemental methods of reform were urgently needed to turn the promises of the Revolution concerning land reform into a nationally relevant social reality.

The transition from ejidal agrarianism to a broader land reform necessitated a break with ejidal legislation's narrow definitions of expropriatable property and its beneficiaries, and an orientation that adapted land reform to the economic situation of the village rather than the political whims of legislators. This realization provided the stimulus for expanding the concept of "the public interest" ("*utilidad pública*") both theoretically and practically, and for implementing a supplementary, parallel reform grounded in the states' statutory powers. This kind of agrarianism was a true test of ideology and leadership, since its very existence depended on state initiative and the ability of the state political system to implement ideas.

It should be noted here that the creation of small private family landholdings—the Mexican Homestead—as a National project and as a part of a large agrarian project the Constitution propagated and legally enabled, had already been politically blocked as early as 1921 when the National Chamber of Representatives rejected Obregon's promulgating law of the breakup of the Latifundios and their division into small family plots that were to be given to the peasants as private owners in return for payment spread out over 20 years, bypassing already existing or in process federative states' laws on that matter. In the long and boisterous debate that extended over 84 sessions, it was apparent that the representatives of the states were not willing to relinquish the prerogative that the constitution granted to the states to handle this particular reform from the stage of the breakup of the Latifundios to the division of the land into homesteads for the peasants by themselves. What was left in the hands of the Governors were other legal procedures from the realm of laws for the public benefit, through them there was a possibility of building a small family property. However, these laws, in contrast to the Latifundios division laws of the States which were exempt from court intervention, were liable to court intervention, that is, they were subjugated to the *amparo* juridical laws and therefore their implementation was slow and very limited.

Cárdenas and Tejeda approached this sphere, or the little that remained of it, in diametrically different ways. Cárdenas contented himself with very minor, moderate action, never putting any stress on the status quo. Tejeda, in contrast, beat the status quo to a pulp, exploiting both his political influence and his statutory powers—as he understood them—to the utmost. Since Revolutionary Mexico, wanting to avoid direct conflict with the *hacendados*, was loath to promote reform based on individual ownership, anything deviating from the government-controlled ejidal formula (which landowners saw as least threatening), was considered a gross and reprehensible attack on private property. Accordingly, the decision to act in this sphere required a certain political hardiness and a kind of ideological faith uncommon in the Mexican political culture of that time.

The Return of the Forest Land to the Meseta Tarasca Communities in Michoacán

Until the railroad was laid from Morelia to Uruapan and from the Guaracha-Zamora region to Los Reyes at the beginning of the century, the richly wooded Meseta Tarasca region was of no special interest to anyone but its inhabitants, since it had no economic importance.[1] Although a Michoacán law (*Ley de Reparto de Tierras de las Excomunidades de Indígenas*) was passed on 18 June 1902 to oblige the Indian communities to divide up their communal lands (meaning most of the agricultural land held by the communities of the Tarascan mountain forests) among the village inhabitants, the Tarascos paid little attention to it.[2] They continued to hold the Meseta lands in common, as they always had.[3]

The inauguration of the railroad to Uruapan and Los Reyes, however, changed everything. The railroad made it possible to exploit the commercial potential of the rich woodland, and lumber companies began to move in. During the period from November 1907, to March 1913, a total of 220,000 hectares of land were leased from the reluctant inhabitants for up to 30-year terms, at ridiculously low rents spread over 20 years.[4]

These lease contracts, having been forced upon the Indians by means of fraud, inveiglement, and intimidation, were illegal under the terms of the 1917 constitution.[5] Until the beginning of the 1930s, however, no politician stepped forward to point this out and remedy the situation. What is more, in February 1928, the contract of one of the five big logging companies, the Michoacán Transportation Company, was extended for another 10 years, under the same distorted leasing terms as before.

Cárdenas was the first of the revolutionary governors to take notice of this situation. The Revolution, he said,

> which had given rise to the Agrarian Laws so that the villages might acquire and demand their ejidal patrimony, destroyed or pillaged by the legal maneuvers of attorneys or individuals . . . had not made its benefits felt by the other disinherited classes, since private interests continued to take precedence over the collective economy of the masses.[6]

It was clear, however, that the ejido was not the answer to this problem, since the communities in question were considered property owners.[7] Instead, the basis for action was to be what Cárdenas called "the promise we made at Pátzcuaro"—a resolution passed by the CRMDT's founding convention.[8] A committee was set up, comprising the engineer Carlos Peralta, Cárdenas's lawyer friend Gabino Vázquez, and the government secretary, Leopoldo Gallegos. They were to study the history and legal aspects of property relations in the Uruapan region, and to submit recommendations to the government based on their findings.[9] In December 1929, Cárdenas called on the forest communities to send representatives to Michoacán's first agrarian congress, which was to open on 5 January 1930 in Morelia, and at which, as described earlier, a league of Indian forest communities (Liga de Comunidades Indígenas de Bosques) was supposed to be founded. In issuing this invitation, Cárdenas spoke of the need to link the establishment of an Indian league with action to cancel the forest leasing contracts and replace the big lumber companies with local Indian logging cooperatives. Although the proposed league was never established, Cárdenas continued to wrestle with a plan for a comprehensive solution to the problem, and in June 1931, he introduced a draft bill in the Michoacán Congress canceling the contracts imposed on 20 communities and providing for a possible extension of the law's application to other communities in the same situation.[10] In theory this law was designed to restore 360,000 hectares of land, 220,000 hectares of that being forest land. In practice, the scope of the law expanded over the years, and by 1950 1,517,698 hectares had been restored to their former owners.[11]

The next challenge was to organize an indigenous logging operation. Since the forests were owned in common by all the inhabitants and could not be divided among them, a cooperative organization seemed the most logical way to harvest the forest products. Cooperatives were also the only significant means of preventing individuals from leasing or even selling their agricultural land, as they had done legally since the Reform (*la Reforma*) 1856 had privatized communal agrarian property, and illegally in the case of forest land, which had remained communal property even after the Reform.[12] In Cárdenas's view, cooperation was in this case a tool "to prevent [forest] products from ending up in the hands of contractors who, taking advantage of the owners' lack of knowledge and capital, enjoy the profits that should go only to the Communities."[13]

Accordingly, on 6 July 1931, Cárdenas published a "Plan of Action" for organizing a federation of lumber-producing cooperatives involving 20 mountain communities. This plan required that each village send five representatives to the federation's founding convention, which was to take place in the village of Paracho on 5 October 1931. At the same time, Cárdenas began to work on instilling an awareness of cooperative principles in 600 students, mostly from mountain villages, who attended the Álvaro Obregón, Josefa Ortiz, and José María Morelos industrial schools in Pátzcuaro. The plan was that after they completed their studies they would return to their communities prepared to organize and manage cooperative enterprises themselves.[14]

The Paracho convention apparently never took place. In the speech Cárdenas made upon leaving office, he referred to it as something yet to come. Nor did he say anything about a "cooperative federation"—an omission suggesting that no organized cooperative movement existed at that point, although no concrete data are available for the year 1931–1932 to confirm this hypothesis.[15] Figures for 1933 show that only one cooperative existed in the region at that time, a 42-member cooperative in Turícuaro; while figures for the first half of 1936 indicate that by then five more forest cooperatives had been established, in Cherán (437 members),[16] Zirosto (57 members), Paricutín, San Felipe, and Quinceo. It seems probable that a number of cooperatives were set up in the mountain region between the years 1933 and 1936, of which Turícuaro may have been the first. This assumption is reinforced by a 1933 report by Benigno Serrato, who succeeded Cárdenas as governor.[17] Whatever the number established, they did not survive long enough to leave any real impression on the collective memory of the residents of the area.[18]

The reform did provide a substantial boost to the lumber industry in the region. From 13,000 cubic meters of wood in 1933, production rose to some 33,000 cubic meters in 1934, while revenue rose from about 1 million pesos to 2.5 million pesos over the same period. The Uruapan region increased its share in the statewide production of wood from 15% to 35% in those years.[19] These figures indicate a much bigger profit than Cárdenas's plan of action had foreseen. Even without intensive cooperative organization, economic prosperity had been created in the area. Unfortunately, however, since the development of the region had not been scientifically managed, the boom ended in economic and ecological disaster. The forests were overrun by private contractors who, having obtained personal concessions from the community committees, embarked on a completely unregulated frenzy of timber-cutting, particularly pine, until they had irreversibly destroyed most of the forest. According to Luis González, 90% of the rich forests of Michoacán have been exterminated since the 1930s.[20]

Tejeda gave the Indians' problems only cursory attention. On 27 November 1930, the local Congress enacted Law #71, which restored to interested communities all lands originally granted to them by the Spanish crown, or other lands which were inalienable to third parties, and that had passed into the hands of the local *municipios* as a result of the law of 25 June 1856. These communities were entitled to apply to the appropriate agrarian authorities for permission to form administrative committees that would represent them in all matters pertaining to these lands.[21] The next day the state government sent out a circular to all the municipios, asking them to withdraw their jurisdiction from the lands governed by Law #71 (under an arrangement know as the *Plan de Arbitrio*, or Arbitration Plan), which would then be rezoned as rural properties instead of municipal land and restored to the inhabitants of the villages from which they had been taken.[22] This land was in fact community land that had been taken away by the municipios but not defined as *fundos legales* (urban zones) for municipal development. In this respect they were in the same category as the forest lands of the Michoacán Tarascos. Some of the land was being exploited (leased to companies or individuals), some remained unused. The law, aimed at those lands that did not come into the purview of restitutional agrarian legislation because they had never been converted into private property, was designed to restore them to their former owners under the provisions of subsection VII of constitutional Article 27. My sources indicate that Tejeda did not take advantage of Law #71, confining himself to a declaration of intentions rather than embarking on any practical action. This is partly attributable to the scarcity of such lands in Veracruz, and the difficulty of confirming the community's original title to them.

Thus, there are no grounds for comparison between Michoacán's and Veracruz's respective policies on Indian lands, since this area of supplementary reform featured prominently in Michoacán and hardly at all in Veracruz. Tejeda did not invest any reformist fervor in this direction, probably not out of any "ideological lapse," but because the issue was irrelevant to the agrarian problem in Veracruz. The problems of the Veracruz Indians were more easily solved through the usual channels of agrarian reform.

Preparing the Way for the Creation of Private Smallholdings in Michoacán

Back to the Old Laws

In contrast to Michoacán's scanty legislative provision for sharecropping, tenancy, and unused land, the legal infrastructure for creating private smallholdings was already well-established when Cárdenas took office as governor. Its foundations had been laid in the Michoacán constitution of February 1918, which instituted family ownership of smallholdings formed from the break-up of haciendas. This principle was enforced by enabling legislation, Laws #45 (March 1919) and #110 (February 1920), counterparts of similar laws in most of the other states. Until 1932, however, nothing whatever was done with either of these laws, which seemed to have been enacted only *"para archivarlas"* ("to file them away") as Moisés T. de la Peña put it.[23] As mentioned in Chapter 4, Cárdenas noted this situation in May 1932, and took action, publishing a draft edict that instructed the state agrarian reform administration and the municipios to enforce Laws #45 and #110 and to publicize them among the *campesinos*. The decree also obliged these authorities to encourage potential petitioners to request land under the provisions of the two laws and to help them draft their requests in the required form.[24]

This step seemed to indicate an intention to break up landholdings larger than 50 irrigated hectares and to distribute them without any federal intervention. If this intention had been put into practice, Michoacán would undoubtedly have changed beyond recognition very quickly. In fact, however, nothing much happened. Even by the beginning of the 1930s, the political center had not changed its views on land reform; it did not want to break up *latifundia* except in the limited ejidal framework. Nor did it have any intention of aiding a process that would have given the federated states great power as initiators and implementers of an extensive agrarian reform that lay beyond the reach of federal supervision. In other words, the center could not tolerate a flagrant display of progressive, energetic federalism. This was evident from the fact that no federal law had ever defined the concept of "the public interest"—an omission that inevitably held up direct expropriations of large properties in the law courts. And, as stated above, the régime did not allow the governors to run the *latifundia* confiscation laws which were in their control, except in rare cases of very modest proportions. Another indication was the flaccid federal circular distributed to the state governors and the governors' circulars to the municipios, which merely "advised" landowners to break up their properties, as being in their own interests, rather than ordering them to do so.[25]

Whether or not the administration actually believed that landowners would take this "advice" of their own free will, it could hardly have expected them to do so in large numbers. Cárdenas himself certainly did not contemplate any crusade on behalf of private smallholdings that would entail systematically breaking up the *latifundia*, mainly because it would have been contrary to the wishes of the federal government—wishes that he was not the man to challenge, particularly not just when he was about to run for the presidency. Since something had to be done nevertheless (this was undoubtedly the motive of Cárdenas's edict in May 1932), the administration began to collect petitions for land. Requests came in from El Huaco, in the Ario de Rosales district; La Angostura, La Cofardía, and Cantabria in the Pátzcuaro district; and others. All of them were personally approved by Cárdenas.[26]

At the same time, Cárdenas began to plan the break-up of a number of haciendas, notably Santa Ana Mancera, San Martín, and Zurumuato and its annexed farms in the Puruándiro district, which were divided up and distributed among peasant petitioners on 27 April 1933. The results of this operation were impressive—24,000 hectares of land were divided among 3,878 families living in 27 different settlements in the district—and were an indication of what could have been achieved had individual distribution been carried out on a larger scale. These expropriations also benefited the local communities generally, since some of the expropriated land was allocated for agricultural experiments and the construction of four schools, a pig-breeding and pork-processing plant, chicken coops, and sheep and goat pens.[27]

Cárdenas's initiative encouraged many to request private land for themselves. In September 1933, 31 new cases of expropriation were in the works as a result of the dozens of petitions submitted since the previous September, and a year later 50 more petitions had been received. Benigno Serrato's administration continued the policy of encouraging this trend. "There are currently sizable groups of *campesinos*," Serrato wrote, "who because of special circumstances have not been able to acquire lands by means of the Agrarian Law, and it is vital that they be provided with this important element by other means in order to resolve their difficult situation. . . ."[28]

Thus, under Cárdenas Michoacán began the process of breaking up *latifundia* and distributing the land among the peasants. This movement, however, began too late and never exceeded what the central government was willing to tolerate—a controlled and limited redistribution of hacienda lands. Since no specific research has been done on the subject, we know little about the haciendas that were broken up: whether they consented to the expropriation or were forced to it; whether they lost all their lands or only part of them; and, in the case of partial expropriations, whether they gave the peasants their best or worst land. The fact that these expropriations took place after Cárdenas left office and at a relatively slow pace for this type of reform suggests that they were partial and voluntary. If so, they probably were not meant to set a precedent for a systematic and comprehensive divestment of all the haciendas in the state in order to establish a system of small and medium-sized private farms that would compete with or replace the ejido.

Law #75: Towards a New Definition of "the Public Interest"

The moderate nature of agrarian reform in Michoacán was also reflected in Law #75, a piece of legislation sponsored by Cárdenas and enacted on 21 January 1932. This law represented a drastic revision of the 1924 law of expropriation on grounds of public interest (*Ley de Expropriación por Causa de Utilidad Pública*), which was a municipal law with no agrarian significance.[29] In the fervor of the agrarianist awakening that characterized the last year of his governorship, Cárdenas had decided to draft a completely new law that would circumvent all the existing restrictions in both ejidal and other land reform legislation, and permit expropriation based solely on the needs of the petitioner and granted at the governor's discretion, thus bypassing all the potential obstacles of court proceedings.

That law was Law #75, an expropriation law that widened the definition of the public interest to include not only infrastructural requirements, but also the demands of settlement and agricultural development, providing remedies for people unable to benefit from other agrarian legislation. Compensation for expropriated land was spread over 20 years, making the law's aims more easily attainable. The courts were given no role in enforcing the law—a process that took up to 28 days at the most, record speed in the field of agrarian reform—except to adjudge issues connected with the payment of compensation. Instead, the CLA bore primary responsibility for the implementation of the law—an indication of the law's popular-agrarianist orientation. The law provided that all expropriations for public purposes other than settlement (municipal development and infrastructure) must be indemnified within 10 years or less, half the time allowed for expropriations to create private farms. It also allowed any individual to initiate expropriation proceedings "in the public interest" by the simple expedient of sending the state governor a written petition describing the property he or she thought should be expropriated and indicating to what use it should be converted.[30] The state administration, and particularly the man who headed it, gained great power virtually overnight, since the law stipulated: "The only authority competent to recognize, establish, and declare the public interest administratively and to decree the expropriation of the property covered by the present Law is the Governor of the State." By law the governor also stood guarantor for the payment of compensation and was authorized to regulate it.[31]

This draconian law is difficult to reconcile with Cárdenas's usual prudence. He scarcely needed such a law, since all he did with it was to announce, on 18 June 1932, the expropriation of all rural and urban property in the Chilchota valley, in the Zamora district—property that had been abandoned during the Revolution and had been handed over to the local peasants for safekeeping in 1917.[32] The law seemingly heralded a change not in the operative approach to agrarian reform so much as in the concept underlying it—a change emerging in other states of the Republic as well as Michoacán. This was clear from Cárdenas's criticism of the previous law. Law #74, he said, did not "correspond to the social necessities of the moment, . . . nor [did it] reflect the relevant provisions of Article 27 of the General Constitution of the Republic. . . ."[33] The law was not intended for enforcement, but rather to reinforce and support the local administration's authority to expropriate land for private farming on the basis of other laws designed for the purpose.

From this perspective, the definition of "the public interest" contained in the law was its most significant aspect. Such a definition was vital, since, as mentioned, the central government had not as yet provided one. The new law also served as a safety net for all those who could not benefit from either the ejidal reform or reform based on private ownership, offering them yet another means of obtaining land. It should therefore be seen more as a conceptual and moral framework for reform than a law focused on actual operative goals. In fact, Cárdenas relied on manipulative tactics to block all land petitions based on the new law and to divert them into the usual channels of agrarian reform—possibly with a warning to the owners of the land that if they were uncooperative the government would be forced to expropriate their holdings directly on the basis of Law #75.

Thus, Law #75 had a clear political purpose: to deter *hacendados* from obstructing agrarian reform, particularly the ejidal reform. Faced with the constant threat of direct and speedy expropriation under the terms of Law #75, landowners naturally were quick to part with a little of their land for the benefit of neighbors living within a radius of seven kilometers, thereby earning peace and security in the form of certificates of inaffectability for the remainder of their land. Ironically, the mere existence of a law that Cárdenas's personality and political purposes would not allow him to use created the conditions for the speedy completion of the agrarian reform in Michoacán.

The *hacendados*, however, did not trouble to analyze Cárdenas's motives, and, together with their similarly placed counterparts in Hidalgo and Veracruz, they appealed to President Ortiz Rubio. The latter urged the federal Congress to demand amendments to the radical laws enacted in the three states. Tejeda, as usual, ignored the congressional command, but

Cárdenas, predictably, cooperated, and on 28 June 1932 he presented the local Congress with a draft amendment transferring all the powers he had assumed to the Congress.[34] The conservative Benigno Serrato went one step further; on 27 June 1933, he introduced a law of his own that canceled Law #75, thereby returning Michoacán to the 1924 status quo for all practical purposes.[35]

Undoubtedly Cárdenas seriously intended to promote the creation of private smallholdings. This was the reason that he sent out circulars and distributed posters informing the public about the new provisions governing expropriation, and the reason that he began to collect land petitions from groups and individuals and to plan the expropriation of several large haciendas. It was also what had motivated him to introduce Law #75, which was intended as a spur to agrarian reform. In this context, the restitution of the forest land to the Indians was also highly significant. The operation on behalf of the Indians, in conjunction with the legislation relating to ejidal and individual land reform, represented the creation in Michoacán of a more integral agrarianism, capable of providing more solutions than in the past to the problems of the *campesinos*. Nonetheless, the decision to expand the reform came too late except as far as the Indians were concerned to effect any substantial change in land tenure in the state. The reform did not even begin until Cárdenas noted a change in the federal center's attitude to private-land reform—the change that would result in the campaign to eradicate ejidal agrarianism. It is a fairly safe assumption that Cárdenas would not have embraced this type of reform if it had not been endorsed by the center. He was not built to break down walls in an edifice so delicate.

Despite his adoption of alternative routes of agrarian reform, Cárdenas remained a great believer in the ejido. He believed that it could provide answers to all the needs of both the peasants and the national economy, if only certain improvements were made with respect to the size of the land parcel assigned to each peasant, eligibility requirements (to allow the inclusion of *peones acasillados*), the speed of implementation, and additional factors such as credit, water use, technical assistance, mechanization, cooperative organization, and so on.

In addition, the ejido offered Cárdenas definite political benefits in his campaign for the presidency, since it was an excellent tool for winning the massive public support that Cárdenas needed. All he had to do was promote the ejidal reform, using threatening laws like Law #75 as prods. In his valedictory speech as governor, Cárdenas explained himself by saying that he had not enacted Law #75 in order to create any kind of "radical conditions" (as the conservative press had claimed), but only to establish "the legal channel for the universal right [to land]."[36] He intended to implement that universal right primarily by means of ejidal agrarianism, as long as it was integrative, purposeful, and efficient. Serrato's subsequent amendment of the law reflected the federal government's contrary view that the ejido had to be suppressed.

On the Way to Another Revolution: The Creation of Private Smallholdings in Veracruz

Workers and Peasants in a Definitive Battle over Property

Although Michoacán made significant strides in alternative means of agrarian reform, its efforts were puny in comparison with what was going on in Veracruz. Veracruz was the scene of a political drama that made waves throughout Mexico. Whereas in Michoacán Cárdenas he had initiated all the non-ejidal reform measures, in Veracruz the initiative for most supplementary legislation, particularly the more radical laws, came from the Agrarian League. Later, the CROM joined its efforts to push the administration into still more radical projects, which culminated in the declaration of all property in the state, even property devoted to personal use, as expropriatable assets. This radicalization was akin to a second revolution, bringing the state to the brink of socialism, or an elimination of the gap between labor and capital.

The Veracruz administration was adamantly hostile not only to capitalism, but also to the PNR, which, in its view, had betrayed the Revolution in order to cuddle up with foreign interests and the Mexican bourgeoisie. In its demonization of the PNR the agrarianists again found a loyal partner in the CROM, with which it happily joined forces to promote the cause of turning Veracruz into a state of workers and peasants—a cause completely contrary to the PNR's integrative vision. In this respect, it is crucial to analyze Veracruz's "home-grown" supplementary measures of agrarian reform in terms of the Tejedist ideology and to examine their importance as a new revolutionary alternative.

The Birth of the Tenant Movement (1929–1930)

Individual land distribution in Veracruz began innocuously enough giving no indication of the direction it would take. Tejeda already had at his disposal Law #3 of 1898 on expropriations in the public interest, which generally resembled the parallel Michoacán law of 1924. Law #3 permitted expropriations for municipal purposes with immediate compensation. Decree #355 (6 July 1922) amended the 1898 law in order to address the tenancy problem, which was particularly severe in the city of Veracruz. This decree declared it to be in the public interest to expropriate urban properties for the benefit of the workers of the city of Veracruz (and, in theory, workers in other cities as well), most of whom, for lack of comfortable and inexpensive housing, lived, "to the shame not only of the city but also of the State and even the entire Nation, in foul shacks or in the so-called '*patios*,' which are perhaps even worse, given the incredible number . . . of people housed in each one . . . these '*patios*' or shacks constitute a focus of infection that is a constant danger to public health."[37]

Despite the amendments introduced by Decree #355, up until 1928 enforcement of the law was completely inadequate relative to the magnitude of the housing problem.[38] Tejeda, however, got the ball rolling, and at top speed. Soon expropriation orders were being issued on the basis of Law #3 and its 1922, 1925, and 1926 amendments and extensions against many city properties for the purpose of expanding factories and building hundreds of workers' housing projects in Veracruz, Jalapa, and Minatitlán. To justify this wave of expropriations, Tejeda remarked that landlords neither built housing for workers nor allowed others to do so, since it was to their personal advantage to keep rents high.[39]

Tejeda did more than simply enforce this law, however. To ease the burden of the debts the workers incurred in building their new homes, Tejeda declared a three-year moratorium on their debts by means of Decree # 38 (23 January 1929). Five months later, on 18 June, he extended this moratorium for two more years by means of Decree #108. The new decree represented a fierce attack on speculative capital in general—capital that, in Tejeda's view, put "a large part of society in oppressive conditions, to the benefit of a minority dedicated to accumulating small fortunes by means of speculation and in conditions that cannot be considered moral."[40] Decree #108 also extended the moratorium to the owners of individual smallholdings in rural areas, where borrowers had a particularly difficult time owing to the custom of concluding agreements orally and changing them to the disadvantage of the borrower when the time came to pay, or imposing draconian penalties on delinquent payers.

On 2 July 1929, Tejeda made another leap forward in implementing constitutional Article 27—the quintessential expression of the primacy of collective interests over private ones—when he presented the local Congress with a draft law governing the expropriation of private city plots for the purpose of building worker housing. Designed as a comprehensive solution to the rental problem, Law #118 permitted any individual to request a plot of land on which to build a house for himself. Permanent residents in the area and household heads of either sex, provided they were Mexican by birth, were given preference. They paid for the land in accordance with the usual terms of constitutional Article 27—over a period of 20 years at most, at a yearly interest rate of 5%.[41]

Law #118, which took effect on 20 July, did not address the issue of land reform in the country. It was apparently too early, in the current state of Tejeda's power, status, and ideological views, to promote such a law, although the issue was constantly present, and was even examined in the local paper, *El Dictamen*, on 13 May. The article, headlined "Break-up and Sale of Land in the State," noted that the government would soon present for approval in Congress a new draft law that would permit the expropriation of state lands and unused private lands in order to foster small-scale agriculture in the state.[42] That draft law was not, in fact, forthcoming. At the time, Tejeda was concentrating on the rental problem, since some sort of solution was important for his support base in the struggle for control of the city of Veracruz, as well as to alleviate the great sufferings of the workers there, occasioned by what he termed the "expanding" world economic crisis.[43]

On 11 January 1930, Tejeda amended Law #118 in order to adapt it to the demands of the Veracruz city labor unions. The amendments lowered the interest rate to 3%; canceled various duties on the transfer to the workers of properties expropriated by the state; permitted organized workers to file group petitions for urban plots and, by giving them priority, recognized their legal status, both at the time of the petition and in the ensuing years of repayment; defined the minimum size of a city lot suitable for construction as 100 square meters (with a maximum of 700 square meters); prohibited prostitution, alcohol sales, and other questionable occupations within the precincts of the worker neighborhoods build on expropriated land; and ordered the closure of any such businesses already operating within three months—a requirement that gave the organized workers de facto control over their neighborhoods.[44] In May the workers' problems were alleviated still further with the cancellation of surcharges (up to 50% of the property's value) on lots facing on main streets. The fact that many of the lots fell into this category made expropriation almost impossible for the workers, Tejeda explained in the preamble to Decree #264 (27 May 1930), thereby injuring the very class that the law was designed to assist.[45]

A year and a half after taking office, Tejeda had revolutionized urban expropriations. For the first time, the workers—particularly organized workers—had become the focus of legislation. As mentioned earlier, Tejeda had never seen himself as a labor leader; but he felt he owed the workers his support as part of his general commitment to "the proletariat." This commitment was expressed in Decree #264, which was wholly and solely designed to provide for the tenancy needs of organized workers. Although up to May 1930, Tejeda confined his expropriation efforts to the urban sector his radical proceedings there represented a first stage in the process of making land reform a universal value, relevant to city and country dwellers alike. Yet he made no unbridled attack on private property as such; in fact, he was careful to protect it as long as it was used fairly. When landlords petitioned him for tax relief on account of losses they had incurred as a result of the tenants' strike in 1922 and the Aguirre revolt in 1923, he granted exemptions immediately.[46]

Extending Land Reform to Rural Property (1930–1931)

On 22 July 1930, Tejeda changed tack by passing Law #323 concerning expropriation in the public interest. This law revoked the 1898 law and all the post-revolutionary additions and amendments governing rental housing, and provided a legal infrastructure for expropriating private rural land in addition to urban land. Its aim was to provide land for all who needed it, whether in the city or in the country, for housing or for agricultural purposes. Law #323 was the first significant step in the radicalization of Tejeda's land reform program.

This law, however, gave no special status to organized peasants and workers; applicants were all treated strictly as individuals, and to enjoy the benefits of the law they were obliged to prove they possessed enough money to invest in the assets for which they were applying. They also had to prove that the expropriation requested was essential to the public interest. Moreover, despite the law's express aim of expediting the expropriation process, it entrusted the courts with the job of determining the amount of compensation, its mode of payment, and the procedure for handing the property over to the new owners—a perfect recipe for red tape. It is unlikely that exempting "notably urgent" (*notoriamente urgentes*) cases from this procedure went very far towards remedying the problem.[47]

This abdication to the court reflected Tejeda's realistic assessment of the limits of his own political power and his realization that at that stage he could not afford to disregard or circumvent the judiciary. At the end of 1931, when he was in a much stronger position, Tejeda cancelled the litigants' obligation to appear in court as a condition for authorization of the administration's expropriation decisions. In this way he deprived the *latifundistas* of a great advantage which they had exploited to the full, since they had been able to prevent the expropriation of their assets by simply failing to appear in court.[48]

The growing power of Tejeda and the Veracruz Agrarian League as the municipio elections of September 1931 approached, together with the maturation of Tejeda's general ideology during this period, encouraged him to venture still further into the province of individual land reform. He went ahead with a law designed specifically to create smallholdings, which replaced the problematic Aguilar Law of 1918 and amplified Law #323.

The original impetus for this law had been an official appeal from the Agrarian League to Tejeda on 2 December 1930, asking him to legislate for a new enabling law to create small farms. According to the League, not one of the admittedly numerous expropriations carried out on the basis of the Aguilar Law ever ended with the delivery of a deed of ownership, meaning that the expropriation could be canceled at any moment. This dismal situation, claimed Agrarian League representatives, could be attributed to the vagueness of the Aguilar Law's provisions concerning compensation. Accordingly, Manuel Almanza, the League president, suggested that Tejeda expedite the enactment of the new law, since "it is on any account vital that the property rights of peasants benefiting from expropriations be guaranteed before the Law and Society, thereby ending all the difficulty caused them by the landowners who continue to believe that they will regain their former domains."[49]

The letter from the League noted three important points. First, the 1918 law gave rise to problems not at the actual stage of expropriation and provisional delivery of the land to the peasants, but at the stage of registering title to the land. This situation offered landowners considerable scope for exerting pressure, while the peasants had no security concerning the property they received. Second, although the initiative to change the law had been presented in December 1930, the government was dragging its feet; and third, the League itself fervently supported the principle of giving land to peasants on the basis of private ownership, seeing it as an important tool for promoting agrarian reform.

In June 1931, Tejeda found the courage to push the desired law forward. In the letter he enclosed with the draft law that he submitted to the Congress at the end of the month, he justified the initiative as follows:

> My office, in accordance with its aim of creating small farms in the State as quickly as possible, establishing them on the firmest bases of equity and justice and thereby fulfilling the postulates of the Revolution as expressed in Article 27 of our Magna Carta, considers this to be the right time to issue a new Law to promote smallholdings . . .

He then repeated the League's arguments and promised that the proposed law would address not only the problem of compensation, which prevented peasants from acquiring title to the land, but also the issues of access to modern agricultural equipment after expropriation, advanced farming techniques, and cooperative labor organization, the aim being to promote agriculture as a "source of national wealth that should be the object, as it is in Veracruz, of delicate care." Tejeda also noted that the new law would establish a local agrarian credit fund designed to finance compensation, easing the burden on the federal government. The institution of this entity, he said, was based on the federal law passed on 7 January 1925, which authorized states to establish such funds and to "issue laws facilitating the break-up of *latifundia* that, owing to special circumstances, have evaded the application of the *Ley de Dotaciones y Restituciones de Tierras y Aguas* [Law of Endowments and Restitution of Lands and Water—the ejidal law]."[50]

Thus, for Tejeda the proposed law was not merely a means of creating private smallholdings, but also a tool for breaking up the *latifundia* that had managed to avoid ejidal expropriation, whether legally or illegally. The wording of the law supports this interpretation, since it obliged all owners of more than 75 irrigated hectares or 200 hectares of agriculturally unproductive land to divide their land up into units measuring up to 50 hectares within 180 days and to offer them for sale, payment to be stretched over 30 years (!) at an interest rate of only 3%. If the big landowners refused to comply with these conditions, the state would sell their land for them, handing it over to peasants in exchange for 30-year bonds with an interest rate of 4%.[51] In addition, priority was to be given to the best plots in terms of soil quality, climate, territorial contiguity, and infrastructure in order to reduce to a minimum the investment in money and labor required to prepare them for use. Priority would also be given to land that had hitherto been used for crops with a lower "social value" than the crops that the petitioners planned to grow.

The law was not intended for the sole benefit of impoverished *campesinos*; it was also meant to assist moderately prosperous farmers, as long as the value of their properties did not exceed 5,000 pesos and their monthly income was no more than 500 pesos. These were very high figures, compared with a teacher's wage, which averaged 60 pesos a month in the country and 100 pesos in the city. The law gave priority to collective petitions from organized groups of at least 10 people, since the government wanted to encourage cooperative organization and efficient use of public aid. This provision was reminiscent of the similar discrimination in favor of organized tenants made by Law #240 of January 1930. The recipients of expropriated land were exempted from all local and state taxes for a period of one year, and enjoyed complete protection from any subsequent expropriation as long as they paid their debt to the state treasury. In exceptional cases of *force majeure*, the government waived even this condition, unless the *campesino* left the area indefinitely for no compelling reason or without government permission.

Although Law #269 was radical, it nevertheless conformed to the provisions of Law #323 in giving the courts the final authority to transfer assets after the determination of compensation—a stipulation guaranteed to delay the expropriation process, particularly since the courts, being ill-disposed to the law, were quick to accord *amparo*. On one occasion, while ruling on a petition for *amparo* brought by the owners of the Cuautlapan hacienda in the Ixtaczoquitlán municipio, the court declared the law to be unconstitutional both with respect to the dimensions of land exempted from expropriation and in its encouragement of *latifundistas* to break up their estates voluntarily even if those particular lands were not really needed. The presiding judge was Manuel Bartlett, the critical, meticulous, and independent district judge of the city of Veracruz, who at the time was also in the thick of the Church's struggle against Tejeda's draconian Law #197.[52]

Under the circumstances, Tejeda was obliged to amend Law #269. On 19 October 1931, the maximum reserve that could be exempted from expropriation was increased to 200 hectares—even more, if the excess were proved to be under cultivation; the practice of automatically parceling out all private lands was stopped, and expropriation was limited to land that was specifically needed.[53] At the same time, to make Laws #269 and #323 easier to enforce, Tejeda initiated a new property-tax law in September 1931, that analyzed every detail of landed property in the state, establishing the criteria for an exact determination of property values and hence the amount of compensation required for expropriation.[54] Interestingly, despite the wide variety of possibilities Law #269 offered for expropriation, it did not attract any attention in the national press, and very little in the local press. Even the American consul, who was sensitive to any kind of attack on private property and normally reported to Washington at length on any legislation of this kind, did not take much interest. In his 21-page report for September 1931, he devoted only a few lines to the subject.[55] Despite its content, the amended Law #269 was considered to reflect a consensus.

The enforcement of the law produced visible results. From the time Tejeda took office up to the enactment of Law #269, only two parcels of land had been expropriated to create smallholdings, one at the end of March and one at the end of April in 1931, for a total area of 546 hectares.[56] In contrast, from the time of the law's enactment up to the end of Tejeda's term, it was enforced on 13 occasions, to expropriate a total of 13,043 hectares.[57] The area expropriated was not, objectively speaking, particularly large, but Tejeda saw it as a great accomplishment, particularly in view of the fact that "the predicted crop yields of the *colonos* [the beneficiaries of the reform] have not only been met, but surpassed." In his view, this was solid proof that in the agrarian sphere his government was taking correct and effective measures "for the satisfactory resolution of the problem of unemployed workers in the Republic." The successful implementation of the law, said Tejeda, provided strength and motivation for continuing to implement it.[58]

Crossing the Rubicon: Towards Total Agrarianism (June 1932)

The most dramatic move in the field of agrarian reform was made on 31 May 1932, when the Veracruz Congress legislated for a complete socialization of private property in the state. Again the initiative came from the Agrarian League, beginning with a bill drafted by all 14 congressional deputies, most of whom were prominent leaders and members of the League. In the preamble to their proposal, the deputies made a fierce but reasoned attack on the accumulation of wealth in its various forms and the cynical and speculative use made of it in Mexico. Capital, they concluded, could not be relied upon; instead, the state must be given the responsibility of acquiring assets for the good of all. In this way, they claimed, the full potential of wealth would be exploited, and the economic crisis—artificially induced, in their view, by the speculative activity of local and foreign private capitalists—would disappear.[59]

The parliamentary draft law which these deputies presented to the Congress declared it to be in the public interest to expropriate all agricultural, industrial, commercial, and other assets "regardless of their size and organization" under certain circumstances, including strikes, poor management, underdevelopment and neglect of equipment, waste of raw materials, and injury to workers' rights or income. Expropriation would be admissible for all productive tools and installations used in farming, industry, and fishing, including storage and refrigeration facilities, housing, and the like which stood idle or in ruins without any prospect of rehabilitation, productive use, or rental as workers' housing. Also eligible for expropriation were urban and rural properties that had lost their fiscal value; rented houses for which the tenants had already paid an accumulated rent of more than 133% of the property's value; and all accumulation on capital deriving from its use for loans at an interest rate exceeding 2% per month. The draft law described the task of locating all these kinds of properties and many others as an *acción popular* ("grassroots action") that would lead to their expropriation and sale under conditions very advantageous to the workers actually employed on these holdings, who would organize in cooperatives.[60]

The law's broad interpretation of the concept of public interest strongly reflected the Veracruz labor leaders' rejection of the idea that post-revolutionary Mexico might achieve social justice and class equality on liberal or neo-liberal foundations. This position had been part of the local Agrarian League's platform since 1924, but now Tejeda had adopted it as well.[61] The radicalization of the Tejeda administration, the serious repercussions of the world economic crisis on the Veracruz economy, and the marked decline in labor's bargaining power against capital all helped create the conditions for the League, the labor movement, and the government to join forces in enacting a socialistic legislative initiative. This powerful coalition was essential to extend the principles of constitutional Article 27 governing rural property to property in general as a preparation for the complete socialization of property in Veracruz.

Tejeda responded to this new challenge just as he had with Law #269. Only four days after receiving a copy of the Congress's proposal he came up with a draft law of his own governing expropriation in the public interest. His law, he wrote, incorporated all the same basic principles and ideas as the legislature's draft.[62] Apparently preferring to appear as a leader rather than a follower in this sensitive sphere, he pointed out that Veracruz already had several expropriation laws, which were often used to build municipal housing projects for workers, to establish urban zones (*fundos legales*) in various communities, to break up *latifundia*, and for many other purposes. The new law, he said, would combine all these purposes under one rubric, and by defining property more generally it would expand immeasurably the possibilities of expropriation.

Containing only three articles, the draft law he presented was much shorter than the legislature's proposal, but it was equally trenchant. The first article made all types of property susceptible to expropriation for reasons of *utilidad social* ("social utility," replacing the notion of "the public interest"). In the second article Tejeda defined the concept of "social utility": From now on, the benefits of expropriation in the public interest would be enjoyed not only by the state, the municipios, and the citizenry in the broad sense, but also the state's labor and peasant organizations in their capacity as organizations. In the third article, Tejeda described in the same terms as the parliamentary draft law the various configurations of "social property" that would be eligible for expropriation.[63]

The third article contained an interesting innovation that reflected the generally socialistic orientation of the law. Along with the concept of "sources of wealth" (*fuentes de riqueza*), enshrined in Article 27 of the constitution and various pieces of agrarian legislation, it spoke of "sources of labor" (*fuentes de trabajo*) as affectable for expropriation. In using this term to cover the range of expropriatable assets enumerated in the parliamentary draft, Tejeda gave the word "wealth" its Marxist interpretation as the product of labor rather than nature, a product that consequently had a deep social significance, particularly for those who created it: the workers and peasants.[64] On 31 May 1932 the Veracruz legislature passed Tejeda's law in its entirety as Law #66, although it replaced the concept of "social utility" with the old and "safer" phrase of "the public interest."[65]

The next task was to adapt Law #323 to the social orientation of Law #66. Law #323 still provided the legal basis for assessing indemnities for expropriated assets, and it governed the procedure for handing the property over to the beneficiaries. In ten closely printed pages sent to the Congress on 30 June 1932, Tejeda clarified the factors that in his view mandated a change in Law #323. The provisions of Law #323, he said, in fact constituted an obstacle to organized workers and peasants, because neither the workers nor their organizations, "always lacking resources," were able to display in advance the "means necessary for the work they intended to carry out [on the expropriated property]," nor could they make a preliminary deposit on the compensation owing to the original owners of the property, as required by the law.[66]

Tejeda devoted most of his letter, however, to the question of the relations between the executive and the judiciary during the implementation of expropriation procedures in the public interest. He recognized the contradiction implicit in the executive's being empowered to order an expropriation but not to enforce it. This contradiction, he noted, in fact derived from the gap between Article 27 of the constitution, which entrusted the expropriation procedure to the executive authority, and Article 14, which stated that only the judiciary was authorized to divest a person of property, liberties, or life. The federal Supreme Court was aware of this contradiction, Tejeda wrote, and accepted the thesis that in any conflict between a private interest and a collective one the executive authority would take precedence over the court. The court would decide all issues involved in determining compensation, but would have nothing to do with the actual processes of expropriation and property transfer, which derived their legal status from the administrative order of expropriation.[67]

Tejeda believed that all the time wasted because of the court's heavy involvement in the expropriation process abused the spirit of the law, eliminating the social benefit it was "designed to produce."[68] Accordingly, he suggested a new procedure to deal with the proliferation of *amparo* proceedings. Under the terms of his proposal, landowners wishing to appeal against the expropriation of their property would have to submit a petition to the governor within five days from the day the expropriation decision was published before they could apply for relief from the court. This, he believed, would prevent hasty, systematic applications for *amparo* that bypassed the governor.[69]

This batch of amendments was incorporated in Law #119 of 4 July 1932. The new law gave preference to organized workers and peasants, and cancelled the court's jurisdiction over expropriation proceedings. The court now retained only the power to assess the property's value for purposes of compensation.[70] Moreover, Tejeda again included a procedure for expropriation on "notably urgent" grounds, which gave the governor the authority, in cases he deemed urgent, to expropriate any property and transfer it to those who needed it (probably organized peasants and workers) by means of an accelerated five-day procedure. This provision caught the attention of the US consul in Veracruz, who wrote with some asperity to Washington: "It is considered locally that the majority of cases will be considered 'notably urgent.'"[71]

The enabling law for Law #66, enacted on 22 July 1932, reaffirmed the preferential treatment that Law #66 extended to unionized workers and peasants. It also provided that until the beneficiaries of the law had paid their debt to the state for the asset they had received as an organized group, the governor would be entitled to intervene in their internal affairs—for example, in questions of financing and professional guidance—whether the workers or peasants were organized in cooperatives or not. During that period they would enjoy possession of the asset, but not title to it. This provision consolidated state control of organized labor as a means both of advancing social welfare and of serving the future political needs of Tejeda himself.[72]

The end of all this legislative evolution was expressed in an interesting letter that Tejeda sent to General Juan José Ríos, the interior minister, with the obvious intention of mollifying the fierce criticism he expected from the political center, particularly with respect to the law's constitutionality.[73] Law #66, he explained to the interior minister, while completely faithful to existing constitutional principles, also answered the need for a short, swift, and logical administrative procedure that would make "the benefits of the law in question accessible to the proletarian classes in particular." He then appealed to the minister's "broad, firm, revolutionary viewpoint," which was "undoubtedly one of his outstanding qualities," and expressed his hope that the minister would appreciate the sincere efforts of the Veracruz administration.[74]

The "Tejeda Law" Undergoes the Test of Public Opinion

The letter to General Ríos and other public-relations efforts were not enough to silence criticism of what the American consul in Veracruz called "nothing more or less than high-way robbery."[75] Although the "Tejeda law" aroused great enthusiasm among unionists and agrarianists, who took the opportunity to attack capitalist "plutagogues," false revolutionaries, and the PNR ("that party devoid of revolutionary principles"),[76] it also provoked great consternation in the political center and the conservative public. Dozens of newspaper articles denounced the law, on three grounds: its constitutionality, its economic logic, and its social motives. Its critics were unanimous in their belief that it went much further than was warranted by constitutional Article 27 and the legal interpretations and precedents that had built up around Article 27 over the years. This sort of law, said the critics, threatened to turn Mexico into a communist, Leninist, or Soviet state (as it was variously described by the press), or, alternatively, into a duplicate of the "feudal satrapies of the more backward states in ancient Asia."

The critics also objected to the law on economic grounds, expressing fear of a cessation of local and foreign investments, a drop in the value of the Mexican currency, and a deep economic depression. Moreover, they argued, such a drastic law was not required in order to put Veracruz's affairs in order and prevent a decline in workers' living conditions. The governments of other states, such as Nuevo León, México, Yucatán, and San Luis Potosí, had managed to cope with similar crises without such extreme laws. Virtually all the detractors concluded that the law was motivated by political and dogmatic ideological considerations more than economic ones, considerations rooted in Tejeda's own "Soviet" views and his ultimate political aspirations which would not allow him to lag behind Vargas Lugo, the governor of Hidalgo, who had also sponsored a radical expropriation law.[77]

These arguments, of course, might have been correct if the man in question had not been someone with Tejeda's outlook. To him, this law was neither a means of furthering his bid for the presidency nor an ideological aberration, but a direct continuation of the ideological development he had undergone since 1931—a development based on the realization that the situation of the Mexican peasant would not improve in any substantial respect unless rural land reform was extended to include all types of property. Accordingly, Tejeda, the state legislature, and Veracruz's parliamentary delegation to the federal legislature all stood firm under the rain of criticism, resisting even the heavy pressure that President Ortiz Rubio brought to bear against Tejeda—and against Vargas Lugo in Hidalgo and Cárdenas in Michoacán.[78] Tejeda embarked on a public relations campaign in which he presented the law as an unavoidable but completely legal emergency measure. The irresponsible behavior of capital, he explained, had created an unbearable situation in which workers, who by organizing had achieved "a level of dignity that allowed them to live as human beings, part of the culture and civilization demanded by the Revolution by means of its laws," were left with nothing. Under these circumstances, the government was compelled to order the expropriation of factories and their transfer to those who worked in them, relying on the moral and professional maturity of the Veracruz working people and the state's successful experiences with cooperatives in running the electric light and power companies of Jalapa and the city of Veracruz, a number of flour mills in those same cities, consumer cooperatives in the industrial zones of Jalapa and Orizaba, and "to a lesser degree, in a number of ejidos."[79]

Moreover, Tejeda claimed, comparison of Article 27 with its counterparts in the constitutions of Germany, Ireland, Romania, Yugoslavia, and Spain showed these countries to be much more radical than Mexico in agrarian issues. This led him to argue that the expropriation laws (including Law #66) transcended Mexico's specific interests with universal messages for humankind in general.[80] The spokespersons of the local Congress made similar statements in the course of a public-relations campaign paralleling Tejeda's own.[81]

The Veracruz, Michoacán, and Hidalgo delegations to the federal legislature defended expropriation even more fiercely. In their view, the expropriation laws of their respective states conformed to "the contemporary legal doctrine that invests property with a social value," and were paralleled by similar laws in countries considered moderate that had not undergone revolutions, such as Germany and Czechoslovakia. Such laws, they said, did not justify the anxiety about "radicalism" that had developed in Mexico and that capitalists were purposely and artificially inflating in their efforts to do away with Law #66. In addition, the members of the three delegations heatedly protested that the federal constitution was not sufficiently progressive and no longer answered the social needs of the times, and that it should be amended to meet the demands of the Mexican people. This was the first glimmer of an acknowledgement that the Mexican constitution, in its accepted interpretation, was by 1932 no longer relevant to the peasants and workers.[82]

While Law #66 ran a gauntlet of *amparo* proceedings in the courts, Carlos Dario Ojeda, the activist federal deputy from Veracruz, defended Tejeda against his critics, insisting, "Tejeda is not a communist."[83] On 17 June, Ortiz Rubio sent a circular to all the state governors asking them not to enact controversial laws that might be misinterpreted and undermine faith in Mexico's political and economic system.[84] This missive prompted a wave of solidarity from many governors, who expressed support for the government's position and the principles of the existing constitution, and promised to behave.[85] Ortiz Rubio's well-wishers included Cárdenas and Vargas Lugo, who were already busy toning down their own expropriation laws.[86]

The president's campaign, aided by *Excelsior,* was effective. Tejeda was completely isolated, the only governor left with a radical expropriation law—which he could hardly amend at that point, after all his resolute declarations and successful mobilization of support in local and national political circles. He was equally unmoved by the president's letter and by talks with Calles, Ortiz Rubio, and the ministers of the interior, the treasury, and foreign affairs. His letter in response to Ortiz was submissive and polite, but "vague," as *Excelsior* put it. In it, he reiterated his firm views concerning the need for Law #66, enumerating the economic factors that had led him to introduce the law, his sense that he had a mission to defend the working class, an ideological commitment to the proletariat in general. This commitment, he explained, derived from his interpretation of the Revolution (as a proletarian revolution) and of the constitution (as the legal formulation of the government's political and moral commitment to the working class).[87]

The publication of the enabling law for Law #66 at the end of July was confirmation that Tejeda did not intend to back down. He continued to go his own way, as he did in every controversial issue that arose during his tenure, largely unperturbed by both his isolation and the political price he was bound to pay. Trapped by his own extremism, he would have found it difficult to comply with the president's wishes even had he wanted to. His political flexibility was severely limited by the inextricable linkage he had established in both law and concept between expropriation in the public interest (Law #66) and expropriation to create small farms (Law #269), since he could not now renounce one without the other.

The real winner in all this was the Agrarian League, which was responsible for Tejeda's predicament. In this situation, where the League was the initiator (thanks to the free rein Tejeda gave it) but Tejeda bore the consequences, any attempt at retreat on his part would compromise his reputation and prove futile in any case, given the League's power and influence. The League, as the faithful voice of the people, was almighty. Another factor that reduced Tejeda's maneuvering ability was his ambivalence towards the PNR, since to keep the PNR in check he needed the support of the CROM. The CROM had its own good reasons for supporting Tejeda's law, since the law favored it as an organization, as well as alleviating the misery of urban workers. Any retreat in this respect would have undermined the support Tejeda received from the Agrarian League for his agrarian policy and lose him the CROM's backing in his campaign for the presidency. All these considerations were ultimately negligible, however, since Tejeda's conduct previous to the enactment of Law #66 was a clear indication that he would have adhered to his principles in any case, though they ended up isolating him completely among Mexican politicians and pitched him into a feud with the worried federal government.

Despite the criticism, Law #66 went into effect. However, like Law #75 in Michoacán, it was actually enforced on only a few occasions, almost none of them involving rural properties. Of roughly 80 expropriations carried out in 1932, most of them to free urban land to build schools or workers' housing, only one case mentioned Law #66, and even then it was in conjunction with Law #323.[88]

The law itself was used to expropriate a small number of properties, such as an abandoned radio station which was to be used to broadcast Agrarian League and LNCUG propaganda and educational programs; 55 urban land parcels, "derelict and overrun with mosquitoes" (the owners claimed the land was a coconut plantation), in Boca del Río, south of the city of Veracruz, which were to be used for worker housing; and, in the Jalapa area, a medium-sized textile factory (La Paz Textil) employing 124 workers that had closed but was to be reopened as a cooperative.[89] Inevitably, however, the owners of this factory, like those of other urban and rural assets expropriated under Law #66, managed to obtain a court order for its return at the end of November that same year.[90]

Although it was so sparingly used, the law inspired deep anxiety in property owners, who feared that their property would be summarily confiscated with no possibility of defense—what the belligerent *Excelsior* called "a definitive death blow."[91] These fears were reinforced by the anti-oligarchic unrest that had gripped the masses in towns such as Altotonga, Huatusco, and Tlapacoyan, but particularly in the city of Veracruz, which was waiting for its day of reckoning with "*los ricos*" (the rich). Large posters that the various workers' unions had put up around the city, declaring support for Law #66 and promising that "the wealth possessed, unjustly, by the rich" would soon be expropriated added to the general tension. Another source of anxiety was the rumor that a rally held at Altotonga by supporters of the law, in the presence of the governor-elect, Vásquez Vela, would be calling for *"socialización de las tierras y las industrias"* ("socialization of land and industry").[92]

The feeling prevailing in financial circles was that a revolution was brewing in Veracruz. This fear led the various chambers of commerce, supported by the Confederación de Cámaras de Comercio (Confederation of Chambers of Commerce), to close ranks and do all they could to undermine the law, fully supported in their efforts by a worried federal administration. One major step was the federal government's decision to offer substantial tax rebates to large companies, including the petroleum companies of Veracruz, and to provide guarantees for private property. This policy was designed to undercut Law #66, since it meant assets could not be expropriated on account of delinquent tax payment or previous debt accumulation, two of the main grounds for expropriation under the Tejeda law.[93]

Although the latifundist oligarchy and the commercial bourgeoisie did manage to neutralize Law #66 to some extent, Veracruz was nevertheless the scene of an unprecedented surge of expropriations during Tejeda's last two years in office, as shown in Table 5.1. The table shows that 85% of the decisions to expropriate were made in the last two years of Tejeda's governorship. At the same time, the average dimensions of each expropriated property were growing as well, reaching their peak in the last two years.

Table 5.1 Direct Expropriation of Land and Other Types of Private Property on Grounds of Public Interest in Veracruz, 1929–1932

Year	Number of expropriations	% of total
1929	18	9.2
1930	11	5.6
1931	71	36.2
1932	96	49.0
Total	196	100.0

Source: *Gaceta Oficial*, 1929–1932.

The properties included land for municipal purposes, urban plots for workers' housing and colonies, and parcels for the creation of small farms. Particularly interesting for our purposes was the fact that from August 1931, all expropriations were justified on ideological grounds.

The Motives for Alternative Reform: Between Ideology and Politics

The main motive for the enactment of Law #66 was, in *Excelsior*'s opinion, Tejeda's designs on the presidency. A review of the long route that Tejeda had carefully and consistently plotted from his first days in office up to July 1932, however, indicates the centrality of other motives. Law #66 represented an effort by an idealistic statesman to provide a suitable solution to the problems of the working class. This purpose led him to define property as "social property," whether rural or urban, and as such subject to expropriation, since in his view "society" was proletarian society, and property was the business of the entire proletariat. This view was not based on a logical syllogism but was rather the product of Tejeda's own internal ideological development, a development influenced by the circumstances of Veracruz's history and socioeconomic infrastructure, particularly the deep economic crisis and the battle with the political center over foreign capital and property rights in the state. All factors contributed to Tejeda's attempt to organize a proletarian revolution in Veracruz and even a new, participatory model for Mexican democracy. From that moment Tejeda became a pariah in national politics, inevitably bound for complete political annihilation.

Realistically, if Tejeda had nourished any serious, long-range political aspirations, he would not have quarrelled so determinedly with the federal center. He would certainly not have done so over a law passed at the end of his governorship. His actions were rather an expression of ideological and political belief that challenged the conservative constitutional outlook of the federal government, the feebleness of the battle against capitalism and the economic depression that capitalism had created, and the abandonment of organized labor, urban and rural, in their losing battle against capital. His actions may also have represented a final lament over the betrayal of the Revolution, by someone who knew his political days were numbered. At the same time, Law #66 represented the culmination of the solidarity between Tejeda and his League, and, to a slightly lesser degree, between Tejeda and the other organized labor groups foundering in the morass of the economic crisis.

Law #66, although couched in the phraseology of socialist theory, was in fact a logical response to a difficult and specific economic situation created by the world depression. It was not some product of Jalapa freemasonry, radical for the sake of radicalism. Nor could it be put down to lack of intelligence on Tejeda's part, as the press claimed. Clearly if Tejeda had not truly believed that the socialization and cooperative exploitation of property were the right response to the economic distress in his state and in the country in general, he would not have sought such far-reaching measures. He certainly would not have taken steps guaranteed to cut himself off completely even from his fellow governors (who were anxious not to be identified with him). Instead, he would have contended with Veracruz's problems in the same ways

Table 5.2 Decisions to Expropriate Agricultural and Non-Agricultural Private Assets on the Grounds of Public Interest in Veracruz, 1924–1935

Year	Governor	Number of expropriation decisions	Total decisions by governor
1921–1924	A.Tejeda	3	15*
1925–1928	H. Jara	8	20*
1929–1932	A. Tejeda	196	196
1933–1936	G. Vázquez Vela	40	80*

* Estimated figures.
Source: *Gaceta Oficial*, 1924–1935.

that those other governors had dealt with similar problems, with varying degrees of success.

Law #66, ultimately, reflected one basic truth: Mexico at the beginning of the 1930s did not offer the conditions necessary to implement the social promises of the constitution. Mexico was too firmly established as a bourgeois, class-based state in which property rights were omnipotent and inequality was omnipresent. This realization led Tejeda to institute this last piece of legislation without regard for the little time left him as governor. To those who complained that his actions were unconstitutional, Tejeda answered: Change the constitution! (Indeed in July 1932 the CROM had suggested making the Tejeda law into an article of the constitution.)[94]

Cárdenas never came close to Tejeda's level of activism. His restraint was possible because his focus was on the long term, because the repercussions of the world depression were more lightly felt in Michoacán, and because the CRMDT did what he told it to do. Cárdenas never dreamed of going as far as Tejeda did, because he did not envision Mexico undergoing a class war, but only, at most, a process of class equilibration. This contrast was reflected in the difference between the two men's respective achievements: one, a solid but ultimately limited program of agrarian reform; the other, a soaring ideal that had the potential, at least, to establish social equality in Mexico.

The destruction of Tejeda's power base almost immediately after he left office and the reaction against his agrarian policies cut off the momentum of expropriations in Veracruz (see Table 5.2). The drop in expropriations after he left office was the result not of a change in the laws, but a change in outlook. The total number of expropriations implemented during Vázquez Vela's governorship amounted to only 360 hectares.

Thus, while Tejeda became a national burden, Cárdenas became a national asset. While Tejeda fell from grace in his last year in power, Cárdenas managed to remain in good standing and to make important advances in the political process that would end in the selection of the PNR candidate for the presidency. Political considerations had won out over social ones.

6

The Eradication of Tejeda's Power and the Contest for the Presidency

The Eradication of Tejedism and the Consolidation of Cardenism

The end of Tejeda's governorship was the signal for a mass attack on everything that Tejeda and his administration symbolized. The federal center had had enough of Tejeda; two months before he left office, in October 1932, it had already begun the task of eliminating him. Although its main target was Veracruz, it also destroyed the power bases of at least 12 other outgoing governors—including the governor of Michoacán. The federal government had clearly decided to use the full weight of its authority to rid itself of the radical agrarianist sector, which had entered an accelerated process of politicization and organization in preparation for the approaching presidential election.

In this respect, there was no substantive difference between Michoacán and Veracruz. In both states, excessive independence was curbed by the federal offensive launched by Calles and carried out by his protégé, Abelardo Rodríguez, who was elected provisional president of the Republic by both chambers of the Congress early on September 4, 1932, after Ortiz Rubio's resignation the day before. Veracruz, however, took priority, being the first to be declared as a national emergency; the methods used against it subsequently served as guides for dealing with the other states. Michoacán was of secondary importance. Reflecting this, the onslaught on Veracruz was greater than on Michoacán. Two months after it began, Tejeda, who had relied mainly on a local power base, was left with nothing. Not only had he lost all influence in his state, he could not even find respectable accommodation for himself and his family. Under these circumstances, his attempt to run for the 1934–1940 presidential term was pathetic. Cárdenas, in contrast, having taken the precaution of establishing himself on the national level, not only avoided injury but emerged from the maelstrom stronger than ever. As defense minister in Abelardo Rodríguez's government (beginning on 1 January 1933), he was a senior partner in the federal offensive against Veracruz, and demonstrated remarkable self-control when that same offensive crushed his own power centers in Michoacán. That self-control showed Calles that he could be trusted with the presidency.

The purging of Veracruz took a year or more. Its targets were all the power centers that Tejeda had cultivated during his governorship: the Agrarian League; the municipios, especially that of the city of Veracruz; the agrarianist *guerrilla*; the local PNR institutions under his control; the tenants' movement of the city of Veracruz; the ejidos; the Liga Nacional Campesina Ursulo Galván; the local Congress, which was controlled by the agrarianists; and the Veracruz delegation in the federal Congress. Other targets were the labor movement of Veracruz, with which Tejeda had considerable influence, and, in particular, the local and national branches of the CROM. The federal government used every possible means to destroy these power centers: It broke up organizational frameworks, dismissed employees, encouraged defections and internal divisions, and, through the national press, denounced daily everything that was done in Veracruz, "Tejeda's communist stronghold."

The wide range of participants in this effort guaranteed its success. Besides the army, the ministry of agriculture, and the ministries of the interior and defense, the collaborators recruited for the anti-Tejedist campaign included all the national and local branches of the PNR, Tejeda's adversaries in Veracruz financial and commercial circles, one-time friends whose tastes had changed—such as the new governor of Veracruz, Gonzalo Vázquez Vela, Tejeda's former protégé—and even most of the members of the Veracruz delegation to the federal Congress. Only a few friends stood fast under the heavy pressure—and of those only three were prominent League members: the federal deputies Eugenio Méndez, Carolino Anaya, and Eduardo Cortina. Their loyalty cost them their political careers.

The first step in eliminating "the last redoubt of communism in Mexico" (as *Excelsior* put it) was to parcel out the ejidal lands in Veracruz.[1] At the beginning of October 1932, the engineering staff of the local branch of the CNA was increased by 100 army engineers, dozens of civilian engineers from various government ministries, and engineering students from the national polytechnic. Their mission was to implement President Rodríguez's plan (actually devised by Calles) to parcel out the land of all the 4,000 communal ejidos in the Republic that had already received presidential authorization for their grants but had not yet divided the land among the members as required by the 1925 law of ejido patrimony. A total of 219 military engineers, protected by 6,000 soldiers, were eventually assigned to the project, which was supposed to end the age of "graft and intrigues by *caciques* and local *liderillos* [self-styled leaders]."[2] Although initially it focused primarily on Veracruz, which was seen as most urgent, it was later extended to other states, notably Morelos, Puebla, Chihuahua, Hidalgo, Michoacán, Querétaro, and Guanajuato.[3]

Since the campaign was supposedly part of a nationwide clamp-down on radicalism, Rodríguez was able to begin moving against Tejeda two months before the latter left office on 30 November.[4] At that time dozens of articles appeared in the national press denouncing the communal ejido, which was presented as both, a failure and a primitive, archaic, corrupt, and distorted economic entity. Only parcelization could salvage something of its trampled honor and turn the ejido into a liberated, modern, and successful economic unit. With the exception of protests by the Veracruz Agrarian League and the LNCUG, the project met virtually no opposition,[5] and by the beginning of 1934, the press was able to proclaim the endeavor a success. It was considered a great achievement not because of the (only!) 259 ejidos that had been divided up by the end of 1933, but because many of these *ejidatarios* belonged to the Veracruz Agrarian League. Critics in the conservative national press naturally took the opportunity to point out that land tenancy in the ejidos had not hitherto conformed to the law, and did not reflect true ejidal agrarianism. Instead, the ejidal law was often abused, with land going to politicians (such as Tejeda's followers) instead of to the peasants themselves. Budgetary difficulties ultimately crippled the ejidal land division program, but the federal center did not lose hope of fully implementing it.[6]

The next stage was to eliminate Tejeda's military force, estimated at 20,000–30,000 men (although its exact size was Veracruz's best-kept secret).[7] For this purpose, the communications and public works minister, General Miguel Acosta (who had been military governor of Veracruz up to October 1931, and was unsympathetic to Tejeda), was called back to active military service in mid-December 1932, to lead a task force of some 12,000 soldiers into Veracruz to disarm the agrarianists. Veracruz was declared a single military jurisdiction (instead of three), and the military engineers already in the field coordinated their efforts with those of the army to break up the agrarianist infrastructure more efficiently.

The military operation actually began with Cárdenas's inauguration as minister of war on 1 January 1933. On the 5th of the month, Acosta reported that he had taken command of the expeditionary force, which in the meantime had reached Veracruz, and on the 10th Cárdenas announced the beginning of the campaign. In the name of the president he guaranteed the safety of the peasants, who would be allowed to return to their fields once they had laid down their arms, liberated from "the manipulation of professional agitators." The army, Cárdenas explained, was well able to keep the peace in Mexico, and no additional force was required. All that the president wanted to do was to defend the interests of the peasants.

Cárdenas, on the point of announcing his candidacy for the PNR nomination in the upcoming presidential election, was, as usual, passing up no opportunity to demonstrate his support for the incumbent president, even if by doing so he dealt a substantial blow to his friend Tejeda and to the survival of the agrarianist movement in his own state. His loyalty to the institution of the presidency took precedence over personal friendships and perhaps even ideology.[8] In addition, Cárdenas had greater faith in the federal army than Tejeda did, and strongly identified with it, besides needing its support in his campaign for the presidency.

Like the operation to divide up the ejidal lands, the disarmament operation ran into tough opposition from the Veracruz *guerrilla* forces, which the press described as completely political organizations led by professional propagandists—bandit groups that warped the peasants' minds, instilling hate. Not only did they constitute a "permanent threat" to them, said the press, but they "cut the peasants off from the land and turned Veracruz from . . . a rich state into a poverty-stricken one," having been created not so much to achieve Veracruz's economic and social rehabilitation as to further Tejeda's aspirations to the presidency.[9]

About a year after the disarmament operation began, the PNR party organ reported that the Veracruz agrarianists had been completely disarmed.[10] General Acosta could return to the ministry of communications and public works, and Manuel Parra's Mano Negra was free to reestablish control throughout central Veracruz, where it promptly embarked on a vigorous campaign of revenge against the agrarianists. The local deputies had betrayed the suffering *campesinos*, Tejeda wrote in despair to Deputy Josafat Márquez. The peasants were helpless against soldiers and gangs "like that of Manuel Parra from Almolonga."[11]

The next step was to divide and conquer the Veracruz Agrarian League. President Rodríguez began this process on 11 January 1933, when he set up a League "organizing" committee under the chairmanship of Sóstenes M. Blanco, a member of the Veracruz League and a former local deputy who had been expelled from the Congress in July 1931, in connection with a dispute over the best way to take over the council of the city of Veracruz. The embittered Blanco's aim was "not . . . to form a new organization separate from the existing one, but to work hard to purge those we call directors [who] have made that organ into a political apparatus and, deviating from their true social mission . . . [are] endangering the *campesinos*' organization and [are] thereby creating uncertainty and disorientation . . . among the *campesino* groups." The declared aim was to purge the League of all the elements that were violating the laws of the state—meaning, of course, Tejeda's followers. Tejeda's men, unlike Blanco's men, were unwilling to follow Rodríguez's directives concerning the patrimonial division of the ejidos, which at the time were being vigorously implemented.[12]

The organizing committee of Blanco's "purge" was headed by Abel Rodríguez, who had been provisional governor of Veracruz for a few months before Tejeda took office, and was headquartered not in Veracruz but in Mexico City, close to the president. On 20 February 1933 Blanco called an "emergency convention" in Jalapa, attended by 2,000 peasants and representatives of all levels of federal, state, and local government, as well as representatives of peasant organizations and parties from all over the country, all of whom had one thing in common: their opposition to the Tejedist League. This convention gave rise to Blanco's new Veracruz agrarian league, which, by *El Nacional*'s reckoning, even at its inception could already claim the allegiance of about half the agrarian committees of Veracruz.[13]

The establishment of this new league was a heavy blow for Galván and Tejeda's original local League (then under the leadership of Isauro Acosta), forcing it to moderate its views, draw closer to Governor Vázquez Vela, and join the national Confederación Campesina Mexicana (CCM—Mexican Peasant Confederation) that Cárdenas established at the end of May. Now two parallel agrarian leagues were operating in Veracruz both espousing generally moderate views, but constantly fighting with each other often physically.[14] The agrarianist radicalism of the original Veracruz Agrarian League had given up the ghost. Another federal government ploy against Tejeda implemented with the close cooperation of the PNR had succeeded.[15]

The federal government's anger was also directed against the LNCUG. At the LNCUG's eleventh convention, which took place in Mexico City on 1 June 1933, Cárdenas's supporters managed to gain control of the organization's central institutions, squeezing out the Veracruz contingent led by the Tejedist Antonio Echegaray. At the same time, the Tejedists were accused of having caused a schism in the LNCUG by trying to put it at the service of Veracruz politics. The convention passed a resolution, clearly directed against the Veracruz Tejedists, which declared that "the League [would] not be a political party or an anarchist organization." This ended the process of the emasculation of the LNCUG that had started off at full steam back in January of the same year and even earlier in February 1931 (see Chapter 2).[16]

At the same time, *Tejedismo* was being eliminated on the local level, particularly in the cardinal city of Veracruz. At the beginning of 1933, Epigmenio Guzmán, the city mayor, requested a leave of absence to clear up the accusations being made against him with regard to the murder of the businessman Antonio Celís of Villa Cardel and his wife during the Aguirre revolt in March 1929. His temporary replacement was initially Ignacio Campos and later Victorio Góngora. The strong involvement of the local PNR under the leadership of the federal deputy and candidate for the post of senator from Veracruz, Carlos Darío Ojeda, led, in March 1933, to the dissolution of the entire governing council, which was made up primarily of Agrarian League members. A temporary *junta* was set up to govern the city, composed of local PNR men.

In June 1933, the election campaign began for the 1934–1935 municipio council. Two parties were competing: the Cardenists and the Tejedists, whose mayoral candidate was Heriberto Jara, the former governor of Veracruz. Tension in the city ran high, producing frequent violent clashes between the rival camps. In September the Cardenists won the election, and the new mayor, Santos Pérez Abascal, took office on 1 January 1934. Thus Tejeda lost his former ascendancy in that city, and a similar process took place in other cities. The overthrow of Tejedist municipal councils was paralleled by a decline in the influence of the tenants and *colonos* (the workers who received expropriated land for housing) that Tejeda had favored in the city of Veracruz.

Vázquez Vela contributed more than a little to the Tejedists' eclipse on the municipio level, declaring in his annual speech in September 1933, that he would calm the municipios and further the PNR's interests there—in other words, drive the Tejedists out. To do so, he used a well-known Tejedist stratagem: the systematic dissolution of uncooperative municipio councils and their replacement by temporary *juntas* until new elections could be held to "correct" the situation.[17]

The battle in the municipios was paralleled by a similar parliamentary battle to purge the state Congress of Tejeda supporters, the members of the original Agrarian League. These seven or eight members[18] occupied half the seats in the house, and had done much to establish Tejedism in Veracruz—in particular by refusing to confirm the results of any municipio elections in which Tejedist candidates had been defeated, a proceeding facilitated by their control of the internal affairs committee of the Congress, which supervised electoral matters. If the Congress did not confirm the results of an election, the outgoing council continued to exercise its functions until new elections could be held, a prolonged and complicated process that gave the Tejedists a long ride in office.

This problem led the federal center to decide to remove the Tejedists from the local Congress. Its chosen method was to lead them to create a division in the Congress, denounce them for it, and eject them. This effort was spearheaded by the governor's brother, Luis Vázquez Vela, who was the leader of the anti-Tejedist faction. The stratagem was put into effect on 20 September 1933, when the winter session of Congress convened. In less than a month—by 11 October—it had been successfully completed, and the Tejedists were replaced by PNR members and supporters of Cárdenas, who was then busily garnering support for his campaign as the official party's presidential candidate.[19]

Once the bases of Tejeda's power had been weakened, the federal center began purging Tejedists from the PNR. Since the party was a confederation of autonomous parties and organizations at all political levels of the Mexican periphery, Tejedists were also members. Their membership, however, was based on practical considerations: where it helped them to put representatives in the federal Congress or in the state governor's office, they declared their support for the PNR; where it got in their way, as in the elections to the local Congress or local government, they worked outside the party.

This inconsistent behavior was tolerated as long as the Tejedists had no obvious political apparatus of their own; but once they established one, in the form of the Partido Socialista de las Izquierdas (PSI—Socialist Party of the Left), in April 1933, they were immediately characterized as enemies of the PNR, and a vigorous campaign began to eliminate them from all the local and federal PNR institutions, including the federal Congress. The first people to feel the effects of this campaign were the Tejedists in the municipal and regional party committees in Veracruz and in the party faction in the local Congress.[20]

The whole campaign took on the aspect of a witch-hunt; anyone who had ever been associated with Tejeda now had to prove he was not a Tejedist. Many announcements disowning Tejeda, sometimes including harsh attacks on the things he had done as governor, streamed into the PNR secretariat and newspaper editorial offices—in many cases from former friends, such as Cándido Aguilar, Carlos Darío Ojeda, and most of the members of the Veracruz delegation to the federal Congress.[21]

The last stage of the purge came during the days leading up to the party congress that was to meet in Querétaro in December 1933, to choose the party's candidate for the presidency. All 14 Veracruz members in the PNR faction in the federal chamber of deputies were asked to declare their loyalty to the party within three days. Eleven of them did so. The remaining three, Eugenio Méndez, Carolino Anaya, and Eduardo Cortina, declared their allegiance to Tejeda and the PSI. After a series of vociferous and insulting arguments within the faction and in the Congress plenum, the three were thrown out of the faction, and Eugenio Méndez was expelled from the chamber of deputies as well. The Veracruz delegation that attended the party congress in December did not include any of Tejeda's supporters. The Tejedist opposition to Cárdenas's nomination as the party's presidential candidate was no more.[22]

The Elimination of the Tejedist Ideology

The federal government was not content to eliminate Tejeda's political power; it also sought to undermine the social ethos he had created. It took a major step towards this objective immediately after he left the governor's office, when it broke up Veracruz's radical educational administration. The director, Gabriel Lucio, was the first to go—labeled as a communist, he was fired and expelled from Veracruz. In an emotional letter to Calles on 29 December 1932, Tejeda tried to clear Lucio of any suspicion of communism and to obtain permission for him and others expelled like him to return to Veracruz, claiming that Lucio had been engaged in designing a new, rehabilitative educational program together with the state teachers, not in any communist activities. The accusations against him and other liberals like him, wrote Tejeda, were nothing but incitement by extremist religious elements "who miss no opportunity to injure liberal elements. . . ."[23]

Another ploy was to present everything Tejeda had done in Veracruz as total anarchy and destructive misrule that had plunged a prosperous state into strife, contention, and civil war. The anti-Tejedists' views were reflected in an *Excelsior* editorial dated 28 April 1933 that excoriated Tejeda's administration as a pathetic, destructive farce that lacked a clear ideology and a social base, and was unsuited to Mexico, being an inappropriate imitation of foreign regimes.[24]

The local oligarchy—Tejeda's implacable adversaries—and all those former friends who had turned against him enthusiastically joined his denigrators. In 1933, innumerable denunciations of his government in Veracruz were issued by such elements, receiving wide coverage in both the local and national press. At the same time some of the tax ordinances that had weighed on businesses were canceled, as were the sanctions on the oil companies, and the land Tejeda had expropriated from the latter was returned to them. All public officials were now told to expropriate land "in strict accordance with the law," a phrase that in fact called for a narrow interpretation of legislation concerning forced land sales, such as Law #208. Every "achievement" marking "a return to normality," as the de-Tejedization process was described, was prominently featured in the press.[25]

By the beginning of December 1933, when Cárdenas was preparing to declare his candidacy for the presidency, Tejeda had been completely stripped of all power and influence. The few people who remained loyal to him were persecuted. Senior officials of the Veracruz state administration and faithful agrarianist leaders lost their jobs, and were asked to leave the state. Tejeda himself was persona non grata in Veracruz as accusations and denunciations were hurled at him from all directions, giving him no chance to respond. The culmination of this period of character assassination was probably the extended debate by the PNR faction of the federal chamber of deputies which took place on 16 October 1933 and ended with the expulsion of Eugenio Méndez from the Congress. Every sentence in the speech Méndez made in defense of Tejeda and Tejedism elicited jeers and catcalls. When, for example, he spoke of Tejeda's battle against the Church, General Agapito Barranco of Veracruz, who was a candidate for the governorship in the 1932 elections, remarked that Tejeda had had his own son baptized in the Jalapa cathedral, and that Barranco himself had stood godfather. When Méndez praised Tejeda's revolutionary integrity, and the fact that he had never taken even one peso for himself, in contrast to the "palaces, haciendas, and businesses" that "many honorable revolutionaries" had appropriated for themselves, Barranco replied, "And I'll tell you that if Colonel Tejeda does not have any of that, it is because he doesn't know how to manage even one peso." This sally provoked extended guffaws from the hundreds of faction members.[26] And thus the debate continued. The tone more than the content indicated the extent to which *Tejedismo* had been discredited not only in Veracruz, but all over Mexico.

Tejeda's troubles were attributable to many factors. He had based his power exclusively on local institutions that he had never troubled to unite in a single front, and he had not sought to cultivate ties with the federal center during his years as governor, the way Cárdenas had. Not only did he fail to establish himself with the PNR, but, in many instances, he even embraced its rivals. His operating methods were heavy-handed and radical; he openly expressed his dissatisfaction with the Revolution and its achievements, calling for far-reaching changes in its conceptual, organizational, and constitutional bases. He assailed the Veracruz bourgeoisie, including the business and entrepreneurial communities, large landowners, the students of some faculties, and elements in the government bureaucracy that he considered conservative, and he embarked on a confrontation course against the army, and insulted its honor. He initiated a controversial anti-clerical campaign that was overly harsh even for his own supporters; and he conducted a policy of overt discrimination in favor of the proletariat, based on the theory of class war. This combination of factors gave rise to such a strong backlash that it was even able to halt the accelerated emancipation of the Veracruz workers and peasants as they approached full political hegemony in the state, and to stamp out Tejeda's special revolutionary ethos, eliminating any chance that his particular brand of popular democracy would ever gain national acceptance.

The Elimination of Cárdenas's Power Bases in Michoacán

A similar political emasculation took place in Michoacán. Benigno Serrato, Cárdenas's successor as governor, was in effect assigned to Michoacán as Calles's agent in order to dissolve Cárdenas's power bases.[27] He divided the CRMDT, expelled all Cárdenas's supporters from the local Congress and the state administration, and won over some of Cárdenas's followers—including Victoriano Anguiano, the secretary of the new government, who became the severest critic of Cárdenas and *Cardenismo*.[28]

None of this, however, was sufficient to undermine Cárdenas's increasing power. Cárdenas knew that the periphery had no influence over the center, and accordingly he had invested considerable effort, as we have seen, in fortifying his position in the federal arena. Accordingly, during the many visits he made to Michoacán after leaving the governor's office, he had no trouble paying court to Serrato with a stately graciousness even though Serrato was working against him. Cárdenas was not concerned with Serrato, but rather with the best way to gain support in the institutions of the PNR. When he arrived in Morelia at the beginning of January 1934, to attend the CRMDT's fifth congress, a few days after the PNR convention where he was elected as the party's presidential candidate, the festive mass welcome he received at the Morelia train station made a mockery of the pathetic attempt to destroy his local bastions of power.

Concerned for his position in the federal government, Cárdenas did not hesitate to take on the task of wiping out Tejeda on behalf of Rodríguez and Calles; it was just one more test on the way to the top. Shrewd, clear-sighted politician that he was, he was not a man to waver, even if he felt some pain on Tejeda's account. In his view, the problem was not Tejeda personally, but rather the way he had chosen to build his power; if that way ran counter to the norms dictated by the center, Tejeda had to pay the price. On a personal level, Cárdenas respected Tejeda; and when, in early January 1933, the latter asked Cárdenas to authorize him and his companions to carry weapons that he said they needed to defend their lives from landowners and Church activists, Cárdenas immediately provided the requested permit.[29]

The Contest for the Presidency

From the outset the contest between Cárdenas and Tejeda for the presidency was an unequal one, in which each man continued to employ exactly the same political tactics he had used as governor. Cárdenas was restrained, cautious, radical in rhetoric but legalistic in practice, magnanimous to defeated rivals and reticent concerning his intentions. He industriously built his political power on as wide a base as possible, laying precise, secret plans to establish for himself new and different organizational frameworks. He was also careful not to step into the electoral arena until the right political moment (5 June 1933), when he was already assured of Calles's official support—just as he had waited for Calles's support before plunging into Michoacán politics at the beginning of 1928.[30] Tejeda, in contrast, was an extrovert who trumpeted his radical non-conformist ideas boldly and without editing, antagonizing the establishment by calling for a proletarian revolution. Not only was all his power vested in local institutions devoid of national influence, he had not thought out an electoral strategy.

Since Cárdenas was the PNR's candidate, his election may have been certain from the start, but he nevertheless took his campaign seriously. Tejeda's defeat was a foregone conclusion even before he declared his candidacy, and in fact he waged a pessimistic campaign, begun very late and never much more than a rearguard operation. Lacking both a real political party and an adequate budget, rarely benefiting from any press coverage and rejected on all fronts, he was more than once compelled to beat a hasty retreat from the impromptu election assemblies he organized in various states, to escape the audience's wrath at his attacks on the government and his "Red" ideas.

It was not until 14 April 1933 that Tejeda founded, with the help of a handful of friends and supporters, the PSI and its organ, *El Globo*. The red shirts worn by party supporters together with the new party's platform, which called for a gradual socialization of the means of agricultural and industrial production, nationalization of transportation and electricity, expropriation of all foreign property in the country, the organization of consumer cooperatives, and similar reforms, created a wall between the PSI and all the parties that defined themselves as "legitimate." The press gave the PSI the stigmatizing moniker of "*camisas rojas*" ("red shirts"). By August some of the main activists had begun to leave the party, tired of waiting for the constantly delayed publication of the party platform and pressured by the PNR, which had categorically stated that it wanted nothing to do with the PSI. It had also made clear that not only would it deny Tejeda the chance to compete for the presidential nomination within the official party—something he may have wished for—but that the political future of anyone who continued to support him would be very doubtful.[31] In June, Tejeda had been informed that the CROM's Partido Laborista Mexicano (Mexican Labor Party) would endorse not him, but Cárdenas. Meanwhile, the press kept up a steady stream of reports on Tejeda's "Red propaganda," describing it in apocalyptic terms to disabuse its readers of any illusions they might harbor concerning the true nature of the man and his party. In July, a number of leading activists headed by Epigmenio Guzmán clashed with police and were put in jail on charges of publicly defaming the president of the Republic at campaign rallies in the city of Veracruz.

The news reaching Tejeda from the field was very discouraging; the party's organizational and propaganda work was foundering on budgetary problems, confusion as to whether the PSI belonged to the PNR or not, the reluctance of the federal deputies from Veracruz to identify themselves with Tejeda, and the party's irrelevance to a public already won over by Cardenism.[32]

Although the PSI's official election campaign was not launched until 2 April 1934—under heavy attack from anti-Tejedists and pro-Cardenists—Tejeda's electoral propaganda actually began about six months before his election as the PSI's candidate for the presidency at the PSI convention in the city of Veracruz on 14 January 1934.[33] The party began by holding rallies in cities around central Veracruz; in light of the treatment they had received in the past, party activists requested government guarantees against detention. Fear of bloody confrontations between Tejeda's supporters and Cárdenas's supporters led the federal government to provide constant army protection for Tejeda personally and for his rallies.

During the following months, Tejeda traveled from state to state, accompanied by a handful of faithful supporters led by his close friend Eugenio Méndez. Fearing attack, Tejeda would appear without any advance publicity—in fact, with no warning of any kind. He would then gather together a few listeners, most of them chance passersby, and tell them his opinions on capitalism, the current regime, the government's social and agrarian policy, the PNR's six-year plan, the machinations of foreign capital in Mexico, and the Soviet-socialist state model he wished to see instituted in Mexico.[34]

At best, Tejeda would be allowed to have his say and even to tour the state for a while, meeting with some of the peasants and workers. More often, however, he was forced to speak quickly and flee before he was chased out by angry citizens, an ordeal he had undergone in Guaymas and other places.[35] The opposition to Tejeda had grown so great that on the eve of the elections the PSI had trouble distributing its ballot slips to some of the states (Tabasco, for example). The election committees refused to accept them, although they were legally bound to do so.[36]

Cárdenas's election campaign had begun, for all practical purposes, on 5 June 1933, the day he announced to the press his acceptance of the PNR nomination. He had at his disposal an efficient electoral apparatus to which many Michoacán residents contributed—for example Gabino Vázquez and Enrique Ramos. He was also supported by many PNR members, including most of the federal Congress, all the PNR committees, all the state governors and most of the municipios in the Republic—including the municipio of Veracruz. In the meantime, Cárdenas turned his attention to winning the support of organized workers. In places with no labor organizations, he established them himself.

Cárdenas's skill in achieving control over existing labor organizations was exemplified in May 1933, when he managed to win the support of most of the leagues belonging to the LNCUG, forming them into the Confederación Campesina Mexicana (CCM—Mexican Peasant Confederation), which competed on one hand with the Partido Nacional Agraria (PNA—National Agrarian Party), a more conservative, Obregonist agrarian party, constituted and led by former Zapatistas, and on the other with the LNCUG. This move virtually eliminated the only two popular peasant frameworks that operated on the national level outside the PNR. As the first mass organization to be included within the framework of the PNR, the CCM filled a void. Now Cárdenas had at his disposal a party machine, a broad base of support, and a widely distributed newspaper. During his campaign *El Nacional* regularly published the names of all the organizations that joined the CCM, the long lists of hundreds of organizations giving the impression that the entire rural population of Mexico supported Cárdenas.[37] He carried out a similar operation in the urban labor movement, by encouraging his friend Vicente Lombardo Toledano to found the Confederación General de Obreros y Campesinos de México (CGOCM—General Confederation of Workers and Peasants of Mexico) at the end of 1933 as a counterweight to the CROM.[38]

Meanwhile, a publicity campaign had been launched to build up and promote Cárdenas's image. From the beginning of January 1933, when Cárdenas took up his duties as war minister, the national conservative and partisan newspapers seemed to be trying to outdo each other in praising every aspect of Cárdenas's personality and of his performance as an officer and a statesman. In the military sphere, he was described as a superb officer of great moral integrity, held in high esteem by Calles since the time of the Revolution, and remembered as the man who had instituted compulsory military service for the purpose of "reducing social gaps." In the political sphere, he was described as an industrious worker both in the framework of the PNR and the organized revolutionary labor movement. In the personal sphere he was presented as a sensible man who had made the army into a body that served the citizens, the Revolution, and the state, and who had made soldiers in general into involved and responsible citizens. In general Cárdenas was described as a man endowed with outstanding civic qualities who had fought against the perversions of the Mexican social establishment—prostitution, alcoholism, and gambling—since his days as a young officer in the Revolutionary army.[39]

As soon as Cárdenas had agreed to present his candidacy for the approval of the PNR's central committee, he resigned from his post as Minister of War and devoted himself entirely to his election campaign. Up to the time he received that approval, in December 1933, he had been promoting his candidacy in other forums as well, although the PNR was the most important in this respect. Throughout this period he issued uncontroversial statements that carefully reflected Calles's views. One typical example was a statement released to the national press on 31 July 1933, the day that Calles returned to Mexico City after an absence of four months. In that statement, Cárdenas said:

> during the presidential term of 1934–1940, . . . the agrarian problem will be solved integrally. All workers will be organized in a single front . . . , the educational program our masses need will be developed; in short, we will see the implementation of the whole doctrine that General Calles has been supporting [i.e., the Six-Year Plan] in order to make Mexico a strong and responsible state, in a period when peoples are fighting for real prosperity for the workingman and for their homes.[40]

During these months, Cárdenas instructed the PNR technical committee to develop, on behalf of the party, a working plan for the coming six years. The order of the day was now to express loyalty to the proposed Six-Year Plan, although everyone could see that it was simply a regulatory plan devised by Calles in order to control Cárdenas's government—if Cárdenas deviated from it, Calles could oust him on the grounds that he had betrayed the principles of the Revolution "as expressed in the Six-Year Plan of the revolutionary party." Interestingly, the US ambassador in Mexico seemed to grasp nothing of what was going on behind the political scenes, writing to Washington that Calles had imposed the plan on Cárdenas because the latter was known to be, as mentioned yet in the introduction, an outstanding soldier but an untalented statesman.[41] Cárdenas, in any case, intended to play the game out—he would continue to express commitment to the plan, while actually bending it to his own purposes. By quietly working behind the scenes in the technical committee, he had already managed to insert provisions much more radical than Calles ever intended, particularly with respect to the agrarian and education sectors.[42]

From June to December 1933, Cárdenas toured the country unflaggingly, and in particular paying many visits—not by chance—to Veracruz. His aim was to gain control of as many political power centers, in the state and in the party, as possible. His strategy was to set up pro-Cardenist committees in all the party branches, in order to promote the candidates he preferred for posts in the party apparatus and in the 1933 elections for the municipios and both chambers of the local and federal Congresses.[43] In the municipal elections at the end of 1933, PNR-sponsored Cardenism reaped victory in all the states of the Republic, including Veracruz, while the Tejedists lost control of most of their former centers of power.[44]

On 7 December 1933, Cárdenas was elected as the PNR's candidate for the upcoming presidential race. The assembled party members stood on their feet for seven whole minutes cheering and applauding him when the party's secretary-general, Carlos Riva Palacio, declared him the victor.[45] Soberly triumphant, Cárdenas began the second phase of his election campaign, which ended in July 1934. In mass rallies and hundreds of visits to various areas of the national periphery, Cárdenas began to build up the support he needed against his rivals from the three small opposition parties.[46] At that point his speeches became more purposeful. Their main message was the need to organize the rural and urban proletariat in a single front in order to facilitate a solution to their problems and promote agrarian reform, which Cárdenas described as "the main problem that must be solved as soon as possible."[47]

The speeches he made along the campaign trail helped him fine-tune what became known as Cardenist socialism—a doctrine that was in fact the same brand of reformist socialism that he had adopted in principle, and, to a limited extent, in practice, while governor of Michoacán.[48] It was a model that did not exceed the strictly interpreted limits of the 1917 constitution and the revolutionary ethos expressed in it—in fact, it is doubtful whether he could have won the PNR nomination or the elections if he had presented a more radical outlook. As it was, when the election finally came around in July, he won 98.2% of the vote.[49]

The biggest loser in the elections was Tejeda, who garnered a laughable 15,755 votes (0.68% of the total). His failure put an end to the last serious attempt to constitute a comprehensive revolutionary alternative designed to shape a different Mexico—decentralized, egalitarian, much more participatory and prosperous. Tejeda was defeated because he entered the governor's office without a clear ideological vision and without any definite aim of running for the presidency in the future. Although he finally clarified his views and his plans, he realized that his term as governor was all the time that he would have. As that term drew to an end, just as he was reaching ideological maturity, he did his utmost to implement as many reforms as possible in the little time he had left. For a brief interim he toyed with the hope that he would succeed in turning Veracruz into a model for other states; but after being stripped of all his political assets in the course of 1933, he realized this was impossible. The dilatoriness of his preparations for the presidential campaign and the politically foolhardy extremism with which he presented his views suggest that he had lost hope of success in this sphere as well. To a certain degree, Tejeda duplicated the failure of Emiliano Zapata, who, although a great idealist and the builder of a popular movement never managed to become a state-builder. It is possible that just as Zapata's populist approach prevented him from making the transition to statesman, Tejeda had trouble making the leap from the local to the national sphere, a difficulty that would have sealed his fate as a presidential candidate regardless of when he decided to run, or alternatively, keeping alive his achivements in Veracruz and turning them to become a national model and ethos, that non of the Presidents to come could ignore.[50]

Why did Tejeda enter a presidential race that he was from the outset bound to lose? He did so because he had trouble admitting that an approach he considered so just and so appropriate a solution to the ills of Mexico, an approach that would make Mexico a truly egalitarian state, had not managed to get past the barriers of the establishment to reach the masses. Tejeda took up that last, lost cause because he could not acknowledge that

Mexico did not permit the free movement of ideas or open public debate on alternatives. It was a closed Mexico, whose rulers had surrounded it with institutionalized barriers preventing the entry of radical ideas of any kind. Tejeda embarked on this battle because he had something to say, and felt obligated to his loyal supporters, a small group of people (members of agrarian committees, the original Agrarian League of Veracruz, and the LNCUG) who believed in him and encouraged him, in endless meetings and letters, to run for president—among other reasons, because the situation in the villages had deteriorated considerably after he left office, as his innovations gradually disappeared. He felt an obligation to all those people, and to himself, to make that pathetic but brave attempt, whatever the outcome— just so he would not feel he had betrayed his ideal or the people who believed in it.[51]

Cárdenas, in contrast, proved the power of ambition conditioned by restraint, of patient planning, of cautious perseverance, of discrimination based on integration, of independence based on obedience, and of liberty based on subordination. All of these qualities were such as to dull the boldness of Cárdenas's vision in the short term, yet sufficient to prepare the ground for its implementation in the long term. Tejeda must have been pleased by many of the measures President Cárdenas took for the benefit of the rural population of Mexico—more than a few of them bore his own fingerprints. Nonetheless, the Mexico of 1934 probably still required a prudent leader who understood that the country was, in many respects, in a pre-modern stage of development, and accordingly needed a controlled popular government with corporate characteristics that would guide it towards democracy and integration in a slowly evolving rather than revolutionary process.

Conclusion

The Triumph of the Agrarianist Ethos and the Fading Away of Participatory Democracy

Both Tejeda and Cárdenas reached the governor's office through politics. Calles backed them because he saw them as loyal men who would mobilize peasant support for the regime and for himself as a possible candidate for the next presidency (1934–1940). Their aid was crucial during the strong political unrest of 1926–1927, years that encompassed the outbreak of the Cristero Rebellion and Obregón's decision to ignore the principle of *no-reelección* in order to run for another presidential term.

From the beginning, Cárdenas was better placed than Tejeda was. He had the advantage of being able to enter local politics without betraying the principle of non-reelection or clashing with Obregón's supporters. Cárdenas was also better prepared for the governorship. Even before he began his campaign, he was able to present an impressive program of social reforms that offered a new political discourse in Mexico, after years of compromise and retreat from Revolutionary ideals. Tejeda did not reach this level of organizational maturity until about 1930. After a rather hesitant and ideologically nebulous beginning, he began to transmit more clearly defined messages. The world depression's economic repercussions in Veracruz and the federal center's declining enthusiasm for agrarianism contributed to his maturation: By mid-1931 Tejeda had begun to rely completely on Marxist analytical tools and to select mechanisms for change accordingly.

The year 1932 marked the culmination of this coming-of-age process, as Tejeda made the conceptual and practical transition to explicit socialism (or radical social democracy, depending on one's perspective). This transition was very clearly reflected in his words and his deeds. His long-term political goals indicated a desire to see Veracruz become a secular workers' state and a select model for national emulation. Although his ideological awakening was manifest in all his political action, it was undoubtedly most influential in the agrarian sphere, which received a creative boost unprecedented in the modern history of Mexico. Tejeda's actions in this sphere reflected his wish to abandon not only the existing constitution but the liberal-social state model established by the Revolution, and to replace it with a vaguely defined popular state. Cárdenas, in contrast, never went this far. Although in his last year as Michoacán's governor he pursued agrarian reform energetically, his agrarianism was nothing more than a minor radicalization of the existing constitutional order.

Both men wielded considerable power based on efficient grassroots organization and, in Tejeda's case, on effective control of the local authorities. However, their respective attitudes to that organization and the ways they used it were different. Tejeda took a democratic approach, giving the organizations he sponsored considerable freedom of action, while Cárdenas preferred a corporative approach combined with strict supervision.[1] Their different methods also produced different results. While Cárdenas managed to retain his influence over the activities of the CRMDT and to keep them in line with his own largely moderate views, Tejeda's Agrarian League got free rein and therefore became a cardinal and leading player in the initiation and direction of Tejeda's radical programs.

Underlying the political differences between the two men were different social concepts. Cárdenas viewed society in national-integrative terms, as a pluralistic entity obligated to coordinate inter-class relations in order to achieve social justice, which he saw as a fundamental condition for healthy development. In his eyes, a primary condition for inter-class dialogue was internal peace. Tejeda, on the other hand, conditioned by his class-based (or proletarian) national ideology, perceived society as a competitive body riven by differences and lacking in solidarity, a society in which the poor could advance only through struggle. According to this logic, internal peace would be the result of rather than a precondition for that struggle. Consequently, Tejeda rejected cooperation with the bourgeoisie and emphasized the unique interests of the proletariat and the mechanisms of the class war, while Cárdenas strove to bring the bourgeoisie around to the realization that significant social reform was unavoidable in any society that aspired to nationhood.

The two governors' different styles were also conditioned by the different social and economic circumstances of their states. Since Porfirio Díaz's day, Veracruz had stood at the forefront of Mexican capitalism. Industrialization had given rise to a modern division of labor that fostered rapid unionization and a greater sensitivity than in most other states to the fluctuations of capitalism. Michoacán, in contrast, stood at the sidelines of modern capitalist development; the division of labor was relatively primitive, unionization exiguous, and sensitivity to capitalist crises negligible. These structural factors undoubtedly had a defining influence on the two governors' basic social and economic views and on their ideological development. While Tejeda, who was basically moderate, had to turn radical in order to tackle the social economic pressures of the late twenties in his state, Cárdenas, in contrast, could hold his basically radical outlook in the short term, and act moderately while governing his state.

The two governors' differing ideological views were also shaped by the federal government's efforts to shrug off its explicit social commitments at the beginning of the 1930s and its ongoing campaign to neutralize the states' power in favor of an increasingly strong center. This centralizing tendency had particularly severe repercussions for Veracruz, given its special socioeconomic circumstances and well-developed unions. It affected Michoacán

less strongly owing to that state's more backward socioeconomic development and scant syndicalist awareness up until the beginning of the 1930s. It
is no surprise, then, that Tejeda reacted particularly strongly to the change
in the federal government's social policy and the reinforcement of the center
at the expense of the states, since these factors prevented him from coping
efficiently with Veracruz's problems. He was unable to take a sufficiently
firm line with the foreign corporations that operated in Veracruz under the
protection and patronage of the federal center; and he was unable to correct
to any significant extent the distorted system of land tenure as long as the
center controlled agrarian matters by means of the ejidal reform and
prevented the states from implementing other forms of agrarian reform.
These factors shed some light on Tejeda's socioeconomic radicalism, his
strong federalist bias, the class-struggle perspective he espoused, his hatred
of the Church as a conservative perpetuator of the status quo and its uncompromising position regarding the sanctity of private property, and his
exhortations concerning the need to implement the provisions of the
Constitution without compromise, or to replace it in case it wouldn't be
possible.

The two men's different priorities—Cárdenas's concern for political
considerations and Tejeda's emphasis of ideological considerations—were
not only a reflection of their different governing challenges and social and
national views, but also a function of their different political life expectancies. Since Cárdenas had decided early in his career to run for president, he
could afford the luxury of long-term plans. Tejeda, in contrast, had not yet
made such a decision when he returned to Veracruz in 1928, and thus had
to compress what he could into a much shorter political time-frame. This
factor influenced the degree of urgency with which each governor translated
his ideology into practice—particularly once the altered trend of federal
policy and the increasing dominance of the center became clear. This was
also the factor that ultimately decided the political fate of each man.[2]

Tejeda's failure to implement his dream represented the end of an interesting attempt to create a participatory democracy in Mexico—an attempt
that had begun with his "trilogy" and ended with a "Soviet" society. He was
not inspired by the Russian model, which had already lost any democratic
content, but by the unitary-decentralized democracies of France, England,
and Denmark, which he thought well-suited to Mexican federalism. Tejeda
envisioned a Mexican regime based on worker unions that would elect representatives to a constitutional convention. That convention would draft a new
constitution establishing a parliament composed of trade-union representatives and convening from time to time rather than on a permanent basis. The
president would be nothing more than a coordinator and a figurehead,
similar to the king of Denmark, the president of France, or the king of
England. The union representatives managing the country would be subject
to popular referendum, as in Switzerland "and many other states of democratic structure." Eventually even this federal structure would disappear, to
be replaced by a functionalist, economic structure that would give society

clear priority over the state. This idea was almost identical to the Marxist utopian concept of the withering away of the state.[3]

Tejeda could not find the terms he needed to describe his ideal in the Mexican political lexicon. Every word he chose was eroded in the obdurate campaign to eliminate the social achievements of the Revolution, as the leaders of that Revolution continued to talk about democracy while concealing the corporative and authoritarian foundations of Mexican life in the post-Revolutionary period. In Tejeda's opinion, democracy could be understood only in pluralistic European terms, as it had developed in the Swiss cantons, Soviet Russia—before the revolution eliminated the soviet as an autonomous popular force—the constitutional monarchies of England and Denmark, "[whose] King is a good man who travels along the road on a bicycle, who obeys the stop and go signals . . . and who is not an extraordinary citizen . . . ," and France's presidential republic, "whose president does not govern in any way, and is only a symbolic representation of the Nation." What Tejeda had in mind, then—although even he had trouble defining it clearly—was a genuinely—rather than nominally—pluralistic, democratic government combining all the advantages of the contemporary European democracies. He described this government as a "sociocracy" or, a government "which would try in every way to arrive at the progressive and exemplary governing of the masses."[4]

Although the dynamic Tejedist model was interesting, conceptually varied, and had begun to put down roots locally in Veracruz, it was divorced from the "Mexican experience" and did not recognize the discipline of reality. Cárdenas once remarked, in a conversation with Ramón Beteta in November 1950, "An uncivilized county like ours, where the majority lives in poverty, must be governed tolerantly in accordance with the principles of the Constitution"[5]—and this was in fact the principle that guided him. Born into a milieu socially and intellectually inferior to that of Tejeda, he had deep roots in that "Mexican experience" (and memory), which was based on Hispanic rather than generally European foundations. Thus, even though, in January 1934, he described Mexico as socialist, he did not envision a proletarian state, but rather a state in which there would be neither magnates nor mendicants, and in which "a just distribution of public wealth would provide well-being to all homes and would bring peace..."[6] In his search for structural models with which to build a more progressive Mexico, he turned to Mexican sources, which were and would remain politicized, corporative, and regulatory rather than democratic in the European sense.

Tejeda was short handedness to revolutionize the revolutionary model and make it really popular, diversified, adjusted to different farmers' aspirations and economically effective, as it has been envisioned by the authors of article 27 of the Constitution. Nonetheless, his stubborn battle on behalf of total agrarianism contributed undoubtedly to the 1934 change of government, which ensured not only a radical change in agrarian policy—the spearhead of Revolutionary commitment—but also the consolidation of the reform on firm ideological bases that perpetuated it as a sacred national revolutionary ethos. Although agrarian reform continued to be bureaucratic, manipulative, politicized, narrow dimensioned and not particularly cost-effective, it preserved its revolutionary potential for the next 60 years.[7]

Cárdenas and Tejeda helped renew the national debate over the shape the ideal Mexican state should take, and placed it in the context of ideological values that gave priority to the poor sectors of society. This achievement ensured that the suffering Mexican peasant would not be forgotten, and that the Revolution would not go down in history as an empty vessel. Cárdenas, elected president in 1934, proved the thing could be done; once liberated to some extent from political constraints he was able to put into practice his radical social views and promote an agrarian reform without precedent in the history of Mexico, as well as such other pioneering reforms as the nationalization of the oil industry in 1938.

On balance, the agrarianists' victory stemmed from the federal center's indecisiveness to move quickly and forcefully enough to shape a rural middle class by dividing up the *latifundia* wholesale and distributing their lands to individuals. The central government's efforts to avoid any conflict with the rural oligarchy led it to opt for a "bourgeois" solution, the privatization of the weak ejido, which could not hold up under the burden imposed on it. The central government's maneuvers aroused the agrarianists' suspicions that it intended to jettison the entire reform and return Mexico to the pre-Revolutionary status quo. Their forceful reaction reflected this reasonable fear. First they reinstated an ideological discourse that restored legitimacy to the principle of redistributing national land, and then they developed the sophisticated political and practical mechanisms necessary for a relatively large-scale distribution of land. Cárdenas and Tejeda reinforced this enterprise by shaping a new civil consciousness that recognized the indispensability of agrarianism, syndicalism, and rational and technical education, as well as the importance of limiting the Church's influence on private and national life.

Cárdenas and Tejeda represented a new generation of leaders that arose to contend with problems unknown to the first generation of the Revolution: political and economic crisis, the religious awakening, and a Revolution that was proving disappointing and irrelevant for most of the rural population of Mexico. It was no time for additional compromises. The peasants, organized and mobilized in the 1920s to support the state, began in the early 1930s to demand concrete solutions to their problems, fueling the outbreak of the intergenerational struggle between the Revolutionary old guard and the agrarianists that ended with Calles's exile in 1935. This popular mobilization was the basis for the popular myth of the Revolution and the definition of the latter as a revolution of social justice. It was this definition that lent validity to the demand for the establishment of a balance between capital and labor in Mexico. Thus were laid the foundations for a model of national integration and social stability unique in Latin America and which has endured since 1929, even though the issue of social justice is far from being resolved.

Notes

Introduction

1 Andrés Molina Enriquez, *Los grandes problemas nacionales* (1909) (México, Era, 1978), pp. 305–308, 344–356, 392–404.

2 The term "Mexican Homestead" appeared in discussions in the second session, on 18 April 1921 in the National Chamber of Representatives (the lower house- Cámara de Diputados), when the law for the division of estates and for the establishment of small private family landholdings was debated, following a bill on this matter, President Álvaro Obregón submitted to the Congress at the beginning of December 1920. See Ley sobre fraccionamiento de latifundios, *Diario de los debates de la Cámara de Diputados del Congreso de Los Estados Unidos Mexicanos*, Primer Período Extraordinario, XXIX Legislatura, tomo 2, nu. 26, Sesión de Apr. 18 de 1921, p. 8 (for further discussion of the issue see chapter 5); Pedro Castro, *Álvaro Obregón: Fuego y ceniza de la Revolución Mexicana* (México, Era, 2009), p. 157. Andrés Molina Enríquez used the term "hogar" or "pequeña propiedad individual" for homestead. See: Enríquez, *Los Grandes Problemas Nacionales*, pp. 129, 359, 378–379, 395–396.

3 Miguel Bustos Cerecedo, *Adalberto Tejeda Olivares: Dimensión del hombre* (Xalapa, Verarcuz, Gobierno del Estado de Veracruz, 1983), pp. 20–21.

4 The structural attributes that Veracruz and Michoacán acquired during this period are still evident today. With respect to land tenure, for example, Veracruz is Mexico's strongest agrarianist state, with some 3,714 communities established under the agrarian reform and inhabited by 523, 660 people (12.4% of all existing reform communities in México), followed by Michoacán, with 1,873 communities and 258,895 inhabitants (6.2% of total reform communities) (2012). See "Veracruz, el Estado con más ejidos y comunidades en México", *Boletín*, no. 61 (May 2012), Secretaría de Desarrollo Agrario, Territorial y Urbano: http://www.sedatu.gob.mx/sraweb/noticias/noticias-2012/mayo-2012/ 11168; "El 48% del territorio de Michoacán es propiedad social", *Boletín* 79 (June 2012). http://www.sedatu.gob.mx/sraweb/noticias/noticias-2012/junio-2012/12333/ See María de la Luz Aguilera Mejía (coord.), *Veracruz: cifras y perfiles 1970–1990* (Xalapa, Universidade Veracruzana, 1995), Vol. III, Tomo 1, pp. 67–70; "Las comunidades agrarias", in: *VII Censo Agropecuario, 1991* (INEGI y el Colegio de Postgraduados, México, 1998), p. 16.

5 In Verarcuz there was a long tradition of federalism. However, in the opinion of Karl Koth, the Federalist issue had definitely died already by 1927 and couldn't be recovered anymore. See Karl B. Koth, *Waking the Dictator. Veracruz, the Struggle for Federalism, and the Mexican Revolution, 1870–1927* (Calgary, Alberta, University of Calgary Press, 2002), p. 251.

6 Helga Baitenmann argues, with no direct evidence, that Tejeda built his rural guerrillas while having in mind the idea of presidency. See Helga Baitenmann,

Rural Agency and State Formation in Postrevolutionary Mexico: The Agrarian Reform in Central Veracruz, 1915–1992 (Doctoral Thesis, New York, The New School for Social Research, 1997), pp. 81–82.

7 Among the numerous well-known initiatives we can list, for instance, clerical socialism, independent campesino leagues (the *Liga Nacional Campesina*, LNC), Indian communality as well as a panoply of parties, labor organizations and syndicates that were independent of the *Confederación Regional Obrera Mexicana* (CROM) and, after 1929, of the PNR.

8 See for example Gilbert M. Joseph and Daniel Nugent, "Popular Culture and State Formation in Revolutionary Mexico," in: *Everyday Forms of State Formation: Revolution and Negotiation of Rules in Modern Mexico* (Durham, Duke University Press, 1994), pp. 9–13; Alan Knight, "Weapon and Arches in the Mexican Revolutionary Landscape," *ibid.*, pp. 45–49, 63–66..

9 With respect to settlements that displayed little inclination for uniform state agrarianism, like Namiquipa, for example, William Roseberry comments on the geographic and social alienation from agrarian policy formation felt by the villagers described by Nugent and Alonso. Everything was determined "there," in Mexico City, far from Namiquipa. Every aspect of policy was decreed by other actors, few of whom had matured within the revolutionary movement. Villagers were certainly excluded. For these peasants, policymaking was an abstract activity, conducted according to alien meanings and objectives. Implementation was carried out according to purely legal concepts, categories, and formulas— in a "foreign" language and in the name of a diffuse body called "the homeland". The campesinos were thus incapable of identifying with either these entities or their agents. See: William Roseberry, "Hegemony and the Language of Contention", Gilbert M. Joseph and Daniel Nugent (eds.), *Everyday Forms of State Formation*, p. 362; Daniel Nugent and Ana María Alonso, "Multiple Selective Traditions in Agrarian Reform and Agrarian Struggle: Popular Culture and State Formation in the Ejido of Namiquipa, Chiuhauha", *ibid.*, pp. 228–229; Daniel Nugent, *Spent Cartridges of Revolution: An Anthropological History of Namiquipa, Chihuahua* (Chicago, University of Chicago Press, 1993), pp. 22–30, 91–105, 150–165.

10 Typical is the ousting of Francisco José Múgica, the governor of Michoacán, who ignored Obregón's orders in the first regard. On this incident, see Martín Sánchez, *Grupos de poder y centralización política en México. El caso Michoacán 1920–1924* (México, Instituto Nacional de Estudios Históricos de la Revolución Mexicana, 1994), pp. 211–29; Verónica Okión Solano, *Los hombres del poder en Michoacán, 1924–1962* (Zamora, El Colegio de Michoacán, 2004), p. 45 y notas 2–4; Héctor Ceballos Garibay, *Francisco J. Múgica. Crónica política de un rebelde* (México, Ediciones Coyoacán, 2004), p. 100.

Quite the same happened with Aurelio Manrique from San Luis Potosí (1923–1925). See Romana Falcón, *Revolución y caciquismo: San Luis Potosí 1910–1938* (México, El Colegio de México, 1984), pp. 161–162.

11 The seeds of this process were already observed in the constitutional camp during the military struggle. Indications include the distributional agrarian policy initiated by Gen. Lucio Blanco and his supporters in 1913, the zapatista and villista agrarianism of 1911–1915; and even the controlled agrarianism of Medero's Ministry of Development in 1912. All were cancelled or denied any effective implementation. The neo-zapatista agrarianism offered to Obregón by

former zapatistas in 1921 met a similar fate. The latter model attempted to integrate communal (*ejidal*) with particularist agrarian distribution. The proposed legislation was debated in the lower house and confirmed, but blocked in the senate, later that same year.

12   Gilbert M. Joseph and Daniel Nugent, "Popular Culture and State Formation in Revolutionary Mexico", in: Gilbert M. Joseph and Daniel Nugent (eds.), *Everyday Forms of State Formation*, p. 12.

13   *Historia documental del Partido de la Revolución* II, Año de 1933 (Instituto de Capacitación Política (ICAP) del PRI, México, 1981), pp. 258–272; 279–284.

14   The following works mention some of these features although they also show some of the extreme characteristics of revolutionary propaganda that stimulated resistance. See for example Jan Rus, "The 'Comunidad Revolucionaria Institucional': The Subversion of Native Government in Highland Chiapas, 1936–1968", in: Gilbert M. Joseph and Daniel Nugent (eds.), *Everyday Forms of State formation*, pp. 278–284; Marjorie Becker, *Setting the Virgin on Fire: Lázaro Cárdenas and the Redemption of the Mexican Revolution* (Berkeley, University of California Press, 1995), pp. 116–119, 134–142, 158–162; Daniel Nugent, *Spent Cartridge of Revolution: An Anthropological History of Namiquipa*, University of Chicago Press, Chicago, 1993; Daniel Nugent and Ana María Alonso, "Multiple Selective Traditions in Agrarian Reform and Agrarian Struggle: Popular Culture and State Formation in the Ejido of Namiquipa, Chiuhauha", pp. 209–246; Adrian A. Bantjes, *As If Jesus Walked on Earth: Cardenismo, Sonora, and the Mexican Revolution* (Wilmington, Delaware, Scholarly Resources, 1997); Ben Fallaw, *Cárdenas Compromised: The Failure of Reform in Postrevolutionary Yucatán* (Durham, Duke University Press, 2001).

15   The peasants found this confrontation, which reached extreme proportions in Veracruz under Tejeda, to be offensive. While in the Tehedista case we can vouch that in the absence of any selectivity in the documentation retained (Tejeda's deliberate policy as relayed in an interview by his close friend and associate, Dr. Javier Tavera Alfaro, former Director and Coordinator, Comité de Biblioteca y Archivo del H. Congreso de Michoacán), it is nonetheless difficult to substantiate the same policy in Michoacán. Cárdenas saw to a punctilious selection of his political and personal documents. His personal diaries lack any important chapters that might portray a more complex though less commanding personality. The State archives relating to the period are particularly lean, with many files missing among those that might contribute to our understanding of his socio-political program. Copies of local newspapers from the period of his governance are totally lacking. The lack of local press reports during the period of his presidency is quite suspicious.

16   Discussed in Daniel Nugent, *Spent Cartridges of Revolution*, pp. 91, 153.

17   James Scott, *Domination and the Art of Resistance: Hidden Transcripts* (New Haven, Yale University Press, 1990), esp. chapters 1–3 and 5–7.

18   During my visits in the last 25 years to the various ejidos, the Veracruz and Michoacán areas showed signs of distress. In the ejido of Actopan for example, in March, 1992, I interviewed a farmer who had to leave for the fields. He took a machete and left. After an hour of walking we arrived at his small plot of land which was near a tributary of the Actopan River, a place called El Descabezadero. When we arrived he asked my forgiveness and using his machete he began uprooting the weeds in his field, a hectare or two in size (and so close

to the gushing spring). A fairly common picture, I came upon it many times in different places, especially where the fields were on very steep slopes or full of stones.

During the summer of 2010, I conducted a series of conversations with farmers in the San Rafael Coapa ejido, located half way between Morelia and Pazcuaro in the state of Michoacán. In this ejido, which I had chosen at random, I found a typical picture, one I was very familiar with from my comprehensive studies of rural Mexico in the 1990s. One of the campesinos (unfortunately, I did not ask his name) I spoke with was working in a neat, well-tended corn field, although dressed in the clothes of a construction worker. He said that he had two hectares of land out of three or four that his grandfather had received in the 1930s. He had water rights but he didn't have the money to put in irrigation lines from the well at the bottom of the village to his plot. This was why he was cultivating his land as 'temporal', that is, by means of rain water only, and with a once-a-year planting cycle. The plot gives him about 20 per cent of the annual income his family needs, he said. The rest he supplements with construction work. I spoke to another ejidatorio, Jaime Rogelio Salinas, the father of the ejido's leader, or the comisariado ejidal, Benjamin Salinas García, in the court-yard of his home, which serves as a very neglected and crowded corral for his cattle. He told me that his extended family has a total of four hectares of land, which his father received at the time, two hectares are irrigated and two are temporal, but they lease eight more hectares of temporal land. On the farm they raise 20 head of cattle, which they sell every three months. 'All of this, he added, 'is still not enough to maintain the family'.

On September 2014, I returned to Ejido Capula near Morelia, Michoacán for a conversation with the veterans of that ejido. At the home of one of the legendary ejido leaders, now deceased, I spoke at length with his daughter. The woman, now aged 70 or so, continues to run the family's plot of four non-irri-gated hectares, which was always a substantial area of corn and beans (Frijol), irrigated only by rainwater the year round. When asked why no irrigation systems had been installed in the fields, she could only say that the community never organized such a request since they knew that they would have to partic-ipate in the cost and the community could not reach any consensus concerning this. The greatest difficulty came to light when more of her story unwrapped. In fact, her husband very early in his and the family's life went to work in the United States and rarely returned, leaving her and their common child in Capula. From her comments, you could understand that he had built himself a new life without bothering to divorce her. A similar story was related by her sister-in-law who joined the conversation. Her husband left her when she was a very young mother of five children and has never returned since. Until today she runs the small plot of four hectares by herself. The sister-in-law continued and related that 45 years ago when she was 23 years old her father was killed in front of her as they were going to the fields in the early morning. That is to say, he was murdered by particulars who quarreled with the father concerning the ejido he had inherited from his father. "Even though I knew who these murderers were and was acquainted with them," she continued, "they were never brought to trial". "Real security we never had here" she concluded.

19   Carlos Salinas de Gortari, *Diez puntos para dar libertad y justicia al campo mexicano*, Los Pinos, Nov. 14 de 1991, copia del documento publicado por la Presidencia de la República, Dirección General de Comunicación Social y el

Instituto de Capacitación Agraria, Talleres Linotipográficos de la Secretaría de la Reforma Agraria, México D.F., 1991, p. 6.

20 For Baitenmann real democray eventually appeared in the Veracruzan camp only after the agrarian reform was terminated. See Helga Baitenmann, "Las reformas al artículo 27 y la promesa de la democratización local: el sector ejidal en la región central de Veracruz", in Julio Moguel and José Antonio Romero (coords.), *Propiedad agrarian y el Procede en: Veracruz, Chiapas y Sonora* (Juan Pablo Editor, S.A., y la UNAM, México, 1998), pp. 20–36.

1 Jeracruz and Michoacán on the Threshold of a New Era

1 *Primer censo agrícola—Ganadero 1930, Resumen general* (México: Secretaría de la Economía Nacional, Dirección General de Estadística, 1936), pp. 40–44; Moisés T. de la Peña, *Veracruz económico* (México: Gobierno del Estado de Veracruz, 1946), vol. I, pp. 128–137.

2 Heather Fowler Salamini, *Movilización campesina en Veracruz (1920–1938)* (México: Siglo XXI Editores, 1979), pp. 22–25; David Skerritt Gardner, *Una historia agraria en el centro de Veracruz 1850–1940* (Xalapa: Centro de Investigaciones Históricas, Universidad Veracruzana, 1989), pp. 29–32; Romana Falcón, *El agrarismo en Veracruz: La etapa radical 1928–1935* (México: Colegio de México, 1977), pp. 28–29; De la Peña, *Veracruz económico*, vol. I, pp. 137–139.

3 David Franco Rodríguez (ed.), *Programa de Gobierno del Estado de Michoacán: Proyecto de 1958* (México: Secretaría de Economía, Talleres Gráficos de la Nación, n.d.), pp. 18–19.

4 *Ibid.*, pp. 78–79.

5 *Quinto censo de población (1930), Resumen general* (México, Secretaría de la Economía Nacional, Dirección General de Estadística, 1934), p. 3; *Primer censo agrícola—Ganadero*, pp. 40–45; 64–69; 70–73; and 224–227.

6 *Quinto censo de población (1930), Resumen general*, pp. 39–40; *Quinto censo de población (1930), Estado de Michoacán* (México, Secretaría de la Economía Nacional, Dirección General de Estadística, 1935), pp. 16, 21–24; *Quinto censo de población (1930), Estado de Veracruz* (México, Secretaría de la Economía Nacional, Dirección General de Estadística, 1935), p. 18.

7 *Quinto censo de población (1930), Resumen general*, pp. 27, 55–64, 78; *Quinto censo de población (1930), Estado de Michoacán*, p. 167; *Programa de Gobierno del Estado de Michoacán: Proyecto de 1958*, pp. 46–51; De la Peña, *Veracruz económico*, vol. I, pp. 239–243; *Quinto censo de población (1930), Estado de Veracruz*, p. 246; *México económico 1928–1930: Anuario estadístico de la Oficina de Estudios Económicos de los Ferrocarriles Nacionales de México* (México: Editorial Cultura, 1932), in *Clásicos de la economía mexicana* (México: Facultad de Economía de la UNAM, 1989), p. 42; and *Primer censo agrícola—Ganadero 1930, Resumen general*, pp. 34–38.

8 By 1911 Veracruz already produced nearly a half of the entire coffee output of Mexico and with its 44% of the spindles in the country, it was one of the most important textile centers. Besides, Veracruz produced and exported big quantitives of sugar, tabacco, lumber, vanilla, textile, rubber and minerals. See Koth, *Waking the Dictators*, pp. 22–24; Karl B. Koth, "La modernización de Veracruz, 1870–1905", in: Barnardo García Díaz y David Skerritt Gardner (eds), *La Revolución Mexicana en Veracruz, Antología* (Veracruz, Comisión Estatal del

Bicentenario de la Independencia y del Centenario de la Revolución Mexicana: Gobierno del Estado de Veracruz, 2009), pp. 21–89.

9   *Mexico económicó 1928–1930*, p. 78;

10 In 1935, 1.2% of the work force was employed at the four main mining sites in Michoacán, in the regions of Tlapujahua and Angangueo, at an average wage of 0.74 pesos per worker. Production value was about 8,692,000 pesos. The Veracruz oil fields provided employment for some 5% of the labor force and produced some 35,000,000 pesos' worth of oil (the combined production of Veracruz and Tabasco was 65,000,000 pesos). See *Mexico económico 1928–1930*, pp. 48–50, 68, 73–75, 155; *Censo industrial de 1935—Resumen general* (México, Secretaría de la Economía Nacional, Dirección General de Estadística, 1941), pp. 61, 230–231, 237–239; María Benítez Juárez, "La organización sindical de los trabajadores petroleros en la Huasteca veracruzana 1917–1931," in *Anuario 5* (Jalapa: Centro de Estudios Históricos, Instituto de Investigaciones Humanísticos, Universidad Veracruzana, 1988), pp. 16, 30–33; and Fernando Foglio Miramontes, *Geografía económicó agrícola del Estado de Michoacán* (México: Editorial Cultura, 1936), vol. II, pp. 49–50, 54, 248.

11 See "Informe leido al 15 de septiembre de 1932, ante la H. Legislatura del Edo. de Veracruz" (Informe 1931–1932, Primer Semestre), in Archivo Adalberto Tejeda [hereafter AAT], vol. 197 (1932), pp. 474–476; and *Censo industrial de 1935—Resumen general* (México, Secretaría de la Economía Nacional, Dirección General de Estadística, 1941), pp. 25–26; 74–83, 124–125, 132–133, 144–147, 184–185.

12 See Alberto J. Olvera Rivera et al., "Balance sobre la investigación de la formación de la clase obrera veracruzana: 1850–1932," in *75 años de sindicalismo mexicano*, ed. Alejandra Moreno Toscano and Samuel L. González (México: Instituto Nacional de Estudios Históricos de la Revolución Mexicana, 1986), pp. 204–219; Heather Fowler Salamini, "Origines laborales de la organización campesina en Veracruz," *Historia Mexicana* 20, 2 (Oct.–Dec. 1970): 235–264; Moisés González Navarro, *La Confederación Nacional Campesina en la reforma agraria mexicana*, 3rd ed. (México : Publicaciones Mexicanas S.C.L., 1985), p. 90.

13 See Soledad García Morales, "Análisis de estadística de 1907. Haciendas y hacendados," in *Veracruz, un tiempo para contar*, memoria del Primer Seminario de Historia Regional, ed. Mirana Benítez, Carmen Blázquz, et al. (México: Instituto Nacional de Antropología e Historia, Universidad Veracruzana, 1989), pp. 138, 144–146, 153–158, 170–178; *Quinto censo de población (1930), Estado de Michoacán*, p. 156; *Primer censo agrícola— Ganadero*, pp. 46–50, 160–161.

14 See Frank Tannenbaum, *Peace by Revolution: Mexico after 1910* (New York: Columbia University Press, 1968), p. 92.

15 Fowler, *Movilización campesina*, p. 28.

16 Christopher R. Boyer, "Revolución, reforma agraria e identidad campesina en Michoacán", Verónica Oikión Solano y Martín Sánchez Rodríguez (coords.), *Vientos de rebelión en Michoacán: Continuidad y ruptura en la Revolución Mexicana* (Morelia y Zamora, Gobierno del Estado de Michoacán, El Colegio de Michoacán, 2010), pp. 174–182; Christopher R. Boyer, "Old Loves, New Loyalties: Agrarismo in Michoacán, 1920–1928", *The Hispanic American Historical Review*, Vol. 78, No. 3 (Aug., 1998), pp. 430–39. The main argument Boyer had in the above mentioned article is that although reform went

slowly in Michoacán prior to Cárdenas's era, agrarian consciousness began to take shape thanks to the dedicated political and conscious work rural teachers and local caciques have done among the suspicious and sometime reluctant Michoacán's peasantry.

17 Comisión Nacional Agraria, *Estadística 1915–1927* (México: Secretaría de Agricultura y Fomento, 1928), pp. 35, 48, 51.

18 *Ibid.*

19 Fowler, *Movilización campesina*, pp. 22–25; De la Peña, *Veracruz económica*, vol. I, pp. 137–139; Falcón, *El agrarismo en Veracruz*, pp. 28–29; Skerritt, *Una historia agraria*, pp. 29–33, 33 n5, 153.

20 Skerritt, *Una historia agraria*, pp. 153–179; Andrew Grant Wood, *Revolution in the Street: Women, Workers, and Urban Protests in Veracruz, 1870–1927* (Wilmington Delaware, Scholarly Resources, 2001), pp. 71–84, 93–98.

21 The Puente Nacional incident was the culmination of months of friction between landowners in the Puente Nacional area and local agrarianists and ejidatarios. Initial skirmishes had taken place between peasants and the *guardias blancas* employed by the wealthy Lagunes family back in October 1922, but matters came to a head on 9 March 1923, when tension between *guardias blancas* being escorted to Jalapa for questioning and the Tejedist civil guards escorting them erupted in a pitched battle that left eight people dead. The affair reached major proportions, eventually involving Obregón himself, who ordered an investigation and ultimately placed the blame on Tejeda. The incident convinced Tejeda of the importance of an armed, organized peasant body, and was a spur to the establishment of the Veracruz Agrarian League 15 days later. See Skerritt, *Una historia agraria*, pp. 183–185; and Romana Falcón and Soledad García Morales, *La semilla en el surco: Adalberto Tejeda y el radicalismo en Veracruz (1883–1960)*, (México: El Colegio de Mexico, 1986), pp. 153–164.

22 Skerritt, *Una historia agraria*, p. 185; Falcón and García Morales, *La semilla en el surco*, p. 158; and Fowler, *Movilización campesina*, pp. 58–64.

23 Falcón, *El agrarismo*, p. 42. Falcón relies on a report by the head of the CLA, Salvador de Gortari, which was sent to Tejeda on 25 June 1930. The figures in the agrarian survey carried out by the CNA (Comisión Nacional Agraria) for the years 1915–1927 are not corroborated by these data. The CNA report gives a total of 299 communities for the period under discussion, 189 of which had received final presidential approval. See Comisión Nacional Agraria, *Estadística 1915–1927*, pp. 35, 48.

24 *Ibid.*

25 On the history of Tapia's League and its problems, see Jesús Múgica Martínez, *La Confederación Revolucionaria Michoacana del Trabajo* (México: Eddisa, 1982), p. 88; Paul Friedrich, *Revueltas agrarias en una aldea mexicana* (México: Fondo de Cultura Económica, 1981), pp. 136, 141–142; Guillermo Bermejo and Laura Espejel L., "Conflicto por el poder y contradicciones de clase: El caso de Michoacán 1920–1926," *Boletín*, Centro de Estudios de la Revolución Mexicana "Lázaro Cárdenas" [hereafter CERMLC] (May, 1982): 28; letter from L. Cárdenas to F.J. Múgica, 24 May 1982, in "Correspondencia entre Lázaro Cárdenas y Francisco J. Múgica desde 1928 a 1939," *Desdeldiez* [CERMLC] (July, 1985): 109; Gerardo Sánchez Díaz, "Los pasos al socialismo en la lucha agraria y syndical en Michoacán 1917–1938", en Jaime Tamayo y Patricia Valles (coords.), *Anarquismo, socialism y sindicalismo en la regions* (Guadalajara, Jalisco, Universidad de Guadalajara, 1993), pp. 42–49

26 Friedrich, *Revueltas agrarias*, pp. 117–118.

27 *Ibid.*, pp. 157.

28 On Tapia's assasination, see Alejo Maldonado Gallardo, "La Confederación Revolucionaria Michoacana del Trabajo: Lázaro Cárdenas y el problema agrario en Michoacán 1928–1932," *Jornadas de Historia de Occidente* 4, [CERMLC] (1981): 93; Friedrich, *Revueltas agrarias*, pp. 134–135.

29 See Tzvi Medin, *El Minimato presidencial: Historia política del Maximato 1928–1935* (México: Ediciones Era, 1983), pp. 22–23.

30 Pérez Morteo to Tejeda, 7 April, 12 May, and 5 Sept. 1927, in AAT, tomo 128, vol. 152, fojas 410–412, 413–414; "Una consulta sobre la reelección de gobernadores," 22 April 1927, in AAT, tomo 128, vol. 152, foja 408; John Dulles, *Yesterday in Mexico: A Chronicle of the Revolution, 1919–1936* (Austin: University of Texas Press, 1967), p. 345; Pérez Morteo to Tejeda, 7 April 1927, in AAT, tomo 128, vol. 152, foja 412.

31 Obregón needed Tejeda but disliked him. He put innumerable obstacles in his path when he ran for governor the first time, characterizing Tejeda on one occasion as a man who did not "work with integrity," who did not fulfill his duties, and who sowed "seeds of discord" in the city and state of Veracruz. He termed Tejeda's social orientations "a road paved with irregularities and unjustified riots." Quoted in Soledad García Morales, *La rebelión delahuertista en Veracruz* (1923) (Xalapa, Veracruz: Universidad Veracruzana, 1986), pp. 95–96.

32 Rufino Jara to Tejeda, 31 March 1927, in AAT, tomo 129, vol. 153, foja 323.

33 Manuel Pérez Valesco to Tejeda, 30 August 1927, in AAT, tomo 129, vol. 153, foja 301.

34 Tejeda to Obregón, 9 Nov. 1927, and Obregón to Tejeda, 25 Nov. 1927, in AAT, tomo 115, vol. 139 (unnumbered pages).

35 Hernán Laborde to Tejeda, 1 Jan. 1928, and Tejeda's response to Hernán Laborde, 16 Jan. 1928, in AAT, tomo 119, vol. 143 (unnumbered pages).

36 *El Dictamen*, 4 May 1928; letters to Tejeda, 12 Jan. 1929, in AAT, tomo 124, vol. 148, fojas 53–55; Tiburcio Sedano to Tejeda, 23 Nov. 1927, in AAT, tomo 129, vol. 153, foja 304.

37 *El Dictamen*, 4 May and 18 July 1928.

38 Marte Gómez to Portes Gil, 27 Nov. 1927, in Marte R. Gómez, *Vida política contemporanea: Cartas de Marte R. Gómez* (México: Fondo de Cultura Económica, 1978), p. 171.

39 On the effectiveness of Tejeda's electoral power, see *ibid.*; letter from the Presidente Municipal to Tejeda, 17 Nov. 1927, in AAT, tomo 128, vol. 152, foja 415; María Eugenia Adela Terrones López, "Un ensayo radical: Los proyectos del Tejedismo en Veracruz (1928–1932)," B.A. thesis (Universidad Iberoamericana, México D.F., 1986), p. 26; Enrique Meza to Tejeda, 3 Dec. 1927, in AAT, tomo 128, vol. 152, doc. 436; and Tejeda's response, 20 Dec. 1927, in AAT, tomo 128, vol. 152, foja 438..

40 "El Coronel Tejeda ha iniciado su propaganda," *El Dictamen*, 4 May 1928.

41 "Diversos problemas del Estado serán atendido por el Gobernador Tejeda," *El Dictamen*, 29 Nov. 1928.

42 *Ibid.*

43 See letter from L. Cárdenas to José Valdovinos Garza, 28 Feb. 1927, in Archivo del Centro de Estudios de la Revolución Mexicana "Lázaro Cárdenas" [hereafter ACERMLC], Fondo Lázaro Cárdenas [hereafter FLC], caja 30, carpeta 20, doc. 5; Nathaniel and Silvia Weyl, "La reconquista de Mexico (los años de

Lázaro Cárdenas)," *Problemas Agrícolas e Industriales de Mexico* VII, no. 4 (Oct.–Dec., 1955): 166; and William Cameron Townsend, *Lázaro Cárdenas, Mexican Democrat* (Ann Arbor: George Wahr Publishing Co., 1952), p. 50.

44 For example, the Gran Partido Jiquilpense Pro-General Lázaro Cárdenas of Jiquilpán (founded at a constitutional convention on 1 January 1928), and the Unión de Partidos Unidos de Puruándiro. See "Acta constitutiva del Gran Partido Jiquilpense Pro-General Lázaro Cárdenas," in ACERMLC, FLC, caja 30, carp. 20, doc. 2; and letter from General Lázaro Cárdenas to the Partidos Unidos de Puruándiro, 15 Jan. 1928, in ACERMLC, FLC, caja 30, carp. 14, doc. 4. See also: Oikión Solano, *Los hombres del poder*, pp. 97–98;

45 Manuel Diego Hernández, *La Confederación Revolucionaria Michoacana del Trabajo* (Jiquilpán, Michoacán: CERMLC, 1982), pp. 28–29; letter from Múgica to Cárdenas, 24 April 1928, in "Correspondencia entre Lázaro Cárdenas y Francisco J. Múgica desde 1928 a 1939," *Desdeldies* (July 1985): 104. According to Oikión Solano the Michoacán socialist parties bloc was headed by Gonzalo N. Santos and not Silvestre Guerrero. According to her, it was Melchor Ortega who actually led the Socialist party bloc. See: Oikión Solano, *Los hombres del poder*, pp. 94–101.

46 See Victoriano Anguiano Equihua, *Lázaro Cárdenas, su feudo y la política nacional* (México: Editorial Referencias, 1989), p. 30; Townsend, *Lázaro Cárdenas, Mexican Democrat*, pp. 9–39; Lázaro Cárdenas, *Obras I: Apuntes 1913–1940* (México: UNAM, 1972), vol. I, pp. 9, 145, 150–151, 163; interview with Amadeo Betancourt Villaseñor, Proyecto de Historia Oral, ACERMLC, caja 1, carp. 5, no. 5, p. 173; María del Carmen Nava Nava, "Relaciones Múgica–Cárdenas," *Jornadas de Historia de Occidente* 7 [CERMLC] (1984): 265–267; Froylan C. Manjarrez and Hernán Gustavo Ortiz, *Lázaro Cárdenas, soldado de la Revolución, gobernante, político nacional* (México: Talleres de Editorial Patria, 1933), p. 52; Weyl, "La reconquista de Mexico," p. 162; Enrique Krauze, *Lázaro Cárdenas, general misionero* (México: Fondo de Cultura Económica, 1987), pp. 21–25. On the plight of the Michoacán economy, see Doc. #9, "Concediendo condonación de un 50% a los causantes por rezagos de contribuciones," 19 Oct. 1928, in *Periódico Oficial del Gobierno Constitucional del Estado Libre y Soberano de Michoacán de Ocampo* XLIX, no. 24 (25 Oct. 1928): 1; "Acta de sesiones #14, XLII Legislatura Michoacana, sesión de 17 de octubre de 1928," *Periódico Oficial* XLIX, no. 33 (25 Nov. 1928): 1; Jean Meyer, *La Cristiada* (México: Siglo XXI Editores, 1991), vol. I, pp. 257–259.

47 Nava Nava, "Relaciones Múgica–Cárdenas," pp. 265–267; Múgica to Ernesto Soto Reyes, 16 Feb. 1932, in ACERMLC, Fondo José Múgica, anexo 3, doc. 475, pp. 2–3.

48 Nava Nava, "Relaciones Múgica–Cárdenas," p. 292, *n*78; and Múgica to Cárdenas, 24 and 30 April 1928, in "Correspondencia entre Lázaro Cárdenas y Francisco J. Múgica desde 1928 a 1939," *Desdeldiez*, pp. 103–107.

49 Townsend, *Lázaro Cárdenas, Mexican Democrat*, p. 50; Weyl, "La reconquista de Mexico," p. 166; and Javier Romero, "Cárdenas y su circunstancia," in *Palabras y documentos públicos de Lázaro Cárdenas, 1928–1970*, vol. I: *Mensajes, discursos, declaraciones, entrevistas y otros documentos, 1928–1940* (México: Siglo XXI Editores, 1978), p. 18.

50 See Medin, *El Minimato presidencial*, p. 28. Cárdenas's reaction to Obregón's murder showed that Calles had judged correctly. As soon as Obregón's death

was known, Cárdenas quickly organized all the state congresses to send a joint petition to Calles asking him to remain president until new elections were held, "out of consideration for the national will, expressed in all social classes, particularly the revolutionary class." See Cárdenas to Rafael Sánchez, 18 Aug. 1928, in ACERMLC, FLC, caja 27, carp. 10, doc. 9. With the outbreak of the Escobar rebellion in March, 1929, and the offensive against the Cristero Rebellion in June, Cárdenas offered his services, and was one of the three leading generals who put down these rebellions. See Medin, *El Minimato presidencial*, p. 132; and Falcón, *El agrarismo*, pp. 116–117.

51 At the time (June 1923–March 1924) Cárdenas was military governor of Michoacán. Just as he took up this position, Múgica returned from the "leave" he had received from Congress a year earlier with an order from the federal Supreme Court upholding his right to resume the governorship. Taking his cues from the federal center, Cárdenas decided not to respect the order, even though he undoubtedly identified with Múgica more than he did with Sidronio Sánchez Pineda, Múgica's replacement. See Weyl, "La reconquista de Mexico," p. 166; Jesús Romero Flores, *Historia de la Revolución en Michoacán* (México: Biblioteca del Instituto Nacional de Estudios Históricos de la Revolución Mexican, 1964), p. 18; and Nava Nava, "Relaciones Múgica–Cárdenas," pp. 276–277.

52 See "Manifesto del General Lázaro Cárdenas al Pueblo de Michoacán," delivered at Villa Cuauhtemoc, Veracruz, 10 Jan. 1928, in Cárdenas, *Palabras* I, p. 85.

53 Letter from Cárdenas to F.J. Múgica, 24 May 1928, in "Correspondencia entre Lázaro Cárdenas y Francisco J. Múgica desde 1928 a 1939," *Desdeldiez*, p. 108.

54 *Ibid.*, p. 109.

55 *Ibid.*

56 See Cárdenas, *Apuntes*, vol. I, p. 171. This short period was not enough to put down the revolt, which was then at its height. Cárdenas continued his efforts, however, even after his inauguration as governor. He achieved a major triumph when, in January 1929, he signed the first agreement with Simón Cortéz, one of the rebel leaders, through the mediation of the widow of the famous General Luviano, with whom both Cárdenas and Cortéz had served during the Revolution (Cortéz from 1912 to 1920, Cárdenas for a shorter period). According to Jean Meyer, Cortéz consented to sign the agreement only after his family had fallen into the hands of federal troops and were being used as hostages to exert pressure on him. Meyer writes that Cortéz was very ill at the time and liable to die without treatment. See Meyer, *La Cristiada*, vol. I, p. 285. This unproven version minimizes Cárdenas's role—understandably, since Meyer takes a critical view in general of Cárdenas and *cardenismo*.

In fact this was a very clever political move on the part of Cárdenas, which was revealed by Jorge Zepeda Patterson. According to Patterson, the principal reason for asking for a military appointment parallel to the political appointment was Cárdenas's attempt to establish his rule and civil authority in Michoacán. Since 1922, asserts Patterson, Michoacán rulers lost their authority in favor of the military commanders. The idea of the federal political center was to use the force of the *jefes militares*—"warlords". These aggressors used different modus operandi in controlling the power of the governors (which was always a concern should they abuse their position in order to consolidate their own centripetal power centers, eventually moving away from the influence of the political center and calling it a challenge). The method was therefore to appoint military commanders to balance and even weaken the governors. The arrival of Cárdenas to Michoacán damaged the standing of the military commander at the time, Juan Espinoza Córdova, who had commanded the country since 1925, and who certainly did not like the novelty. Therefore, when the time came for the great offensive against the Cristeros, Cárdenas requested to also be appointed military commander of the country, lest another commander would take control and weaken his political position as governor of the state. As Patterson put it, Cárdenas "no deseaba el encumbramiento de otro militar dentro de su territorio" (did not want the rise of another army within his territory). Cárdenas, therefore, did not take the military command of Michoacán because the state of affairs there was pitiable and in need of an authoritative command of affairs, as Meyer stated. Indeed, the situation was complicated, but Cárdenas wanted it to be himself who would establish his authority in Michoacán and not someone else who would steal this opportunity by accomplishing it by his method. See: Jorge Zepeda Patterson, "Michoacán en la época de Lázaro Cárdenas", en: *Historia general de Michoacán*, Vol. IV, Enrique Florescano (Cood.) (Morelia, Gobierno de Estado de Michoacán, Instituto Michoacano de Cultura, 1989), p. 147.

Veronica Oikión Solano offered an equally convincing explanation, placing Cardenas' appointment in another context. According to Solano, Plutarco Elías Calles, who was the Minister of War in the administration of Emilio Portes Gil, and Portes Gil himself who appointed Cárdenas. Calles's intention was primarily to gain the support of the peasants of the country who were very appreciative of Cárdenas. Portes Gil looked forward to the end of the Cristero struggle, but at the same time wished to consult with Cárdenas as a constraint against the influence of Gilberto Valenzuela who saw himself as the next presidential candidate (1930–1934), and began to propagate his candidacy in the country, much to the chagrin of Calles and Portes Gil, who supported Ortíz Rubio as the next president. Surprisingly, Valenzuela was favored by no one less than the outgoing military commander of Michoacán, General Roberto Cruz, who apparently replaced Juan Córdova, and was presumed clearly an unsympathetic personality among the senior national leadership. Indeed, Solano states, with the appointment of Cárdenas as army commander of Michoacán, Valenzuela's camp dissolved. See Oikión Solano, *Los hombres del poder*, pp. 109–111.

57 Álvaro Ochoa Serrano, "Miguel de la Trinidad Regalado y la lucha por la tierra", *Relaciones* 4, 14 (Spring, 1983): 109–118; Jesús Tapia Santamaria, *Campo religioso y evolución política en el bajio zamorano* (Zamora, Michoacán: El Colegio de Michoacán, Gobierno del Edo. de Michoacán, 1986), pp. 188–199; Alvaro Ochoa Serrano, "Miguel Regalado y la sociedad unificadora de la raza indígena," in Gerardo Sánchez Díaz (coord.), *La Revolución en Michoacán 1920–1926* (Morelia, Michoacán: Departamento de Historia, Universidad Michoacana, 1987), pp. 53–80; Gerardo Sánchez Díaz, "Los elementos y las acciones de la contrarrevolución en Michoacán, 1918–1923," in *La Revolución en Michoacán 1920–1926*, pp. 110–112; and "Carpeta especial sobre el asesinato del Diputado Rafael Picazo (24 de febrero de 1931), protestas de varios pueblos," in Archivo Histórico del Congreso de Michoacán del Ocampo [hereafter AHCMO], Legislatura LXIII, "Especiales," caja I.

58 See Liga de Comunidades Agrarias y Sindicatos Campesinos del Estado de Veracruz, *Ursulo Galván, 1893–1930: Su vida—su obra* (Jalapa-Enríquez: CNC, 28 July 1966), p. 24; Skerritt, *Una historia agraria*, pp. 155–156, 180–193; Olivia Domínguez Pérez, *Política y movimientos sociales en el Tejedismo* (Xalapa: Centro de Investigaciones Históricas, Universidad Veracruzana, 1986), p. 136; and Antonio Santoyo, *La Mano Negra: Poder regional y Estado en Mexico* (Veracruz, 1928–1943), (México: Consejo Nacional para la Cultura y los Artes, 1995), pp. 123–150.

2 Towards Reform: The Development of Leadership Patterns and Political Infrastructure

1 Leafar Agetro, *Las luchas proletarias en Veracruz: Historia y autocrítica* (Jalapa: Editorial Barricada, 1942), p. 101.

2 "Liga de Comunidades Agrarias de Veracruz: Datos acerca de su formación e ideología revolucionaria," *El Nacional* (edición conmemorativa), 20 Nov. 1931.

3 *Ibid.*

4 "Liga de Comunidades Agrarias del Estado de Veracruz—Convocatoria," *El Machete*, 30 Oct.–6 Nov. 1924; "Liga de Comunidades Agrarias de Veracruz: Datos acerca de su formación e ideología revolucionaria," *El Nacional* (edición conmemorativa), 20 Nov. 1931; "El IV Congreso de la Liga de Comunidades Agrarias del Estado de Veracruz," *El Machete*, 17 Dec. 1927; "Resoluciones del IV Congreso de la Liga de Comunidades Agrarias del Estado de Veracruz," *El Machete*, 24 Dec. 1927.

5 Fowler, *Movilización campesina*, p. 94.

6 The League's agendas, resolutions, and protocols are testimony to its organizational sophistication. See, for example, "IV Congreso de la Liga de Comunidades Agrarias de Veracruz," *El Machete*, 11 Nov. 1927; "El IV Congreso de la Liga de Comunidades Agrarias del Estado de Veracruz," *El Machete*, 17 Dec. 1927; and Pedro Pérez, Delegado Regional de la 2a zona de Medellín, to the Sub-Jefe del Departamento de Gobernación, 1 Aug. 1932, in Archivo de Adalberto Tejeda (AAT), vol. 220, foja 39.

7 Reuben Clark, Jr., to the Secretary of State, "Disarming of Agrarian or 'Defence' Organizations of the State of Veracruz," 30 Dec. 1932, in US National Archives, Records of the Department of State Relating to the Internal Affairs of Mexico, 1929–1939, Washington, DC [hereafter NA/RDS], doc. 812.52/1781 (10 Jan. 1933), p. 3; Leonard G. Dawson, American Consul, to the Secretary of State, "Disarmament of 'Guerillas' in Veracruz State," 13 Jan. 1933, in NA/RDS, doc. 812.00, Veracruz/45, p. 3; and "Las anárquicas defensas rurales de Veracruz," *El Universal*, 11 Jan. 1933.

8 "La Liga trata de readquirir su preponderancia en la legislatura," *El Dictamen*, 5 Oct. 1931.

9 Expediente de Ley #66 de1 4 de marzo de 1929: "Concede facultades extraordinarias al ejecutivo del Estado en los ramos de hacienda, gobernación y milicia," in Archivo General del Estado de Veracruz (AGEV), Fondo Legislatura.

10 "Ley expedida por el Ejecutivo del Estado, con fecha 10 de abril, estableciendo en el Estado cuerpos de defensa pública con el nombre de 'guerrillas,'" *Gaceta Oficial* XXI, no. 52 (30 April 1929): 1–2.

11 "Reglamento de la Ley de las Guerrillas de junio 24 de 1929," *Gaceta Oficial* XXII, no. 79 (2 July 1929): 2–4.

12 Antonio Echegaray, Presidente de la Liga de Comunidades Agrarias, to Tejeda, 24 May 1932, in AAT, vol. 220, foja 18; Tejeda to the Jefe de la Guerrilla de Zongolica (no number, no date), in AAT, tomo 124, vol. 148; and expediente 885, paquete 3130 (1932), exp. 996, pq. 3183 (1932), exp. 994, pq. 3165 (1932), and exp. 225, pq. 3171 (1932), all in AGEV, Fondo de Gobernación y Justicia.

13 "El campesino organizado, dice el Gobernador, ha traido la tranquilidad del campo," *El Dictamen*, 6 May 1931.

14 In Fowler's estimation, without the *guerrillas*, not only would Tejeda not have been able to implement the agrarian reform, but he would also never have been able to achieve such a central role in the federal sphere. See Fowler, *Movilización campesina*, p. 121.

15 On some of the League's actions in the fields of morality and criminal justice, see Comunicación de novedades de las fuerzas de reserva to Tejeda, 9 Feb., 31 March, 10, 16, and 18 April, 3, 11, and 25 May, and 9 and 22 June 1932, in AAT, vol. 220 (1932); Comandante de Martínez de la Torre to Tejeda, 15 Dec. 1931, in AAT, tomo 167, vol. 191 (1931), foja 172; and General Samuel A. Kelly to Tejeda, 9 Nov. 1931, in AAT, tomo 167, vol. 191 (1931), doc. 33.

16 Tejeda to C. Diputado Secretario de la H. Legislatura del Estado, 8 Aug. 1932, in AAT, tomo 197 (1932), pp. 379–380; and exp. 225, *pq.* 3171; exp. 561, *pq.* 3128; exp. 798, *pq.* 3105; exp. 995, *pq.* 3165; exp. 1012, *pq.* 3125; exp. 1495, *pq.* 3125; and exp. 2062, *pq.* 3167, all in AGEV, Fondo Gobernación y Justicia (1932).

17 David Skerritt G. "El papel de Adalberto Tejeda en la cuestión agraria," *La palabra y el hombre, Revista de la Universidad Veracruzana* (Nueva Epoca) 32 (Oct.–Dec. 1979): 16–17; "Expediente de Decreto #108 de junio 30 de 1932 facultando al Ejecutivo del Estado para ceder a la Liga de Comunidades Agrarias del Estado una finca propiedad del Estado," in AGEV, Fondo Legislatura, doc. 4-1-108-1932; "Expediente de Decreto #109 de junio 30 de 1932 facultando al Ejecutivo del Estado para ceder una finca al Comité Agrario de Atoyac," in AGEV, Fondo Legislatura, doc. 4-1-109-1932; and Secretario Particular de Tejeda to the Liga de Comunidades Agrarias, 6 April 1932, in AAT, vol. 220, foja 36.

18 Quoted in Fowler, *Movilización campesina*, p. 108.

19 Skerritt, "El papel de Adalberto Tejeda en la cuestión agraria," pp. 20–21.

20 Falcón and García Morales, *La semilla en el surco*, p. 240.

21 On Tejeda's devotion to the Veracruz labor movement, see Alberto J. Olvera Rivera et al., "Balance sobre la investigación de la formación de la clase obrera veracruzana: 1850–1932," in Alejandra Moreno Toscano and Samuel L. González (eds), *75 años de sindicalismo mexicano* (México: Instituto Nacional de Estudios Históricos de la Revolución Mexicana, 1986), p. 213; Olivia Dominguez Pérez, *Política y movimientos sociales en el tejedismo* (Xalapa: Centro de Investigaciones Históricas, Universidad Veracruzana, 1986), pp. 40–56, 134–141; Terrones, *Un ensayo radical*, pp. 88–100; and "Informe leido al 15 de septiembre de 1932 (Informe 1931–1932: Primer semestre) ante la H. Legislatura del Estado de Veracruz," in AAT, tomo 197 (1932), fojas 473–476.

22 In the port, for example, Tejeda tried to weaken various unions, such as the Liga de Trabajadores de la Zona Marítima of Veracruz which was headed by Rafael García, an activist who had competed with him for control of the city. See Skerritt, "El papel de Adalberto Tejeda en la cuestión agraria," pp. 20–21. On

other occasions, he would reinforce one particular (independent) proletarian organization among all those in Veracruz—for example, the port dockers' union (Unión de Carretilleros del Puerto de Veracruz)—by offering it generous government financial guarantees, while undermining another—in this instance, another, larger dockers' union (Unión de Cargadores y Abridores de la Zona Marítima). This policy brought him very close to unlawful discrimination at times, and indeed in the case of the dockers' unions he was obliged by court order to cancel the financial guarantees. See "Expediente de Decreto #136, derogando el Decreto 327 del 5 de agosto de 1930" (15 Jan. 1931), in AGEV, Fondo Legislatura, expediente 4-136 (1931).

23   Olivia Domínguez Pérez, "Un estudio de caso: Los comunistas de San Bruno," in *Anuario* II (Jalapa: Centro de Estudios Históricos, Universidad Veracruzana, 1979), pp. 227–252.

24   "Unificación obrera y campesina en el Estado de Veracruz," *El Nacional*, 18 Jan. 1931. It should be noted, however, that *El Nacional*'s reports on this subject tended to exaggerate.

25   In response to the accusation by one of the Communist representatives at the League's sixth congress (which took place at the end of May, 1929) that Galván had "sold his soul to the state," Galván firmly insisted that the League did not belong to the state, and operated independently of it. See *El Universal* and *Excelsior*, 1 June 1929. Fifteen out of the 17 prominent leaders of the first generation of the League who were active between 1923 and 1933 were of peasant origin, and eight of them remained *campesinos* even after they became leaders. In the second generation, post-Tejeda, the situation was reversed. See Fowler, *Movilización campesina*, pp. 179–181.

26   One of the few times Tejeda is known to have intervened was at the League's founding convention in 1923. On that occasion he used his influence to have Ursulo Galván rather than José Cardel elected head of the organization, even though Cardel was considered the League's natural leader. See Heather Fowler Salamini, "Los orígines de las organizaciones campesinas en Veracruz: Raíces políticas y sociales," *Historia Mexicana* 22, no. 1 (July–Sept., 1972): 71–72.

27   Women had a master roll in the tenants movement of the city of Veraruz and in other working issues of this city from free sex trade to reasonable rent prices to strikes and public humiliation of civil servants and money collectors and until domestic workers rights, which Tejeda knew very well from his first governship. See: Wood, *Revolution in the Street*, pp. 75–80, 113, 164.

28   "Del triunfo de la Revolución responde el Estado de Veracruz," *El Dictamen*, 8 April 1931.

29   "Convocatoria que el Ciudadano Governador del Estado haga a los trabajadores de Michoacán," in Archivo Municipal de Zamora (AMZ), Fondo de Fomento, exp. 2, caja 1929 (varios); and Gabino Vázquez, Jefe del Centro Organizador de la Convención to the Presidente Municipal de Zamora, 11 Jan. 1929, in AMZ, Fondo de Fomento, exp. 2, caja 1929 (varios).

30   Jesús Múgica Martínez, *La Confederación Revolucionaria Michoacana del Trabajo* (México: Eddisa, 1982), p. 98.

31   *Ibid.*, Estatutos, arts. 1, 3, and 6.

32   Manuel Diego Hernández, *La Confederación Revolucionaria Michoacana del Trabajo* (Jiquilpán, Michoacán: Centro de Estudios de la Revolución Mexicana "Lázaro Cárdenas", 1982), p. 43; and "Programa Sindical de la Confederación

Revolucionaria del Trabajo," art. VI, in Múgica Martínez, *La Confederación*, pp. 105–106.

33 "Quedó integrada en Michoacán una confederación de los trabajadores," *El Universal Gráfico*, 6 Feb. 1929; Diego Hernández, *La Confederación*, pp. 33–34; and Múgica Martínez, *La Confederación*, pp. 107–109.

34 Diego Hernández, *La Confederación*, p. 32; and Múgica Martínez, *La Confederación*, pp. 103–105.

35 "La tercera convención de la Confederación Revolucionaria Michoacana de Trabajo," *El Nacional*, 27 July 1931.

36 We must relate to the number of members of the organization carefully. One of the listed members of the Movement was the father of the historian Luis González y González. He received his membership certification but never acknowledged his desire to be a member or identified with anything in the organization. From a discussion with Luis González y González, Mexico City, January 1992.

37 The new law stipulated that when a new union was established in a factory or other work place, all individual contracts would be provisionally cancelled and a collective labor agreement would be signed between the union and the employer. Workers who did not want to join the union could sign individual agreements as long as they were carefully based on the existing labor law. If two or more unions were set up in one work place, the largest one would negotiate the collective labor contract on behalf of all the others. See Ley #28: "Sobre reforma a la ley de trabajo vigente en el Estado," 18 Jan. 1929, in AHCMO, XLII Legislatura, caja 2, carp. 3.

38 *Ibid.*

39 "Reglamento a que deben sujetarse los trabajos preparatorios y los discusiones del primer congreso agrario michoacano," *Impresos michoacanos*, no. 7 (Morelia: Biblioteca del H. Congreso del Edo de Michoacán); "Convocatoria del Gobernador constitucional del Estado de Michoacán a las comunidades agrarias, sindicatos campesinos y hacendados del Estado de Michoacán," Morelia, 3 Oct. 1929, in Lázaro Cárdenas, *Palabras* I, pp. 86–87; "Convocatoria del Gobernador constitucional del Estado de Michoacán a las comunidades indígenas forestales del Estado," Morelia, Dec., 1929, in Lázaro Cárdenas, *Palabras* I, pp. 87–88.

40 Mora Tovar, for example, was appointed as the deputy of the president of the central survey committee. Later he was the sole representative of the government in Michoacán's central body for conciliation and arbitration. He was also a reporter for *El Nacional*, the official organ of the PNR, and editor of *El Estado*, the Michoacán edition of *El Nacional*. See Luis Mora Tovar to Presidente Municipal de Zamora, 13 Aug. 1929, in AMZ, Fondo de Fomento, exp. 16: "Censos de habitantes, industrias y agrupaciones," caja 1929; and "Directorio oficial," in *Periódico Oficial* LIII (20 June 1932).
José Solórzano was, in addition to his position in the CRMDT, one of five workers' representatives in the central board of conciliation and arbitration, and first secretary of the PNR's state executive committee (*comité ejecutivo estatal*) in Michoacán. In 1932 he was elected local deputy for the years 1932–1934. See *Periódico Oficial* XLIX, no. 51 (27 Jan. 1929); "Directorio oficial," *Periódico Oficial* XLIX, no. 51 (27 Jan. 1929); and "Acta de sesiones #2, sesión de 17 de junio de 1932, XLIII Legislatura," *Periódico Oficial* LIII, no. 21 (15 Aug. 1932). Antonio Mayés Navarro, a founder and leader of the CRMDT, was a member

of the Michoacán PNR's executive, and in 1932 was elected to the local Congress. Augusto Hinojosa was also a founder of the CRMDT, had helped set up the Liga Agraria de Michoacán, and served as head of the federal agricultural-ejidal bank in Michoacán. Alberto Coria was the second secretary of the CRMDT's first executive (the CCC) and a member of the state executive committee of the PNR. See "Directorio oficial," *Periódico Oficial* LIII, no. 21 (15 Aug. 1932); Múgica Martínez, *La Confederación*, p. 97; "Acta de sesiones no. 2, sesión de junio 17 de 1932, XLIII Legislatura," *Periódico oficial* LIII, no. 21 (15 Aug. 1932).

Gabino Vázquez, Cárdenas's right hand in organizing the CRMDT, was government secretary throughout Cárdenas's term of office in Michoacán, his permanent deputy, and a member of the state executive committe of the PNR. He stood in for Cárdenas on a number of occasions as provisional governor, and also spent some time as one of the five state Supreme-Court judges. See "Directorio oficial," *Periódico Oficial* LIII, no. 21 (15 Aug. 1932); "Acepta a los C.C. Licenciados Agustín Leñero y Gabino Vázquez las renuncias que presentan de la carga de magistrados propietario y supernumerario respectivamente, y nombrando a los substitutos," *Periódico Oficial* L, no. 82 (1 May 1930): 1–2; and "Magistrados del Supremo Tribunal de Justicia," *Periódico oficial* LI, no. 7 (28 July 1930).

41   "Defensas sociales en Zitacuaro, *El Universal*, 30 March 1929.

42   For some of the violent incidents in the Michoacán countryside that necessitated the intervention of the rural guards, see "Una gevilla de bandolero ha sembrado el espanto en todo el Estado de Michoacán," *El Nacional*, 2 Sept. 1930; "El clero reorganiza en Michoacán," *El Nacional*, 26 Sept. 1930; and "Fue inhumada la víctima de un crimen," *El Nacional*, 24 Sept. 1931.

43   Reuben Clark, Jr., to Secretary of State, "Disarming of Agrarian or 'Defence Organizations' of the State of Veracruz," NA/RDS, 812.52/1781 (10 Jan. 1933), p. 3.

44   Cárdenas, *Apuntes* I, p. 182.

45   "Amplia defensa de los agraristas del Estado de Michoacán," *El Nacional*, 26 Feb. 1933.

46   Author's interview with Jesús Múgica Martínez, Morelia, Michoacán (July, 1992); and Múgica Martínez, *La Confederación*, pp. 128–129.

47   "Citatorio del Presidente Municipal de Zamora a los CC. miembros de la Junta de Mejoras Materiales del municipio," 10 July 1931, in AMZ, Fondo de Fomento, exp. 8/IBID 1931, caja 1930–1931/2°.

48   See, for example, Cárdenas, *Informe 1929–1930*, p. 19; "Informe del General de División Lázaro Cárdenas, Gobernador del Estado de Michoacán, ante la XLIV Legislatura Local, correspondiente al ejercicio comprendido entre 1928–1932," Morelia, Michoacán, 16 Sept. 1932, in *Palabras y documentos públicos de Lázaro Cárdenas 1928–1940*, vol. II (México: Siglo XXI Editores, 1978), p. 36; and "Respuesta del Dr. Enrique Ramos, el C. Diputado Presidente del H. Congreso, al informe de 1932," in AHCMO, XLIII Legislatura, exp. 5, caja 2, "Varios," pp. 2–3.

49   On this serious episode, which aroused a storm in Congress, see "Acta #14 de 24 de julio de 1931, primer período extraordinario de sesiones," *Libro de actas de sesiones*, XLIII Legislatura (1931–1932), 14 Sept. 1931–29 Aug. 1932, in AHCMO.

50   Cárdenas, *Informe 1928–1932*, p. 33.

51 "Informe que rinde el C. Ing. Adalberto Tejeda, Gobernador constitucional del Estado, ante la H. Trigesimacuarta Legislatura," 16 Sept. 1932, in *Estado de Veracruz: Informes de sus gobernadores 1826–1986*, comp. by Carmen Blázquez Domínguez, vol. 12 (Xalapa: Gobierno del Estado de Veracruz, 1986), pp. 6071–6072; Fowler, *Movilización campesina*, p. 103; and letter from Tejeda to Carlos Tejeda, quoted in Terrones López, *Un ensayo radical*, pp. 236–237.

52 H.N. Branch, trans., *The Mexican Constitution of 1917 Compared with the Constitution of 1857* (Philadelphia: The American Academy of Political and Social Science, 1917), pp. 89–90.

53 "Constitución política del Estado libre y soberano de Veracruz-Llave," Edición oficial (Orizaba, Veracrus: Tipografía del Gobierno del Estado, 1917), in *150 años de constitucionalismo veracruzano, 1825–1975: Origenes e instituciones 2* (Estado Libre y Soberano de Veracruz-Llave: 1975), pp. 191–192; "Constitución libre y soberano de Michoacán de Ocampo," Articles 94–108, in Xavier Tavera Alfaro (ed.), *Recopilación de leyes, decretos, reglamentos y circulares expedidas en el Estado de Michoacán*, Vol. XLIV, *Período preconstitucional y XXXVI Legislatura del 1 de enero de 1917 al 25 de septiembre de 1918* (Morelia, Michoacán: H. Congreso del Estado, 1978), pp. 523–528.

54 On the local authorities' powers, see "Constitución política de Veracruz," Art. 28/I; and "Constitución política de Michoacán," Arts. 103, 104/IX-XII. The Veracruz constitution and the Veracruz *Ley de Municipio Llibre* did not emphasize the agrarian issue as the Michoacán constitution did, although in fact its tasks in this field were identical to those of Michoacán. See "Ley Orgánica del Municipio Libre del Estado de Veracruz," 14 Jan. 1918, in Gobierno Constitucional del Estado de Veracruz-Llave, *Colección de leyes, decretos y circulares* (Orizaba, Veracruz: Tipografía del Gobierno del Estado, 1918), p. 117. Tejeda demanded full committment to agrarianism from the municipios. The agrarian laws themselves expressed this, since they gave the municipios the main responsibility for implementing them. On the municipios' role in agrarian reform, see Salvador Robles Quintero, "La reforma agraria actual y el nuevo municipio mexicano," *Estudios municipales* (Centro Nacional de Estudios Municipales [CNEM], Secretaría de Gobernación) 2, no. 7 (Jan.–Feb., 1986): 43–50.

55 Anguiano cites at least three instances of this. See Victoriano Anguiano Equihua, *Lázaro Cárdenas, su feudo y la política nacional* (México: Editorial Referencias, 1989), pp. 57–58. See also "Acta #21, sesión de 19 de diciembre de 1931, XLIII Legislatura," in *Periódico oficial* LII, no. 88 (21 April 1932): 4–6.

56 "Actas de sesiones del Congreso Michoacano, XLII Legislatura, sesiones 44, 50, 51, 57, and 65," *Libro de actas de sesiones*, Vol. I (1928–1930); Proyecto de Ley #2, XLIII Legislatura, in AHCMO, caja 1 carp. 2; and Proyecto de Ley #92, XLIII Legislatura, in AHCMO, caja 5, carp. 19. Cárdenas claimed to have established 12 municipios during his governorship, though this is not borne out by the facts. See Cárdenas, *Informe 1928–1932*, pp. 32–33.

57 "Vecinos de Tocumbo al Ciudadano Presidente del H. Congreso del Estado," 27 Nov. 1929, in Expediente del Ley #76, AHCMO, LXII Legislatura, caja 4, carp. 8; and Ley #76: "Elevado a la categoría de municipio libre la tenencia de Tocumbo," "Acta #57, sesión de 11 de febrero de 1930, segundo período ordinario de sesiones, XLII Legislatura Constitucional," *Libro de actas de sesiones* (1928–1930), in AHEMO.

58   See, for example, a letter from the inhabitants of Tacatzcurao, included in a letter from Lic Augustín Leñero, secretario general de Gobierno, to H. Congreso del Estado, "Asunto: Se transcribe mensaje del C. Presidente municipal de Tinguindín," 13 Feb. 1930, Expediente del Ley #76, AHCMO, LXII Legislatura, caja 4, carp. 8.

59   Francisco Quijano de la Parra, Hacienda de la Esperanza, to the C. Secretario del Congreso del Estado, Morelia, 6 Feb. 1930, Expediente del Ley #76, AHCMO, LXII Legislatura, caja 4, carp. 8.

60   Proyecto de Ley #76 de la 1/a Comisión de Gobernación (11 Feb. 1930);

61   A similar spirit was revealed in the establishment of Ocampo, Churumuco, Alvaro Obregón, and Tarímbaro. See Expediente del Ley #68 (Ocampo), AHCMO, XLII Legislatura, caja 3, carp. 23; Expediente del Ley #94 (Alvaro Obregón), AHCMO, XLII Legislatura, caja 5, carp. 5; Expediente del Ley #71 (Churumuco), AHCMO, XLII Legislatura, caja 4, carp. 3; and Expediente del Ley #89 (Tarímbaro), AHCMO, XLII Legislatura, caja 4, carp. 22.

62   Guaracha: Expediente del Ley #60, AHCMO, LXII Legislatura, caja 3, carp. 13, and *Periódico Oficial* LII, no. 13 (3 Aug. 1929); Ibarra: *Periódico oficial* LII, no. 13 (3 Aug. 1929); Sorumbeneo: Expediente del Ley #72, AHCMO, LXII Legislatura, caja 4, carp. 5; Cuto and Tejaro: Expediente del Ley # 89, AHCMO, LXII Legislatura, caja 4, carp. 22; Pastor Ortíz: Expediente del Ley #124, AHCMO, LXII Legislatura, caja 6, carp. 16; Mariano Escobedo: *Periódico Oficial* LII, no. 23 (7 Sept. 1931); Copándaro: *Periódico Oficial* LIII, no. 27(5 Sept. 1932); Salto de Tepuxtepec: *Periódico Oficial* LIII, no. 22 (18 Aug. 1932); and Nueva Italia, Lombardía, Tepenahua, Pedernales, Briseñas, Chaparro, Cantabria: *Periódico Oficial* LIII, no. 30 (suplemento) (15 Sept. 1932).

63   Carta de Juan Chamio, Jefe Municipal de Charo, al H. Congreso Local, 22 Nov. 1929; carta de los vecinos del Rancho de Surumbeneo al H. Congreso Local, 28 Oct. 1929; Proyecto de Ley #72, 24 Jan. 1930, in Expediente de Ley #72, AHCMO, LXII Legislatura, caja 4, carp. 5.

64   Proyecto de Ley #124, 24 July 1930, in Expediente de Ley #124, AHCMO, LXII Legislatura, caja 6, carp. 16; and "Acta #5, sesión de 24 de julio de 1930, tercer período extraordinario de sesiones," in *Libro de actas de sesiones*, vol. 1, p. 6, AHCMO.

65   "Acta #14, sesión de 24 de octubre de 1929, segundo período ordinario de sesiones," in *Libro de actas de sesiones* I (1929–1930), pp. 2–3, AHCMO, XLII Legislatura.

66   See, for example, "Continuará la deposición de ayuntamientos," *El Dictamen*, 12 Dec. 1930; "Con ayuda de la fuerza tomó posesión el Ayuntamiento de Pánuco," *El Universal*, 7 Jan. 1932; and "Maniobra de un grupo político en México contra el Gobernador Tejeda," *El Dictamen*, 1 Aug. 1929.

67   On the Veracruz municipio, see *Excelsior*, 1 and 4 Jan. 1929; on Pánuco, see "Cultivo obligatorio en las tierras repartidas," *Excelsior*, 26 June 1932.

68   "Discusión de la sesión efectuada el día 1° de julio de 1930," XXXII H. Legislatura del Estado (de Veracruz), p. 12, in AGEV, Fondo Legislatura, Paquete de actas de sesiones de la XXXII Legislatura (Sept. 1928–Sept. 1930).

69   For a few instances among many, see Expediente de Decreto #84 (20 March 1929), AGEV, Fondo Legislatura; Expediente de Decreto #85 (22 March 1929), AGEV, Fondo Legislatura; Expediente de Decreto #86 (9 April 1929), AGEV, Fondo Legislatura; Expediente de Decreto #137 (13 Aug. 1929), AGEV, Fondo Legislatura; Expediente de Decreto #138 (22 Aug. 1929), AGEV, Fondo

Legislatura; and Expediente de Decreto #334 (30 July 1930), AGEV, Fondo Legislatura.

70 See, for example, Lázaro Cruz to Diputado Marcos C. Licona, 2 June 1932, AAT, vol. 220 (1932), foja 63; José R. Bravo a Tejeda, 4 Nov. 1931, AAT, tomo 167, vol. 191 (1931), foja 295; carta sin nombre a Tejeda, 12 Sept. 1929, AAT, tomo 128, vol. 152 (1929); Promovente "Junta de Administración Civil de Tlacolulán," AGEV, Fondo de Gobernación y Justicia, exp. 2161, pq. 3219.

71 Promovente: "Junta de Administración Civil de Tomatlán—Nombramientos," AGEV, Fondo de Gobernación y Justicia, exp. 21045, pq. 3219.

72 It is important to note that the city and especially the fleet that was harbored there were central to the support in the Escobar–Aguirre revolt. From the city, more accurately the military government situated there, the September 1927 revolt brought about the downfall of Governor Heriberto Jara who preceded Adalberto Tejada. The importance of controlling this major port city of the Republic was essential for the control of Veracruz and to establish a bargaining position against the Federal Center that had always endeavored to take control of the city and weaken its Governor. See: Erasmo Hernández García, *Redes Políticas y Sociales: Consolidación y Permanencia del Régimen Posrevolucionario en Veracruz, 1920–1970* (Doctoral Thesis, Universidad Veracruzana, 2010), pp. 13, 68–70, 85, 93, 103.

73 Decreto #80 (20 March 1929): "Suspensión definitiva a los miembros del ayuntamiento de Veracruz," AGEV, Fondo Legislatura, 1929; "Fue suspendido ayer el Ayuntamiento del Puerto de Varacruz," *Excelsior*, 1 Jan. 1929; *Excelsior*, 4, 6, 8, 10 January 1929; and telegrama de Tomás Pérez Morteo, Presidente Municipal de Veracruz, a Tejeda, AAT, tomo 134, vol. 158 (1929), foja 58.

74 *Excelsior*, 10 and 12 Jan. 1929.

75 Decreto #80 (20 March 1929): "Suspensión definitiva a los miembros del Ayuntamiento de Veracruz," AGEV, Fondo Leg. (1929). On the many appeals received by the Congress from all quarters and the ensuing debate, see "Acta de Sesiones del H. XXXII Legislatura Veracruzana de 1 y 2 de enero de 1929," *Gaceta Oficial* XXIII, no. 54–55 (6–10 May 1930).

76 On the many commendations Tejeda received for his prompt and decisive action against the revolt, and on the view that the revolt's quick termination in Veracruz compared with other places was due to the speedy mobilization of the agrarianists, see "El Coronel Tejeda ha sido ya localizado," *El Universal*, 6 March 1929; "Resumen sobre la situación militar en Veracruz," *El Universal*, 7 March 1929; "La campaña de Veracruz se estima terminada desde ayer," *El Universal*, 8 March 1929; "Más adhesiones de los partidos agraristas," *El Universal*, 12 March 1929; and "El Gobernador Tejeda llegó ayer al puerto con ochocientos agraristas," *El Dictamen*, 9 March 1929. Aguirre himself was caught on 21 March in the city of Veracruz by General Miguel Acosta, the commander of the military troops sent to Veracruz, summarily tried, and executed on the same day. See "Hoy será ejecutado J.M. Aguirre y en un encuentro murió Alemán," *El Dictamen*, 21 March 1929.

77 The American consul in the city of Veracruz, Leonard Dawson, wrote on this subject to the Secretary of State in Washington on 1 July 1931: "The city of Veracruz has been free from any element representing the agrarian party, as the territory included within the municipal jurisdiction is of little importance agriculturally. The municipal governments have been composed almost exclusively of the leaders of the labor organizations. . . ." Leonard G. Dawson, American

Consul, to Secretary of State, "Political Report for June 1931," NA/RDS, Doc. 812.00, Veracruz/22, 1 July 1931.

78 "¿Qué ayuntamiento es que desean los vecinos de Veracruz?" *El Universal*, 16 April 1929.

79 "Gran actitud política en la ciudad de Córdoba," *Excelsior*, 8 July 1929.

80 Arnulfo Gómez (agente confidencial de Tejeda) to Tejeda, 30 Oct. 1929 and 9, 18, and 21 Nov. 1929, AAT, tomo 130, vol. 154 (1929), fojas 588, 586, 584.

81 Joaquin López, secretario general del Gran Partido Socialista Veracruzano, to Ing. Pascual Ortiz Rubio, 5 Aug. 1929, AAT, tomo 135, vol. 159 (1929), foja 128; Pascual Ortiz Rubio to Tejeda, 9 Aug. 1929, AAT, tomo 135, vol. 159 (1929), foja 127. On the breach between Galván and the Communist party, see "La verdad sobre la expulsión de Galván del Partido Comunista," *El Machete* V (27 May 1929, extra edition); "Sobre la expulsión de Ursulo Galván," *El Machete* V, no. 168 (8 June 1929); "Galván contra la Liga Nacional Campesina," *El Machete* V, no. 170 (22 June 1929); "Galván se quita la máscara," *El Machete* V, no. 171 (29 June 1929); and "Galván contra la LNC," *El Machete* V, no. 172 (6 July 1929).

82 Tejeda to Pascual Ortiz Rubio, 29 Aug. 1929, AAT, tomo 135, vol. 159 (1929), foja 121.

83 Tejeda had many sources of information in the city of Veracruz. One of them was the city treasurer, José del Carmen López, and another was a professional agent by the name of Arnulfo Nieves who sent him a report every few days. See, for example, José del Carmen López, tesorero municipal de Veracruz, to Tejeda, 26 and 30 June 1929 and 11 and 28 July 1929, AAT, tomo 130, vol. 154 (1929), fojas 357, 358, 346–348, and 361, respectively.

84 "Parecen tener un solo programa de gobierno los candidatos a la presidencia municipal," *El Dictamen*, 24 June 1929.

85 "Protestas contra un líder ortizrubista (Altamirano) en Veracruz," *El Universal*, 27 May 1929; "Fue desaforado ayer el Sr. Gobernador de Zacatecas," *El Universal*, 30 May 1929; and "Maniobra de un grupo político en Mexico contra el Gobernador Tejeda," *El Dictamen*, 1 Aug. 1929.

86 "En candente sesión protesta la legislatura por la anunciada maniobra," *El Dictamen*, 11 Aug. 1929; "El Gobernador A. Tejeda exhortó para que se consideren con serenidad, prudencia y patriotismo las versiones sobre el atentado a la soberanía de Veracruz," *El Dictamen*, 12 Aug. 1929.

87 "Petición de Manlio Fabio Altamirano desechada con una rechifla general," *El Dictamen*, 18 Sept. 1929.

88 Expediente de Decreto #157: "Declarando nulas las elecciones verificadas en el Puerto de Veracruz al 22 de septiembre próximo pasado," AGEV, Fondo Legislatura, 4-1-1929, 24 Oct. 1929; and "Anulan la elección municipal en este puerto, por unanimidad y sin discusión," *El Dictamen*, 25 Oct. 1929.

89 Decretos #91, #157, #182–186, #192–194, #199, #207–213 (24–27 Oct. 1929), *Gaceta Oficial* XXII, pp. 131, 149–150, 154–155, and *Gaceta Oficial* XXIII, no. 2 (31 Oct. 1929–4 Jan. 1930)

90 In a congressional debate on 14 December 1928 concerning the temporary status of the Orizaba council, serious charges were made against the administration over the methods of the administrative *juntas*. Some claimed that these provisional councils created pressure on government workers to take part in them. Ultimately, seven Congress members supported the holding of elections and seven opposed it, leaving the situation in Orizaba unchanged. See "Acta de

sesiones del H. Legislatura Veracruzana, 14 y 21 de diciembre de 1928," *Gaceta Oficial* XXI, nos. 61, 62, and 66 (21 and 33 May and 1 June 1929).

91 Leonard G. Dawson to Secretary of State, "Political Report for June, 1931," NA/RDS, Doc. 812.00, Veracruz/22 (1 July 1931), pp. 15–20.

92 On criticism of his methods, see, for example, a variety of headings that appeared in one newspaper article that Tejeda received from a friend or agent, and that was filed in his archive at the end of September, 1929, without mention of the name of the newspaper: "No quieren ya cambios en Pueblo Viejo," "Parece que el Gobernador de Veracruz trata de nombrar autoridades por enésima vez," "Un telegrama al Sr. Presidente de la República," and "Las maniobras giran alrededor de las elecciones que se efectuarán hoy," AAT, tomo 133, vol. 157 (1929), foja 159. For other criticism in the local and national press, see "Continuará la deposición de ayuntamientos," and "Para tener el absoluto dominio electoral estando entre los amenazados, Puerto México [Coatzacoalcos] y Tlalixcoyan," *El Dictamen*, 12 Dec. 1930; and "Con ayuda de la fuerza tomó posesión el Ayuntamiento de Pánuco," *El Universal*, 7 Jan. 1932.

93 Leonard G. Dawson to Secretary of State, "Political Report for April, 1931," NA/RDS, Doc. 812.00, Veracruz/18 (1 May 1931), pp. 7–8. On the agrarianists' opposition to the dissolution of the council of Atoyac, which had given every proof of its good will towards them and had even helped organize them in agrarian committees, see Expediente de Decreto #274 del 20 de agosto de 1931: "Suspendiendo provisionalmente en sus funciones al Ayuntamiento de Atoyac," AGEV, Fondo Legislatura, 1931.

94 Leonard G. Dawson to Secretary of State, "Political Report for June, 1931," NA/RDS, Doc. 812.00, Veracruz/22 (1 July 1931), p. 20.

95 "Un atentado a la vida del Coronel Adalberto Tejeda," *Excelsior*, 26 July 1931; "Atentado al Gobernador de Veracruz, Coronel A. Tejeda," *El Nacional*, 27 July 1931; and Leonard G. Dawson to Secretary of State, "Attempt on Life of Governor Tejeda and Assassination of Priest at Veracruz," NA/RDS, Doc. 812.00/29629, Veracruz/24 (28 July 1931), pp. 1–7.

96 The consul, too, had expected Guzmán to win the election for head of the governing council, since he had won the nomination as the PNR's local candidate. Perhaps to illustrate Guzmán's potential as a fearless man unswerving in the pursuit of his goals, the consul recounted an episode that had taken place a month earlier, when Guzmán and another deputy had been attacked by a band of religious extremists near Tlalixcoyan. Guzmán had escaped without harm, but only after a gun battle that lasted all night.

97 Leonard G. Dawson to Secretary of State, "Political Report for September, 1931" NA/RDS, Doc. 812.00, Veracruz/27 (30 Sept. 1931), p. 2.

98 "La Liga de Comunidades Agrarias de Veracruz," Edición conmemorativa de *El Nacional Revolucionario*, 20 Nov. 1931; and "El ejemplo del Estado de Veracruz," *El Nacional*, 26 Dec. 1931.

99 "El Gobernador felicitó a la Liga por su tendencia moralizadora y a los electos por su triunfo," *El Dictamen*, 23 Dec. 1931.

100 "La Liga de Comunidades Agrarias de Veracruz," Edición conmemorativa de *El Nacional Revolucionario*, 20 Nov. 1931

101 "El ejemplo del Estado de Veracruz," *El Nacional*, 26 Dec. 1931.

102 Wood, *Revolution in the Street*, pp. 197–198.

103 Leonard G. Dawson to Secretary of State, "Political Report for October, 1931,"

NA/RDS, Doc. 812.00, Veracruz/28 (4 Nov. 1931), pp. 12–13, NA/RDS, LC 812.00, Veracruz/28, 1931; Sóstenes Molina, Secretario de Finanzas del Sindicato Revolucionario de Inquilinos, to Tejeda, 18 April 1929, AAT, tomo 131, vol. 155,(1929), foja 262; Antonio Martínez to Tejeda, undated, AAT, tomo 131, vol. 155, foja 277; Enedin Valdés, Colonia Comunista de la Ciudad de Veracruz, to Tejeda, undated, AAT, tomo 131, vol. 155, foja 279; Juan Perea, Encargado del Departamento Inquilinario Municipal de Veracruz, to Secretario General de la Federación del Mar y Tierra, 1 Jan. 1929, AAT, tomo 134, vol. 158, fojas 484–485; Octavio García Mundo, *La etapa radial del movimiento inquilinario en Veracruz*, pamphlet (Veracruz: Facultad de Historia de la Universidad Veracruzana, Biblioteca del COLMEX, n.d.); and Leafar Agetro, *Las luchas proletarias en Veracruz*, pp. 67–93.

104 "El ejemplo del Estado de Veracruz," *El Nacional*, 26 Dec. 1931.

105 On the risk to his position, see "Maniobra de un grupo político en Mexico contra el Gobernador Tejeda," *El Dictamen*, 1 Aug. 1929; "El Gobernador Adalberto Tejeda exhorta para que se consideren con serenidad, prudencia y patriotismo las versiones sobre el atentado a la soberanía de Veracruz," *El Dictamen*, 12 Aug. 1929.

106 Expediente de Decreto #221: "Creando un municipio con el nombre de Tenochtitlán" (1 July 1931), AGEV, Fondo Legislatura, carp. 4-1-221; and Expediente de Decreto #223: "Creando el municipio de Angel R. Cabada" (3 July 1931), AGEV, Fondo Legislatura, carp. 4-1-23, 1931.

107 In this respect, see the fascinating and stormy affairs of Chontla, Temapache, Texcatepec, Córdoba, Fortín, and others: Expediente de Decreto #221: "Establece la cabecera municipal de Chontla en el Pueblo de San Francisco" (17 Dec. 1929), AGEV, Fondo Legislatura, carp. Ni-4-1/D; Decreto #81: "Suspendiendo provisionalmente a los miembros del Ayuntamiento de Chontla" (20 March 1929), AGEV, Fondo Legislatura, carp. Ni-4-1/D; Expediente de Decreto #39: "Reestablece la cabecera de municipio de Temapache en el pueblo de su nombre" (16 Jan. 1929), AGEV, Fondo Legislatura, carp. Ni-4-1/D; Expediente de Decreto #90: "Deroga el Decreto #39 de 16 de enero del presente año, que restituía al pueblo de Temapache su carácter de cabecera, la cual por consiguiente continuará residiendo en Álamo" (29 May 1929), AGEV, Fondo Legislatura, carp. Ni-4-1/D; Expediente de Decreto #90: "Memorial que elevan los habitantes del Municipio de Temapache, con cabecera en Álamo, a la H. Legislatura del Estado, pidiendo que no sea transladada a Temapache aquella cabecera municipal" (Jan., 1929), AGEV, Fondo Legislatura, carp. Ni-4-1/D; Expediente de Decreto #217: "Establece la cabecera del Municipio de Texcatepec en la Congregación de Amaxac" (16 Dec. 1929), AGEV, Fondo Legislatura, carp. Ni-4-1/D; Expediente de Decreto #221, AGEV, Fondo Legislatura, carp. Ni-4-1/D; Expediente de Decreto #307: "Segrega a los municipios de Córdoba e Ixtaczoquitlán, los congregaciones de Fortín, Monte Blanco, Zapoapita, y Cuapichapán, formando con ellas un municipio con el nombre de Fortín" (4 July 1930), AGEV, Fondo Legislatura, carp. Ni-4-1/D; letter from Adolfo Campos to Tejeda, 11 Aug. 1931, AAT, tomo 166 (1931), foja 27; Expediente de Decreto #364: "Derogando el Articulo 2° del Decreto #209 de fecha 30 de junio del año en curso, restituye a la villa de Tlalixcoyan su carácter de cabecera municipal" (17 Dec. 1931), AGEV, Fondo Legislatura, Expediente 4-1-364; Expediente de Decreto #203: "Restituye al pueblo de San Antonio Tenejapan su carácter de cabecera del municipio de su nombre" (17 Dec. 1929),

AGEV, Fondo Legislatura, Expediente 4-1-203; and Expediente de Decreto #355: "Concediendo carácter de cabecera del municipio de San Antonio Tenejapan al pueblo de Omatlán" (8 Dec. 1931), AGEV, Fondo Legislatura, expediente 4-1-355, 1931.

108 In 1930 there were 1,481 *congregaciones* in Veracruz, a number which may make Tejeda's contribution seem small; but when compared with parallel figures for his predecessors and successors, his totals indicate the relative magnitude of his contribution to reducing latifundist influence in the sphere of local government. See Secretaria de la Economía Nacional, Dirección General de Estadistica, *Quinto censo de población (1930), Resumen general* (México, 1934), Cuadro I: División política de las entidades, p. 5, and Cuadro VI: Localidades clasificadas según sus categorías políticas, pp. 21–24.

109 "Acta de sesiones #43, 27 de diciembre de 1928," *Periódico Oficial* XLIX, no. 51 (27 Jan. 1929): 4–5; "Acta de sesiones #53, sesión de 14 de enero de 1929," *Periódico Oficial* XLIX, no. 59 (25 Feb. 1929): 6–7; "Acta de sesiones #6, sesión de 20 de abril de 1931," *Periódico Oficial* LI, no. 10 (27 July 1931): 3; "Acta de sesiones #21, sesión de 19 de diciembre de 1931, XLIII Legislatura," *PeriódicoOficial* LII, no. 88 (24 April 1932): 1–7; and "Acta de sesiones #28, sesión de 2 de febrero de 1932," *Periódico Oficial* LII, no. 95 (16 May 1932): 4–6.

110 Townsend, *Lázaro Cárdenas, Mexican Democrat*, pp. 53–67.

111 *Ibid.*, p. 73. See also Cárdenas, *Apuntes* I, pp. 185–188; "Asamblea del ejecutivo del PNR," El Nacional, 28 Aug. 1931; "El General Cárdenas en gobernación," *El Nacional*, 29 Aug. 1931; and "La Revolución mexicana no puede ni podrá dividirse," *El Nacional*, 30 Aug. 1931.

112 Terrones López, *Un ensayo radical*, pp. 21–40M

113 José A. Ronzón León, "La campaña presidencial de Adalberto Tejeda" (Master's thesis, Universidad Veracruzana, 1991), p. 96; Fowler Salamini, *Movilización campesina*, p. 105.

114 "Entrevista #16, con Manza Silva Federico," in Centro de Estudios de la Revolución Mexicana "Lázaro Cárdenas" [CERMLC], "Entrevistas de Historia Oral," CERMLC, caja 2, carpeta 5, p. 80; "Entrevista #111 con José González Cisneros," in CERMLC, "Entrevistas de Historia Oral," CERMLC, caja 7, carp. 14, pp. 4–5; and "Entrevista #135 con Flores Ceja Esperanza," in CERMLC, "Entrevistas de Historia Oral," CERMLC, caja 9, carp. 3, p. 83; Entrvista con la hija del difunto comisariado ejidal da Capula, Michoacán, 13 de Septiembre de 2014. In the ultimate case the first issue this woman told me while presenting myself as an historian who work on Cárdenas was that once he visited the village and hearing the need for drinking water, he immediately ordered to dig a well in the village—still there to exhibit everyone the great contribution this man endowed the village.

115 "Fructífica jira del C. Cárdenas," *El Nacional*, 23 Nov. 1930; "Va Michoacán el General Cárdenas," *El Nacional*, 16 Dec. 1930; "Espontáneos demostraciones de admiración y respeto al destacado político de Michoacán," *El Nacional*, 25 Dec. 1930; "Frente al PNR la vigorosa personalidad del General Cárdenas," *El Nacional*, 25 Dec. 1930; "Se inaururó en Zamora un congreso agrarista," *El Nacional*, 20 June 1932; Cárdenas, *Apuntes* I, pp. 188–189, 193, 197, 204; and letter from Lázaro Cárdenas to F.J. Múgica, 14 Sept. 1931, ACERMLC, Fondo Múgica, vol. 16, doc. 26. See also: Eitan Ginzberg, "La intimidad cardenista: Hacia una política de diálogo multisectorial en michoacán

posrevolucionaria". In Oikión Solano & Sánchez Rodríguez (coords.), *Vientos de rebelión en Michoacán*, pp. 218–222.

116 See the following quarterly reports from the beginning of 1931 up until 1933: National Archives/Microfilm Publications [hereafter NA/MP] 1370, Roll no. 1, Docs. 812.00/29540 (1930); NA/MP, Docs. 812.00/29603, 29631, 29648, 29684 (1931); NA/MP, Docs. 812.00/29714, 29740, 29800, 29823 (1932); and NA/MP, Docs. 812.00/29845, 29913 (1933).

117 Author's interviews with the following: Moisés Lagunes González, Cerro Gordo, Veracruz (24 March 1992); Pedro Pérez Cervantes and Ignacio Hernández Cervantes, Mozomboa, Veracruz (29 March 1992); and Federico Fabián Zapata, Almolonga, Veracruz (2 April 1992).

118 Although Tejeda's secret service employed some 100 agents, in July, 1932, economic pressure forced him to cut this force down by 25%—according to the explanation given in the letters of dismissal the 28 redundant agents received at the beginning of the month: Pedro Tagal to Pablo Pailles, 19 July 1932, AAT, tomo 197 (1932), foja 31; Santiago Mota Barrientos to C. Jefe del Departamento Confidencial, 1 July 1932, AAT, tomo 197 (1932), foja 27; and P. Pailles to Gonzalo Hernández, AAT, tomo 197 (1932), foja 28.

119 Tejeda to C. Diputado Secretario de la H. Legislatura del Estado, 8 Aug. 1932, AAT, tomo 197 (1932), fojas 379–380.

120 Tejeda to Esteban Pous Cházaro, 25 Jan. 1932, AAT, tomo 166 (1931), fojas 220–221; Informe Confidencial, 22 Jan. 1932, AAT, tomo 166 (1931), fojas 749–750; Agente Confidencial (PGA) to Tejeda, 27 July 1931, AAT, tomo 168, vol. 192 (1931), docs. 200–201.

121 Secretario del Departamento Confidencial to José Muñoz, Proprietario del Cine "Lux," 2 March 1932, AAT, vol. 220 (1932), foja 22.

122 Letter from Agente Confidencial Facundo Tello to Pablo Pailles, 10 Feb. 1932, AAT, tomo 197 (1932), foja 646.

123 See, for example, letter from Agente Confidencial to Tejeda, 27 July 1931, AAT, vol. 192, tomo 168 (1931), fojas 200–201; confidential letter to Tejeda, 3 Sept. 1931, AAT, tomo 168, vol. 192 (1931), foja 350; letter from Lázaro Cárdenas to Tejeda, 21 Oct. 1931, AAT, tomo 168, vol. 192 (1931), foja 169; confidential letter to Tejeda, 23 Nov. 1931, AAT, tomo 168, vol. 192 (1931), fojas 207–208; and Tejeda to Esteban Pous Cházaro, 25 Jan. 1932, AAT, tomo 166 (1931), fojas 220–221.

124 Cuauhtémoc González Pacheco, *Organización campesina y lucha de clases. La Confederación Nacional Campesina* (México: Instituto de Investigaciones Económicas, U.N.A.M., 1979), pp. 67–68; Romana Falcón, "El surgimiento del agrarismo cardenista—Una revisión de las tesis populistas," *Historia Mexicana* 27 (1977–1978), no. 107 [3] (Jan.–March, 1978): 360–361.

125 "Quejas de campesinos," *El Nacional*, 14 Jan. 1933; "Explica las causas de la escisión la Liga Nacional Campesina 'Ursulo Galván'," *El Nacional*, 23 Jan. 1933; "Segunda sesión de la reunión plenaria de la 'Ursulo Galván'," *El Nacional*, 2 June 1933; and "Trabajará por separado la Liga Ursulo Galván," *Excelsior*, 6 June 1933.

126 Falcón, "El surgimiento del agrarismo cardenista," pp. 381–384.

127 Leopoldo Zea, *The Latin American Mind*, Translated from Spanish by James H. Abbott and Lowell Dunham (Norman, University of Oklahoma Press, 1963), pp. 269–289.

128 Cárdenas, *Apuntes* II, p. 417.

129 Arthur Bliss Lane to Secretary of State, 17 Oct. 1930, NA/RDS, 812.00/29532, MP 1370, Roll No. 1 (17 Oct. 1930).

3 The Shaping of a New Civil Consciousness

1 "Informe que rinde el C. Ing. Adalberto Tejeda, Gobernador Constitucional del Estado, ante la H. Trigesimacuarta Legislatura, 16 de septiembre de 1932 (Memoria del Gobierno de Tejeda 1928–1932)," in *Estado de Veracruz: Informes de sus Gobernadores 1826–1986*, vol. 12, comp. by Carmen Blázquez Domínguez (Xalapa: Gobierno del Edo. de Veracruz, 1986), p. 6068.

2 Cárdenas, *Palabras* I, p. 110.

3 See for example: Alfredo Pureco Ornellas, *Empresarios lombardos en Michoacán. La familia Cusi entre el Porfiriato y la posrevolución (1884–1938)* (México, Instituto Mora-El Colegio de Michoacán, 2010); Paul Garner, *Leones británicos y águilas mexicanas. Negocios, política e imperio en la carrera de Weetman Pearson en México, 1889–1919* (México, FCE-Instituto Mora-El Colegio de México-El Colegio de San Luis, 2013 [Stanford University Press, 2011]); Emilio Kourí, *Un pueblo dividido. Comercio, propiedad y comunidad en Papantla, México* (México, FCE-El Colegio de México, 2013 [Stanford University Press, 2004]); Francie Chassen-López, *Oaxaca: entre el liberalismo y la revolución. La perspectiva del sur (1867–1911)* (México, UABJO-UAM Iztapalapa, University of Kentucky, 2010 [Penn. State Press, 2004]); Mauricio Tenorio y Aurora Gómez G. *El Porfiriato* (México, FCE-CIDE, 2006); Beatriz Rojas (coord.), *Mecánica política: para una relectura del siglo XIX mexicano* (México, Universidad de Guadalajara-Instituto Mora, 2006); Eduardo Mijangos Díaz y Marisa Pérez D. (cords), *Voces del antiguo régimen. Representaciones,sociedad y gobierno en México contemporáneo* (Morelia, Universidad Michoacana-Instituto Mora, 2009); Sergio Miranda Pacheco (coord.), *Nación y municipio en México. Siglos XIX y XX* (México, UNAM, 2012); Emilio Kourí, "Los pueblos y sus tierras en el México porfiriano: Un legado inexplorado de Andrés Molina Enríquez", en: Emilio Kourí (coord.), *Cien años de los grandes problemas nacionales* (México, El Colegio de México, 2009), pp. 253–330; Molina Enriquez, *Los grandes problemas nacionales* (esp. chapters A–IV, V and B I, IV and V); César Moheno, *Las historias y los hombres de San Juan* (México: Colegio de Michoacán and CONACYT, 1985), pp. 52–55, 91–94; Luis González y González, *San José de Gracia, Mexican Village in Transition* (Austin, TX, and London: University of Texas Press, 1974), pp. 87–93; Jennie Purnell, "'With All Due Respect': Popular Resistance to the Privatization of Communal Lands in Nineteenth-Century Michoacán", *Latin American Research Review* 34, 1 (1999); Donald J. Fraser, "La política de desamortización en las comunidades indígenas, 1856–1872", *Historia Mexicana* Vol. XXI: 84, 4 (Abril–Junio de 1972): 615–652; T.G. Powell,"Los liberales, el campesinado indígena y los problemas agrarios durante la Reforma", *Historia Mexicana*, Vol. XXI 84, 4 (Abril–Junio de 1972): 653–675; Robert Knowlton, "La individualización de la propiedad corporativa civil en el siglo XIX—notas sobre Jalisco", en: *Los pueblos de indios y las comunidades. Lecturas de Historia Mexicana* 2 (México: El Colegio de Mexico, 1995), pp. 181–218; Robert Knowlton, "La individualización de la propiedad corporativa civil en el siglo XIX—notas sobre Jalisco", en: *Historia Mexicana*, Vol. XXVIII: 1 (109) (Julio–Septiembre de 1978): 24–61. See the excellent bibliographical list

of major studies on the agrarian policy of the Porfirian regime, published until 2000 in Kourí, "Los pueblos y sus tierras", note 3 pp. 254–255.

4 According to Marjorie Becker, a prominent present-day representative of this school of criticism, the state created an official revolutionary ethos that negated the traditional rural way of life without proposing any creditable alternative. In her view, that ethos was supported by the writings of the major historians of the Revolution, who thereby helped the revolutionary regime to make it part of the national heritage—for example, Eyler N. Simpson, Frank Tannenbaum, Arthur Womack, Friedrich Kats, Alan Knight, Silvia and Nathaniel Weyl, Adolfo Gilly, and Nora Hamilton. See Marjorie R. Becker, *Setting the Virgin on Fire: Lázaro Cárdenas, Michoacán Peasants and the Redemption of the Mexican Revolution* (Berkeley: University of California Press, 1995).

5 See for example: Molina Enriquez, *Los grandes problemas nacionales*, pp. 278–302

6 Author's interview with Dr. Luis González y González, Mexico City, June, 1992. Alongside Cárdenas several other radicals were active including former members of Partido Socialista Michoacano, the Partido Comunista and the Liga de Comunidades y Sindicatos Agraristas del Estado de Michoacán, and individuals like Alfonso Soria, Jesús Rico, Jesús Ramírez Mendoza, Ernesto Soto Reyes, Alberto Coria, and Luis Mora Tovar, who became the founders and leaders of the CRMDT. See Tamayo y Valles, *Anarquismo, socialismo y sindicalismo en las regiones*, p. 48

7 See, for example, "Decretos de expropiación por causa de utilitdad pública, 1931," in *Ediciones de la Gaceta Oficial* (1931); *Ley #323 de expropiación que regirá en el Estado de Veracruz-Llave* (Jalapa-Enríquez: Talleres Linotipográficos, 1930); Expediente [hereafter Exp.] de Ley #208: "Reformando la Ley #291 de 8 de julio de 1926, que declara de utilidad público el cultivo y aprovechamiento de tierras propias para agricultura y o ganadería," in AGEV, Fondo Legislatura [hereafter Fondo Leg.], doc. 4-1-208 (26 June 1931); and Exp. de Decreto #269: "Estableciendo la creación y fomento de la pequeña propiedad," in AGEV, Fondo Leg., doc. 4-1-269 (13 Aug. 1931).

8 "Informe que rinde el C. Ing. Adalberto Tejeda," 1928–1932, pp. 6071–6072; Fowler, *Movilización campesina*, p. 103; letter from Tejeda to Carlos Tejeda, quoted in Terrones López, *Un ensayo radical*, pp. 236–237.

9 "El candidato comunista," *Excelsior*, 19 July 1933.

10 An interesting discussion on this topic could be found in: Alan Knight, 'The Ideology of the Mexican Revolution, 1910–40', *Estudios Interdisciplinarios de América Latina y El Caribe* (EIAL) 8, 1 (Enero–Junio de 1997): 77–109.

11 In 1921, Obregón established the Secretaría de Educación Pública (Secretariat of Public Education), headed by José Vasconcelos. See Leopoldio Zea, "Hacia un nuevo liberalismo en la educación," in Josefina Zoraida Vázquez (coord.), *La educación en la historia de México* (México: El Colegio de México, 1996), pp. 291–311; Engracia Loyo, "Lectura para el pueblo 1921–1940," in *La educación en la historia de México*, pp. 243–290; and Renate Marsiske, "Universidad y educación rural en México (1924–1928)," in Pilar Gonzalbo Aizpuru (coord.), *Educación rural e indígena en Iberoamérica* (México: El Colegio de México and Universidad Nacional de Educación en Distancia, 1996), pp. 123–137; Jürgen Buchenau, *The Last Caudillo: Álvaro Obregón and the Mexican Revolution* (Oxford: Wiley-Blackwell, 2011), pp. 123–125.

12 In 1929, when Portez Gil began his Presidency, schools could accommodate only

1.19 million children out of 2.94 million children in education age. At that time there was a lack of 40,000 schools. See Engracia Loyo Bravo, "Los mecanismos de la "federalización" educative, 1921–1940", in Pilar Gonzalbo Aizpuru (coord.), *Historia de la educación y enseñanza de la historia* (México: El Colegio de México, 1998), p. 122. Anyway, attendance was very poor, especially in the agriculture sector. See Francisco Arce Gurza, "En busca de una educación revolucionaria, 1924–1934", in Josefina Zoraida Vázquez et al. (coords.), *Ensayos sobre historia de la educación en México* (México, El Colegio de México, 1996), p. 159.

13 "Informe para el año de 1927–1928, rendido por el C. Gobernador interino Luis Méndez," AHCMO, XLII Legislatura [hereafter Leg.], exp. 6, caja 1, "Varios," p. 17.

14 *Ibid.*, "Contestación del Lic. Silvestre Guerrero".

15 "Informe de Gobierno de 1928–1929, que rinde el General de División Lázaro Cárdenas del Río," AHCMO, XLII Leg., exp. 19, caja 1, "Varios," pp. 12–13.

16 "Informe de Gobierno de Dámaso Cárdenas de 1929–1930," AHCMO, XLIII Leg., exp. 5, caja 2, "Varios," p. 16; Lázaro Cárdenas, *Informe 1928–1932*, p. 29.

17 "Informe de Gobierno, rendido por el C. Benigno Serrato, en el período de 1932–1933," AHCMO, XLIV Leg., exp. 13, caja 1, "Varios."

18 David L. Raby, "Los principios de la educación rural en México: El caso de Michoacán, 1915–1929," *Historia Mexicana* XXII, 4 (April–June, 1973): 553–581.

19 "Se presenta una seria dificultad," *Excelsior*, 11 Jan. 1929.

20 *El Universal*, 17 April 1929.

21 *Ibid.*

22 "Proyecto para que los niños reciban educación," *El Universal*, 6 April 1929; "Solución al problema de las escuelas," *El Universal*, 22 April 1929; De la Peña, *Veracruz económico* I, pp. 303–304; and "Un escalafón justiciero para profesores rurales," *Excelsior*, 11 Jan. 1931.

23 Jacinto Lara to Tejeda, 22 Nov. 1928, AAT, tomo 130, vol. 154, foja 92; Jacinto Lara to Tejeda, 10 Dec. 1928 and 8 Feb. 1929, AAT, tomo 130, vol. 154, fojas 90 and 83, respectively.

24 The law required every owner of a business or a farm employing at least 10 families with one or more children to establish and equip a rural school, and to maintain one teacher for every 50 pupils. In addition to his or her daily teaching duties, this teacher would be called upon to spend an additional two hours every evening teaching adults and children unable to attend school during the day. See Decreto #21: "Se reforma el Capítulo XVII de la Ley Orgánica de Educación Primaria del Estado de Michoacán . . . ," in "Acta de sesiones #32, sesión del 31 de diciembre de 1930, XLIII Leg.," *Periódico Oficial* LII, no. 74 (19 March 1931): 5–8.

25 The statistics cited by Foglio Miramontes show a discrepancy between the percentages and the absolute figures. In 1932, for example, he claims that close to 42% of the children between the ages of 6 and 14 were enrolled in the education system, yet he also says that only 80,000 were enrolled, meaning only some 30% of the total. See Foglio Miramontes, *Geografia económicó* II, p. 205.

26 Cárdenas, *Informe 1928–1929*, p. 29.

27 Author's interview with Jesús Múgica Martínez, Morelia, Michoacán, July, 1992. On the important contribution of the teachers organized in the frame-

work of the Bloque de Maestros Socialistas de Michoacán (Bloc of Socialist Teachers of Michoacán), to promote socialist education in the rural villages, see Gallardo, *La lucha por la tierra*, pp. 49–51, 96n.144.

28   Cárdenas, *Informe 1928–1929*, p. 7.

29   *Ibid.*, pp. 7–8.

30   *Ibid.*, p. 8.

31   *Ibid.*, pp. 11–12.

32   "Ley #76 reglementaria de la educación pública del Estado de Michoacán de Ocampo" (21 Jan. 1931), *Libro de Actas de la XLIII Leg.* (Sept., 1930–Aug., 1931), Articles 9–44, pp. 2–16, AHEMO.

33   *Ibid.*, Art. 20.

34   *Ibid.*, Arts. 100–108.

35   "Es festejada una maestra," *El Nacional*, 10 Oct. 1930.

36   Cárdenas, *Informe 1928–1929*, p. 9.

37   Exp. de Decreto # 5: "Se reforma al art. 130 de la consitutición particular del Estado, aprobado el 9 de octubre de 1930," AHCMO, XLIII Leg., exp. 5, caja 1, "Decretos." In fact, a specific law for the training colleges was never enacted. The subject was included in the new education law passed in January, 1931.

38   Letter from F.J. Múgica to Cárdenas, 14 July 1931, in ACERMLC, FJM, vol. 16 (1931), doc. 28.

39   Cárdenas, *Apuntes* I, p. 184.

40   "Acta de sesiones #17, sesión del 4 de agosto de 1931, XLIII Leg.," *Periódico Oficial* LII, no. 62 (21 Jan. 1932): 1–4.

41   Decreto-Ley #84 "que faculta al ejecutivo del Estado para que suspenda, cierre o prohiba el funcionamiento de centros de enseñanza, cuando haya pletora de profesionistas" (16 Feb. 1932), *Periódico Oficial* LII, no. 77 (14 March 1932): 1–2.

42   "Informe de Gobierno de 1930–1931 que rinde el Lic. Gabino Vázquez," AHCMO, XLII Leg., exp. 5, caja 1, "Varios," p. 13.

43   Gallardo, *La lucha por la tierra*, pp. 49–50.

44   For an account of the murder of a rural teacher, see "Entrevista al Sra. Bertha Méndez Ramírez," ACERMLC, #49, caja 3 carp. 16, p. 15. On an attack made on a large cultural mission, see "Una misión cultural balaceada en Arteaga, Michoacán, por bandoleros," *El Nacional*, 29 Dec. 1931.

45   Cárdenas, *Informe 1928–1932*, pp. 27–28.

46   Ezequiel Mendoza Barragán, *Testimonio cristero* (México: Editorial Jus, 1990), pp. 381–382.

47   The Cardenist enterprise did not bear immediate fruit. The shortage of teachers and schools, the high drop-out rate, and the large number of children who were not even enrolled in the school system continued to plague Michoacán for years. In 1957, for example, 108,400 of the total 347,526 school-aged children in the state were not enrolled (about 30%). There was a shortfall of 2,168 teachers and a similar number of classes (on a basis of 50 children per class!). At that time, 268 communities still lacked both schools and teachers. See Jesús Romero Flores, *Geografía del Estado de Michoacán* (Morelia: Gobierno del Estado, Talleres Tipográficos de la ETI Álvaro Obregón, 1958), p. 109. Even by 1980 Michoacán's education system was one of the worst in Mexico, rated 29 in reading and writing levels out of 31 state school systems covered in a survey conducted by the Instituto Nacional de Estadística y Geografía (INEGI). See Jorge Zepeda Patterson, *Michoacán: Sociedad, economía, política, y cultura*

(México: Centro de Investigaciones Interdisciplinarias en Humanidades, UNAM, 1990), p. 26.

48 "Informe que rinde el C. Ing. Adalberto Tejeda," 1931–1932 (segundo semestre), pp. 6310–6311. Undoubtedly Tejeda included in the number 789 the federal rural schools, which, according to data collected from the Education Ministry by *Excelsior*, numbered 381. See "Funcionan en el país 6,480 escuelas rurales," *Excelsior*, 30 July 1933.

49 Letter from Tejeda to Diputado Secretario de la H. Leg. del Estado, 7 Jan. 1932, in Exp. de Ley #50 de Egresos del Estado (1932), AGEV, Fondo Leg..

50 Diputado Jesús Ramírez Ordóñez to H. Leg. del Estado de Veracruz, 22 Dec. 1931, in Exp. de Ley #50, AGEV, Fondo Leg.

51 Comisión de Instrucción Pública del H. Leg. del Estado to H. Leg., in Exp. de Ley #50.

52 Moiés de la Torre to Tejeda, n.d., in Exp. de Ley #50.

53 "Informe que rinde el C. Ing. Adalberto Tejeda," 1928–1932, pp. 6093–6094; *Ley de ingresos y egresos del Estado libre y soberano de Veracruz-Llave (1931)* (Jalapa-Enríquez: Talleres Linotipográficos del Gobierno del Estado, 1931); and *Gaceta Oficial* XXV, no. 7 (15 Jan. 1931): 68–69.

54 "Para ayudar en la educación del campesino en el Estado, a los comités agrarios les dirige el governador una exitativa," *El Dictamen* (19 June 1929).

55 Decreto #345: "Modificando el Decreto 254 de 21 de enero último, relativo a la partida #160 del ramo Veracruz del presupuesto de egresos" (1 Aug. 1930), AGEV, Fondo Leg., exp. 4-1-345; and "Informe que rinde el C. Ing. Adalberto Tejeda," 1928–1932, p. 6090.

56 "Acta extraordinaria de sesiones de la H. XXXII Leg. del Estado de Veracruz de 3 de enero de 1929," *Gaceta Oficial* XXIII, no. 56 (10 and 13 May 1929): 20–22.

57 *Ley de ingresos y egresos del Estado libre y soberano de Veracruz-Llave (1929)* (Jalapa-Enríquez: Talleres Linotipográficos del Gobierno del Estado, 1929), p. 37, in AGEV, Fondo Leg..

58 Memorandum from Lorenzo García, Secretario Particular de Tejeda, to Subtesorero del Estado, 22 Jan. 1929, in AAT, tomo 125, vol. 149, foja 121; A. Tejeda to Francisco Tejeda, Visitador de Administración, 17 April 1929, in AAT, tomo 130, vol. 154 (1929), fojas 210–211.

59 Presidente Municipal de Pánuco to Tejeda, 12 Sept. 1929, in AAT, tomo 124, vol. 148, foja 560; and Tesorero Municipal de Veracruz to Tejeda, 11 July 1929, in AAT, tomo 130, vol. 154 (1929), fojas 346–349, 361.

60 Circular #9, *Gaceta Oficial* XXIII, no. 71 (14 June 1930): 3.

61 Decreto #91, *Gaceta Oficial* XXV, no. 2 (3 Jan. 1931): 1–2.

62 See, for example, Decreto #325: "Se suspende provisionalmente, por tres meses, al ciudadano Guillermo Hernández en sus funciones de presidente municipal de Papantla . . ." (15 July 1930), AGEV, Fondo Leg., exp. 4-1-325; Decreto #11: "Se suspende provisionalmente poer el término de 3 meses a los miembros del Ayuntamiento de Tlacotalpan" (21 Sept. 1931), AGEV, Fondo Leg., exp. 4-1-11 (1931); Decreto #298: "Suspendiendo provisionalmente . . . el Ayuntamiento de Villa Cuahuatémoc" (20 Oct. 1931), AGEV, Fondo Leg., exp. 4-1-298 (1931); and Decreto #199: "Suspendiendo provisionalmente . . . al C. José Azuara, Presidente Municipal de Tempoal" (11 Oct. 1932), AGEV, Fondo Leg., exp. 4-1-199 (1932).

63 Ley #222: "Reformando la fracción XLIV del Artículo 68 de la Constitución

Política del Estado" (24 Nov. 1932), AGEV, Fondo Leg., exp. 4-1-222 (1932). See also the Constitución Política del Estado libre y soberano de Veracruz-Llave, Art. 157/XLIV/f, p. 212.

64 "La colonia agrícola del maestro quedará establecida en la ciudad de Córdoba, Veracruz," *El Nacional* (10 June 1932).

65 Decreto #213 (30 June 1931), *Gaceta Oficial* XXIV, no. 82 (9 July 1931): 3; and Circular #65 (18 May 1931), *Gaceta Oficial* XXV, no. 64 (28 May 1931): 2–3.

66 Leonard Dawson to Secretary of State, "Political Report for January, 1932," NA/RDS, 812.00/Veracruz 32 (3 Feb. 1932), pp. 2–4.

67 Tejeda seldom cited statistics in his speeches, and never in any systematic, organized fashion. The only orderly set of data he ever provided on the education system appeared in a report on the 1930–1931 school year, which recorded 97,054 pupils in the state primary-school system and another 6,824 pupils in private primary schools. The question, of course, is what percentage of total children these figures represented. In 1930, there were 340,911 children aged 5–14 in Veracruz. Primary-school age being 6–12, statistical extrapolation gives us a total of 227,274 children in that age range. On the basis of Tejeda's figures, it can be estimated that only about 38% of school-aged children were enrolled in school in Veracruz in 1931. Even worse was the drop-out rate, which Tejeda never mentioned at all but which is well presented in *Veracruz económico* by Moisés de la Peña, who provides data for 1945. De la Peña writes that of the total children who enrolled in first grade in the rural schools, only 1.3% were still attending school after four years. Not one was still in school by the sixth grade, the last year of primary school. The situation was slightly better in the urban schools, though still very bad in absolute terms. There, 19% of first-grade enrollees continued to attend school through the sixth grade. See *Quinto censo de población (1930), Estado de Veracruz*, p. 184; De la Peña, *Veracruz económica* I, pp. 313, 322; "Informe que rinde el C. Ing. Adalberto Tejeda," 1930–1931, pp. 6261–6262; "Informe que rinde el C. Ing. Adalberto Tejeda," 1928–1932, p. 6093.

68 "Informe que rinde el C. Ing. Adalberto Tejeda," 1930–1931, pp. 6255–6257.

69 *Ibid.*, pp. 6305–6306.

70 The debate on the third article of the constitution which deals with education, was the first of many debates of the sitting assembly and one of its most intensive. The wording of the article was presented on the 11th of December 1916 by Francisco José Múgica, the chairman of the legislative committee, and 18 members signed up to speak. There was a sense of great tension between the Obregonistas and the Carrencistas whose suggestion to article 3 was a milder version than the one Múgica had tabled. The Carrencistas proposed secular and free education that would be mandatory for the State schools only. Múgica's suggestion, in the spirit of Obregón's followers, was mandatory secular education in all schools—both State and private (including religious). Diario de los debates del Congreso Constituyente de 1917 (Edición de la Comisión Nacional para la Celebración del Sesquicentenario de la Proclamación de la Independencia Nacional y del Cincuentenario de la Revolución Mexicana, México 1960), Vols V. I, pp. 503–733; Francisco José Múgica, *Hachos no palabras* (México, INEHRM, 1986), Vol. I, p, 97; Marcelo Blidstein, *The Constitution as a Tool for National Integration: Revolutionary Mexico, 1917–1924* (Doctoral Thesis, Tel Aviv University, 2000 [Hebrew]), pp. 131–134.

71 *Ibid.* The initiative for the pedagogical congress was born in February, 1931, at the third congress of the Confederación Sindicalista del Estado (State Syndical Confederation), which was affiliated with the CROM. The idea of socialist schools had already been raised back in November, 1924, in a speech by Lombardo Toledano at the sixth congress of the CROM. At that time he spoke of a "socialist education at the service of the proletariat" and of an "affirmative" school, since it was impossible to educate without implanting ideas. See Ragueb Chain Revuelta, "El programa de la educación socialista en Veracruz," in *Veracruz, un tiempo para contar*, p. 250.

72 "Informe que rinde el C. Ing. Adalberto Tejeda," 1931–1932 (primer semestre), AAT, tomo 197, fojas 493–494.

73 "Informe que rinde el C. Ing. Adalberto Tejeda," 1928–1932, p. 6097.

74 *Ibid.*

75 *Ibid.*, p. 6096.

76 This was also the impression of the US ambassador to Mexico. See Josephus Daniels to Secretary of State, Washington, 10 May 1939, NA/RDS, 812.00/30740, pp. 2–3.

77 Revuelta, "El programa de la educación socialista en Veracruz," pp. 253–255.

78 Dirección General de Educación Popular, *Programa de educación primaria* (Xalapa, Veracruz: Oficina Tipográfica del Estado, 1932), quoted in Revuelta, "El programa de la educación socialista en Veracruz," p. 253 and 259 *n*23.

79 Exp. de Ley #222: "Reformando la fracción XLIV del artículo 68 de la Constitución Política del Estado" (24 Nov. 1932)," AGEV, Fondo Leg., doc. 4-1-222.

80 See Josafina Z. Vázquez de Knauth, "La educación socialista de los años treinta," *Historia Mexicana* 71, 3 (Jan.–March, 1969): 408–423; Jorje Mora Forero, "Los maestros y la práctica de la educación socialista, *Historia Mexicana* 113, 1 (July–Sept., 1979): 133–162; Guadalupe Monroy Huitrón, *Política educativa de la Revolución (1910–1940)* (México: Secretaría de Educación Pública, 1975); Jorge H. Portillo, *El problema de las relaciones entre la iglesia y el estado en México* (México: Costa-Amic Editores, 1982), p. 54; Lázaro Cárdenas, *Ideario político* (México: Era, 1984), pp. 206–211; interview with Vicente Lombardo Toledano, 6 May 1984, in *Mexico visto en el siglo 20: Entrevistas de historia oral*, W. Wilkie and Edna Monzón de Wilki (eds), (México, Instituto Mexicano de Investigaciones Económicas, 1968), pp. 336–340; Martaelena Negrete, *Relaciones entre la Iglesia y el Estado en México 1930–1940* (México: El Colegio de México y La Universidad Iberoamericana, 1988), pp. 151–189, 337; and Tzvi Medin, *Ideología y praxis política de Lázaro Cárdenas* (México: Siglo XXI Editores, 1987), pp. 178–189.

81 De la Peña, *Veracruz económico* I, p. 296.

82 "Informe que rinde el C. Ing. Adalberto Tejeda," 1931–1932 (primer semestre), AAT, tomo 197, foja 486.

83 Prof. Gabriel Lucio to Tejeda, 28 Sept. 1931, in AAT, tomo 168, vol. 192 (1931), foja 435.

84 On this affair see "Actas de sesiones del XXXIII Legislatura del Estado de Veracruz, sesiones de 4, 11, and 13 noviembre de 1930," in AGEV, Fondo Leg., 1930.

85 Genaro Ángeles, is remembered as the founder of Symphony Orchestra of Jalapa (Orquestra Symfonica de Xalapa OSX). The orchestra still operates today. See: http://www.uv.mx/universo/365/reportaje/reportaje.htm

86 "Más protestas por los ataques al Cor. Tejeda," *El Nacional*, 15 Sept. 1930; "Hay en Veracruz una pugna entre los estudiantes," *Excelsior*, 15 Sept. 1930; and "Desaire a Tejeda en Veracruz," *Excelsior*, 18 Sept. 1930.

87 "Actas de sesiones del XXXIII Leg. del Estado de Veracruz, sesión de 12 de septiembre de 1930," AGEV, Fondo Leg. (1930), pp. 11–12, 46–47.

88 Terrones López, *Los proyectos del tejedismo*, p. 179.

89 Tejeda to C. Diputado Secretario de la H. Leg. del Estado, 6 Jan. 1932, in Exp. de Ley #50: "Ley de egresos del Estado de Veracruz por el año de 1932," AGEV, Fondo Leg., n.d.

90 "Informe que rinde el C. Ing. Adalberto Tejeda," 1928–1932, p. 6096.

91 "Informe que rinde el C. Ing. Adalberto Tejeda," 1931–1932 (primer semestre), AAT, tomo 197, foja 485.

92 Exp. de Decreto #278: "Facultando al ejecutivo del Estado para ceder gratuitamente a la Unión de Obreros de Minatitlan una casa para oficinas, escuelas, bibliotecas y establecimientos de beneficiencia" (1 July 1930), AGEV, Fondo Leg. (1930); Confederación Sindicalista de Obreros y Campesinos de la región de Córdoba, Veracruz, adherida al CROM, to C. Gabriel Lucio, Director General de Educación, 12 Dec. 1931, in Exp. de Ley #50: "Ley de Egresos del Estado de Veracruz por el año de 1932," AGEV, Fondo Leg.; and Lista de alumnos pensionados dependientes del Departamento Universitario del Estado, mandada por Dr. Genaro Ángeles, Jefe del Departamento Universitario, 12 Jan. 1932, in Exp. de Ley #50.

93 On all these issues, see De la Peña, *Veracruz económico* I, pp. 312–327.

94 Domínguez Pérez, *Política y movimientos sociales en el tejedismo*, p. 140.

95 Ragueb Chain Revuelta, "El programa de la educación socialista en Veracruz," pp. 245–246.

96 "El Coronel Tejeda dice que Rusia no es comunista," *El Universal*, 4 Jan. 1933.

97 This report in fact noted everything Cárdenas did in his four years as governor: for example, the transfer of the teachers' colleges to the state administration, the linkage of the universities to the state educational enterprise, the closure of private schools, the anti-alcoholism campaign that was incorporated into educational activities, pedagogical supervision of private schools, and so on. See Cárdenas, *Informe 1928–1932*, pp. 28–29.

98 One of these was the congress convened in March, 1931, in Jalapa, by the workers' unions of Veracruz in order to "learn the corrections required in the existing system of education in the state, on the assumption that the system now used in the local schools does not accord with the thinking of the workers." Following a congress of its own the same month, the Veracruz Agrarian League demanded that Tejeda reinforce the rural schools and expand their teaching staff significantly. See "El Congreso Pedagógico de Jalapa," *El Nacional*, 15 March 1931; and "En la Convención Agraria no se trató de política," *El Dictamen*, 13 March 1931.

99 "La educación rural," *El Nacional*, 21 Oct. 1932.

100 Cárdenas, *Informe 1928–1932*, pp. 27–28.

101 "Se ha logrado ya la rendición de todos los rebeldes en Michoacán," *El Universal Gráfico*, 4 Jan. 1929; *El Universal*, 12 June 1929; letter from L. Cárdenas to F.J. Múgica, 24 May 1928, in "Correspondencia entre Lázaro Cárdenas y Francisco Múgica desde 1928 a 1939," *Desdeldiez*, CERMLC (July, 1985): 109; Jean Meyer, *La Cristiada* I, p. 258; and "Rendición de más rebeldes

en Michoacán: Simón Cortés Vieyra, uno de las jefes de alzados se sometía al gobierno federal," *Excelsior*, 31 Jan. 1929.

102 Gerardo Sánchez D. and Gloria Carreño A., "El movimiento Cristero en el distrito de Coalcomán, Michoacán, 1927–1929," *Boletín*, CERMLC (Aug., 1979): 113–114; Townsend, *Lázaro Cárdenas, Mexican Democrat*, p. 40; and *Informe de la Contaduría General de Glosa, 1930–1932*, in AHCMO, XLIII Leg., exp. 10, caja 1, "Varios"; Eitan Ginzberg, "Una labor de convencimiento: La culminación de la Guerra cristera en Michoacán", Julia Preciado Zamora y Servando Ortoll (coords.), *Los guachos y los mochos: Once ensayos cristeros* (Morelia, Jitanjáfora, 2009), pp. 179–188.

103 Jorge H. Portillo, *El problema de las relaciones entre la Iglesia y el Estado en México*, p. 45; letter from Jefe del Departamento de Gobernación to Cárdenas, 26 June 1929, Archivo del Poder Ejecutivo del Estado de Michoacán de Ocampo [hereafter APEEMO], Ramo: Gobernación, Subramo: Religión: "Remisión de sacerdotes al Dpto. de Gobernación," exp. 7-2, carpeta 5, caja 83; "Acta levantada ante el personal del juzgado de esta villa (de Morelos) . . . ," 26 Jan. 1929, APEEMO; José Solórzano, Presidente de la Liga de Comunidades y Sindicatos Agrarias del Estado de Michoacán de Ocampo, to Cárdenas, 4 June 1929, APEEMO, exp. 7-53-B4; Agustín Lañero, Secretario General de Gobierno, to Secretario de Gobernación en México D.F., 7 Feb. and 17 June 1929, APEEMO; Circular 53: "Sobre la entrega de templos en Chilchota," exp. 7-53, carpeta 12, caja 3, APEEMO; letter from Isaac Prado, Presidente Municipal de Chilchota, to Secretario General de Gobierno, 27 July 1929, APEEMO; and Cárdenas, *Informe 1928–1929*, p. 28.

104 On Law #62, see "Proyecto de limitación de número de ministros de los cultos que pueden ejercer su ministerio en el Estado libre y soberano de Michoacán de Ocampo," 5 March 1926, AHCMO, Exp. de Ley #62, XL Leg., exp. 3, caja 4.

105 Letter from Tejeda to Portes Gil, 23 June 1929, cited in Soledad García Morales, "El conflicto clerical en Veracruz en 1931" (Master's thesis, Universidad Veracruzana, 1974), p. 9.

106 *Ibid.*, p. 11.

107 "El Obispo Guizar atribuye a lento trámite la demora en la entrega de templos," *El Dictamen*, 13 July 1929; "Pide el desafuero del Gobernador del Estado el Lic. Emilio Sedas Rivera," *El Dictamen*, 5 Aug. 1929; García Morales, *El conflicto clerical*, pp. 21, 63–64; and William John Baker, "Church and State in Veracruz, 1840–1940: The Concord and Conflicts of a Century" (Ph.D. diss., University of St. Louis, 1971), p. 274.

108 See, among many other examples, Ley #197 in *Gaceta Oficial* XXV, no. 73 (18 June 1931): 3; "Sólo 11 sacerdotes en todo el Estado de Veracruz," *El Dictamen*, 11 June 1931; Leonard G. Dawson, American Consul, to Secretary of State, "Political Report for June, 1931," NA/RDS, 812.00, Veracruz/22 (1 July 1931), pp. 5–6; Leonard Dawson, American Consul, to Secretary of State, "Law Fixing Number of Religious Ministers in Veracruz State," NA/RDS, 812.00, Veracruz/21 (22 June 1931), pp. 3–5; "Informe acerca de los hechos ocurridos en Huatusco," 25 June 1931, AAT, tomo 167, vol. 191 (1931), foja 16; Baker, "Church and State in Veracruz," pp. 351–372; García Morales, "El conflicto clerical," pp. 88–104; Moisés de la Torre to Tejeda, 11 Nov. 1931, AAT, tomo 168, vol. 192, fojas 469–472; Tejeda to General Samuel Kelly, Jefe de los Fuerzas Rurales del Estado, Nov., 1931, AAT, tomo 166, foja 81; reports by Samuel Kelly, Carolino Anaya, and Gonzalo Hernández to Tejeda, 19–21 Oct. 1931,

AAT, tomo 167, vol. 191 (1931), fojas 1–6; and Rafael Guizar Valencia to Tejeda, 23 and 25 July 1931, AAT, tomo 168, vol. 192, fojas 293–294 and 248–249.

109 Baker, "Church and State in Veracruz," pp. 376, 383–384; Dr. Genaro Ángeles, Vicepresidente de la Dirección General de Beneficencia Pública, to Dr. José María Flotes, Presidente de la Junta Municipal de Beneficencia de Veracruz, 22 Sept. 1931, AAT, tomo 167, vol. 191, foja 110.

110 Baker, "Church and State in Veracruz," pp. 439–443; Martaelena Negrete, *Relaciones entre la Iglesia y el Estado*, pp. 75–79, 92; "Ante el reto del clero, un frente de la Revolución," *El Nacional*, 15 Dec. 1931; "La mazorca de la cuenta," *El Nacional*, 17 Dec. 1931; and "La escuela acabará con el fanatismo religioso," *El Nacional*, 18 Dec. 1931.

111 "Actas de sesiones: Acta 2 del primer período extraordinario de sesiones, de 10 de mayo de 1932, XLIII Legislatura," AHCMO, Tomo de las Actas del 14 de sept. de 1931 al 29 agosto 1932.

112 Letter from Leopoldo Ruiz to Lopoldo Lara y Torres, Obispo de Tacambaro, 16 May 1932, in *Documentación para la historia de la persecución religiosa en México* (México: Editorial Jus, 1954), pp. 1011–1012; Enríque Guerra Manzo, "Católicos y agraristas en Michoacán: Del conflict al modus vivendi", Oikión Solano y Sánchez Rodríguez (coords.), *Vientos de rebelión en Michoacán*, p. 201.

113 Telegram from Múgica to Cárdenas, Islas Marías, 16 May 1932, and telegram from Cárdenas to Múgica, Michoacán, 17 May 1932, both in ACERMLC, Fundo Lázaro Cárdenas, rollo 17, primera parte.

114 Author's interview with Domingo Jiménez Chavez, Capácuaro, Michoacán, 12 July 1992.

115 Author's interview with Padre Daniel, Párroco de Nauatzen, formerly Rector del Santuario de Totolán, Nauatzen, Michoacán, 12 June 1992.

116 Carlos Martínez Assad, Ricardo Pozas Horcasitas, and Mario Ramírez Rancano, *Revolucionarios fueron todos* (México: Fondo de Cultura Económica, 1982), pp. 170–171.

117 See letter from Tejeda to Roberto Yañez and Manuel Padilla, 4 Aug. 1931, AAT, tomo 166 (1931), fojas 93–94; Tejeda to Manuel Padilla, 18 June 1931, AAT, tomo 167, vol. 191 (1931), fojas 286–288; Tejeda to Carlos Dario Ojeda, 20 June 1931, AAT, tomo 167, vol. 191 (1931), foja 276; and "Informe que rinde el C. Ing. Adalberto Tejeda, 1930–1931."

118 The unfortunate Ramón Huesca, for example, a nine-year-old pupil at the Luis J. Jiménez elementary school in Jalapa, insisted on adhering to his faith and refused to listen to the mandatory school lectures denouncing the Church and religion. As a result he was expelled from the school, though subsequently re-admitted. On this peculiar episode, see Profesora Isabel Ochoa to Francisco Andrade, Síndico Primero, Encargado del Ramo de Educación, 12 Sept. 1931, AAT, tomo 168, vol. 192 (1931), foja 348.

119 Author's interview with Pedro Pérez Cervantez and Ignacio Hernández Cervantez, Mozomboa, Actopan, Veracruz, 29 March 1992. The historian Xavier Tavera Alfaro, a personal friend of Tejeda's in his last years, confirms that a whole "underground" existed for hiding and smuggling priests in all sorts of strange disguises, including women's clothing, in order to continue holding religious ceremonies after the churches were closed on 25 July 1931. See author's

interview with Dr. Xavier Tavera Alfaro, Coordinador de la Comisión de Archivo y Biblioteca del H. Congreso del Estado de Michoacán, Morelia, Michoacán, Aug., 1991.

120 Vecinos de la Villa de S.J. Evangelista to José Aguilar y Maya, Procurador General de la República, 27 Feb. 1930; "Criterio de la Comisión de gobernación del Congreso," April, 1931, in Exp. de Decreto #245: "Cambia el nombre de la villa de San Juan Evangelista por el de Santana Rodríguez," AGEV, Fondo Leg., 1930.

121 Leonard Dawson to Secretary of State, "Law Fixing Number of Religious Ministers in Veracruz State," 22 June 1931, NA/RDS, 812.00, Veracruz/21, pp. 3–5; "Informe acerca de los hechos ocurridos en Huatusco, 25 June 1931, AAT, tomo 167, vol. 191 (1931), foja 16; Decreto #258: "Suspendiendo en sus funciones al Ayuntamiento de Huatusco . . . ," AGEV, Fondo Leg., doc. 4-1-258 (30 July 1931); García Morales, *El conflicto clerical*, pp. 70–104; Carlos Gómez, Secretario General del Sindicato de Panaderos de Huatusco, to Tejeda, 7 Oct. 1931, AAT, tomo 168, vol. 192 (1931), fojas 193–194; Moisés de la Torre to Tejeda (on events in Tlapacoyan), 11 Nov. 1931, AAT, tomo 168, vol. 192 (1931), fojas 469–472; Javier Jara, Receptor de Rentas de Coscomatepec, to Tejeda, 9 Nov. 1931, AAT, tomo 168, vol. 192 (1931), fojas 46–47; and AGEV, Fondo Gobernación y Justicia, exp. #760, pq. 3122 (March, 1932).

4 The Salvation of Agrarianism: The Ejido Issue

1 During the period 1928–1930, yearly income from land, including agricultural products, cattle, wood, mining, and oil, came to some 1.145 billion pesos, while industrial production was roughly 900,333,000 pesos. Thus, land and its products accounted for some 56% of Mexican production during those years even without taking into account the role of agricultural products in industry. See *México económico 1928–1930*, Cuadro 1, p. 14.

2 Although land reform officially ended more than 20 years ago, the ejido is still an element of identity and belonging which are very important to its residents. Even though practically they can sell the property they have to all comers for residential purposes, many continue to hold the fields they have not bothering to cultivate them.

Last September (2014) I made a visit to the ejido Ocolusen in the outskirts of Morelia, Michoacán, still an ejido for all intents and purposes. Ocolusen is in the process of privatization and sale of residential buildings. Despite its excellent location on the slopes of a ridge overlooking the city of Morelia, ejido members, with whom we spoke, still prefer to hold their tiny agriculture porperties and not sell them in order to keep their ejidal status.

3 Smallholders were farmers who had a piece of land or preferred to buy it by their own in order to be free of any State tutelage. But, we can relegate to this group also many peasants from different agrarian ranking and ideological (or theological) tendencies like *peones acasillados*—most of them sharecroppers or tenants and day labourers who preferred to continue living this way even under the possibility of getting land through the agrarian process. Other non-interested village dwellers were what are generically called "particulares" mostly artisans who preferred non-ager works or some combinations of the two ways of life on a totally private basis. And there were the *comuneros*—Indians who expected

to get back their lost community land, taken from them by the 19th century liberal Reform, on a restitution process the reform limitedly enabled, inter alia, because it prevented it from any further intervention in the community life.

4   Artículo 27 de la constitución de 1917, in Arnaldo Córdova, *La ideología de la revolución mexicana: la formación del nuevo régimen* (México: Ediciones Era, 1985), pp. 488–490; Fernándo González Roa, 'El artículo veintisiete constitucional', in *Problemas Agrícolas e Industriales de México*, 5: 3 (julio-sep., de 1953), pp. 115–16; Luis Cabrera, *Veinte años después: el balance de la Revolución. La campaña presidencial de 1934. Las dos revoluciones* (México: Ediciones Botas, 1938), p. 278; Adolfo Gilly, *The Mexican Revolution* (Thetford, Norfolk: Thetford Press, 1983), p. 230; Carlos Elizondo, *The Concept of Property of the 1917 Mexican Constitution* (México: Centro de Investigación y Docencia Económicas, 1993), pp. 9, 11; Ivan Resprepo and Salomón Eckstein, *La agricultura colectiva en México: la experiencia de La Lguna* (México: Siglo XXI Editores, 1975), p. 149.

5   "Ley de Ejidos de 30 de Diciembre de 1920", en: Antonio Villareal Muñoz, *Restitución y dotación de ejidos: el problema agrario en México* (México Comisión Nacional Agraria, 1921), pp. 177–190; the 1915 particual legislation of Veracruz, for example, proposed the break-up of latifundios and their redistribution as irrigated family plots of 1–50 hectares, as a basis. The Yucatan law of 1915 offered 10 hectares of irrigated agave land, 25 irrigated hectares for regular farming or 200 for grazing. In Zacatecas, 3–25 hectares of irrigated land was offered as a basis in the 1917 law, while in Durango 10–20 was proposed (in 1922). In Chihuahua (1922), 6–10 hectares of irrigated land was offered, in Michoacán (1919, 1920) 25–50 hectares of irrigated land, and so on in the states of Colima, Sonora, San Luis Potosí, Hidalgo, Guerrero and others. These units served as a basis for more widespread distribution of unirrigated plots that reached dimensions of 44,000 hectares of poor quality pasture land in the state of Chihuahua (!). The dimensions of the plots were determined by the soil conditions, and general living conditions in each region. Despite what might seem like 'federal anarchism', in most of the states the legislators planned agrarian redistribution that would provide reasonably sized, but not extravagant plots, which could support a family. The land was given to interested potential farmers in exchange for payment, spread out over 20 to 44 years, the amount determined according to the fiscal value of the expropriated land with the addition of 5 per cent annual interest. On the other hand, the private estate properties (the former latifundios) were granted 50 to 200 hectares of irrigated land as a basis. A table that summarises the scope of land expropriation implemented according to the state laws on a comparative basis can be found in Gilberto Fábila and Francisco A. Ursua, *Fraccionamiento de latifundios: bases para la ley federal sobre esta materia, reglamento del Articulo 27 Constitucional* (México: Imprenta de la Cámara de Diputados, 1925), pp. 56–57. For a general discussion on all the aspects of the state legislation, see *ibid.*, pp. 43–69. For further discussion, see also Frank Tannenbaum, *The Mexican Agrarian Revolution* (Hamden, Connecticut: Archon Books, 1968), pp. 432–50.

6   "Anteproyecto de Decreto: Fraccionamiento de latifundios y fomento agrícola," *Periódico Oficial* LII, no. 97 (23 May 1932): 1.

7   Tejeda to Diputado Secretario de la H. Legislatura del Estado, 22 June 1931, in Exp. de Decreto #269: "Estableciendo la creación y fomento de la pequeña propiedad," 10 Aug. 1931, AGEV, Fondo Legislatura, exp. 4-1-269, 1931. The

reason that neither Michoacán nor Veracurz could operate their laws on the breaking up of the latifundios and the distribution of their land in small plots to private farm families, emanated from the failure of 1921's legislative attempt to nationalize the regulation of the Mexican homestead, given constitutionaly, as mentioned earlier, to the federative states. Since, by using polical pressures, the Center prevented all Federative State from operating their smallholding distributive laws. See: Ley sbore fraccionamiento de los latifunidios, sesiones de.19 de abril, 25 de abril y 20 de mayo 1921.

8 *Gaceta Oficial* XVIV, no. 85 (17 July 1930): 7–8; Moisés T. de la Peña, *Mito y realidad de la reforma agraria en México* (México: Cuadernos Americanos, 1964), p. 318.

9 On the obstacles to this mode of agrarian reform in Veracruz and Michoacán alone, see, for example: Decreto #222 (2 July 1931): "Suspendiendo provision-almente en sus funciones al C. Antonio Berlin, Presidente Municipal de Villa Jara," AGEV, Fondo Legislatura, exp. 4-1-222, 1931; Exp. de Decreto #165 (30 April 1931): "Suspendiendo por 3 meses al Ayuntamiento de Tlapacoyan," Fondo Legislatura, exp. 4-1-165, 1931; exp. 796, pq. 3125, AGEV, Fondo Gobernación y Justicia, 1932; exp. 885, pq. 3130, Fondo Gobernación y Justicia, 1932; exp. 2, pq. 3078, Fondo Gobernación y Justicia, 1932; exp. 2196, pq. 3215, Fondo Gobernación y Justicia, 1932; Exp. de Ley #110: "Reglamentaria de tierras ociosas del Estado de Michoacán de Ocampo, XLII Legislatura, 19 May 1930, AHCMO, exp. 2, caja 6; Tejeda to C. Diputado Secretario de la H. Legislatura del Estado, 3 Aug. 1931, in Exp. de Ley #265: "Reglamentaria de la Ley Federal de Tierras Ociosas del 1 de agosto de 1931," AGEV, Fondo Legislatura, exp. 4-1-265, 1931.

10 Luis Cabrera, "Balance de la Revolución," in *Historia documental del Partido de la Revolución*, vol. I (México: Partido Revolucionario Institucional and Instituto de Capacitación Política, 1986), p. 188.

11 Quoted in Medin, *El Minimato presidencial*, pp. 101–102.

12 Letter from Cárdenas to F. J. Múgica, Puruándiro, Michoacán, 20 Nov. 1929, ACERMLC, Fondo J. Múgica, vol. 9, doc. 211, pp. 1–3.

13 Cárdenas, *Informe 1929–1930*, p. 21.

14 "Discurso del Gobernador Constitucional del Estado de Michoacán al separarse del Gobierno del Estado por los obligaciones de su nuevo cargo en la presidencia del PNR," 7 Nov. 1930, in L. Cárdenas, *Palabras* I, pp. 93–95.

15 "Palabras del Gobernador Constitucional del Estado de Michoacán al inaugurar el Instituto de Investigaciones Sociales," 6 Nov. 1930, in *ibid.*, pp. 91–93.

16 "Declaraciones del Presidente del PNR a representantes de las Camaras de Diputados y Senadores con la relación al posible retiro del Gobernador del Estado de Tamaulipas," 30 Nov. 1930, in *ibid.*, p. 95.

17 "Declaraciones del Presidente del PNR a la prensa nacional en apoyo de los Gobernadores," 3 Dec. 1930, in *ibid.*, pp. 95–97.

18 "Discurso del Presidente del PNR sobre el programa de trabajo para el año de 1931," 31 Dec. 1931, in *ibid.*, pp. 98–101.

19 Luis Cabrera, "Balance de la Revolución," p. 189; Lázaro Cárdenas, "No ha fracasado la Revolución," response by Lázaro Cárdenas, Presidente del Comité Ejecutivo Nacional Revolucionario, to Luis Cabrera, published in *El Nacional* (1 Feb. 1931), in *Historia documental del Partido de la Revolución*, I, p. 202;

"Respuesta del Presidente del PNR a los ataques lanzados al régimen de la Revolución . . . ," 31 Jan. 1931, in *Historia documental del Partido de la Revolución*, I, pp. 101–106.

20   "Excitativa del Presidente del PNR para lograr el ejercicio de la democracia dentro del partido," 28 April 1931, in *ibid.*, pp. 106–108.

21   "Fructífera jira del C. Cárdenas," *El Nacional*, 23 Nov. 1930; "Va a Michoacán el General L. Cárdenas," *El Nacional*, 16 Dec. 1930; "Unión de los educadores," *El Nacional*, 24 Dec. 1930; "Frente al PNR la vigorosa personalidad del General Cárdenas," *El Nacional*, 25 Dec. 1930; "Hoy llegará el C. Cárdenas: Regresa de una interesante jira que realizó al estado de Michoacán," *El Nacional*, 11 Feb. 1931; "Reciente jira del Sr. Gral. Cárdenas en el Edo. de Michoacán," *El Nacional*, 13 Feb. 1931; "Agasajos en Morelia al Primer Magistrado," *El Nacional*, 18 Feb. 1931; "Visita el Sr. Presidente Pátzcuaro y Uruapan," *El Universal*, 25 Feb. 1931; "Una carretera en Michoacán: El General Lázaro Cárdenas va a inaugurar la de Uruapan-Apatzingan," *El Nacional*, 16 May 1931; "Fructíferos resultados de la jira del Gral. Cárdenas," *El Nacional*, 20 July 1931; "Benefica ha sido la visita del Gral. Cárdenas a Michoacán," *El Nacional*, 20 July 1931; "En todo su estado natal homenajado el Gral. de División Lázaro Cárdenas," *El Nacional*, 22 July 1931; "Arriba ayer a la capital el Gral. L. Cárdenas," *El Nacional*, 14 Aug. 1931; "Seis meses de licencia al General Lázaro Cárdenas," *El Nacional*, 11 Nov. 1931; "No existe fracaso del ejido: Sensacional discurso del Gral. Lázaro Cárdenas en Morelia, Michoacán," *El Nacional*, 20 Nov. 1931.

22   See, for example, "Ampliación de ejidos a los campesinos de San Joaquín, Morelia, Edo. de Michoacán," *El Nacional*, 22 Dec. 1930; "Cooperativa de ejidatarios de Tanhuato, Michoacán," *El Nacional*, 22 Dec. 1930; "Varias rancherías solicitan dotaciones de tierras en los estados del país," *El Nacional*, 22 Dec. 1930; "Dotación ejidal en Apúndaro, Michoacán," *El Nacional*, 13 Feb. 1931; "Un atentado latifundista en Michoacán (Guaracha)," *El Nacional*, 6 March 1931; "Un ejido modelo en Michoacán," *El Nacional*, 2 May 1931; "El gobierno de Veracruz fomenta la agricultura ejidal," *El Nacional*, 24 May 1931; "Otro ejido modelo," *El Nacional*, 25 May 1931; "Comentario: El agrarismo y la crísis," *El Nacional*, 25 May 1931; "Una visita a los ejidos de Michoacán," *El Nacional*, 13 July 1931.

23   "Informe que rinde el C. Ing. Adalberto Tejeda," 1928–1932, p. 6139.

24   "Informe que rinde el C. Ing. Adalberto Tejeda," 1931–1932 (primer semestre), AAT, tomo 197, foja 531.

25   "Exposición de motivos de various Diputados, que originó el proyecto de una nueva ley de expropiación por causa de utilidad pública," 26 May 1932, in Exp. de Ley #66 sobre Expropriación, AGEV, Fondo Legislatura, exp. 4-1-66, 1932; and "Formula observaciones a proyecto de ley sobre expropiación," Tejeda to C. Diputado Secretario de la H. Legislatura del Estado, 30 May 1932, in *ibid.*

26   "Informe que rinde el C. Ing. Adalberto Tejeda," 1931–1932 (primer semestre), AAT, tomo 197, fojas 531–534; Tejeda, *Informe 1928–1932*, p. 6139.

27   "Que no cese el reparto de tierras mientras el campesino las necesite", *El Dictamen*, 19 Feb. 1930; and "El reparto ejidal para los peones de hacienda pide la Liga Campesina", *El Dictamen*, 20 Feb. 1930.

28   "El reparto de tierras continuará conforme a la ley. Las cámaras de comercio no pueden dar orientaciones en materia agraria al Gobierno de Ortiz Rubio", *El Universal*, 3 Oct. 1930.

29 "El Congreso Campesino de Jalapa y la lucha de las facciones burguesas," *El Machete Ilegal* 187 (Nov. 1930): 2.

30 *Ibid.*

31 "La legislatura veracruzana propone que se aplace el proyecto de la reforma agraria," *El Dictamen*, 4 Dec. 1930; "Aplazar la reforma agraria sería aplazar y agravar la situación," *El Dictamen*, 5 Dec. 1930; and "Tejeda y la nueva ley agrariaa," *El Machete Ilegal* 188 (Dec., 1930): 1, 3.

32 Comisiones Unidas de Justicia y Puntos Constitucionales, Trabajo y Previsión Social de la Legislatura Veracruzana to the H. Asamblea Local, 14 Dec. 1931, in Exp. sobre las referencias al Art. 10 de la Ley de 6 de enero de 1915, AGEV, Fondo Legislatura, 14 Dec. 1931; and "Aprobó el Senado la reforma de la Ley del 6 de enero de 1915," *El Nacional*, 3 Dec. 1931.

33 "La tierra y la libertad de los pueblos," *El Nacional*, 30 Dec. 1931; "La Ley Agraria de 6 de enero," *El Universal*, 14 Jan. 1932.

34 "El ejercito y los agraristas en el concurso social," *El Nacional*, 15 Oct. 1931; "El floreciente Estado de Michoacán," *El Nacional*, 20 Nov. 1931; "Rechazó los certificados de liberación agraria la Cámara," *El Nacional*, 18 Dec. 1931; "La Revolución alerta: El ejido es conquista definitiva," *El Nacional*, 20 Dec. 1931; "Los agricultores gestionan el pago de la deuda agraria," *El Nacional*, 22 Dec. 1931; "El ejemplo del Estado de Veracruz," *El Nacional*, 26 Dec. 1931; and "Michoacán tierra de promisión," *El Nacional*, 29 Dec. 1931.

35 "La Revolución alerta," *El Nacional*, 20 Dec. 1931; "Si Cristo volviera sería agrarista," cartoon in *El Nacional*, 21 Dec. 1931; and "La emancipación económica traerá la del espiritu: Declaraciones del Gobernador Constitucional del Edo. de Puebla," *El Nacional*, 21 Dec. 1931.

36 CNA, *Estadística 1915–1927* (México: Secretaría de Agricultura y Fomento, 1928), p. 35; Cárdenas, *Informe 1928–1932*, p. 25; Falcón, *El agrarismo en Veracruz*, Table VII, pp. 76–77; *Atlas ejidal del Estado de Veracruz, Encuentra nacional agropecuaria ejidal, 1988* (Aguascalientes: Instituto Nacional de Estadística Geografía e Informática and ORSTOM, 1991), p. 1.

37 "Acta de sesiones de la Legislatura Michoacana, #42: Sesión del 26 de diciembre de 1928" [in two parts], in *Periódico Oficial* XLIX, nos. 49 and 50 (20 and 24 Jan. 1929): 5 and 4, respectively.

38 Cárdenas, *Informe 1929–1930*, p. 20.

39 *Ibid.*, pp. 1–2.

40 Francisco S. Elías, "Agrarismo organizado," *El Nacional*, 3 Dec. 1931.

41 "Discurso del Gobernador Constitucional del Estado de Michoacán al inaugurar el Instituto de Investigaciones Sociales," 6 Nov. 1930, in Cárdenas, *Palabras* I, p. 92.

42 "Decreto #17: Los gastos del Estado durante el período del 1 de enero al 31 de diciembre de 1931," *Periódico Oficial*, supplement (2 Feb. 1931): 4; "Decreto #52: Presupuesto del Estado de Michoacán durante el período del 1 de julio al 31 de diciembre del presente año, modifica el Decreto #17 del 31 de diciembre de 1930," *Periódico Oficial*, supplement (1 July 1931): 4–5.

43 "Ley de egresos (año de 1929)," in *Leyes de ingresos y egresos del Estado libre y soberano de Veracruz-Llave que han de regir en el año de 1929* (Jalapa-Enríquez: Talleres Linotipográficos del Gobierno del Estado, 1929), p. 12; *Ley #241 de egresos del Estado libre y soberano de Veracruz-Llave, que ha de regir en el año de 1930* (Jalapa-Enríquez: Talleres Linotipográficos del Gobierno del Estado, 1930), p. 55; *Ley de ingresos y egresos del Estado libre y soberano de*

Veracruz-Llave (1931) (Jalapa-Enríquez: Talleres Linotipográficos del Gobierno del Estado, 1931), in *Gaceta Oficial* XXV, no. 7 (15 Jan. 1931), p. 55; and "Ley de egresos #50 (1932)," in *Leyes de ingresos y egresos del Estado libre y soberano de Veracruz-Llave que han de regir en el año de 1932* (Jalapa-Enríquez: Talleres Linotipográficos del Gobierno del Estado, 1932), p. 48. This achievement remained after Tejeda left office. In 1934 the staff of the CLA totaled 59 people, 35 of them technicians. This indicates that the agrarianist movement continued to hold its ground in Veracruz even after Tejeda's departure. See "Ley de egresos #24 (1934)," in *Leyes de ingresos y egresos del Estado libre y soberano de Veracruz-Llave, que han de regir en el año de 1934* (Jalapa-Enríquez: Talleres Linotipográficos del Gobierno del Estado, 1934), p. 63.

44   "Actas de sesiones de la H. Legislatura Veracruzana, sesión extraordinaria de día 3 de enero de 1929," in *Actas y discusiones de la XXXII H. Legislatura del Estado de Veracruz-Llave* (Jalapa-Enríquez: Talleres Linotipográficos del Gobierno del Estado, 1929), pp. 9, 16–17.

45   Grupo de Diputados to H. Legislatura, Jalapa-Enríquez, 11 Jan. 1932, in Exp. de Ley #50 de egresos del año de 1932.

46   Deputy Isaac Fernández to H. Legislatura, 9 Jan. 1932, in Exp. de Ley #50.

47   Gallardo, *La lucha por la tierra*, pp. 44–45 and 96*n*.125–126; Salmerón Castro, "Proceso político y estructuras de poder en una micro región canera de Michoacán: Taretan 1880–1980" (Master's thesis, El Colegio de Michoacán, 1988), pp. 261–262; Los vecinos de Tocumbo to Ciudadano Presidente del H. Congreso del Estado, 27 Nov. 1929, in Exp. de Ley #76, LII Legislatura, AHCMO, caja 4, carp. 8; Exp. de Ley #94, LXII Legislatura Michoacana, caja 5, carp. 5; letter from Carolino Anaya, Presidente de la Liga de Comunidades Agrarias de Veracruz, to Adalberto Tejeda, 15 Feb. 1929, AGEV, Fondo de Agricultura, Fomento y Obras Públicas, exp. II.153 (7-2), 1117, pq. 3852 (1929), in re: "Lo relacionado con las dificultades surgidas entre los arrendatarios (del Pueblo de San Nicolás, Mpio. de Actopan) y el terrateniente, Sr. Manuel Galván"; Exp. 625: "Dotación, Ranchería de San Nicolás, Mpio. Actopan, ex-cantón de Jalapa, in ASRA, Delegación Veracruzana; author's interview with the veterans of the former hacienda de Guaracha (now Emiliano Zapata), Michoacán, June, 1989; and *Periódico Oficial*, 13 March 1930, p. 4, 25 June 1931, p. 6, 6 July 1931, p. 2, 5. As concerns murder, Jesús Múgica Martínez found that during the years 1924 and 1925 alone 250 "soldiers of agrarianism" (as he called them) were killed in Michoacán. See Múgica Martínez, *La Confederación*, pp. 146–150. The culmination of this series of killings was the murder of the agrarianist federal deputy Rafael Picazo. On this affair see Carpeta Especial: "Asesinato de Diputado Rafael Picazo (24 de febrero de 1931), Protestas de varios pueblos," AHCMO, LXIII Legislatura, "Especiales," caja 1.

48   "Solicitud de ejidos presentada por los vecinos de La Estancia de la Trinidad, Municipio de Puruándiro," *Periódico Oficial*, 9 March 1931, p. 9.

49   "Solicitud de ejidos presentada por los vecinos de Agostitlan, Municipio de Hidalgo," *Periódico Oficial*, 24 March 1930, p. 3.

50   "Acta #15 de la XLIII H. Legislatura Michoacana, sesión del 24 de julio de 1931," in *Libro de las actas del H. XLIII Legislatura local*, 11 Sept. 1930–12 Sept. 1931.

51   On the range of coercive measures and inducements employed, see the following examples: "Asunto: Tramitación de ejidos en el Municipio; dotación de ejidos

a los vecinos de las haciendas de 'La Rinconada' y de 'La Ladera'," AMZ, exp. 5, Caja de Fomento 1930–1931/2°, Sección de Agricultura; and Caytano Reyes García, "Los empresarios Noriega contra la Comisión Local Agraria de Michoacán, 1922," *Relacciones* [Estudios de Historia y Sociedad, El Colegio de Michoacán] XI, no. 43 (Summer, 1990): 157–174.

52 Tejeda to Pedro Palazuelos, 9 April 1929, AAT, tomo 131, vol. 155, doc. 11 (1929).

53 Heather Fowler Salamini, "The Agrarian Revolution in the State of Veracruz, 1920–1940: The Role of Peasant Organizations" (Ph.D. diss., Washington, D.C.: American University, 1970), vol. II, p. 249; "Informe que rinde el Comité Central Executivo ante la Asamblea del VII Congreso Ordinario de la Liga de Comunidades Agrarias del Estado de Veracruz," in Manuel Almanza García, "La historia del agrarismo en el Estado de Veracruz" (manuscript), vol. IV, ch. XXV, p. 42.

54 Letter from Cárdenas to Manuel Pérez Treviño, Secretario de Agricultura, 22 March 1931, ACERMLC, Fondo L. Cárdenas, caja 27, carp. 11, doc. 1.

55 "Informe de Gobierno, rendido por el C. Benigno Serrato, en el período de 1932–1933" (Sección de la Labor Agraria), AHCMO, XLIV Leg., exp. 13, caja 1, "Varios"; "Directorio Oficial del Estado de Michoacán," *Periódico Oficial* LIII, no. 5 (20 June 1932): 1–2.

56 Decreto #125: "Facultando al Ejecutivo del Estado para expedir durante el período de receso de esta H. Legislatura una ley de responsabilidades de funcionarios y empleados públicos del Estado," 5 July 1932, AGEV, Fondo Legislatura, exp. 4-1-125 (1932); Decreto #125 in *Gaceta Oficial* XXVIII, no. 84 (14 July 1932): 2; "La responsabilidad de los funcionarios en asuntos agrarios comprendida en una ley," *Excelsior,* 28 Aug. 1932; "Responsabilidad por la dotación de ejidos," *Excelsior*, 20 Sept. 1932.

57 "Circular a los Presidentes Municipales y Agentes del Ministerio Público, sobre la correcta aplicación de las Leyes de Tierras Ociosas," *Periódico Oficial* LII, no. 97 (23 May 1932).

58 The institution of the Procuraduría de Pueblos was established in 1922 by CNA circular #22, published on 17 April of that year. See "Procuraduría de Pueblos" in Antonio Luna Arroyo and Luis G. Alcérreca, *Diccionario de Derecho agrario mexicano* (México: Porrúa, 1982), p. 690.

59 Raúl Wilber Delgado, Procurador de Pueblos, to Pedro Torres Ortiz, Presidente Municipal de Zamora, 20 Feb. 1931, AMZ, exp. 5, Caja Fomento 1930–1931/2°, Sección de Agricultura: "La tramitación de ejidos en el municipio."

60 "Informe que rinde el C. Ing. Adalberto Tejeda," 1928–1932, p. 6139.

61 "Solicitud de ejidos presentada por los vecinos de la Hacienda de Zincuirán, Mpio. de La Huacana," *Periódico Oficial*, 6 July 1931, pp. 5–6.

62 *Ibid.*, p. 4.

63 "Solicitud de dotación de ejidos presentada por los vecinos de la Hacienda de Zinciro," *Periódico Oficial*, 25 June 1931, p. 6.

64 See, for example, Ranchería de Rinconada, *Periódico Oficial*, 8 May 1931, p. 2; Hacienda de Lombardía, *Periódico Oficial*, 25 June 1931, p. 4; Rancho de las Pierdas, *Periódico Oficial*, 10 Oct. 1931, p. 9; Ranchería de la Loma, *Periódico Oficial*, 7 Dec. 1931, p. 4; and Colonia Lázaro Cárdenas, *Periódico Oficial*, 10 Dec. 1931, p. 4.

65 Interview with David Lúa Castañeda, ACERMLC, Entrevistas, caja 9, carp. 10,

no. 141, pp. 20–21; Enrique Krauze, *General misionero—Lázaro Cárdenas,* Biografía del Poder, no. 8 (Mexico: FCE, 1987), p. 61–62.

66 For a detailed account of the whole episode, see "Atentado latifundista en Michoacán," *El Nacional,* 6 March 1931; and Exp. agrario #500 de las Zarquillas, Mpio. de Villamar, Archivo Estadístico de la Secretaría de la Reforma Agraria [AESRA], Morelia, Michoacán.

67 "Un rico hacendado que trata inutilmente de sostener su feodalismo en el E. de Michoacán," *El Nacional,* 21 Aug. 1931; Exp. agrario #540 de Emiliano Zapata, Mpio. de Villamar, AESRA, Morelia, Michoacán; Heriberto García Moreno, *Guaracha, tiempos viejos, tiempos nuevos* (Zamora: El Colegio de Michoacán, 1980), pp. 165–166; Eric Van Young, "Crítica del libro de Heriberto Moreno, Guaracha, tiempos viejos, tiempos nuevos (Fonapas-Michoacán/El Colegio de Michoacán, 1980)," *Relaciones,* Vol. 3, no. 12 (Fall, 1982): 150–155.

68 "Una felicitación al señor General L. Cárdenas," *El Nacional,* 6 March 1931.

69 "Resumen estadístico de los datos agrarios del Edo. de Michoacán, años 1928–1932," AESRA, Delegación Michoacana, Morelia and Uruapán, Michoacán.

70 "Solicitud de restitución de tierras presentada por los vecinos de la comunidad de San Miguel," *Periódico Oficial* L, no. 57 (3 Feb. 1930): 8.

71 "Solicitud de dotacíon de ejidos presentada por los vecinos de la congregación de la Manzana de Guadalupe, Mpio. de Tlalpujahua," *Periódico Oficial,* 2 Jan. 1930, p. 9.

72 Presidente de la Liga de Comunidades Agrarias de Veracruz to Tejeda, 9 March 1931, AAT, vol. 192, tomo 168, doc. 6 (1931); report by confidential agent "Merino" to Tejeda, n.d., AAT, vol. 192, tomo 168, foja 206 (1931); Diputado Isaac Fernández to H. Legislatura, 9 Jan. 1932, AAT, Exp. de Ley #50 de 1932.

73 Author's interviews with: Moisés Lagunes González, Cerro Gordo, Mpio. de Actopan, 23 March 1992; Gabriela Tejeda, widow of Félix Díaz, Palmas de Abajo, Actopan, 29 March 1992; Ignacio Hernández Cervantes and Pedro Pérez Cervantes, Mozomboa, Actopan, 29 March 1992; Jacinto Vásquez Casas, Actopan, Actopan, 30 March 1992; Federico Fabian Zapata, Almolonga, Alto Lucero, 2 April 1992; and Alegario Utrera Cardeña, San Nicolás, Actopan, 2 April 1992.

74 "Informe que rinde el C. Ing. Adalberto Tejeda," 1930–1931 (primer semestre), p. 6246; "Informe que rinde el C. Ing. Adalberto Tejeda," 1931–1932 (primer semestre), fojas 531–534.

75 See data for the years 1924–1928 and 1933–1936 in Falcón, *El agrarismo en Veracruz,* pp. 76–77.

76 "Informe que rinde el C. Ing. Adalberto Tejeda," 1928–1932, p. 6141.

77 Ortiz Rubio resigned on 18 August 1932, although Calles had been dissatisfied with him for some time already; Calles had decided, however, not to precipitate his resignation before he had served two years, not wanting to have new elections before the end of Ortiz Rubio's legal term, at the end of November, 1934. See Medin, *El Minimato presidencial,* p. 112; and Lorenzo Meyer, *Las crísis en el sistema político mexicano (1928–1977)* (México: El Colegio de Mexico, 1977), p. 23.

78 The case of Las Zarquillas was representative. For other examples in Veracruz, see Campesinos de San Nicolás Ixtayuca to Tejeda, 30 July 1931, AAT, vol. 191, tomo 167 (1931), foja 168; and the following, all in AGEV, Fondo Gobernación y Justicia, 1932: exp. 12127, pq. 1175, April, 1932; exp. 1149, pq. 3168, 1932;

exps. 1293 and 1319, pq. 3175, 1932; exps. 2200 and 1684, pq. 3185, 1932; exp. 1340, pq.3216, 1932; exp. 6, pq. 4626, 1932; exp. 67, pq. 3112, 1932; exp. 96, pq. 3188, 1932; and Exp. de Ley #1, pq. 3078, 1932.

79　Segundo Maldonado, el Perito Agrario "D," to Ing. Castulo Villaseñor, Delegado en el Edo. del Dpto. Agrario, Jalapa, 5 Oct. 1942, in exp. agrario #124 del Pueblo de Actopan, ASRA, Delegación Veracruzana, Jalapa, Veracruz. A letter sent by a colleague of Segundo Maldonado to the Office of Agrarian Reform in Mexico City in February, 1943, indicates that Maldonado's life was indeed in danger from certain landowners, and that he was accordingly replaced by another engineer. See Ing. Elías Lizardi Sánchez to Jefe del Dpto. Agrario, Secretaría General en México D.F., Jalapa, 9 Feb. 1943, in exp. agrario #124 del Pueblo de Actopan, ASRA, Delegación Veracruzana, Jalapa, Veracruz.

80　Every warning by the governor was normally repeated by the president of the municipio. See, for example, two letters from Pedro Torres Ortiz, Presidente Municipal de Zamora, to Manuel Zavala de la Hacienda de "El Cerrito," 8 May 1931, in AMZ, exp. 5, Caja Fomento 1930–1931/2°, Sección de Agricultura: "Tramitación de ejidos en el municipio."

81　See "Familia asaltada por un grupo de pillos que logró huir," *El Nacional*, 3 Jan. 932; "Se hallan presos los probables authores de un asesinato," *El Nacional*, 20 Jan. 1932; "Reparto de tierras a vecinos de Huetamo, Edo. de Michoacán," *El Nacional*, 20 Jan. 1932. See also the following agrarian cases: Exp. #777 de San Ignacio, #387 de San Jerónimo, #513 de La Mesa de Totolán, #546 de Ojo de Agua de Uro, #364 de Sanchiqueo, #488 de Turitzio, #533 de Uspio, all in ASRA, Delegación Michoacana, Morelia, Michoacán. Substantial factual discrepancies are notable between press accounts and archival sources. Whereas the press reported 20 ejidos, the archives list only eight. A number of communities may have been put together in a single file, a common practice at the time which would explain the discrepancy.

82　See, for example, "Iniciativa de realización de una guerrilla en la región de Tuxtepec," 3 April 1929, AAT, vol. 148, tomo 124 (1929), fojas 141–143; and Pedro Ponce, Presidente del Comité Ejecutivo Particular de "Loma de los Hoyos," Mpio. de Cotaxtla, to Tejeda, 6 June 1932, concerning the formation of a "*guerrilla*" in the area, AAT, vol. 220 (1932), fojas 85–86.

83　See the following examples: Vicente Rincón, Presidente del Comité P.A.A. de San Nicolás to Delegado de la CNA en Jalapa, 21 July 1930, in Exp. #625: "Dotación de ejidos a los vecinos de la Ranchería de San Nicolás, Mpio. de Actopan, Veracruz, SRA, Delegación Veracruzana, Jalapa, Veracruz; Abelardo Hinojosa to Tejeda, Jalapa, 21 Aug. 1931, in AAT, tomo 168, vol. 192, doc. 199; exp. #746, Departamento de Agricultura y Ganadería, Gobierno de Veracruz: "Vecinos de Pueblo de Xitalpa solicitan tierras en arrendamiento, de conformidad con la Ley #297 del predio denominado de la Hacienda de Almolonga," AGEV, exp. 0.0.(7-9), 1930; letter from Dimas Fernández, Presidente del Comité Particular Administrativo (del Ejido de San Nicolás) to Delegado de la Comisión Nacional Agraria, 12 Dec. 1929, in exp. agrario #625 del Ejido de San Nicolás, Mpio. de Actopan, Veracruz, SRA, Delegación Veracruzana, Jalapa, Veracruz.

The situation changed completely after Tejeda left office. See: interviews with Ignacio Hernández Cervantes and Pedro Pérez Cervantes, Mozomboa, Actopan, 29 March 1992; Jacinto Vásquez Casas, Actopan, Actopan, 30 March 1992; Federico Fabian Zapata, Almolonga, Alto Lucero, 2 April 1992; Alegario Utrera

Cardeña, San Nicolás, Actopan, 2 April 1992; and Martín Contreras Contreras, Paso de la Milpa, Actopan, 30 March 1992.

84 Fowler Salamini reached this conclusion as well. See Fowler Salamini, "The Agrarian Revolution in the State of Veracruz," pp. 246–247.

85 "Oficio 2103 del Congreso Veracruzano, sesión del 11 de diciembre de 1928," *Gaceta Oficial* XXI, no. 58 (14 May 1929).

86 *Ley #297 sobre Arrendamiento de Tierras* (Jalapa, Veracruz: Oficina Tipográfica del Gobierno del Estado, 1926).

87 *Ley de Tierras Ociosas: Cartilla explicativa para los presidentes municipales y para los campesinos*, 4th edition (México: Publicaciones de la Secretaría de Acción Agraria del Partido Nacional Revolucionario, 1937), Art. 9, pp. 19–20; letter from Francisco Cervantez, Presidente del Comité Ejecutivo Agrario de Mozomboa, to Delegado del Dpto. Agrario, 9 July 1934, in ASRA, Delegación Veracruzana, exp. 1202: "Dotación, Congregación de Mozomboa, Mpio. de Actopan, Veracruz."

88 For examples of these applications, see: Letter from Presidente de la Liga de Comunidades Agrarias del Estado to Tejeda, 26 March 1931, AGEV, Fondo Agricultura y Ganadero, exp. 1034 (Arch.), 1931: "Arrendamiento Congregación de Chapote, Mpio. Platón Sánchez"; "Comité Ejecutivo de Zimpizahua (Mpio. de Coatepec) solicita tierras de acuerdo con la Ley 297 . . . " 15 Dec. 1929, AGEV, Fondo Agricultura y Ganadero, exp. 714 (Arch.), 1930; "El Comité Paricular Ejecutivo de Tlapacoyan solicita en arrendamiento la propiedad de los srs. Bello y Fernando Mendoza, de conformidad con la Ley 297 . . . " Jan.-March, 1930, AGEV, Fondo Agricultura y Ganadero, exp. 735 (Arch.), 1930.

89 "El Presidente del distrito agrario de 'Ahuimol,' Mpio. de Chicontepec (representante de la Liga de Comunidades Agrarias del Estado), solicita granjas y tierras de conformidad a la Ley # 297," AGEV, Fondo Agricultura y Ganadero, exp. 0.0.(5), 1930; Guadalupe Osorio, Presidente del Departamento "A" de la Liga de Comunidades Agrarias del Estado, to Tejeda, 15 Dec. 1929; and Salvador Gortari to Jefe del Departamento de Agricultura y Ganadero del Estado, 31 Dec. 1929.

90 "Exposición de motivos por las Comisiones Legislativas de Fomento, Trabajo y Previsión Social y Justicia y Puntos Constitucionales de H. Congreso Veracruzano sobre el Proyecto de Ley #208, 4 de junio de 1931," in Exp. de Ley #208: "Reformando la Ley #297 de 8 de julio de 1926 que declara de utilidad pública el cultivo y aprovechamiento de tierras propias para agricultura o ganadería," AGEV, Fondo Legislatura, exp. 4-1-208, 1931; and Fowler, *Movilización campesina*, p. 128.

91 Oficio #22044: "Exposición de motivos de Tejeda sobre el proyecto de ley que declara obligatoria el cultivo y aprovechamiento de tierras propias para la agricultura y la ganadería, enviado al Diputado Secretario de la H. Legislatura del Edo. en 16 de diciembre de 1930," in Exp. de Ley #208: "Reformando la Ley #297 de 8 de julio de 1926 que declara de utilidad pública el cultivo y aprovechamiento de tierras propias para agricultura o ganadería," AGEV, Fondo Legislatura, exp. 4-1-208, 1931.

92 See, for example, exp. 2196, pq. 3215, 1932, Promovente: Comité Agrario de Comatepec, Mpio. de Cosamaloapan, AGEV, Fondo Gobernación y Justicia; exp. 345, pq. 3134, 1932, Promovente: Procurador General de Justicia, Jalapa, AGEV, Fondo Gobernacíon y Justicia; Exp. de Ley #2, pq. 3078, Promovente:

Jefetura de Operaciones Militares, Veracruz (Ciudad), AGEV, Fondo Gobernacíon y Justicia; and "Queja por despojo de tierras," Sindicato de Jornaleros, Compañía de Tabacos, Mpio. San Andrés Tuxtla, AGEV, Fondo Agricultura y Ganadero, exp. 500 (Arch.), 1932.

93 Tejeda to C. Diputado Secretario de la H. Legislatura del Estado, 3 Aug. 1931, in Exp. de Ley #265 "(que) reglamenta la Ley Federal de Tierras Ociosas," 13 Aug. 1931, AGEV, Fondo Legislatura, exp. 4-1-265, 1931.

94 "Informe de los Diputados Isaac Trigos y Jesús Ramírez Ordóñez a la H. Legislatura Local, acerca de la averiguación de las quejas formadas en contra del Ayuntamiento Constitucional de Tlapacoyan, 27 May 1931," in Exp. de Decreto #165 "que suspende por 3 meses al Ayuntamiento de Tlapacoyan," 30 April 1931, AGEV, Fondo Legislatura, exp. 4-1-165, 1931.

95 See, for example, the following cases: "Vecinos de la Ranchería de Almolonga solicitan tierras en arrendamiento . . . ," April, 1930, AGEV, Fondo Agricultura y Ganadero, exp. 713 (Arch.), 1930; "Arrendamientos Comprendidos de la Congregación 'El Yegual,' Mpio. de Jamapa, Informe del Presidente Municipal," 21 April 1931, AGEV, Fondo Agricultura y Ganadero, exp. 1030 (Arch.), 1931, p. 2.

96 "Informe que rinde el C. Ing. Adalberto Tejeda," 1928–1932, p. 6314.

97 "Ley #110 Reglamentaria de Tierras," 19 May 1930, AHCMO, XLII Legislatura, "Decretos," exp. 2, caja 6.

98 "Exp. relativa a la solicitud de tierras ociosas, que elevaron los vecinos de Sauz de Magaña," AMZ, Caja de Fomento 1931–1932, exp. #7.

99 "Informe de Gobierno de 1930–1931 que rinde el Lic. Gabino Vázquez," AHCMO, XLII Legislatura, exp. 5, caja 1, "Varios"; Lázaro Cárdenas, *Informe 1928–1932*, p. 26; "Circular a los CC. Presidentes Municipales y Agentes del Ministerio Público, sobre la correcta aplicación de las Leyes de Tierras Ociosas," *Periódico Oficial* LII, no. 97 (23 May 1932): 2.

100 Foglio Miramontes, *Geografía económicó* III, pp. 410–411.

101 "Informe de Gobierno, rendido por Benigno Serrato, en el año de 1933 a 1934," AHCMO, XLIV Legislatura, "Varios," exp. 14, caja 1.

102 *Ibid.*

103 For the text of the law, see "Ley de Aparcería Rural," AHCMO, "Acta #1, XLIII Legislatura, tercer período extraordinario de sesiones, 16 July 1932," in *Actas de sesiones*, tomo del 14 de septiembre de 1931 al 29 de agosto de 1932, Arts. 8, 11, 22, 30, pp. 2–8.

104 Serrato, for example, reported 67 new unions registered in the fiscal year 1932–1933 (28 of them peasant unions); out of the 67 new unions 62 (!) joined the CRMDT. See "Informe de Gobierno, rendido por Benigno Serrato, 1932–1933" (Sección: Tribunal de Trabajo), p. 2.

105 *Ley general de sociedades cooperativas, expedida por el Congreso de la Unión con fecha 21 de enero de 1927* (Jalapa: Talleres Linitinográficos del Gobierno del Estado, 1929).

106 Decreto #174: "Autorizando al Ejecutivo del Estado para que de los fondos que el Gobierno mismo reciba de la cooperativa industrial de luz, fuerza y trans-portes de Jalapa, en calidad de anticipo, conceda a la eléctrica de Minatitlán S.C. de R.I. un préstamo por la cantidad de 20,000 = que esta destinará exclusiva-mente para su desembolsimiento," 12 Aug. 1932, AGEV, Fondo Legislatura,, exp. 4-1-174, 1932; "Informe que rinde el C. Ing. Adalberto Tejeda," 1930–1931 (primer semestre), p. 6244.

107 "Congreso de agraristas en Jalapa," *Excelsior*, 30 Oct. 1930.

108 See, in AAT, tomo 197, 1932, the following: Memorandum for el Sr. Lic. Eugenio Méndez, n.d., fojas 561–564; letter from Presidente de la República, el Gral. Ortiz Rubio, to Coronel A. Tejeda, 21 April 1932, foja 543; letter from Empresa Hidro-Eléctrica de Minatitlán to Ing. A. Tejeda, 29 April 1932, foja 541; and letter from Empresa Hidro-Eléctrica de Minatitlán to Ing. A. Tejeda, 6 May 1932. See also "Se proyecta una empresa en Puerto México," *El Nacional*, 6 Dec. 1930.

109 Tejeda to H. Diputado Secretario de la Legislatura Local, 16 Dec. 1930, in Exp. de Decreto #156: "Fundando la Refaccionaria del Edo. de Veracruz," AGEV, Fondo Legislatura, doc. 4-6-156, 1931, 15 Jan. 1931.

110 "Informe que rinde el C. Ing. Adalberto Tejeda," 1928–1932, p. 6129.

111 *Ibid.*, pp. 6130–6131.

112 "Informe que rinde el C. Ing. Adalberto Tejeda," 1930–1931 (primer semestre), p. 6244; "Informe que rinde el C. Ing. Adalberto Tejeda," 1928–1932, p. 6130.

113 Concerning the requests for help, see, for example, the request the El Potrero ejido made during the League's seventh congress for help in setting up a coop-erative: Gregorio Castellanos, Presidente del Comité Agrario de "El Potrero," Mpio. de Atoyac, and Delegado al VII Congreso de la Liga de Comunidades Agrarias del Estado, to the Asamblea del H. VII Congreso de la Liga, 26 March 1932, AAT, vol. 220 (1932), foja 38; Secretario Particular del Gobernador a la Liga de Comunidades Agrarias, 6 April 1932, AAT, vol. 220, foja 37; Secretario Particular to CC. Gregorio Castellanos and Juan Flores, Presidente and Secretario del Comité Agrario de "El Potrero," Atoyac, 6 April 1932, AAT, vol. 220, foja 41.

114 See, for example, in AAT, vol. 220 (1932), the following requests and the responses they elicited: Nemesio Garduño to Tejeda, 14 May and 14 June 1932, fojas 11 and 64; ejidatarios del Paso Moral, Mpio. de Soledad de Doblado, to Tejeda, 6 June 1932, foja 82; Tejeda to Nemesio Garduño, Gerente de la Sociedad Refaccionaria de Estado, 9 and 28 June 1932, fojas 81 and 66; Tejeda to the Liga de Comunidades Agrarias, 10 June 1932, foja 13; and Presidente de la Liga de Comunidades Agrarias to Presidente del Comité Particular Agrario de Soledad de Doblado, 14 June 1932, foja 68.

115 Fowler, *Movilización campesina*, pp. 135–136.

116 "Ayer llegó el Coronel Tejeda," *El Nacional*, 15 June 1932.

117 Secretaría de Prensa y Propaganda del CEN del PNR, *La jira del General Lázaro Cárdenas: Síntesis ideológica* (Nov., 1934), p. 53.

118 Cárdenas, *Palabras* I, p. 105.

119 "Un ejido modelo en Michoacán," *El Nacional*, 2 May 1931; "Otro ejido modelo," *El Nacional*, 21 May 1931; "Fructíferos resultados de la jira del Gral. Cárdenas," *El Nacional*, 20 July 1931.

120 "Fue expedida la nueva ley sobre crédito agrario," *Excelsior*, 25 Jan. 1931; "Seis millones a los ejidatarios," *Excelsior*, 25 Jan. 1931; Ramón Beteta, *Pensamiento y dinámica de la Revolución Mexicana, Antología de documentos políticoso-ciales* (México: Editorial México Nuevo, 1950), p. 209.

121 "Creación del Departamento de Fomento Cooperativo," *El Universal*, 12 Dec. 1932; "Se revisa la Ley de Cooperativas para enviarla al Congreso de la Unión," *El Universal*, 11 Dec. 1932; Circular #341 del Departamento de Agricultura, Fomento y Previsión Social, sent by Victoriano Anguiano to the Presidente

Municipal de Zamora, 24 Nov. 1932, and the response of the latter, 5 Dec. 1932, in AMZ, Caja de Fomento 1930–1931/2°, "Varios," exp. 4.

122 Decreto #179: "Condona hasta el 31 de diciembre de 1928 los contribuciones que adeunen a los municipios los ejidatarios del Estado," 14 Sept. 1929, AGEV, Fondo Legislatura.

123 See, AGEV, Fondo Legislatura: Decreto #190: "Condona a los ejidatarios del Estado la contribución predial rústica que adeunen . . . , siempre que se pagan al corriente antes de 31 de enero de 1930; Decreto #153: "Condonado contribuciones a los ejidatarios hasta diciembre de 1929," 15 Jan. 1931, exp. 4-1-153, 1931; Decreto #187: "Condonado . . . a los miembros del Comité Particular Administrativo Agrario de Pubanco, Papantla," 11 June 1931, exp. 4-1-187, 1931; Decreto #294: "Condonado a los ejidatarios de la Congregación de Poza de Cuero, Mpio. de Coatzintla, los contribuciones . . . tanto al Estado como al Municipio," 20 Oct. 1931, exp. 4-1-294, 1931.

124 Letter from Tejeda to C. Diputado Secretario de la H. Diputación Permanente, 10 April 1931, in Exp. de Decreto #187, "condonado contribuciones a los miembros del Comité Particular Administrativo Agrario de Pabanco, Papantla," 11 June 1931, 4-1-187, 1931.

125 "Acta #19, XLII Legislatura, sesión del 5 de noviembre de 1929," *Periódico Oficial* L, no. 39 (2 Dec. 1929): 2–3.

126 Decreto #70: "Por el cual se condona a las comunidades agrarias el 80 porciento de las contribuciones que adeunan," Acta #47, sesión del 21 de enero de 1930, XLII Legislatura, *Periódico Oficial* L, no. 73 (31 March 1930), p. 3.

127 "Acta #10, sesión del 8 de julio de 1930, XLII Legislatura," *Periódico Oficial* LI, no. 15 (25 Aug. 1930): 3.

128 Cárdenas to Lic. Ezio Cusi, 29 March 1968, in *Epistolario de Lázaro Cárdenas*, vol. I (México: Siglo XXI Editores, 1974), p. 151.

129 "Declarando de utilidad pública la desecación del Valle de Zamora . . . " *Periódico Oficial* LII, no. 4 (2 July 1931): 1–2.

130 The term *pueblo* and its historical and conceptual development since the Spanish colony were taken according to the elaborated analysis of Emilio Kourí in Kourí, "Los pueblos y sus tierras", pp. 266–286

131 Medin, *El Minimato presidencial*, p. 115.

132 Lucio Mendieta y Nuñez, ed., *Código agrario de los Estados Unidos Mexicanos* México: Edición del *Diario Oficial*, 1940), Arts. 41, 51, and 84, pp. 45–48, 64; Falcón, "El surgimiento del agrarismo cardenista," pp. 383–384.

133 Translation of Statements by Coronel Adalberto Tejeda, Transmitted by Josephus Daniels to the Secretary of State in Washington, 10 May 1939, NA/RDS, 812.00/30740, pp. 2–4.

5 From Ejidal Agrarianism to Total Agrarianism

1 Cárdenas, *El Gobierno del Estado y las comunidades de indígenas—Programa de acción y antecedentes históricos y legales* (Morelia: Tipografía de ETI Alvaro Obregón, 1931), p. 23.

2 *Reparto de Tierras de los Excomunidades de Indígenas, Disposiciones Relativas* (Morelia: Tipografía José Sansón, 1919), pp. 3–4.

3 This wasn't the case in the Tarascan communitie of the plains, where privatization processes that took place there wiped out entirely the Indian communities' structure and their collective legal status. See, Jennie Purnell, "With All Due

Respect: Popular Resistance to the Privatization of Communal Land in Nineteenth-Century Michoacán." *Latin American Research Review* 34, 1 (1999): 85–121; *Informe que rinde el C. Mayor de Caballera Lauro L. Guzmán, Prefecto del Distrito de Morelia al C. Gobernador Constitucional del Estado de Michoacán, Aristeo Mercado, referente al estado general de la administración del distrito de Morelia, durante los años de 1907 y 1908* (Morelia: Imprenta Artística de J.M. Jurado, 1909).

4   Cárdenas, *Programa de acción*, pp. 23–26.

5   Proyecto de Ley #46: "Declarando anticonstitucional las diferentes contratos con comunidades indígenas de Estado de Michoacán para la explotación de sus bosques," AHCMO, XLIII Legislatura, caja 3, carp. 8.

6   Cárdenas, *Programa de acción*, p. 3.

7   Their ejidal petitions were always turned down on such grounds as: "Denied because petitioners possess communal property"; "Denied because lacking proof of both title and loss" (responding to a petition for restitution); "Denied because petitioners possess communal land." See Expedientes agrarias #468 (San Felipe de los Herreros), #1270 (Comacuen), #1330 (Arato), #756 (Salvador Paricutín), and #847 (Cocucho), ASRA, Morelia, Mpios. of Nuevo Parangaricutiro, Paracho, and Charapan.

8   Letter from Cárdenas to Múgica, 20 Nov. 1929, in "Correspondencia entre Lázaro Cárdenas y Francisco J. Múgica entre 1929 a 1932," *Desdeldiez* [CERMLC] (Dec., 1985): 171.

9   Cárdenas, *Apuntes* I, p. 183.

10   "Acta 7, sesión del 18 de junio de 1931, y acta 8, sesión del 19 de junio de 1931, primer período extraordinario, XLIII Legislatura," *Libro de actas de sesiones* (11 Sept. 1930–12 Sept. 1931), vol. I.

11   Emilio Alañis Patiño, José López Bermudez, and Manuel Mesa Andraca, "Problemas de la tenencia y aprovechamiento de la tierra en México," *Problemas Agrícolas e Industriales de México* 5, no. 4 (Oct.–Dec., 1953): 105.

12   See Antonio Arriaga, *Organización social de los Tarascos* (Morelia: Publicaciones del Departamento de Extensión Universitaria, 1938), pp. 27–28; and author's interview with Domingo Jiménez Chávez (Capacuaro, 12 July 1992), and with Luis González y González (Mexico City, June 1992).

13   Cárdenas, *Programa de acción*, pp. 5–6.

14   Foglio Miramontes, *Geografía económicó* II, p. 216; Cárdenas, "Convocatoria a las comunidades indígenas forestales", in Cárdenas, *Palabras* I, p. 88.

15   Cárdenas, *Informe 1928–1932*, p. 26.

16   In Cherán the cooperative had the exclusive right to exploit the forest belonging to the community, but any local resident could join it upon payment of 10 pesos. See Rolf L. Beals et al., *Cherán: A Sierra Tarascan Village* (Norman: University of Oklahoma Press, 1988), pp. 60, 63. This monopoly was part of Cárdenas's plan to return the forests to the control of the Indian communities, and in Cherán, at least, no one appears to have tried to circumvent the cooperative in order to cut wood for commercial puposes.

17   "Sociedades cooperativas forestales organizadas en el Estado, y reconocidas por la Secretaría de Agricultura y Fomento, 1933", and "Sociedades cooperativas forestales, 1er semestre de 1936", in Foglio Miramontes, *Geografía económicó* II, pp. 113 and 279–280 repectivamente; and "Informe de Gobierno, rendido por el C. Benigno Serrato, en el período de 1932–1933," AHCMO, XLIV Legislatura, exp. 13, caja 1, "Varios," p. 64.

18   Author's interviews with: Andrés Alvaro Hernández, Vicente González, and Lorenzo Torres (Pichátaro, 11 July 1992); Jesús Leiva Roque (Cherán, 11 July 1992); Cristobal González Colesio (Paracho, 12 July 1992); Domingo Jiménez Chávez (Capácuaro, 12 July 1992); and Dr. Luis González y González (Mexico City, June 1992).

19   Foglio Miramontes, *Geografía económicó* II, pp. 72–113.

20   Author's interview with Dr. Luis González y González (Mexico City, June 1992).

21   Decreto #71 (27 Nov. 1930), *Gaceta Oficial* XXIV, no. 150 (16 Dec. 1930): 1.

22   Circular #25 (28 Nov. 1930), *Gaceta Oficial* XXV, no. 1 (1 Jan. 1931): 1–2.

23   Peña, *Mito y realidad*, p. 318.

24   "Anteproyecto de Decreto sobre fraccionamiento de latifundios y fomento agrícola," *Periódico Oficial del Estado de Michoacán de Ocampo* LII, no. 97 (23 May 1932): 1–2.

25   "Fraccionamiento de tierras," Declaration by Gobernador Constitucional del Estado L. Cárdenas, Morelia, Michoacán (29 April 1932); Circular #21 del Departamento de Agricultura, Fomento y Previsión Social del Estado (27 July 1932), AMZ, Fomento, exp. 18, caja 1931–1932.

26   *Periódico Oficial* (11 Aug. 1932): 1–4.

27   "Informe de Gobierno, rendido por el C. Benigno Serrato, en el período de 1932–1933," pp. 14–15.

28   *Ibid.*; "Informe de Gobierno, rendido por Benigno Serrato, en el año de 1933 a 1934," AHCMO, XLIV Legislatura, "Varios," exp. 14, caja 1, Departamento de Agricultura, Sección de Expropiación y Fraccionamiento.

29   "Ley de expropiación por causa de utilidad pública #74, autorizado por el Art. 27 de la Constitución General de la República," 22 March 1924, XXXIV Legislatura, AHCMO, exp. 24, caja 4.

30   "Ley de expropiación por causa de utilidad pública #75," 21 Jan. 1932, Art. 7, pp. 2–3, AHCMO, XLIII Legislatura, exp. 2, caja 5.

31   *Ibid.*, p. 2.

32   Decreto #113: "Declarando de utilidad pública la ocupación de los inmuebles rústicos y urbanos de la Cañada de Chilchota," *Periódico Oficial* (14 July 1932), pp. 7–9.

33   "Ley de expropiación por causa de utilidad pública #75."

34   "Acta #4, 28 June 1932, XLIII Legislatura, Segundo período extraordinario de sesiones," in *Libro de actas de sesiones* (14 Sept. 1931–29 Aug. 1932).

35   "Ley de expropiación por causa de utilidad pública #34," 27 Dec. 1933, in *Impresos Michoacanos* (Colección de documentos hechos por el Congreso Michoacano), vol. 24 (Morelia: Biblioteca del H. Congreso Local, 1933).

36   Cárdenas, *Informe 1928–1932*, p. 27.

37   *Gaceta Oficial* XI, no. 34 (19 March 1929): 1–3. See also *Gaceta Oficial* XXI, no. 64 (28 May 1929): 3.

38   *Gaceta Oficial* XII, no. 144 (1 Dec. 1923); *Gaceta Oficial* XIII, no. 29 (3 June 1924); *Gaceta Oficial* XIII, no. 30 (7 June 1924)l *Gaceta Oficial* XV, no. 129 (27 Oct. 1925); *Gaceta Oficial* XV, no. 131 (31 Oct. 1925); *Gaceta Oficial* XIV, no. 75 (23 June 1925); *Gaceta Oficial* XIV, no. 1 (2 Jan. 1926); *Gaceta Oficial* XVI, no. 10 (23 Jan. 1926).

39   *Gaceta Oficial* XXI, no. 22 (19 Feb. 1929): 2–3; *Gaceta Oficial* XXI, no. 34 (19 March 1929): 1–3; *Gaceta Oficial* XXI, no. 64 (28 May 1929); *Gaceta*

Oficial XXII, no. 127 (22 Oct. 1929): 2; *Gaceta Oficial* XXII, no. 139 (19 Nov. 1929): 5.

40 Exp. de Decreto #108: "Ley de moratoria sobre pago de créditos hipotecarios," 18 June 1929, AGEV, Fondo Legislatura, 1929.

41 Ley #118, *Gaceta Oficial* XXII, no. 87 (20 July 1929): 1–5.

42 "Fraccionamiento y venta de tierras en el Estado", *El Dictamen*, 13 May 1929.

43 Decreto #240: "Reforma algunos artículos de la Ley #118 de 8 de julio de 1929," 11 Jan. 1930, AGEV, Fondo Legislatura, 1930.

44 *Ibid.*; Ley #240, *Gaceta Oficial* XIII, no. 11 (25 Jan. 1930): 3–4.

45 Exp. de Decreto #264 (27 May 1930): "Deroga el Artículo 25 de la Ley #118 de 8 de julio de 1929", AGEV, Fondo Legislatura, 1930.

46 Exp. de Decreto #132 (5 July 1929): "Condona a la Sta. Dolores Fernández Camacho, el 75% de las contribuciones que adeuda hasta el 31 de diciembre de 1928 a la Tesorería Municipal de este ciudad," AGEV, Fondo Legislatura, 1929; Exp. de Decreto #171 (24 octubre 1929): "Condona al Sr. Feverrardo Sausa contribuciones municipales que adeuda al Municipio de Veracruz," AGEV, Fondo Legislatura, 1929; Exp. de Decreto #173 (26 Nov. 1929): "Condona a la Sta. María Hernández Veta de Coantepec el importe de las contribuciones que adeuda hasta la fecha al Estado y al Municipio por fincas urbanas," AGEV, Fondo Legislatura, 1929.

47 *Ley de Expropiación que Regirá en el Estado de Veracruz-Llave* (Jalapa-Enríquez: Talleres Linotinográficos del Gobierno del Estado, 1930).

48 "Ley #285: Que reforma el Art. 21 de la Ley #323 de 22 de julio de 1930 sobre expropiaciones . . . ," *Gaceta Oficial* XXVI, no. 121 (8 Oct. 1931): 1–2.

49 Manuel Almanza, Presidente del Comité Ejecutivo de la Liga de Comunidades Agrarias, to Tejeda (2 Dec. 1930), in Exp. de la iniciativa para el reglamento de la Ley para fomento de la pequeña propiedad, AGEV, Fondo del Departamento de Agricultura y Ganadero, pq. 5070.

50 Tejeda to Diputado Secretario de la H. Legislatura del Estado (22 June 1931), Exp. de Decreto #269: "Estableciendo la creación y fomento de la pequeña propiedad, AGEV, Fondo Legislatura, exp. 4-1-1931.

51 *Ley Número 269 que declara de utilidad pública el fraccionamiento y expropiación de terrenos para la creación y fomento de la pequeña propiedad* (Jalapa-Enríquez: Talleres Linotinográficos del Gobierno, 1931), Art. 5, p. 4.

52 "Observaciones del Gobernador a la Ley Agraria que votó la Cámara," *El Dictamen*, 12 Oct. 1931; "Leyes en materia agraria aplicadas en el Estado son anticonstitucionales," *El Dictamen*, 18 Oct. 1931.

53 Exp. de Ley #301 (19 Oct. 1931): "Reformando los Artículos 2 y 1 transitorios de la Ley #269 de 15 de agosto del presente año," AGEV, Fondo Legislatura, exp. 4-1-301, 1931.

54 *Ley general del catastro del Estado de Veracruz* (Jalapa-Enríquez: Talleres Gráficos del Gobierno del Estado, 1931), vol. of *Ley de organización fiscal del Estado de Veracruz* (Jalapa-Enríquez: Talleres Linotipográficos del Gobierno del Estado, 1932), pp. 149–162; *Reglamento de la Ley general del catastro del Estado de Veracruz* (Jalapa-Enríquez: Talleres Gráficos del Gobierno del Estado, 1931).

55 See Leonard G. Dawson, American Consul, to the Secretary of State, "Political Report for Month of September 1931," NA/RDS 812.00, Veracruz/27, 30 September 1931, p. 15.

56 "Expropiación por los campesinos de la Congregación de 'Ojital,' Municipio de 'Pueblo Viejo,'" *Gaceta Oficial* XXV, no. 49 (23 April 1931): 2–3; "Expropiación por los campesinos de la Congregación de 'Vista Hermosa de Anaya,' Municipio de Papantla," *Gaceta Oficial* XXV, no. 52 (30 April 1931): 1–2.

57 *Gaceta Oficial* XXVI, no. 140 (21 Nov. 1931): 1–2; *Gaceta Oficial* XXVII, no. 10 (23 Jan. 1932): 3; *Gaceta Oficial* XXVIII, no. 138 (17 Nov. 1932): 1; *Gaceta Oficial* XXVIII, no. 141 (24 Nov. 1932): 2.

58 "Informe que rinde el C. Ing. Adalberto Tejeda," 1928–1932, pp. 6134–6135.

59 "Exposición de motivos de varios diputados, que originó el proyecto de una nueva ley de expropiación por causa de utilidad pública" (26 May 1932), in Exp. de Ley #66, sobre Expropiación, AGEV, Fondo Legislatura, exp. 4-1-66, 1932. See also letter from Agustín Alvarado, Diputado Secretario de la H. Legislatura Local, to Tejeda, 26 May 1932, in Exp. de Ley #66.

60 Exp. de Ley #66.

61 "Resoluciones aprobadas en el Secundo Congreso de la Liga de Comunidades Agrarias del Edo. de Veracruz—La adhesión a la Internacional Campesina de Moscú," *El Machete* (11–18 Dec. 1924).

62 "Exposición de motivos y proyecto de ley de Tejeda" (30 May 1932), in Exp. de Ley #66.

63 Exp. de Ley #66.

64 See discussion in "Exposición de motivos y proyecto de ley de Tejeda" (30 May 1932), in Exp. de Ley #66.

65 Law #66, *Gaceta Oficial* XXVII, no. 66 (2 June 1932): 1. See the recollections of Pastor Rouaiz, the development minister in Carranza's provisional government, who played a prominent role in the drafting of constitutional Article 27 and who ratified the concept of *utilidad social* 50 years after the formulation of Article 27, in Jorge Luis Ibarra Mendívil, *Propiedad agraria y sistema político en México* (México: El Colegio de Sonora and Porrúa, 1989), pp. 111–112.

66 Tejeda to C. Diputado Secretario de la H. Legislatura del Estado (30 June 1932): "Exposición de motivos, relativa a la reforma de la Ley #323," in Exp. de Ley #119, reformando la Ley #323 de julio de 1930, AGEV, Fondo Legislatura, exp. 4-1-119, pp. 2–3.

67 *Ibid.*, p. 4.

68 *Ibid.*, p. 7.

69 *Ibid.*, p. 9.

70 Ley #119 (4 July 1932), in Exp. de Ley # 19; Ley #119, *Gaceta Oficial* XXVII, no. 82 (9 July 1932): 2–7. See also Ley de Expropiación #323 de 22 de julio de 1930 con las reformas hechas por Ley #119, de 6 de julio de 1932," in *Ley de Organización Fiscal del Estado de Veracruz-Llave* (Jalapa-Enríquez: Talleres Linotinográficos del Gobierno del Estado, 1932), pp. 275–284.

71 William Kernes, American Vice-Consul to the Secretary of State, "Political Report for Month of July, 1932," NA/RDS, 812.00, Veracruz/39, 1 Aug. 1932, pp. 2–3.

72 "Reglamento de la Ley #66 de 1 de junio de 1932," in Exp. de Ley #66.

73 *Ibid.*; *Gaceta Oficial* XXVIII, no. 90 (28 July 1932): 1–4.

74 Tejeda to General Juan José Ríos (22 July 1932), in Exp. de Ley #66. See also AGEV, Fondo Gobernación y Justicia, exp. 1516, pq. 3166, Promovente: Ley sobre Expropiación.

75   William Kernes, American Vice-Consul, to Secretary of State, "Political Report for Month of July, 1932." p. 3.

76   See the following, in Exp. de Ley #66: Delegado Regional de la Liga de Comunidades Agrarias por la Segunda Zona de Soledad de Doblado, en nombre de las organizaciones de esta zona, to the Legislatura Local, 9 June 1932; Comité Ejecutivo del Sindicato de Obreros y Similares de Cocolapan to Tejeda, 15 June 1932; Comité Ejecutivo de Santa Cruz, Cosamaloapan, to Presidente del Congreso Local, 15 June 1932; Sindicato de Obreros Costureros de "La Suiza" y Anexos, miembro de la CROM, to Presidente de la Legislatura Local, 17 June 1932; telegram from Presidente del Sindicato de Obreros Molineros y Sociedad Cooperativa de la Ciudad de Veracruz to the Cámara de Diputados, 20 June 1932.

77   "Toda la riqueza de Veracruz bajo la Ley de Expropiación", *Excelsior,* 1 June 1932; "La expropiación en Veracruz," *El Nacional,* 5 June 1932; "La ley de despojo de Veracruz," *Excelsior,* 6 June 1932; "Sólo se puede expropiar las aguas y las tierras: La Cámara de Comercio de Iguala protesta contra Hidalgo y Veracruz," *Excelsior,* 7 June 1932; "No será promulgada la Ley de Expropiación de Veracruz," *Excelsior,* 8 July 1932; "No fue hasta ayer que se publicó en Jalapa la ley que afecta a la propiedad privada," *Excelsior,* 10 June 1932; "Todavía las leyes de expropiación," *Excelsior,* 10 June 1932; "Finalidades que persigue la Ley de Expropiación," *Excelsior,* 13 June 1932; "Propiedad privada o socialización," *El Universal,* 24 June 1932; "No se dará ayuda a los azucareros durante la zafra," *Excelsior,* 25 June 1932; "Como bandera política empleará Tejeda la Ley de Expropiación," *Excelsior,* 25 July 1932; "Mantiene Tejeda su soviética Ley de Expropiación: Ha sido formulado el reglamento que deja al Gobernador facultades omnímodas," *Excelsior,* 3 Aug. 1932.

78   Of the three, the Michoacán law was perceived as the most moderate. *Excelsior,* for example, suddenly remembered it four months after its publication, and *El Universal* did not attribute any special importance to it. See "Desde febrero existe en Michoacán una ley de carácter confiscatorio," *Excelsior,* 10 June 1932; "Propiedad privada o socialización," *El Universal,* 24 June 1932; "Hidalgo y Veracruz ante la Federación," *El Universal,* 24 June 1932.

79   "Ayer llegó el Coronel Tejeda," *El Nacional,* 15 June 1932.

80   *Ibid.*

81   "Contra el criterio de todo el país sostiene Tejeda la funesta ley," *Excelsior,* 24 June 1932.

82   "Protesta de Diputados por las declaraciones de 4 CC. Gobernadores," *Excelsior,* 16 June 1932.

83   "Piden silencio para las leyes de expropiación," *Excelsior,* 17 June 1932.

84   See "Mensaje del Sr. Presidente a los Gobernadores de Estados," *Excelsior,* 18 June 1932.

85   "Nuevo León en contra las leyes confiscatorias," *Excelsior,* 17 June 1932; "Siete gobernadores más ofrecen obrar de acuerdo con el centro," *Excelsior,* 21 June 1932; "La Constitución incolume: Mensajes de felicitación," *Excelsior,* 22 June 1932;"Más mensajes al presidente," *Excelsior,* 25 June 1932; "Contestan los gobernadores," *El Universal,* 25 June 1932; "Desean cooperar con el Presidente Ortiz Rubio: Todos los gobernadores excepto el de Veracruz han contestado cordialmente el mensaje del ejecutivo," *El Universal,* 26 June 1932.

86   "Será corregida la ley de expropiación de Hidalgo," *Excelsior,* 5 June 1932;

"Iniciará el gobierno de hidalgo reformas constitucionales a la ley de expropiación," *Excelsior*, 12 June 1932; "Acta #4, sesión de 28 de junio de 1932, XLIII Legislatura," in *Libro de actas de sesiones* (14 Sept. 1931–29 Aug. 1932), AHCMO.

87 For the complete text of the letter, see "Respuesta vaga del Coronel Tejeda," *Excelsior*, 29 June 1932.

88 "Declaratoria de expropiación del terreno necessario para dotación de fundo legal al poblado marciel," *Gaceta Oficial* XXVII, no. 77 (28 June 1932): 2.

89 "Declaratoria de expropiación por causa de utilidad pública de la estación radiodifusora 'X.E.T.F.' de Veracruz, *Gaceta Oficial* XXVIII, no. 150 (15 Dec. 1932): 1–3; "El primero caso de la aplicación de la Ley de Expropiación ha registrado ya en Veracruz," *Excelsior*, 17 July 1932; "Se aplicó ya en Boca del Río la Ley de Expropiación de Veracruz," *Excelsior*, 22 July 1932; "Declaratoria de expropiación por causa de utilidad pública de la fábrica de hilados y tejidos 'La Paz Textil,' S.A., de esta ciudad," *Gaceta Oficial* XXVIII, no. 111 (15 Sept. 1932): 1–3.

90 "La justicia rescata una fábrica incautada," *El Universal*, 21 Nov. 1932; "El ingenio 'Tenampa' ha sido ya devuelto," *Excelsior*, 8 Feb. 1933; "Ejecutoria cumplida en el Edo. de Veracruz," *Excelsior*, 6 June 1933. On the eviction of the peasants of the *congregación* of Buena Vista in the Córdoba municipio from lands expropriated by the Tejeda laws, see *Excelsior*, 3 July 1933.

91 "El Gobierno y los comunistas," *Excelsior*, 14 July 1932.

92 "Se aplicó ya en Boca del Río la Ley de Expropiación de Veracruz," *Excelsior*, 22 July 1932.

93 "No será llamado por la Cámara el Sr. Secretario de Hacienda, como quería un C. Diputado por Veracruz," *Excelsior*, 21 Oct. 1932; "Respaldo vigoroso a la política del ejecutivo," *El Nacional*, 21 Oct. 1932; "Síntomas de mejoramiento económico," *Excelsior*, 5 Dec. 1932.

94 "Como bandera política empleará Tejeda la Ley de Expropriación: Las agrupaciones cromistas de Veracruz acaban de lanzar un manifiesto pidiendo una reforma constitucional," *Excelsior*, 25 July 1932.

6 The Eradication of Tejeda's Power and the Contest for the Presidency

1 "El último reducto del comunismo en México," *Excelsior*, 9 Dec. 1932.

2 "Fueron nombrados los cincuenta ingenieros para deslindar ejidos," *Excelsior*, 5 Oct. 1932; "El fin del caciquismo," *Excelsior*, 16 March 1933; "Veracruz libre de los lideres," *Excelsior*, 5 May 1933.

3 "La distribución de parcelas comenzara por el Edo. de Veracruz," *El Nacional*, 30 Oct. 1932; "El fraccionamiento para beneficiar al labriego: Tal como se hace ahora en Veracruz, se harán los Estados de Guanajuato . . . Michoacán y Querétaro," *Excelsior*, 19 Dec. 1932; and "Political Report for December, 1932," NA/RDS, Doc. 812.00, Veracruz 44, 31 Dec. 1932.

4 See Rodríguez's plan and his comments in favor of parcelization "as a supplement to the revolutionary program" in "El parcelamiento de los ejidos complementa el programa revolucionario," *Excelsior*, 9 Dec. 1932.

5 "El problema fundamental del país es el campesino," *El Nacional*, 1 Oct. 1932; "Nuevo aspecto de la cuestión agraria," *Excelsior*, 4 Oct. 1932; "Fueron nombradas los cincuenta ingenieros para deslindar ejidos," *Excelsior*, 5 Oct. 1932; "La nueva etapa del agrarismo," *Excelsior*, 29 Oct. 1932; "Cien inge-

nieros para deslindar los ejidos," *El Universal*, 3 Nov. 1932; "El parcelamiento ejidal en el país," *El Universal*, 24 Nov. 1932; "Los agraristas y los ingenieros militares," *El Universal*, 25 Nov. 1932; "Tendrán garantías los ingenieros agrónomos: Las tropas federales apoyarán a los que van a deslindar ejidos en Veracruz," *Excelsior*, 2 Dec. 1932; "Con el fraccionamiento ejidal se creará el derecho de propiedad sobre la tierra," *Excelsior*, 2 Dec. 1932; "El fin del caciquismo," *Excelsior*, 16 March 1933; "Amplia labor de depuración en los ejidos," *Excelsior*, 8 June 1933; Leonard G. Dawson, American Consul, to the Secretary of State, "Political Report for November, 1932," NA/RDS, 812.00, Veracruz 43, 2 Dec. 1932, p. 2; Reuben Clark, Jr., to the Secretary of State, "Law Amending the Law of the Division of Ejidal Lands and the Constitution of the Parcelary Ejidal Patrimony of Dec. 19, 1925," NA/RDS, 812.52/1771, Dec. 1, 1932; Leonard G. Dawson, American Consul, to the Secretary of State, "Political Report for December, 1932," NA/RDS, Doc. 812.00, Veracruz 44, 31 Dec. 1932.

6   "Más de 300,000 agraristas pueden perder sus tierras," *Excelsior*, 24 Dec. 1932; "Eficación en el deslinde," *El Universal*, 12 Jan. 1934.

7   "Disarmament of 'Guerillas' in Veracruz State—Report of General Acosta," NA/RDS, Doc. 812.00, Veracruz 45, 13 Jan. 1933.

8   This loyalty stemmed from his view of the institution of the presidency as a symbol of unity that had to be defended despite any differences of opinion. See in this respect Fernando Benítez, *Lázaro Cárdenas y la Revolución Mexicana*, vol. II (México: Fondo de Cultura Económica, 2013 [1977]), p. 233.

9   On this affair in general, see "Movilización de fuerzas al Estado de Veracruz," *Excelsior*, 9 Dec. 1932; "Hoy debe salir rumbo a Veracruz la columna de tropas federales," *Excelsior*, 12 Dec. 1932; "Desarme de varias guerrillas de agraristas en Veracruz," *El Universal*, 13 Dec. 1932; "El Gral. Cárdenas Ministro de Guerra," *El Universal*, 28 Dec. 1932; "Por acuerdo del ejecutivo de la unión, van a dejar sus armas todos los agraristas del Edo. de Veracruz," *Excelsior*, 10 Jan. 1933; "El General Cárdenas y el desarme de las defensas rurales," *Excelsior*, 11 Jan. 1933; "Informe el Gral. Acosta de su misión en Veracruz," *Excelsior*, 14 Jan. 1933.

10   "Terminó el desarme de agraristas," *El Nacional*, 13 Jan. 1934.

11   Tejeda to Josafat Márquez, Oficial Mayor de la H. Legislatura del Estado, 26 Sept. 1933, in AAT, tomo 207, vol. 231 (1933), fojas 590–591. David Skerritt thinks that the picture wasn't simply a division between bad landowners and good agrarianists. First, main leaders of Parra's organization fought shoulder to shoulder with agrarianists during the La Huerta rebellion in 1923 and on the other hand there were agrarianists who were at the same time Liga members and Mano Negra's members, usually due to personal friendships, pressures and maneces posed by Parras' men on agrarian leaders, combined with promises to provide help in order to stop cattle robbery and rural insecurity. Nonetheless, says Skerritt, the Mano Negra was principally a landowners's organization designed to protect their property and interests from "illegitimate" land expropiation. See David Skerritt Gardner, "¿Que es la Mano Negra?", in *Anuario 3* (Xalapa Centro de Estudios Históricas, Instituto de Investigaciones Humanisticas, Universidad Veracruzana, 1983), pp. 129–138.

12   "Prosperidad y paz en el Edo. de Veracruz," *Excelsior*, 12 Jan. 1933; "Depuración de elementos campesinos," *El Nacional*, 10 Jan. 1933; "El desarme de agraristas," *El Universal*, 13 Jan. 1933; "Para no romper la cohe-

sión de la Liga de Comunidades Agrarias renunció Blanco," *El Dictamen*, 7 July 1931; "La primera sorpresa en la reunión de la Legislatura," *El Dictamen*, 4 Aug. 1931; "La Liga Agraria trata de readquirir su preponderancia en la Legislatura," *El Dictamen*, 5 Oct. 1931.

13 "Asamblea de campesinos," *El Nacional*, 20 Feb. 1933; "La segunda sesión del congreso de campesinos en Jalapa, Veracruz," *El Nacional*, 21 Feb. 1933; "Graves atentados en Edo. de Veracruz, " *El Nacional*, 22 Feb. 1933; "Una tentativa para acarrear campesinos a la política en Veracruz," *El Nacional*, 25 Feb. 1933.

14 See, for example, the following complaints the two leagues made of one other to President Rodríguez: Letter from Adolfo Prieto, Delegado de la LCAEV, to Abelardo Rodríguez, Presidente de la República, 3 Aug. 1933, in Archivo General de la Nación [hereafter AGN], Fondo Abelardo Rodríguez, exp. 541.5/21-8; and the following, in AGN, Fondo Abelardo Rodríguez, exp. 552.5/26: report from Evaristo Pérez, General de Brigada, Jefetura de Operaciones Militares en Veracruz, to Abelardo Rodríguez, Presidente de la República, 28 Jan. 1933; letter from Amador Zarate, Secretario General del Comité Ejecutivo del Partido Veracruzano del Trabajo, to Abelardo Rodríguez, Presidente de la República, 6 Jan. 1933; letter from a group of farmers of Túxpan, Veracruz, to Abelardo Rodríguez, Presidente de la República, 4 Jan. 1933; letter from F. Cedeño to C. Presidente de la República, 3 Jan. 1933.

15 "Tranquilidad en Veracruz," *El Nacional*, 1 Aug. 1933; "Nuevo Congreso de Agraristas," *Excelsior*, 26 July 1934.

16 "Quejas de campesinos," *El Nacional*, 14 Jan. 1933; "Explica las causas de la escisión la Liga Nacional Campesina 'Ursulo Galván'," *El Nacional*, 23 Jan. 1933; "Segunda sesión de la reunión plenaria de la 'Ursulo Galván'," *El Nacional*, 2 June 1933; "Trabajará por separado la Liga Ursulo Galván," *Excelsior*, 6 June 1933.

17 José A. Ronzón León, "La campaña presidencial de Adalberto Tejeda" (Master's thesis, Universidad Veracruzana, 1991), pp. 84–92; "Agitación política municipal hay en el Puerto de Veracruz," *El Nacional*, 20 Jan. 1933; "Fue consignado el Presidente Municipal del Puerto de Veracruz," *El Nacional*, 25 Jan. 1933; "Auto de formal prisión para el Alcalde Guzmán," *Excelsior*, 6 Feb. 1933; "Cargos, en Veracruz, al Diputado Carlos Ojeda," *Excelsior*, 9 March 1933; "Junta administradora en la CD [ciudad] de Veracruz," *Excelsior*, 12 March 1933; "Triunfó en Veracruz la candidatura cardenista," *Excelsior*, 12 June 1933; "Aplastante derrota a los 'Rojos' de Tejeda," *Excelsior*, 13 June 1933; Josephus Daniels, "Political Situation—Holding of Plebiscites," NA/RDS, MP 1370, Roll No. 2, 1930–1939, Doc. 812.00/29905, 9 Aug. 1933.

18 Ronzón León, "La campaña presidencial," p. 93.

19 "Surgió la división en la legislatura formandose dos bloques iguales de las izquierdas y de las derechas," *El Dictamen*, 20 Sept. 1933; "Los derechistas no dieron quorum ayer en la legislatura del Estado," *El Dictamen*, 22 Sept. 1933; "Aunque se conserva igual la división en la Legislatura, hay indicios de que las filas de los Rojos no tardarán en ceder," *El Dictamen*, 23 Sept. 1933; "Los diputados rojos dieron la sorpresa de constituirse tambien ellos en legislatura," *El Dictamen*, 9 Oct. 1933; "Los diputados rojos nombraron un gobernador tratando de creaar conflicto de poderes," *El Dictamen*, 10 Oct. 1933; "Los diputados rojos fueron desaforados y consignados por usurpación de funciones," *El Dictamen*, 11 Oct. 1933; "Los Rojos perdieron en absoluto la

partida en el Estado; la Secretaría de Gobernación sigue reconociendo a la Legislatura; Vázquez Vela se ha afirmado plenamente en su Gobierno," *El Dictamen*, 12 Oct. 1933.

20   "Las camisas rojas no han encontrado eco entre los campesinos," *El Dictamen*, 21 April 1933; "Expulsados del PNR los camisas rojas," *El Dictamen*, 23 April 1933; "Expulsados del PNR los camisas rojas: Cinco diputados y seis ediles de Jalapa," *El Dictamen*, 25 April 1933; telegram from Carlos Dario Ojeda, Presidente de la Convención estatal del PNR [in Veracruz], to Presidente de la República, Abelardo Rodríguez, 20 Aug. 1933, in AGN, Fondo Abelardo Rodríguez, exp. 516.1/12-2; Manuel Olmos Ruíz, Presidente del Comité Confederal Estatal de la Liga de Comunidades Agrarias del Estado de Veracruz, to Presidente del Comité Estatal del PNR, 13 July 1933, in AGN, Fondo Abelardo Rodríguez, exp. 516.1/12-2.

21   "Viene a defenderse el Diputado C.D. Ojeda," *Excelsior*, 4 Aug. 1933; "Visitó al Presidente el General C. Aguilar," *El Nacional*, 16 Aug. 1933; "Candido Aguilar ya no está con el tejedismo," *Excelsior*, 16 Aug. 1933; "Un interesante debate en la cámara popular," *El Nacional*, 11 Oct. 1933.

22   "Van a definir su posición dentro del PNR 3 Diputados," *El Nacional*, 10 Oct. 1933; "Un interesante debate en la cámara popular," *El Nacional*, 11 Oct. 1933; "Plazo a tres CC Diputados," *El Nacional*, 12 Oct. 1933; "El bloque de la cámara popular expulsó de su seno a un diputado," *El Nacional*, 17 Oct. 1933; Josephus Daniels, "Political Situation," NA/RDS, MP 1370, Roll No. 2, 1930–1939, Doc. 812.00/29938 (16 Oct. 1933); Josephus Daniels to the Secretary of State, "Political: Expulsion of Colonel Adalberto Tejeda's Sympathizers from the P.N.R. Bloc of the Chamber of Deputies, NA/RDS, MP 1370, Roll No. 3, 1930–1939, Doc. 812.00/29941 (19 Oct. 1933); and Josephus Daniels to the Secretary of State, "Political Situation," NA/RDS, MP 1370, Roll No. 3, 1930–1939, Doc. 812.00/29942 (24 Oct. 1933).

23   Letter from A. Tejeda to Sr. Gral. Plutarco Elías Calles, 29 Dec. 1932, in AAT, tomo 166 (1931), foja 226.

24   "Agitación extemporanea en Veracruz," *Excelsior*, 28 April 1933.

25   "El último reducto del comunismo en México," *Excelsior*, 9 Dec. 1932; "Acción para que Veracruz vuelva a su antiguo estado floreciente," *El Universal*, 12 Dec. 1932; "Fue derogada la Ley Catastral en Veracruz," *El Universal*, 16 Dec. 1932; "En Veracruz ya no se vivirá sin pagar renta," *El Universal*, 1 Jan. 1933; "El fin del desgobierno en Veracruz," *El Universal*, 19 Jan. 1933.

26   "El bloque de la cámara popular expulsó de su seno a un diputado," *El Nacional*, 17 Oct. 1933. On Tejeda's efforts to find a place to live in Veracruz, see "Llegó al Puerto de Veracruz el ex-Gobernador Adalberto Tejeda," *El Universal*, 27 Dec. 1932; "El Coronel Tejeda se radica en Veracruz, Ver." *El Universal*, 11 Dec. 1932. On the expulsion of Tejeda's staff from the state, see "Empleados tejedistas invitados a salir del Estado de Veracruz," *El Universal*, 18 Dec. 1932.

27   One controversial theory is that Cárdenas himself engineered Serrato's appointment in order to weaken the CRMDT, which he believed was becoming too powerful and might put obstacles in his path to the presidency. See John Gledhill, *Casi Nada: A Study of Agrarian Reform in the Homeland of Cardenismo* (Albany, NY: Institute for Mesoamerican Studies, 1991), p. 64.

28   "El desafuero de diputados en Michoacán," *El Universal*, 8 Dec. 1932; "El desafuero dictado contra varios diputados michoacanos," *El Universal*, 25 Dec.

1932; "La agonía de Michoacán," *Excelsior*, 10 Feb. 1933; "Amplia defensa de los agraristas del Estado de Michoacán," *El Nacional*, 26 Feb. 1933; "Un Congreso agrarista que trabaja bien," *Excelsior*, 29 March 1933; "Son injustificados los cargos hechos al Gobierno de Michoacán," *El Nacional*, 18 June 1933; "Aboga el Gral. Cárdenas por la unificación obrera," *El Nacional*, 1 Jan. 1934; "Aboga el Gral. Cárdenas por la unificación obrera," *El Nacional*, 31 Jan. 1934.

29 Tejeda to Cárdenas, 19 Jan. 1933, in AAT, tomo 199, vol. 223 (1933), foja 24; Cárdenas to Tejeda, 17 Feb. 1933, in AAT, tomo 204, vol. 231 (1933), foja 156.

30 John W.F. Dulles, *Yesterday in Mexico: A Chronicle of the Revolution* (Austin: University of Texas Press, 1961), p. 573.

31 For the PSI platform, see Ronzón León, "La campaña presidencial," p. 96; Fowler, *Movilización campesina*, p. 105.

32 "Tejeda fue desechado por la convención del laborista," *El Universal Gráfico*, 10 June 1933, in AAT, tomo 210, vol. 234 (1933), fojas 81–82; "Lázaro Cárdenas acepta el apoyo del laborista," *Excelsior*, 12 June 1933; "Tejeda no aprobó aún un programa político," *Excelsior*, 13 June 1933; "Aclaración hecha por el Comité tejedista," *Excelsior*, 1 Aug. 1933; "Contestación de la Secretaría de Gobernación al Coronel Tejeda," *El Nacional*, 3 Aug. 1933; "Fueron detenidos anoche 37 comunistas en un mitin," *El Nacional*, 17 Aug. 1933; Ignacio Rosas, Presidente del Partido Revolucionario Radical Tejedista, Dependiente del PSI y Adherido al PNR, to Tejeda, 16 April 1933, in AAT, tomo 204, vol. 231 (1933), foja 581; letter from Antonio Echegaray to Tejeda, 2 June 1933, in AAT, tomo 199, vol. 223 (1933), fojas 374–375; Tejeda's reply to Antonio Echegaray, 8 June 1933, in *ibid.*, foja 373; letter from Manuel Almanza to Tejeda, 11 June 1933, in AAT, tomo 206, vol. 230 (1933), fojas 571–572; Diputado Manuel Jasso to Tejeda, 14 June 1933, in AAT, tomo 211, vol. 238 (1933), fojas 13–14; Tejeda to Presidente de la República, A. Rodríguez, 1 Aug. 1933, in AAT, tomo 198, vol. 222 (1933); letter from Aurelio T. Pérez to Tejeda, 2 Aug. 1933, in AAT, tomo 211, vol. 235 (1933); letter from Dr. Antonio Herrera Bravo to Presidente del Comité Directivo "Pro Tejeda," 3 Sept. 1933, in AAT, tomo 204, vol. 231 (1933), fojas 606–607.

33 "Asamblea tejedista reunida en Veracruz: En ella se designó candidato a la presidencia al Coronel Adalberto Tejeda," *El Universal*, 15 Jan. 1934.

34 "Lo que ofrecía en Villa Cardel el Coronel Tejeda," *El Universal*, 19 Feb. 1934; "Carta aclaratoria del Coronel Tejeda," *El Universal*, 21 Feb. 1934; "Un mitin tejedista se efectuó en Veracruz," *El Universal*, 12 March 1934; "Iniciará su campaña el 12 de abril el Corl. Tejeda," *El Universal*, 12 March 1934; "Demandan garantías los tejedistas de Veracruz," *Excelsior*, 25 March 1934; "Principia su jira el Corl. Adalberto Tejeda," *Excelsior*, 5 April 1934; "El Coronel Tejeda ya en plena campaña," *Excelsior*, 6 April 1934; Josephus Daniels, "Colonel Adalberto Tejeda, Candidate for President, Visits Mazatlán," NA/RDS, MP 1370, Roll No. 3, Doc. 812.00/30045 (4 May 1934).

35 "Rápida partida del Corl. Tejeda," *Excelsior*, 7 April 1934; "Al Corl. Tejeda no le dejó hablar en Guaymas," *El Universal*, 9 May 1934.

36 "En Tabasco rechazaron las boletas de Tejeda," *Excelsior*, 22 June 1934.

37 On the organizational struggle behind the scenes to recruit support for Cárdenas, see "Guanajato decide por el Gral. Cárdenas," *Excelsior*, 8 May 1933; "Tacitamente aceptó el Gral. Cárdenas su candidatura," *Excelsior*, 1 June 1933; Josephus Daniels to Secretary of State, "Political Situation in Regard to

the Nomination of Presidential Candidates," NA/RDS, MP 1370, Roll No. 2, Doc. 812.00/29852 (10 May 1933); Josephus Daniels to Secretary of State, "Political Situation in Regard to the Nomination of Presidential Candidates," NA/RDS, MP 1370, Roll No. 2, Doc. 812.00/29855 (16 May 1933); Josephus Daniels to Secretary of State, "Political Situation," NA/RDS, MP 1370, Roll No. 2, Doc. 812.00/29863 (26 May 1933); and Doc. 812.00/29864 (26 May 1933).

38 Medin, *El Minimato presidencial*, p. 133.

39 "El General Cárdenas en la Secretaría de Guerra," *El Nacional*, 1 Jan. 1933; "No será candidato el Sr. Gral. Lázaro Cárdenas," *Excelsior*, 26 March 1933.

40 *Excelsior*, 1 Aug. 1933; NA/RDS, MP 1370, Roll No. 2, Doc. 812.00/29895, 25 July 1933, and Doc. 812.00/29897, 1 Aug. 1933.

41 Josephus Daniels, "The Six Year Plan Program of Government for 1934," NA/RDS, MP 1370, Roll No. 3, Doc. 812.00/30041 (17 April 1933).

42 PRI, "Plan Sexenal," in *Historia documental del Partido de la Revolución: PNR, 1933* (México: Instituto de Capacitación Política, 1981), pp. 337–373.

43 See in this respect: "La campaña pro Cárdenas en el Edo. de Veracruz," *El Nacional*, 5 July 1933; "Existe completa unificación en el Partido N.R.," *Excelsior*, 4 Aug. 1933; "Movimiento político en pro del Gral. Lázaro Cárdenas en Guanajuato y Veracruz," *El Nacional*, 5 Aug. 1933; "Triunfo del cardenismo," *El Nacional*, 7 Aug. 1933; "Estadística de la campaña por la sucesión presidencial," *El Nacional*, 24 Oct. 1933; "Se inicia una fuerte campaña en favor del Gral. Lázaro Cárdenas," *Excelsior*, 14 Nov. 1933.

44 According to a report by the American consul in Veracruz, at the end of the municipal elections in Veracruz at the end of 1933, Tejeda retained control over only about 10 municipios, while independent parties held another 20 and Cárdenas the remaining 150. See Josephus Daniels, "Political Report," NA/RDS, MP 1370, Roll No. 3, Doc. 812.00/29985 (18 Jan. 1934).

45 Josephus Daniels, "Nomination of General Lázaro Cárdenas as Presidential Candidate of the P.N.R. (National Revolutionary Party)," NA/RDS, MP 1370, Roll No. 3, Doc. 812.00/29972 (7 Dec. 1933).

46 These parties were: Tejeda's Partido Socialista de las Izquierdas, the Confederación Revolucionaria de Partidos Independientes, whose candidate was Antonio Villareal, and the Partido Comunista, with Hermán Laborde. See Stanley Hawks, Second Secretary of Embassy, to Secretary of State, "Political Activities of the Opposition Parties in the forthcoming Presidential Elections," NA/RDS, MP 1370, Roll No. 3, Doc. 812.00/30024 (21 March 1934). Ultimately, Laborde, Tejeda, Villareal, and Cárdenas participated in the election. See Josephus Daniels, "Publication of Final Presidential Election Returns," NA/RDS, MP 1370, Roll No. 3, Doc. 812.00/30096 (3 Aug. 1934).

47 Nelson R. Park, American Consul, to Secretary of State, "Visit to Torreón of General Lázaro Cárdenas, Presidential Candidate of the Partido Nacional Revolucionario," NA/RDS, MP 1370, Roll No. 3, Doc. 812.00/30065 (25 June 1934); Cárdenas's speech in Chihuahua on 24 June 1934, in *La jira del General Lázaro Cárdenas: Síntesis ideológica* (Secretaría de Prensa y Propaganda del CEN [Comité Ejecutivo Nacional] del PNR, 1934), p. 59.

48 As the election campaign lasted Cárdenas intensified his messages and turned them into socialist. He started to speak about "El ideal de la doctrina socialista de la Revolución", to be achieved by a cooperativist efforts of the workers, that would enable them " la conquista de las fuentes de riqueza y de los instrumentos

productivos" and "el sistema de ideas socialistas que sustenta al Revolución Mexicana". See "Discurso del candidato del PNR a la presidecia de la República", Durango, Junio 30 de 1934, in *Palabras* I, p. 132. Cárdenas really believed in the socialist character of the Revolution. Shortly before his death he still insisted on it saying: "Creo que los principios del socialismo son compatibles con las ideas de la Revolución Mexicana en su ulterior e inevitable desarrollo". See Lázaro Cárdenas, *Ideario político*, p. 37. Actually Cárdenas was astute liberal, saying time and again "Nuestra Constitución es democática y liberal, con algunos rasgos moderados de socialismo". See Lázaro Cárdenas, *Ideario politico*, p. 69.

49 NA/RDS, MP 1370, Roll No. 3, Docs. 812.00/29971 (Josephus Daniels, "Statement of General Lázaro Cárdenas Regarding Cooperatives," 5 Dec. 1993), 812.00/29975 (Josephus Daniels, "General Lázaro Cárdenas' Speech of Acceptance of the P.N.R. Candidacy for President of Mexico," 12 Dec. 1933), 812.00/30025 (Stanley Hawks, Second Secretary of Embassy, to Secretary of State, "Campaign Tour of the Southern States of Mexico by General Lázaro Cárdenas, Presidential Candidate of the P.N.R.," 9 Feb. 1934), 812.00/30051 (R. Henry Norweb, Chargé d'Affaires ad interim, to Secretary of State, "Campaign Tour of the States of Guerrero, Morelos and Mexico of General Lázaro Cárdenas, Presidential Candidate of the P.N.R.," 22 May 1934), 812.00/30060 (Samuel Sckobin, American Consul, to Secretary of State, "Visit to Saltillo of P.N.R. Presidential Candidate, General Lázaro Cárdenas," 18 June 1934), 812.00/30073 (R. Henry Norweb, Chargé d'Affaires ad interim, to Secretary of State, "Mexican National Elections," 3 July 1934), 812.00/30096 (Josephus Daniels, "Publication of Final Presidential Election Returns," 3 Aug. 1934), 812.00/30098 (Josephus Daniels, "General Political Report," 17 Aug. 1934); "Declaraciones hechas por Gral. Cárdenas," *El Nacional*, 5 Feb. 1934; "Un gobierno de orden y estrictamente moral," *El Universal*, 11 Feb. 1934; "Gobierno esencialmente revolucionario," *El Nacional*, 11 Feb. 1934; "Animado mitin en Veracruz," *El Nacional*, 12 Feb. 1934; "El General Cárdenas y los chamulas," *El Nacional*, 7 March 1934; "Las tierras henequén eran repartidos para ejidos," *El Universal*, 12 March 1934; "Congreso agrario inaugurado por el General Cárdenas," 6 June 1934.

50 On the factors in Zapata's failure, see Gledhill, *Casi Nada*, p. 29.

51 For some of the many letters of encouragement sent to Tejeda, see: L. Guerrera, Partido Liberal Antireeleccionista de Salvatierra, Guanajuato, to Tejeda, 6 Feb. 1933, in AAT, tomo 204, vol. 231 (1933), foja 468; J. Guadalupe Osorio, en nombre del Comité Particular Administrativo de Ahuimol, Chicontepec, Veracruz, to Tejeda, 14 June 1933, in *ibid.*, foja 248;.Dirigentes del Partido Socialista del Sur to Tejeda, 12 July 1933, in *ibid.*, foja 25; Manuel Hernándes Landa to Tejeda, 3 Sept. 1933, in *ibid.*, fojas 39–40.

Conclusion

1 This point is excellently elaborated in Ernesto Hernández, B.A., *Cafeteras, Molineras*, and Adalberto Tejeda: unveiling negotiation between Women Workers and State Power in Veracruz, México (1920–1932) (Master's thesis, Georgetown University, Washington, 1996), esp. chapters 3 and 4.

2 Eitan Ginzberg, "Ideología, política y la cuestión de las prioridades: Lázaro

Cárdenas y Adalberto Tejeda, 1928–1934," *Mexican Studies/Estudios Mexicanos* 13, no. 1 (1997): 80–85.

3 "Declaration of Colonel Adalberto Tejeda" (a translation of a conversation between Tejeda and Lic. Salvador Mendoza that had been transcribed by *La Prensa*, 24 April 1939), in Josephus Daniels to the Secretary of State, "Transmitting Translation of Statements by Colonel Adalberto Tejeda," NA/RDS, Doc. 812.00/30740 (10 May 1939).

4 *Ibid.*, pp. 2–3.

5 Cárdenas, *Apuntes* II (1941–1956), p. 417.

6 *Ibid.*, pp. 221–222.

7 Not everyone is of this opinion. According to Arturo Warman, one of the sharpest critics of the post-Cárdenist ejido, the latter simply perpetuated the economic enslavement and social isolation of the Mexican peasant. See Arturo Warman, "Sociedad campesina y reforma agraria," in *Ensayos sobre el campesino en México* (México: Editorial Nueva Imágen, 1984), pp. 27–38. This view was shared by President Carlos Salinas de Gortari, who, on 14 November 1991, just before terminating the agrarian reform, told hundreds of representatives of peasant organizations assembled in Los Pinos: "This is the unquestionable reality of the Mexican peasant: there is much injustice and poverty in the country." See Carlos Salinas de Gortari, *Diez puntos para dar libertad y justicia al campo mexicano*, Los Pinos, 14 Nov. 1991 (México D.F.: Presidencia de la República, Dirección General de Comunicación Social y el Instituto de Capacitación Agraria, 1991), p. 6. According to Salinas de Gortari, the agrarian reform's downfall was the system of ejidal distribution, a system that might have had some sort of logic initially, in the era of '*tierra vacante y poca población*' ("vacant land and scant population"), but subsequently became a myth that in fact brought poverty to the country. Those who criticized the end of the reform and wanted to perpetuate the myth, he said, were basically advocating the continuation of poverty and misery for millions of peasants. *Ibid.*, p. 20.

Sources and References

I Primary Sources

Archives

Archivo Particular de Adalberto Tejeda Olivares (AAT).

Archivo del Centro de Estudios de la Revolución Mexicana "Lázaro Cárdenas" (ACERMLC).

Archivo General de la Nación (AGN): Ramo de Presidentes, Fondo Abelardo Rodríguez.

Archivo Histórico del Congreso Constitucional del Estado de Michoacán de Ocampo (AHCMO).

Archivo General del Estado de Veracruz (AGEV): Fondos Legislatura, Gobernación y Justicia, and Agricultura y Ganadero.

Archivo Municipal de Zamora (AMZ).

Archivo del Poder Ejecutivo del Estado de Michoacán de Ocampo (APEMO).

Archivo de la Secretaría de la Reforma Agraria (ASRA): Delegaciones de Michoacán (Morelia) y Veracruz (Jalapa).

Hemeroteca Nacional.

National Archives, Records of the Department of State Relating to Internal Affairs of Mexico, 1929–1939.

Sección de Estadística de la Secretaría de la Reforma Agraria (SESRA): Delegaciones de Michoacán (Morelia y Uruapan) y Veracruz (Jalapa).

Newspapers and Official Periodicals

El Dictamen de Veracruz, 1928–1934.

El Machete, 1923–1929.

El Machete Ilegal, 1929–1934.

El Nacional Revolucionario, 1929–1934.

El Universal, 1929–1934.

Excelsior, 1929–1934.

Gaceta Oficial, official organ of the State of Veracruz-Llave, 1925–1936.

La Sotana, Periódico de Combate, organ of the Revolutionary Anticlerical League México D.F., 1930–1932.

Periódico Oficial, official organ of the State of Michoacán de Ocampo, 1928–1934.

Parliamentary Protocols

Actas de Sesiones del H. Congreso del Estado de Michoacán, 1928–1932, AHEMO, Morelia, Michoacán.

Actas de Sesiones del Congreso del Estado de Veracruz, AGEV, Fondo Legislatura.

Statistical Sources

Anuario Estadístico del Estado de Veracruz (1991). Instituto Nacional de Estadística Geografía e Informática, Gobierno del Estado de Veracruz, México, 1991.

Atlas Ejidal del Estado de Veracruz: Encuesta Nacional Agropecuario Ejidal, 1988, Instituto Nacional de Estadística Geografía Informatica, Instituto Frances de Investigación Científica para el Desarrollo en Cooperación (ORSTOM), México, 1991.

*Censo de Población (1940), Estado de Michoacán (*1943), (México, Secretaría de la Economía Nacional, Dirección General de Estadística).

Censo de Población (1940), Estado de Veracruz (1943), (México, Secretaría de la Economía Nacional, Dirección General de Estado).

Censo General de Habitantes de 1921, Estado de Veracruz (1928), (México, Departamento de Estadística Nacional, T.G. de la Nación).

Compendio Estadístico (1951), Secretaría de Economía, Dirección General de Estadística, México, 1952. Datos Sujetos a Rectificación del Censo General de Habitantes de 1930, por Municipios, Departamento de Estadística Ncional, Dirección de Exposición, México, 1932.

Directorio de Ejidos y de Comunidades Agrarias, V Censo Ejidal (1970), Secretaría de Industria y Comercio, Dirección General de Estadística, México, diciembre de 1972.

Directorio de Ejidos y de Comunidades Agrarias, V Censo Ejidal (1970), Secretaría de Industria y Comercio, Dirección General de Estadística, México, diciembre de 1972.

"División Municipal del Estado de Veracruz" (Marzo de 1933), en: División Municipal de las Entidades Federativas en 1933, Estados Unidos Mexicanos, Secretaría de la Economía Nacional, Dirección General de Estadística, México D.F., 1933, 112–122.

"División Municipal del Estado de Veracruz" (Diciembre de 1964), en: División Municipal de las Entidades Federativas en Diciembre de 1964, Estados Unidos Mexicanos, Secretaría de Industria y Comercio, Dirección General de Estadística, México D.F., 1966, 93–104.

"División Municipal del Estado de Michoacán" (1938), en: División Municipal de las Entidades Federativas en 1938, Estados Unidos Mexicanos, Secretaría de la Economía Nacional, Dirección General de Estadística, México D.F., 1939, 64–141.

Estadística 1915–1927, Comisión Nacional Agraria, Secretaría de Agricultura y Fomento, 1928.

México Económico 1928–1930, Anuario Estadístico de la Oficina de Estudios Eeconómicos de los Ferrocarriles Nacionales de México, Editorial "Cultura", México, 1932: en: Clasicos de la Economía Mexicana, Facultad de Economía de la UNAM, 1989.

Primer Censo Agrícola–Ganadero (1930), Resumen General, Secretaría de la Economía Nacional, Dirección General de Estadística, México, 1936.

Primer Censo Ejidal (1935), Resumen General, Secretaría de la Economía Nacional, Dirección General de Estadística (no fecha).

Quinto Censo De Población (1930), Resumen General, Secretaría de la Economía Nacional, Dirección General de Estadística, México D.F., 1934.

Quinto Censo De Población (1930), Estado de Michoacán, Secretaría de la Economía Nacional, Dirección General de Estadística, México D.F., 1935.

Quinto Censo de Población (1930), Estado de Veracruz, Secretaría de la Economía Nacional, Dirección Nacional de Estadística, México, 1935.

Resumen General del Censo Industrial de 1935, Secretaría de la Economía Nacional, Dirección General de Estadística, México, 1941.

Segundo Censo Ejidal de los Estados Unidos Mexicanos (1940), Resumen General, Secretaría de la Economía Nacional, Dirección General de Estadística, México, 1949.

Private Correspondence

"Correspondencia entre Lázaro Cárdenas y Francisco Jose Múgica desde 1928 y 1939", Desdeldiez, CERMLC, Julio de 1985, 101–132.

"Correspondencia entre Lázaro Cárdenas y Francisco Jose Múgica entre 1929 y 1932", Desdeldiez, CERMLC, Diciembre de 1985, 163–183.

Epistolario de Lázaro Cárdenas, Tomo I, Siglo XXI Editores, México, 1974.

Legal Sources

Código Agrario de los Estados Unidos Mexicanos (1940), Edición del "Diario Oficial", México D.F., 1940.

Constitución Política del Estado Libre y Soberano de Veracruz-Llave, Edición Oficial, Oficina Tipografica del Gobierno del Estado, Orizaba, Veracruz, 1917; en la Colección: 150 Años de Constitucionalismo Veracruzano, 1825–1975, Origines e Instituciones No. 2, Estado Libre y Soberano de Veraruz–Llave, 1975.

Cincuentenario de la Promulgación de la Constitución Política De Veracruz, Debates de los Constituyentes, Editorial del Gobierno de Veracruz, Jalapa, Ver., 1967.

Decreto por el cual Todo Mexicano Mayor de 18 Años Tiene Derecho a Adquirir Gratitudamente Terrenos Nacionales, Secretaría de Agricultura y Fomento, Dirección de Aguas y Colonización, Tacubaya, D.F., México, 1930.

Estatutos de la Camara Nacional de Comercio, Agricultura e Industria de la Ciudad de Morelia, Tipografía Comercial, Morelia, 1923.

Estatutos de la Cámara Agrícola Nacional de Michoacán, Imprenta "José Sansón", Morelia, 1918.

Fábila, Manuel, *Cinco Cientos Años de Legislación Agraria 1493–1940*, Secretaría de la Reforma Agraria, México, 1981.

Fábila, Gilberto y Ursua, Francisco A., *Fraccionamiento de Latifundios*. Bases Para la Ley Federal Sobre Esta Materia, Reglamento del Artículo 27 Constitucional, México D.F., 1925.

Ley de 19 de diciembre de 1925 Sobre Repartición de Tierras y Constitución de Patrimonio Ejidal y Su Reglamento de 4 de Marzo de 1926, Edición Oficial, Comisión Nacional Agraria, 1926.

Ley Orgánica del Municipio Libre, Estado de Veracruz, Enero 14 de 1918, Gobierno Constitucional del Edo. de Ver.–Llave, Tip. del Gobierno del Edo., Orizaba, Ver., 1918, en: Colección de Leyes, Decretos y Circulares, Año 1918.

"Ley Orgánica de División Territorial de Michoacán de 1909", Recopiliación de Leyes, Decretos, Reglamentos y Circulaciones que Se Han Expedidas en el Estado de Michoacán, Tomo XL, XXXII Congreso, Talleres de la Escuela Industrial Militar "Porfirio Días", Morelia,1910.

Ley sobre fraccionamiento de latifundios, Diario de los debates de la Cámara de Diputados del Congreso de Los Estados Unidos Mexicanos, Primer Período Extraordinario, XXIX Legislatura, tomo 2, No. 26.

Ley de Tierra Libre Para Los Mexicanos de 1923 y su Titulación, Talleres Gráficos de la Nación, México, 1926.

Ley de Tierras Ociosas: Cartilla Explicativa para los Presidentes Municipales y para los Campesinos, Cuarta Edición, Publicaciones de la Secretaría de Acción Agraria del Partido Nacional Revolucionario, México D.F., 1937.

Ley de Organización Fiscal del Estado de Veracruz-Llave, Jalapa-Enríquez, Talleres Linotipográficos del Gobierno del Estado, 1932.

Ley General del Catastro del Estado de Veracruz, Talleres Gráficos del Gobierno del Estado, Jalapa-Enríquez, 1931, en: Ley de Organización Fiscal del Estado de Veracruz-Llave, Jalapa-Enríquez, Talleres Linotipográficos del Gobierno del Estado, 1932, 149–162.

Ley de Organización Fiscal del Estado de Veracruz-Llave, Talleres Linotinograficos del Gobierno del Estado, 1930.

Ley Número 269 que Declera de Utilidad Pública el Fraccionamiento y Expropiación de Terrenos, para la Creación y Fomento de la Pequeña Propiedad, Talleres Linotinográficos del Gobierno, Jalapa-Enríquez, 1931.

Ley Número 3 sobre Enajenación Forsoza de Tierras por Causa de Utilidad Pública, de 24 de mayo de 1898, en: Colección de Leyes, Decretos y Circulares Corespondientes al Año de 1898, Xalapa-Enríquez, Tipografía del Gobierno del Estado, 1899.

Ley Para el Fomento de la Pequena Propiedad en el Estado Libre y Soberano de Veracruz-Llave de 15 de Enero de 1918, Oficina-Tipográfica del Gobierno del Estado, 1925.

Ley Número 208 (de 10 de Julio de 1931) que Refunde y Modifica las Disposiciones Contenidas en la Ley Núm. 297, de 8 de Julio de 1926. Folleto, Biblioteca del COLMEX, México D.F..

Ley General del Catastro del Estado de Veracruz, Talleres Gráficos del Gobierno del Estado, Jalapa-Enríquez, 1931.

Ley Nu. 34, de Expropiación por Causa de Utilidad Pública, de Junio 27 de 1933, XLIV Leg. Michoacana, Tip. de E.T.I. Álvaro Obregón, Morelia, 1933, en: Impresos Michoacanos, Vol. 24, Biblioteca del H. Congreso Local, Morelia, Michoacán.

Ley de Expropiación que Regira en el Estado de Veracruz-Llave, Talleres Linotinográficos del Gobierno del Edo., Jalapa-Enríquez, 1930.

Mendieta y Nuñez Lucio, Código Agrario (de 1934), Porrúa, México, 1938.

Recopilación de Leyes, Decretos, Reglamentos y Circulares Expedidas en el Edo. de Mich., Tomo XLIX, XLI Legislatura de Septiembre de 1926 al Septiembre de 1928, Xavier Tavera Alfaro (ed.), H. Congreso del Edo., Morelia, Michoacán, México, 1989.

Recopilación de Leyes, Decretos, Reglamentos y Circulares Expedidas en el Edo. de Mich., Tomo XLVI, XXXVIII Legislatura del 16 de Septiembre de 1920 al 19 de Agosto de 1922, Xavier Tavera Alfaro (ed.), H. Congreso del Edo., Morelia, Michoacán, 1980.

Recopilación de Leyes, Decretos, Reglamentos y Circulares Expedidas en el Edo. de Mich., Tomo XLIV, Periodo Preconstitucional y XXVI Legislatura del 1 de Enero de 1917 al 25 de Septiembre de 1918, Xavier Tavera Alfaro (ed.), H. Congreso del Edo., Morelia, Michoacán, 1978.

Recopilación Agraria: Leyes y Disposiciones, Confedración Nacional Campesina (CNC), Imprenta de la Dirección de Estudios Geográficos y Climatológicos, México, 1924.

Reformas, Adiciones y Rectificaciones a la Ley de Organización Fiscal del Estado, y Reglamento General de la Misma, Talleres Linotinogr ficos del Gobierno del Estado, Jalapa-Enríquez, 1931.

Reglamento Interior de la H. Legislatura (del Estado de Veracruz), Talleres Linotinográficos del Estado, Jalapa-Eneiquez, 1930.

Reglamento de la Ley General del Catastro del Estado de Veracruz, Talleres Gráficos del Gobierno del Edo., Jalapa-Enríquez, 1931.

Informes de Gobierno

Informe que Rinde el Ejecutivo del Estado Ante la XXXIII H. Legislatura el 5 de Mayo de 1931 (Informe 1930–1931 Primer Semestre), Talleres Linotipográficos del Gobierno del Estado, Jalapa-Enríquez, 1931, en: Estado de Veracruz: Informes de sus Gobernadores 1826–1986, Tomo XII, Carmen Blázquez Domínguez (compiladora), Gobierno del Edo. De Veracruz, Xalapa, 1986, 6223–6267.

"Informe Leido al 15 de Sep. de 1932 (Informe 1931–1932: Primer Semestre), Ante la H. Legislatura del Edo. de Veracruz", AAT, Tomo 197, Año 1932, Fojas 468–535.

"Informe que Rinde el C. Ing. Adalberto Tejeda, Gobernador Constitucional del Estado, Ante la XXXIII H. Legislatura", 16 de Sep. de 1932 (Segundo Semestre), Talleres Tipográficos del Gobierno del Estado, Jalapa-Enríquez, 1932, en: Estado de Veracruz: Informes de sus Gobernadores 1826–1986, Tomo XII, Carmen Blázquez Domínguez (compiladora), Gobierno del Edo. de Veracruz, Xalapa, 1986, 6269–6313.

"Informe que Rinde el C. Ing. Adalberto Tejeda, Gobernador Constitucional del Estado, Ante la H. Trigesimacuarta Legislatura", Sep. 16 de 1932 (Memoria del Gobierno de Tejeda 1928–1932), en: Estado de Veracruz: Informes de sus Gobernadores 1826–1986, Tomo XI, Carmen Blázquez Domínguez (compiladora), Gobierno del Edo. De Veracruz, Xalapa, 1986, 6063–6222.

"Informe que Ante la XXXIV H. Legislatura del Estado Rinde el Ciudadano Lic. Gonzalo Vázquez Vela, Encargado del Poder Ejecutivo", 16 de Sep. de 1933 (Informe 1932–1933), Talleres Tipográficos del Gobierno del Estado, Jalapa-Enríquez, 1934, en: Estado de Veracruz: Informes de sus Gobernadores 1826–1986, Tomo 12, Carmen Blázquez Domínguez (compiladora), Gobierno del Edo. de Veracruz, Xalapa, 1986, 6315–6403.

La Jira del General Lázaro Cárdenas: Síntesis Ideológica, La Secretaría de Prensa y Propaganda del Comite Ejecutivo Nacional (CEN) del Partido Nacional Revolucionario (PNR), México D.F., 1934.

Palabras y Documentos Publicos de Lázaro Cárdenas 1928–1940, Tomo 2: Informes de Gobierno y Mensajes Presidenciales de Año Nuevo, 1928–1940, Siglo XXI Editores, México, 1978.

Palabras y Documentos Publicos de Lázaro Cárdenas 1928–1970, Tomo 1: Mensajes, Discursos, Declaraciones, Entrevistas y Otros Documentos 1928–1940, Siglo XXI Editores, México, 1978.

Los Presidentes de México Ante la Nación, 1821–1984, Vol. 4, Cámara de Diputados, Quetzal, Grupo de Comunicaciones, México, 1985.

Seis Años de Gobierno al Servicio de México, 1934–1940, Departamento. de Plan Sexsenal de la Secretaría de Gobernación, México, 1940.

Party Sources

Historia Documental del Partido de la Revolución, Tomo I (PNR, 1929–1932), Edición del PRI y el Instituto de Capacitación Política (ICAP), México, 1986.
Historia Documental del Partido de la Revolución II, Año de 1933.
Instituto de Capacitación Política (ICAP) del PRI, México, 1981.

Political Programs

El Gobierno del Estado y las Comunidades de Indígenas—Programa de Acción y Antecedentes Históricos y Legales, por Lázaro Cárdenas, Tip. de E.T.I. Álvaro Obregón, Morelia, Michoacán, 1931.
The Mexican Government's Six Year Plan 1934 to 1940, Trens Agency News for Newspapers, Mexico City, Mexico. (c. 1934).
Programa de Gobierno del Estado de Michoacán: Proyecto de 1958, Secretaría de Economía y Lic. David Franco Rodriguez, Gobernador de Michoacán, Talleres Graficos de la Nación, México, D.F.
Resolución Integral del Problema Agrario en Lombardía y Nueva Italia, Michoacán, por Lázaro Cárdenas, D.A.P., México, 1938.
Reparto de Tierras de las Excomunidades de Indígenas—Disposiciones Relativas, Gobierno de Michoacán, Tip. Jose Sanson, Morelia, 1919.

Ecclesiastical Sources

Documentación para la Historia de la Persecución Religiosa en México, Editorial Jus, México, 1954.

Private Memories

Cárdenas, Lázaro, *Obras*: I—*Apuntes* 1913–1940, Tomo I, México, UNAM, 1972.
Cárdenas, Lázaro, *Obras*: I—*Apuntes* 1941–1956, Tomo II, México, UNAM, 1972.
Cabrera, Luis, *Veinte Años Despues*: El Balance de la Revolución; La Campaña Presidencial de 1934; Las Dos Revoluciones, México, Edición Botas, 1938.
Gómez, Marte R., Vida Política Contemporánea, México, Fondo de Cultura Económica,1978.
Torres, Manuel, *Memorias*, Manuscrito Privado del Autor.

Interviews

Entrevistas con Andres Álvaro Hernández, Vicente González y Lorenzo Torres, Comuneros Indígenas de Pichátaro, Michoacán, Julio 11 de 1992.
Entrevista con José Jesús Leiva Roque, Comunero Indígena de Cherán, Michoacán, Julio 11 de 1992.
Entrevista con Cristobal González Colesio, Comunero Indígena de Paracho, Michoacán, Julio 12 de 1992.
Entrevista con Domingo Jimenez Chávez, Comunero y Ex-Comisariado Comunal de Capácuaro, Michoacán, Julio 12 de 1992.
Entrevista con el Padre "Daniel", Párroco de Nauatzen, Antes Rector del Santuario de Totolán, Nauatzen, Michoacán, Junio 12 de 1992.
Entrevista con Dr. y Padre Francisco Miranda, Profesor en el Colegio de Michoacán, Zamora, Julio 18 de 1992.
Entrevista con Algunos de los Ex-Peones Acasillados de la Antigua Hacienda de Guaracha (Hoy: Emiliano Zapata), Michoacán, Junio de 1989.
Entrevista con Jesús Múgica Martínez, Morelia, Ex-Secretario de Educación del CREMDT, Mich., Julio de 1989 y Julio de 1992.

Entrevista con el Lic. Emigdio Hernández Ascensi, Ex-Comunero Indígena de Naranja, Zacapú, Michoacán, Julio 16 de 1992.

Entrevista con Moisés Lagunes González, Ejidatario de Cerro Gordo, Mpio. de Actopan, Veracruz, Marzo 23 de 1992.

Entrevista con Gabriela Tejeda, Viuda del Ejidatario Felix Díaz, Palmas de Abajo, Actopan, Veracruz, Marzo 29 de 1992.

Entrevista con Ignacio Hernández Cervantes y Pedro Perez Cervantes, Ex-Agraristas de Mozomboa, Actopan, Veracruz, Marzo 29 de 1992.

Entrevista con Jacinto Vásquez Casas, Comisariado Ejidal de Actopan, Actopan, Veracruz, Marzo 30 de 1992.

Entrevista con Federico Fabian Zapata, Ex-Comisariado Ejidal de Almolonga, Mpio. de Alto Lucero, Veracruz, Abril 2 de 1992.

Entrevista con Olegario Utrera Cardena, Comisariado Ejidal de San Nicolás, Actopan, Veracruz, Abril 2 de 1992.

Entrevista con el Dr. Luis González y González, México D.F., Julio de 1991 y Junio de 1992.

Entrevista con el Padre Manuel Olimón, Profesor en la Universidad Pontificia, Tlalpan, México D.F., Junio de 1992.

Interview with Dr. Luis González y González, México City, June, 1992.

Interview with the daughter of the deceased Capula's (ejido) leader, Capula, Michoacán, September 13, 2014.

II References

Agetro, L. 1942: *Las Luchas Proletarias en Veracruz: Historia y Autocrítica*, Jalapa, Editorial "Barricada".

Alañis Patiño, E., Lópes Bermudez, J. y Mesa Andraca, M. 1955: "Problemas de la Tenencia y Aprovechamiento de la Tierra en México", en: *Problemas Agrícolas e Industriales de México*, Vol. 5, 4, 85–167.

Anguiano Equihua, V. 1989: *Lázaro Cárdenas, Su Feudo y la Política Nacional*, México, Editorial Referencias.

Arriaga, A. 1938: *Organización Social de los Tarascos*, Morelia, Michoacán, Publicaciones del Departamento de Extención Universitaria.

Baitenmann, H. 1997: "Rural Agency and State Formation in Postrevolutionary México: The Agrarian Reform in Central Veracruz, 1915–1992", Doctoral Thesis, The New School for Social Research: New York, 81–82.

Baker, W.J. 1971: "Church and State in Veracruz, 1840–1940: The Concord and Conflicts of a Century", Ph.D. Dissertation, University of St. Louis.

Becker, M. 1995: *Setting the Virgin on Fire: Lázaro Cárdenas and the Redemption of the Mexican Revolution*, University of California Press: Berkeley, California.

Benítez, F. 1978: *Lázaro Cárdenas y la Revolución Mexicana*, Fondo de Cultura Económica: México.

Benítez, F. 1987:" El Agua Envenenada", *Colección Popular, Nu. 27*, México: Fondo de Cultura Eeconómica.

Benítez J., Mirna A. 1988: "La Organización Sindical de losTrabajadores Petroleros en la Huasteca Veracruzana, 1917–1931", en: *Los Trabajadores Ante la Nacionalización Petrolera, Anuario V*, Jalapa: Centro de Investigaciones Históricas, Instituto de Investigaciones Humanisticas, Universidad Veracruzana, 13–33.

Bermejo, G. y Espejel, L. 1982: "Conflicto por el Poder y Contradicciones de Clase: El Caso de Michoacán, 1920–1926", en: *Boletin*, CERMLC, 23–31.

Boyer, C. 2003: *Becoming Campesinos: Politics, Identity, and Agrarian Struggle in Postrevolutionary Michoacán, 1920–1935*, Stanford: Stanford University Press.

Branch, H.N. (ed. and trans.), 1917: *The Mexican Constitution of 1917 Compared with the Constitution of 1857*, Phidladelphia: The American Academy of Political and Social Science.

Buchenau, J. 2011: *The Last Caudillo: Álvaro Obregón and the Mexican Revolution*, Oxford: Wiley-Blackwell.

Cárdenas, L. 1984: *Ideario Político*, México: Era.

Cerecedo, M. 1983: *Adalberto, T. O.: Dimensión del hombre*, Xalapa, Verarcuz, Gobierno del Estado de Veracruz.

Chassen-López, F. 2010: *Oaxaca: entre el liberalismo y la revolución.La perspectiva del sur (1867–1911)*, Iztapalapa, México, UABJO-UAM: University of Kentucky.

Chain, R. R. 1989: "El Programa de la Educación Socialista en Veracruz", en: *Veracruz, Un Tiempo Para Contar, Memoria del Primer Seminario de Historia Regional*, Mirana Benítez, Carmen Blázquez y Otros (coords.), México, Universidad Veracruzana, Instituto Nacional de Antropologia e Historia, 245–259.

Clark, M. R. 1973: *Organized Labor in Mexico*, New York, Russell and Russell.

Córdova, A. 1989: *La Ideología de la Revolución Mexicana: La Formación del Nuevo Regimen*, México, Era.

De La Peña, M. T. 1946: *Veracruz Económico*, México, Gobierno del Estado de Veracruz.

Diego, H. M. 1982: *La Confederación Revolucionaria Michoacana del Trabajo*, Jiquilpan, Michoacán, Centro de Estudios de la Revolución Mexicana "Lázaro Cárdenas", A.C.

Domínguez P. O. 1979: "Un Estudio de Caso: Los Comunistas de San Bruno", en: *Anuario 2*, Centro de Estudios Históricos, Facultad de Humanidades, Universidad Veracruzana, 224–252.

Domínguez P. O. 1981: "El Anarcosindicalismo en el Agro Veracruzano", en: *Anuario 3*, Centro de Estudios Históricos, Instituto de Investigaciones Humanisticos, Universidad Veracruzana, 59–77.

Domínguez P. O. 1986: *Política y Movimientos Sociales en el Tejedismo*, Universidad Veracruzana, Centro de Investigaciones Históricas, Xalapa.

Embriz, O. A. 1984: *La Liga de Comunidades y Sindicatos Agraristas del Estado de Michoacán*, México, Centro de Estudios Históricos del Agrarismo en México.

Embriz, O. A. 1987: "Primo Tapia: Cien Años de su Nacimiento", en: *La Revolución en Michoacán 1920–1926*, Universidad Michoacana, Moerlia, Michoacán, Departamento de Historia, 119–134.

Fábila, G. y Ursua, F. A., 1925: *Fraccionamiento de latifundios: bases para la ley federal sobre esta materia, reglamento del Articulo 27 Constitucional*, México: Imprenta de la Cámara de Diputados.

Falcón, R. y García Morales, S. 1986: *La Semilla en el Surco. Adalberto Tejeda y el Radicalismo en Veracruz (1883–1960)*, México, El Colegio de México y el Gobierno del Edo. de Veracruz.

Falcón, R. 1984: *Revolución y caciquismo: San Luis Potosí 1910–1938*, México: El Colegio de México.

Falcón, R. 1977: *El Agrarismo en Veracruz: La Etapa Radical 1928–1935*, México: El Colegio de México.

Falcón, R. 1978: "El Surgimiento del Agrarismo Cardenista—Una Revisión de las Tesis Populistas", *Historia Mexicana*, Vol. 27 (1977–1978), No. 107 (3), Enero-Marzo, 333–386.

Fallaw, B. 2001: *Cárdenas Compromised: The Failure of Reform in Postrevolutionary Yucatán*, Durham: Duke University Press.

Fernández de Córdoba, J. 1953: "Michoacán: La Historia y Sus Instrumentos", *Historia Mexicana*, Vol. 2, Nos. 5–8, 138–154.

Foglio Miramontes, F. 1936: *Geografía económicó agrícola del Estado de Michoacán*, Secretaría de Agricultura y Fomento, Dirección de Economía Rural, Editorial Cultura, México.

Fowler Salamini, H. 1972: "Los Origines de las Organizaciones Campesinas en Veracruz: Raices Políticas y Sociales", *Historia Mexicana*, Vol. 22 (Jul.–Sep.), No. 1, 52–76.

Fowler Salamini, H., 1970: "Origines Laborales de la Organización Campesina en Veracruz", en: *Historia Mexicana*, Vol. 20 (Oct.–Dic.), No. 2, 235–264.

Fowler Salamini, H. 1970: *The Agrarian Revolution in the State of Veracruz, 1920–1940: The Role of Peasant Organizations*, Phd. Thesis, Submitted to the Faculty of the College of Arts and Sciences of the American University in Parcial Fulfillment of the Requirements for the Degree of Doctor of Philosophy in History, The American University, Washington, D.C.

Fowler Salamini, H. 1980: "Revolutionary Caudillos in the 1920s: Francisco Múgica and Adalberto Tejeda", in: *Caudillo and Peasent in the Mexican Revolution*, D.A. Brading (ed.), Cambridge University Press: Cambridge, 169–192.

Frazer, D. J. 1972: "La política de desamortización en las comunidades indígenas, 1856–1872", *Historia Mexicana*, Vol. XXI: 84(4), (Abril–Junio), 615–652.

Friedrich, P. 1981: *Revueltas Agrarias en una Aldea Mexicana*, México, Fondo de Cultura Económica.

Garcia Morales, S. 1989: "Análisis de Estadística de 1907. Haciendas y Hacendados", en: *Veracruz, Un Tiempo Para Contar, Memoria del Primer Seminario de Historia Regional*, Mirna Benítez, J., Carmen Blázquez, D. y Otros (coords.), México, Universidad Veracruzana, Instituto Nacional de Antropología e Historia, 130–179.

García Morales, S. 1974: *El Conflicto Clerical en Veracruz en 1931*, Tesis para obtener el Título de Maestría En Historia, Jalapa-Enríquez, Universidad Veracruzana, Facultad de Humanidades.

Garibay, H. C. 2004: *Francisco J. Múgica. Crónica política de un rebelde*, México, Ediciones Coyoacán.

Garncr, P. 2013: *Leones británicos y águilas mexicanas. Negocios, política e imperio en la carrera de Weetman Pearson en México, 1889–1919*, México, FCE-Instituto Mora-El Colegio de México-El Colegio de San Luis [Stanford University Press, 2011].

Joseph, G. M. and Nugent, D. 1994: "Popular Culture and State Formation in Revolutionary Mexico," in: Gilbert M. Joseph and Daniel Nugent (eds.), *Everyday Forms of State Formation: Revolution and Negotiation of rules in Modern Mexico*, Durham: Duke University Press, 9–13.

Ginzberg, E. 2009: "Una labor de convencimiento: La culminación de la Guerra cristera en Michoacán", Julia Preciado Zamora y Servando Ortoll (coords.), *Los guachos y los mochos: Once ensayos cristeros*, Morelia: Jitanjáfora, 179–188.

Ginzberg, E. 1998: "State Agrarianism versus Democratic Agrarianism: Adalberto's

Tejeda Experiment in Veracruz, 1928–32, *Journal of Latin American Studies*, Vol. 30, No. 2, 341–372.

Ginzberg, E. 1999: *Lázaro Cárdenas Gobernador de Michoacán, 1928–1932*, Zamora and Morelia, El Colegio de Michoacán and the Universdad Michoacana de San Nicolás de Hidalgo.

Ginzberg, E. 1997: "Ideología, Política y la Cuestión de las Prioridades: Lázaro Cárdenas y Adalberto Tejeda 1928–1934", *Mexican Studies/Estudios Mexicanos*, Vol. 13(1), 55–85.

González y González, L. 1974: *San José de Gracia, Mexican Village in Transition*, Austin, TX, and London: University of Texas Press.

González Navarro, M.1985: *La Confederación Nacional Campesina en la Reforma Agraria Mexicana*, Sociedad Cooperativa (de) Publicaciones Mexicanas S.C.L., tercera Edición, México D.F.

González Navarrro, M. 1969: "Tenencia de la Tierra y Población Agrícola 1877–1960", en: *Historia Mexicana 73*(1), Julio–Septiembre, *Vol. 19*, de 1969–1970, 62–86.

González P. 1979: *Cuauhtémoc, Organización campesina y lucha de clases. La Confederación Nacional Campesina*, Instituto de Investigaciones Eeconómicas, UNAM.

Salinas de Gortari, C. 1991: *Diez puntos para dar libertad y justicia al campo mexicano*, Los Pinos, 14 Nov. 1991 (México, Presidencia de la República, Dirección General).

Guerra Manzo, E. 2008: "The Resistance of the Marginalised: Catholics in Eastern Michoacán and the Mexican State, 1920–40", *Journal of Latin American Studies*, Vol. 40, No. 1, Feb., 109–133.

Guerra Manzo, E. 2010: "Católicos y agraristas en Michoacán: Del conflicto al modus vivendi", Oikión Solano, Verónica y Rodríguez, Sánchez (coords.), *Vientos de rebellion en Michoacán: Continuidad y ruptura en la Revolución Mexicana*, Morelia y Zamora, Gobierno del Estado de Michoacán, El Colegio de Michoacán, 187–208.

Guerra Manzo, E. 1999: "La gobernatura de Lázaro Cárdenas en Michoacán (1928–1932): una vía agrarista moderada", *Secuencia, nueva época, 45*, Sep.–Dic., 131–166.

Gurza, F. A. 1996: "En busca de una educación revolucionaria, 1924–1934, en: Josefina Zoraida Vázquez et al. (coords.), *Ensayos sobre historia de la educación en México*, México, El Colegio de México, 145–187.

Guzmán Ávila, J. N. 1982: *Michoacán y la Inverción Extranjera 1880–1911*, Universidad Michoacana de San Nicolas de Hidalgo, Deptamento de Investigaciones Históricas.

Hernández García, E. 2010: *Redes Políticas y Sociales: Consolidación y Permanencia del Régimen Posrevolucionario en Veracruz*, 1920–1970, Tesis de Doctorado en Historia y Estudios Regionales presentada al Instituto de Investigaciones Histórico-Sociales de la Universidad Veracruzana.

Hernández, M. D. 1982: *La Confederación Revolucionaria Michoacana del Trabajo*, Jiquilpán, Michoacán, Centro de Estudios de la Revolución Mexicana "Lázaro Cárdenas".

Ibarra Mendivil, J. L. 1989: *Propiedad Agraria y Sistema Político en México*, México, El Colegio de Sonora y Porrúa.

Knight, A. 1994: "Weapon and Arches in the Mexican Revolutionary Landscape", Gilbert M. Joseph and Daniel Nugent (eds.), *Everyday Forms of State Formation:*

Revolution and Negotiation of rules in Modern Mexico, Durham: Duke University Press, 24–66.

Knight, A. 1997: "The Ideology of the Mexican Revolution, 1910–40", *Estudios Interdisciplinarios de América Latina y El Caribe (EIAL)*, 8 (1), (Enero–Junio), 77–109.

Koth, K. B. 1999: "La modernización de Veracruz, 1870–1905", in: Barnardo García Díaz y David Skerritt Gardner (eds.), *La Revolución Mexicana en Veracruz, Antología* Veracruz, Comisión Estatal del Bicentenario de la Independencia y del Centenario de la Revolución Mexicana: Gobierno del Estado de Veracruz, 21–89.

Knowlton, R. 1978: "La individualización de la propiedad corporativa civil en el siglo XIX—notas sobre Jalisco", en: *Historia Mexicana*, Vol. XXVIII (1), (Julio–Septiembre), 24–61.

Kourí, E. 2013: *Un pueblo dividido*. Comercio, *propiedad y comunidad en Papantla, México*, México, FCE-El Colegio de México, [Stanford University Press, 2004].

Kourí, E. 2009: "Los pueblos y sus tierras en el México porfiriano: Un legado inexplorado de Andrés Molina Enríquez", en: Emilio Kourí (Cood.), *Cien años de los grandes problemas nacionales*, México, El Colegio de México, 253–330.

Krauze, E. 1987: "General Misionero Lázaro Cárdenas", México, FCE, Serie: *Biografía del Poder*, No. 8.

La Cuestion de la Tierra, Colección de Folletos para la Historia de la Revolución Mexicana, Tomos I–IV, Jesús Silva Herzog (dir.), Instituto Mexicana de Investigaciones Eeconómicas, México, 1960–1962.

Laborde, H. 1952: "Cárdenas, Reformador Agrario", *Problemas Agrícolas e Industriales de México*, Vol. 4, No. 1, Enero–Marzo, 59–86.

Lemus G. R. 1967: "El Amparo en Materia Agraria", *Revista del México Agrario, Año I*, No. 1 (Nov.–Dic.), 35–48.

Lizama Silva, G. 1990: "Los Capitales Zamoranos a Principios del Siglo 20", *Historia Mexicana 156 (4), Vol. 39* (Abril–Junio), 1029–1055.

López Terrones, M. E. 1989: "Un Intento Renovador: Los Proyectos del Tejedismo en Veracruz 1928–1932", en: *Veracruz, Un Tiempo Para Contar, Memoria del Primer Seminario de Historia Regional*, Mirana Benítez, Carmen Bl Vazquez y Otros (coords.), Universidad Veracruzana, Instituto Nacional de Antropologia e Historia, México, D.F., 199–215.

López Terrones, E. A. 1986: *Un Ensayo Radical: Los Proyectos del Tejedismo en Veracruz (1928–1932)*, Tesis para Optar al Grado de Licenciado de Historia, Universidad Iberoamericana, México D.F.

Lombardo García, I. 2007: *La participación política de la prensa en la campaña de 1934. El caso de la candidatura a la presidencia de la república del Coronel Adalberto Tejeda Olivares*, Tesis de Doctorado en Historia y Estudios Regionales, Universidad Veracruzana.

Lombardo Toledano, V. 1974: *En Torno al Problema Agrario*, México, Confederación Nacional Campesina (CNC) y el PPS.

Luna Arroyo, A. y Alcerréca, L. G. 1982: *Diccionario de Derecho Agrario Mexicano*, Porrúa, México.

Maldonado Gallardo, A. 1981: "La Confederación Revolucionaria Michoacana del Trabajo: Lázaro Cárdenas y el Problema Agrario en Michoacán 1928–1932", en: *Jornadas de Historia de Occidente*, No. 4, CERMLC, 91–100.

Maldonado Aguirre, S. 1992: *De Tejeda a Cárdenas: el movimiento agrarista de la*

Revolucion Mexicana, 1920–1934, Universidad de Guadalajara: Guadalajara, Jal.

Maldonado, S. 1989: *Poder Regional y Poder Nacional, El Movimiento Agrarista en Veracruz, 1920–1934*, Tesis para Obtener el Grado de Maestro en Estudios Regionales, Instituto Mora, México D.F.

Malefakis, Eduard E., 1970: *Agrarian Reform and Peasant Revolution in Spain, Origins of the Civil War*, New-Haven and London: Yale University Press.

Manjarrez, F. C. y Ortiz Hernán, G. 1933: *Lázaro Cárdenas, Soldado de la Revolución, Gobernante, Político Nacional*, México, Talleres de Editorial Patria.

Marsiske, R. 1996: "Universidad y educación rural en México (1924–1928)", Pilar Gonzalbo Aizpuru (coord.), *Educación rural e indígena en Iberoamérica*, México, El Colegio de México y la Universidad Nacional de Educación en Distancia, 123–137.

Martínez Apolinar, M. 1946: *Primo Tapia, Semblanza de un Revolucionario*, México, El Libro Perfecto.

Martínez Assad, C. 1981: *La Sucesión Presidencial En México: Conyuntura Electoral y Cambio Político*, U.N.A.M., Editorial Nueva Imagen, México.

Martínez Assad, C. (coord.) 1988: *Estadistas, Caciques y Caudillos*, México, UNAN, Instituto de Investigaciones Sociales.

Martínez Assad, C. 1977: "La Lucha Campesina en Veracruz entre 1923 y 1934: Un Intento de Organización Independiente", en *Cuadernos Agrarios*, Año 2, No. 5, 38–56.

Marván, I. 1988: "Se Que Te Vas a la Revolución . . . ": Lázaro Cárdenas 1913–1929", en: *Estadistas, Caciques y Caudillos*, Carlos Martínez Assad (cood.), México, UNAM, Instituto de Investigaciones Sociales, 97–120.

Medin, T. 1973: "Ideología y Praxis Política de Lázaro Cárdenas", *Siglo XXI*, Editores.

Medin, T. 1983: *El Minimato Presidencial: Historia Política del Maximato 1928–1935*, México, Era.

Melgarejo Vivenco, J. L. 1980: *Adalberto Tejeda*, Unidad Interdisciplinaria de Antropología e Historia de la Universidad Veracruzana, El Gobierno del Estado de Veracruz-Llave, Xalapa, Veracruz.

Mendoza Barragán, E.1990: *Testimonio Cristero*, Editorial Jus, México.

Meyer, J. 1981: "La Segunda Cristiada en Michoacán", *La Cultura Purhe, 2*, Coloquio de Antropologia e Historia Regionales, FONAPAS, Zamora, 14–16 de Agosto de 1980, Francisco Miranda (ed.), Colegio de Michoacán, 246–275.

Meyer, J. 1991: *La Cristiada*, 13a edición, Siglo XXI Editores, México.

Meyer, L. 1982: "La Revolución Mexicana y sus Elecciones Presidenciales: Una Interpretación (1911–1940)", *Historia Mexicana*, 126 (2), Vol. 32, Oct.–Dic., 143–197.

Meyer, L. 1977: "La Etapa del Estado Mexicano Conteporaneo 1928–1940", en: *Las Crisis en el Sistema Político Mexicano (1928–1977)*, Centro de Estudios Internacionales, El Colegio De México, 5–30.

Michaels, A. L. 1971: "Las Elecciones de 1940", *Historia Mexicana*, 81 (1), Vol. 21, 80–134.

Michaels, A. L. 1966: "El Nacionalismo Conservador Mexicano, Desde la Revolución hasta 1940", *Historia Mexicana*, 62 (2), Vol. 16, 213–238.

Mijangos Díaz, E., y Marisa Pérez, D. (coords.), 2009: *Voces del antiguo régimen. Representaciones, sociedad y gobierno en México contemporáneo*, Morelia, Universidad Michoacana-Instituto Mora.

Miranda, F. 1979: *Uruapan*, Monografía Municipal, Gobierno del Estado de Michoacán.

Miranda, F. 1978: *Yurecuaro*, Gobierno del Edo. de Michoacán.

Moheno, C. 1985: *Las Historias y los Hombres de San Juan*, El Colegio de Michoacán, CONACYT,.

Molina Enríquez, A. A. 1985: *Los Grandes Problemas Nacionales (1909)*, Era, México (primera ed. 1978).

Monroy Huitron, G. 1975: *Política Educativa de la Revulución (1910–1940)*, Secretaría de Educación Publica, México D.F.

Mora Forero, J. 1979: "Los Maestros y la Practica de la Educación Socialista", *Historia Mexicana*, 113 (1), Vol. 29, 133–162.

Moreno Sánchez, M. 1955: "Mas Alla de la Revolución Mexicana", *Problemas Agrícolas e Industriales de México*, Vol. 7, No. 2, 217–245.

Moreno, H. G. 1980: *Tiempos Viejos, Tiempos Nuevos*, Morelia, El Colegio de Michoacán.

Morett S., J. C. 1992: *Alternativas de Modernización del Ejido*, México, Instituto de Proposiciones Estrategicas, A.C., Editorial Diana.

Múgica Martínez, J. 1982: *La Confederación Revolucionaria Michoacana del Trabajo*, México, Eddisa.

Muñoz, A. V. 1921: *Restitución y dotación de ejidos: el problema agrario en México*, México: Comisión Nacional Agraria.

Nava Hernández, E. 1987: "Cultura Política y Política Popular en Michoacán: Notas Para su Estudio", *Relaciones*, 31, Vol. 8, 25–60.

Nava Nava, M. del C. 1984: "Relaciones Múgica–Cárdenas", en: *Jornadas de Historia de Occidente*, No. 7, CERMLC, 263–310.

Nugent, D. and Alonso, A. M. 1994: "Multiple Selective Traditions in Agrarian Reform and Agrarian Struggle: Popular Culture and State Formation in the Ejido of Namiquipa, Chiuhauha", Gilbert M. Joseph and Daniel Nugent (eds.), *Everyday Forms of State Formation: Revolution and Negotiation of Rules in Modern Mexico*, Durham: Duke University Press, 209–246.

Negrete, M. 1988: *Relaciones Entre la Iglesia y el Estado en México 1930–1940*, México: El Colegio de México y La Universidad Iberoamericana.

Nugent, D. 1993: *Spent Cartridges of Revolution: An Anthropological History of Namiquipa, Chihuahua*, Chicago: University of Chicago Press.

Ochoa, A. 1983: "Miguel De La Trinidad Regalado y La Lucha por la Tierra", *Relaciones*, Vol. 4, No. 14, 109–118.

Ochoa Serrano, A. 1987: "Miguel Regalado y la Sociedad Unificadora de la Raza Indígena", en: *La Revolución en Michoacán 1920–1926*, Morelia, Michoacán, Universidad Michoacana, 53–80.

Oikión Solano, V. 2004: *Los hombres del poder en Michoacán, 1924–1962*, Zamora, El Colegio de Michoacán.

Olimón Nolasco, M. 1990: *Tensiones y Acercamientos: La Iglesia y el Estado en la Historia del Pueblo Mexicano*, México, Instituto Mexicano de Doctrina Social Cristiana.

Olivera Sedano, A. 1987: *Aspectos del Conflicto Religioso de 1926 a 1929: Sus Antecedentes y Consecuencias*, México, Secretaría de Educación Pública.

Olvera Rivera, A. J., González Sierra, J., Skerritt, D. G., Corzo Ramírez, R., 1986: "Balance sobre la Investigación de la Formación de la Clase Obrera Veracruzana: 1850–1932", en: *75 Años de Sindicalismo Mexicano*, Alejandra Moreno Toscano y Samuel L. González (coords.), México, Instituto Nacional de Estudios Históricos de la Revolución Mexicana, 189–221.

Orive Alba, A. 1970: *Irrigación en México*, México, Editorial Grijalba, S.A.

Ornelas, A. P. 2010: *Empresarios lombardos en Michoacán. La familia Cusi entre el Porfiriato y la posrevolución (1884–1938)*, México, Instituto Mora y El Colegio de Michoacán.

Ortiz, L. F. 1977: *Colectivización Ejidal y Cambio Rural En México*, Juárez, Tabasco, Universidad Autónoma Juárez de Tabasco, Comisión de Grijalva.

Osorio, S., Reyes, C.: "Evolución de la Tenencia de la Tierra en México, Reunión Nacional de Tecnología en la Reforma Agraria, Celebrada del 24 al 27 de Julio de 1968", en el Centro Interamericano de Estudios de Seguridad Social, de la Independencia del IMSS.

Pacheco, S. M. (coord.), "Nación y municipio en México", *Siglos XIX y XX*, México, UNAM, 2012.

Padilla Gallo, J. 1935: *Los de Abajo en Michoacán*, Morelia, Michoacán, México, Tip. de la E.T.I. "Álvaro Obregón".

Peña Roja, G. A.y Marquéz Galicia, J. (Compiladores) 1982: *Adalberto Tejeda y el Artículo 27 Constitucional*, México, Centro de Estudios Históricos del Agrarismo en México (CEHAM).

Portillo, J. H., 1982: *El Problema de las Relaciones entre la Iglesia y el Estado en México*, México, Costa—Amic Editores.

Powell, T.G. 1972: "Los liberales, el campesinado indígena y los problemas agrarios durante la Reforma", *Historia Mexicana*, Vol. XXI 84(4), 653–675.

Purnell, J. 1999: "'With All Due Respect': Popular Resistance to the Privatization of Communal Lands in Nineteenth-Century Michoacán", *Latin American Research Review*, 34(1), 85–121.

Raby, D. L. 1973: "Los Principios de la Educación Rural en México: El Caso de Michoacán, 1915–1929", *Historia Mexicana*, 88(4), Vol. 22, 553–581.

Reyes García, C. 1990: "Los Empresarios Noriega Contra la Comisión Local Agraria de Michoacán, 1922", *Relacciones*, Vol. XI, No. 43, 157–174.

Roa, F. G. 1953: "El Artículo Veintisiete Constitucional", en: *Problemas Agrícolas e Industriales de México*, Vol. 5, No. 3, 95–116.

Rodriguez Sesma, J. 1988: *Historia de la Liga de Comunidades Agrarias y Sindicatos Campesinos*, México, Confederación Nacional Campesina (CNC), CEHAM.

Rojas, B. L. 1980: "La Sucesión Presidencial de 1934 y la Familia Revolucionaria", en: *Relaciones*, 4, Vol. 1, 41–75.

Rojas, B. (coord.) 2006: *Mecánica política: para una relectura del siglo XIX mexicano*, México, Universidad de Guadalajara-Instituto Mora.

Romero Flores, J. 1946: *Historia de Michoacán, Tomo 2*, México, Gobierno de Michoacán, Imprenta "Calidad".

Romero Flores, J. 1958: *Geografía del Estado de Michoacán*, Morelia, Michoacán, Gobierno de Estado, Talleres Tipográficos de la E.T.I. "Álvaro Obregón".

Romero Flores, J. 1964: *Historia de la Revolución en Michoacán*, México, Bibloteca del Instituto Nacional de Estudios Históricos de la Revolución Mexicana.

Romero López, A. L. 1989: "La Batalla Escolar—Estado de Veracruz 1914–1920", en: *Veracruz, Un Tiempo Para Contar, Memoria del Primer Seminario de Historia Regional*, Mirna Benítez, J., Carmen Blázquez, D. y Otros (coords.), México D.F., Universidad Veracruzana, Instituto Nacional de Antropología e Historia, 231–244.

Romero Rincón, S. 1981: *El Ejido Mexicano*, México D.F., Centro Nacional de Investigaciones Agrarias.

Ronzón León, J. A. 1991: "La Campaña Presidencial de Adalberto Tejeda", Tesis de Maestería en Historia, Universidad Veracruzana, Facultad de Historia, Xalapa, Veracruz.

Roseberry, W. 1994: "Hegemony and the Language of Contention", Gilbert M. Joseph and Daniel Nugent (eds.), *Everyday Forms of State Formation: Revolution and Negotiation of rules in Modern Mexico*, Durham: Duke University Press, 355–366.

Salmerón Castro, F. I. 1988: *Proceso Político y Estructuras de Poder en una Micro Region Canera de Michoacán: Taretan 1880–1980*, Tesis de Maestería en Antropología Social, El Colegio de Michoacán, Zamora, Michoacán.

Sánchez Díaz, G. 1987: "Los Elementos y las Acciones de la Contrarrevolución en Michoacán 1918–1923", en: *La Revolución en Michoacán 1920–1926*, Universidad Michoacana, Departamento de Historia, Morelia, Michoacán, 105–118,

Sánchez Díaz, G. y Carreño, G. A. 1979: "El Movimiento Cristero en el Distrito de Coalcomán, Michoacán, 1927–1929", *Boletin*, CERMLC, 98–117.

Sánchez, M. 1994: *Grupos de poder y centralización política en México. El caso Michoacán 1920–1924*, México, Instituto Nacional de Estudios Históricos de la Revolución Mexicana.

Scott, J. 1990: *Domination and the Art of Resistance: Hidden Transcripts*, New Haven: Yale University Press.

Silva Herzog, J. (dir.), 1961: *La Cuestion de la Tierra 1910–1911*, Colección de Folletos para la Historia de la Revolución Mexicana, Tomo I, México, Instituto Mexico de Investigaciones Económicas.

Skerritt Gardner, D. 1983: ¿Que es la Mano Negra?, *Anuario 3*, Xalapa, Centro de Estudios Históricas, Instituto de Investigaciones Humanisticas, Universidad Veracruzana, 129–138.

Skerritt Gardner, D. 1989: *Una Historia Agraria en el Centro de Veracruz 1850–1940*, Xalapa, Veracruz: Universidad Veracruzana, Centro de Investigaciones Históricas.

Skerritt Gardner, D. 1979: "El Papel de Adalberto Tejeda en la Cuestion Agraria", en: *La Palabra y el Hombre*, Revista de la Universidad Veracruzana, *Nueva Epoca*, No. 32, 15–24.

Tapia Santamaria, J. 1986: *Campo Religioso y Evolución Política en el Bajio Zamoran*, México, El Colegio de Michoacán y el Gobierno del Edo. de Michoacán.

Tannenbaum, F. 1968: *Peace by Revolution: México After 1910*, New York: Columbia University Press.

Tannenbaum, F. 1968: *The Mexican Agrarian Revolution*, Hamden, Connecticut: Archon Books.

Tenorio, M. y Gómez, A. G. 2006:, *El Porfiriato*, México, FCE-CIDE.

Toro, A., 1931: *La Iglesia y el Estado en México, Estudio Sobre el Conflicto entre el Clero Católico y los Gobiernos Mexicanos desde la Independencia hasta Nuestros Días*, Jalapa-Enríquez, Secretaría de Gobernación, T.I.P. del Gobierno.

Toro, J., 2010: "Reforma agraria y movilización Campesina en Veracruz (México) durante el siglo XX", *Cesla*, Vol. 2, Num. 13, 579–594.

Townsend, W. C. 1952: *Lázaro Cárdenas, Mexican Democrat*, Ann Arbor, Michgan: George Wahr Publishing Co.

Úrsulo Galvaán 1893–1930: Su Vida—Su Obra, Liga de Comunidades Agrarias y

Sindicatos Campesinos del Estado de Veracruz, CNC, Jalapa-Enríquez, Veracruz, 1966.

Vásquez de Knauth, J. Z., 1969:"La Educación Socialista de los Años Treinta" en: *Historia Mexicana*, 71 (3), Vol. 18, 408–423.

Velasco Gill, C. M. 1953: "Veracruz: Revolución y Extremismo", *Historia Mexicana*, Vol. 2, No. 4(8), 618–636.

Warman, A. 1984: *Ensayos Sobre el Campesinado en México*, México, Nueva Imagen.

Weyl, N. y Silvia, 1955: "La Reconquista de México (Los Días de Lázaro Cárdenas)", en: *Problemas Agrícolas e Industriales de México*, Vol. VII, No. 4, 119–334.

Wilkie, J. W. y Monzón E. de Wilkie, E. 1978: *México Visto en el Siglo 20: Entrevistas de Historia Oral*, México, Instituto Mexicano de Investigaciones Económicas.

Wood, A. G. 2001: *Revolution in the Street: Women, Workers, and Urban Protests in Veracruz, 1870–1927*, Wilmington Delaware: Scholarly Resources.

Wood, A. G., 2009: "Adalberto Tejeda of Veracruz: Radicalism and Reaction", in *State Governors in the Mexican Revolution, 1910–1952: Portraits in Conflict*, Jürgen Buchenau and William H. Beezley (eds.), New York: Rowman & Littlefield, 77–94.

Zea, L. 1996: "Hacia un nuevo liberalismo en la educación," en Josefina Zoraida Vázquez (coord.), *La educación en la historia de México*, México, El Colegio de México, 291–311.

Zea, L. 1963: *The Latin American Mind*, Translated from Spanish by James H. Abbott and Lowell Dunham, Norman: University of Oklahoma Press.

Zepeda Patterson, J. 1986: "Los Pasos de Cárdenas. La Confederación Revolucionaria Michoacana del Trabajo", en: *75 Años de Sindicalismo Mexicano*, Alejandra Moreno Toscano y Samuel L. González (coords.), México, Instituto Nacional de Estudios Históricos de la Revolución Mexicana, 231–262.

Zepeda Patterson, J. 1988: "Los Caudillos en Michoacán: Francisco J. Múgica y Lázaro Cárdenas", en: *Estadistas, Caciques y Caudillos*, Carlos Martínez Assad (cood.), México, Instituto de Investigaciones Sociales, UNAM, 43–267.

Zepeda Patterson, J., 1989: "Michoacán en la época de Lázaro Cárdenas", en: *Historia general de Michoacán*, Vol. IV, Enrique FlorescAño (coord.), Morelia, Gobierno de Estado de Michoacán, Instituto Michoacano de Cultura.

Zepeda Patterson, J. 1990: *Michoacán: Sociedad, Economía, Política, y Cultura*, Centro de Investigaciones Interdisciplinarias en Humanidades, UNAM.

Index

Page numbers in italics refer to tables.

Made in United States
Orlando, FL
18 January 2023